Colbert,
Mercantilism,
and the
French Quest for Asian Trade

Colbert, Mercantilism,
and the
French Quest for Asian Trade

Glenn J. Ames

Northern Illinois
University
Press
DeKalb
1996

© 1996 by Northern Illinois University Press
Published by the Northern Illinois University Press,
DeKalb, Illinois 60115
Manufactured in the United States using acid-free paper
Design by Julia Fauci

Ames, Glenn Joseph.
Colbert, mercantilism, and the French quest for Asian trade /
Glenn Joseph Ames.
p. cm.
Includes bibliographical references and index.
ISBN 0-87580-207-9
1. Colbert, Jean Baptiste, 1619–1683—Influence. 2. Mercantilism—France—
History—17th century. 3. France—History, Military—17th century. 4. France—
Commerce—Asia—History—17th century. 5. Territorial expansion. I. Title.
DC130.C6A84 1996
382'.092—dc20
[B]   95-45429
CIP

In memory of my father

Contents

List of Maps

Preface

> "France will never be powerful, or feared or respected by
> her neighbors if she is not mistress of the sea. . . . [A]n
> army of 20,000 men on this liquid plain would bring
> her more honour and profit than 20,000 men on land.
> In the end, whoever controls the sea controls every-
> thing."
>
> Attributed to Gagnier, *Mémoire*, 1761

The topic of European expansion to the Indian Ocean has attracted extensive historical research over the past century. During that time, the literature
has undergone several transformations. Much of the scholarly work completed from roughly 1880 to 1940 on the topic falls conveniently within the
limits of what M. N. Pearson has aptly described as the "seeds-of-empire"
school of historiography.[1] Eurocentric, Whiggish, even jingoistic, this body
of work was written by English, French, Dutch, and Portuguese civil servants active in the administration of the twilight empires of those countries
and was engendered in part by a need to glorify past colonial adventures as
a means of legitimizing modern European imperialism. Not surprisingly,
such studies were sometimes less than objective. In the decolonization period, the entire field was tainted by this legacy, and it is only within the past
twenty years that renewed interest and more balanced monographs have begun to appear. The dominant trend in the recent historiography has been to
avoid the methodological pitfalls of the traditional nationalist literature and
to utilize an approach that examines the symbiotic economic, social, religious, and cultural interaction between Europe and Asia that began with
Vasco da Gama's arrival in Calicut in 1498.

In this historiographical transformation, the work of C. R. Boxer has
played a seminal role.[2] Boxer's impressive body of scholarly work combines
the best elements of the traditional literature and portends many of the
methodological refinements of the recent historiography. His example has
been followed by a generation of younger scholars such as Pearson, T. R. de
Souza, A. R. Disney, Sanjay Subrahmanyam, K. N. Chaudhuri, and others
who have brought innovative research techniques, including those of the
Annales school, to what hitherto had been viewed as a bastion of traditional
history.[3] This shift in perspective (or paradigm) has gradually led to the
modification of the Eurocentric "seeds-of-empire" school. The field today is
much more multicultural, multilingual, and multifaceted, focusing on what
has recently been described by John E. Wills as the "interactive emergence
of European domination" over the trade of maritime Asia from about 1500

to 1800. As Wills points out, recent studies on the rise of these European merchant empires have been facilitated by dynamic pockets of research located in Leiden, Paris, Delhi, and, one might add, Minneapolis.[4]

The recent decades of revisionism may have succeeded in modifying the accepted orthodoxy in many specific areas and questions relating to European expansion, but this important process is far from over. Even a cursory review of the expanding secondary literature reveals that the work devoted to the Asian empires of the Dutch, English, and Portuguese and their interaction with the culture of maritime Asia by far outweighs that detailing the French experience in the Indian Ocean basin from 1600 to 1800. Boxer's imposing body of work concentrates almost exclusively on the travails of the *Estado da India* and the *Vereenigde Oost Indische Compagnie* (VOC). Pearson, De Souza, Disney, and Subrahmanyam also concentrate almost exclusively on Indo-Portuguese history. Israel and Prakash focus largely on the VOC, and Chaudhuri's impressive body of work examines the London (or English) East India Company (EIC).[5] A crucial factor in this historiographical imbalance is no doubt that the French were simply less successful in the Indian Ocean trade than their European rivals. Colbert's *Compagnie des Indes Orientales* and Dupleix's career—high points in an otherwise undistinguished two-century period—were the focus of studies by French historians of the Third Republic like Paul Kaeppelin, Jules Sottas, and Henry Weber.[6] Virtually no original work has been completed during the past fifty years.[7]

The dearth of recent literature on the French experience in Asia is one reason to undertake a reexamination of the topic. Even more compelling is that the orthodoxy of the Third Republic was heavily influenced by the "seeds-of-empire" methodology to which it subscribed. For all of its considerable merits, the work of Kaeppelin et al. was overwhelmingly nationalist in perspective and, moreover, based almost exclusively on French manuscript sources.[8] This study will redress the lacunae of recent research on the French in Asia by detailing one of the most crucial periods for France's ambitions in the Indian Ocean trade: the ten-year period from 1664 to 1674. In doing so, it will contribute to recent scholarly interest in examining the interactive experience of the European powers in that region and the rise of their merchant empires during the early modern period.

The history of the European powers in Asia is demarcated by critical epochs in which these states either exploited or squandered opportunities to establish themselves in the trade. Albuquerque's epic campaign of the early sixteenth century, for example, exploited a lack of serious rivals and the superiority of European naval firepower to capture Hurmuz, Goa, and Melaka in rapid succession, thus helping to ensure a century of Portuguese dominance in the spice trade. During the first half of the seventeenth century, the entrepreneurial innovations and formidable military strength of the VOC were utilized by Jan Pieterzoon Coen, Anthony Van Diemen, and Johan Maetsuycker to destroy Portuguese pretensions and establish Dutch commercial preeminence. Meanwhile, the commercial and military resilience of the English during the Dutch Wars of the mid-seventeenth century solidified the position of the London Company and portended its future prosperity. I believe that the decade from 1664 to 1674 was such a period of opportunity for French ambitions in the trade, for these years witnessed an unparalleled conjuncture of events in Europe and Asia that favored French advances and engendered Colbert's Asian strategy, the most concerted French effort of the entire seventeenth century to break into this lucrative trade.

In an effort to avoid the interpretive problems of the nationalist approach and to broaden the scope of the analysis, I have based this reexamination on a "comparative" archival approach by utilizing relevant Dutch, English, Portuguese, Indian, and French manuscript sources. Although this new approach to a traditional subject has necessitated more than four years' work in the major archives of Western Europe and India, this methodology and the ability to peruse documentary collections that have hitherto not been consulted by historians in the field has significant advantages. The inherent bias of the French manuscript documents can sometimes be tempered with data from non-French sources available in London, The Hague, Lisbon, and Goa. Moreover, valuable evidence not found in the relevant French collections can often be gleaned from Dutch, English, Portuguese, and Indian archives. Manuscript sources for the indigenous Indian kingdoms of this period found in the India Office Library in London and the Historical Archive of Goa offer valuable information that was overlooked by the historians of the Third Republic.[9] This new evidence allows the historian to transcend the perceptual limits of the orthodox approach and to avoid the alluring tendency to compile a merely "French" history of the French in India or Colbert's Asian strategy.

I have accumulated a long list of professional and personal debts in the process of researching this study and the Ph.D. dissertation upon which it is based. In the United States, I would like to thank Gino Silvestri, who originally encouraged my interest in history. I also owe a debt of gratitude to my professors at the University of Minnesota. A special thanks to my advisor, Paul Walden Bamford, who convinced me that extensive archival research is the basis for writing "good" history. David Kopf was instrumental in demonstrating the need for comparative studies that would overcome the Eurocentric legacy of traditional historiography. I would also like to acknowledge the assistance and advice offered by J. Kim Munholland, Stanford Lehmberg, Ward Barrett, S. Alvi, John Parker, Carol Urness of the James Ford Bell Library, and Henry Scholberg of the Charles Wesley Ames Library. In Paris, M. Etienne Taillemite was helpful in directing my attention to the most important collections in the French archives. In Lisbon, the staff members of the *Filmoteca Ultramarina Portuguesa* were incredibly generous with their advice. In India, Teotonio de Souza S. J., director of the Xavier Centre of Historical Research; P. P. Shirodkar, director of the Historical Archive of Goa; and P. R. Mehendirata of the the American Institute of Indian Studies all facilitated my work. In England, I would like to acknowledge a special debt of gratitude to Professor C. R. Boxer for his advice, encouragement, and offer to utilize documents in his vast private collection. William Doyle of The University of Bristol kindly offered to read an earlier draft of the manuscript. In Australia, I thank A. R. Disney of La Trobe University and M. N. Pearson of the University of New South Wales, who also read through earlier drafts and offered valuable suggestions.

The Graduate School of the University of Minnesota, the Francis E. Andrews-Minneapolis Fund, the American Institute of Indian Studies, the Portuguese Ministry of Education, and the Leverhulme Trust in London all provided generous financial support for which I am most grateful. I must also thank the staff members of the archives I utilized in France, England, Portugal, and India, who were instrumental in allowing me to compile the documentary evidence that serves as the basis for this study. I am most appreciative of the support that Mary Lincoln, director of Northern Illinois University Press, has shown for the project since the outset and of the entire staff at Northern Illinois for their valued assistance in bringing the manuscript to print. Finally, a very special thanks to Beth and Miranda for their inspiration and support.

Colbert,
Mercantilism,
and the
French Quest for Asian Trade

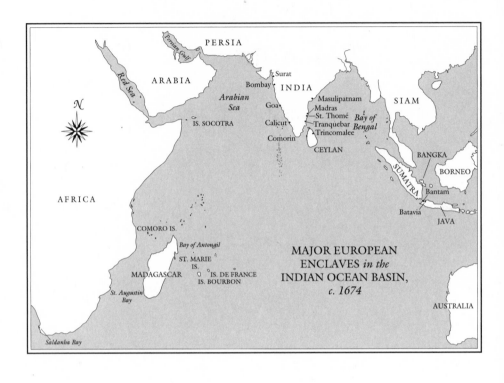

N

PERSIA

ARABIA

Red Sea

Persian Gulf

Surat

Bombay

Arabian Sea

INDIA

IS. SOCOTRA

Goa

Calicut

Comorin

Masulipatnam

Madras

St. Thomé

Tranquebar

Trincomalee

Bay of Bengal

SIAM

CEYLAN

SUMATRA

BANGKA

BORNEO

Bantam

Batavia

JAVA

AFRICA

COMORO IS.

Bay of Antongil

ST. MARIE IS.

MADAGASCAR

IS. DE FRANCE

IS. BOURBON

St. Augustin Bay

MAJOR EUROPEAN ENCLAVES *in the* **INDIAN OCEAN BASIN,** *c. 1674*

AUSTRALIA

Saldanha Bay

Introduction

European Powers and the Asian Trade

"Ye Emperors, Kings, Dukes, Marquises, Earls, and
Knights, and all other people desirous of knowing
the diversities of the races of mankind, as well as
the diversities of kingdoms, provinces, and regions
of all parts of the East, read through this book
and ye will find it."

—Rustigielo,
Prologue to *The Travels of Marco Polo*

India. Persia. Tartary. Zipangu. For centuries these exotic-sounding names
were synonymous in Europe with the wealth, power, and mystery of the
Orient. Rustigielo's stirring prologue promised that the readers of his cell-
mate's *Travels* would find a vivid description of "the greatest and most mar-
vellous characteristics" of these almost mythical kingdoms of the East.[1] Literate Europeans were not disappointed. Polo's *Travels* was the most
complete of all medieval travel journals, a series of accounts made possible
by the conquests of Chingis Khan and the tolerant policies of his successors,
the Tartar Khans, who during the late thirteenth and early fourteenth century encouraged an active, if all too fleeting, religious and mercantile interchange with Europe. Polo's work portended increased European contact
with Asia, which was ultimately fulfilled during the great Age of Discovery a
century and a half later. In the interim, his manuscript was widely copied by
hand in Italian, Latin, and French and first printed in 1483. Thereafter, it
circulated widely in various editions and languages throughout Europe.[2]
Prince Henry the Navigator knew the work in manuscript. Columbus had a
well-worn, printed copy that was instrumental in the formulation of his
geographic calculations on the voyage west in search of Asian riches. The

arduous odyssey of the thirteenth-century Venetian and the even wider appeal of more spurious travelers' tales as those of Sir John Mandeville had served to fire the imagination of European monarchs, nobles, merchants, adventurers, and seamen hungry for Asian wealth.[3] Once ignited, the desire for overseas trade, riches, and empire would, by the mid-seventeenth century, come to dominate the foreign policy and economic calculations of most of the major European states.

The main outlines of the Age of Discovery are well-known. In the mid-fifteenth century, advances in maritime construction, navigation, ship-borne armaments, and finance, combined with certain religious and geopolitical imperatives, prompted the Iberian Crowns of Portugal and Castile and Aragon to act on the long-standing and deeply held desire to establish direct trading relations with the Orient.[4] Bartolomeu Dias rounded what he called the Cape of Storms—a name changed to the Cape of Good Hope by his optimistic monarch João II—during a voyage of 1487–1488. Manoel I would outfit the historic voyage of Vasco da Gama a decade later. Upon his arrival in Calicut, da Gama is said to have declared that the Portuguese had come in search of "Christians and Spices."[5] Although this, perhaps the most famous, statement of the Age of Discovery may be apocryphal, it does summarize Portuguese motives in this quest. Manoel I was anxious to deprive the ubiquitous middlemen of the Italian city-states of their traditional profits earned by transshipping Eastern cargoes from the Levant to a spice-starved Europe. There can be little doubt that the devout Portuguese Crown also saw the voyage as a logical continuation of the *reconquista* against Islam, a means of outflanking that archenemy while searching for Prester John and any Christians that might be found or created along the way.[6]

The epic late-fifteenth-century voyages of Vasco da Gama and Christopher Columbus were rapidly built upon in the decades that followed by the Asian victories of Afonso da Albuquerque, thus establishing the basis of a Portuguese Asian empire, and by the conquests of Hernando Cortés and Francisco Pizzaro, which helped ensure Spanish dominion in the New World.[7] As early as August 1499, Manoel I had rather precipitously taken the title of "Lord of the Conquest, Navigation, and Commerce of Ethiopia, Arabia, Persia, and India."[8] Not to be outdone, Ferdinand and Isabella made grandiose claims in America and granted Cortés a vast *encomienda* in the valley of Oaxaca.[9] By the mid-sixteenth century, the Iberian Catholic powers had seemingly justified the brash claims of the *Inter caetera*, the *Dudum siquidem*, and the Treaty of Tordesillas (1494) to divide the overseas world between them. By 1550, the Portuguese Crown was importing over 40,000 quintals of pepper on the Cape route, and profits of 200 percent were not uncommon.[10] According to E. J. Hamilton's figures, between 1516 and 1560 over 11.9 million ducats of gold and silver flowed into Seville from the mines of New Spain and New Granada, thus helping to engender the price revolution of the sixteenth century.[11] These were seminal events in the creation of a world market economy whose importance was well appreciated by contemporaries. The Spanish chronicler Francisco López de Gómara, when dedicating his *General History of the Indies* to Charles V in 1552, called the discovery of the sea routes to the East and West Indies the "greatest event since the creation of the world, apart from the incarnation and death of Him who created it."[12] As late as the physiocratic revolution of the eighteenth century, Adam Smith, certainly not known for his passionate outbursts, asserted, "The discovery of America, and that of a passage to the East Indies by the Cape of Good Hope, are the two greatest and most important events recorded in the history of mankind."[13]

Iberian dominance over the developing world market economy of the early modern period was destined to be relatively short-lived. The monarchical monopolism of the Iberians was rapidly supplanted during the age of competition for empire that followed. In this fierce global struggle among the European powers, the entrepreneurial structures of merchant capitalism eventually came to dominate, much to the detriment of the Iberians.[14] Philip II's invasion of Portugal in 1580 and the obtainment of that coveted Crown and its vast *imperio* had seemed to portend perpetual Habsburg dominance overseas. But these military victories on the continent were misleading. By 1600, serious cracks had already begun to appear in the imperial facade of Counter-Reformation Spain. The festering wound of the Netherlands' revolt, the Armada debacle, a series of endemic economic problems that were revealed in the frequent bankruptcies of Charles V and Philip II, and the Thirty Years' War all served to undermine Iberian pretensions. In the Escorial, it must have seemed that God, if he had not completely deserted the Habsburg cause, was indeed working in mysterious ways. By 1640, Olivares's desperate gamble to regain the initiative in the long struggle with France had become an utter failure. Catalonia was in open revolt. Portugal had finally risen to throw off the Spanish yoke, and a bloody war for independence ensued, which lasted until 1668.[15] Meanwhile, the rise of merchant capitalism in the Atlantic economies of the north had begun to demonstrate its innovative power, inexorably undermining the imperial position of Spain and Portugal. The death knell for Iberian monopoly ushered in a renascent scramble for territory and trade in the New World and Asia that would continue for the remainder of the *ancien régime*.

It was no accident that the original manifestations of this renewed struggle were the Dutch Wars of the 1650s and 1660s. Once the victory of Atlantic over Mediterranean had seemingly been heralded, the confident Protestant powers had reverted to invidious conflict in an attempt to divide the spoils of the Iberian imperial carcass. These wars were brief maritime struggles fought primarily for mercantile objectives in Europe, the New World, Africa, and the Indian Ocean. They were largely contests for dominance over what was perceived as the most lucrative and strategic components of the developing world market economy. These mid-seventeenth-century wars, following close upon the victory of Parliament over Stuart absolutism in England and burgher capitalism over Habsburg monarchism in the Netherlands, ushered in the age when global conflicts would become the norm, when the quest for overseas trade and empire would become at least as important in dictating the foreign policy of the European states as more traditional dynastic goals on the continent. The quest for Asian wealth therefore attained increasing importance during the course of the "long" seventeenth century and became integrated into European diplomacy and peace settlements in the process. This global conflict for Iberian spoils was, however, open to all comers, and this in part helps explain the origins of the Third Dutch War of 1672–1679, the first major and arguably the most important of all of Louis XIV's wars. For France, after a long bout of somnambulism with respect to this quest for overseas wealth, belatedly awoke to the potential benefits of conquest in *outre-mer* and the necessity of joining this global mercantile contest. Preeminence in Europe was increasingly dependent on economic and political dominion overseas. Bourbon France, despite its demographic advantages and a traditional preference for dynastic gains on the continent, could ill afford to ignore this reality. The man responsible for this fundamental policy shift was Jean-Baptiste Colbert.

Mercantilism was a doctrinal outgrowth of the structures of the early modern state, an economic creed that reached its apogee in Louis XIV's France. The primary form of expansion for the so-called absolutist states of the period remained military conquest. For Colbert, mercantile expansion was grounded in *economic* warfare.[16] In this pre-Smithian age, world wealth was judged to be limited; winning a larger piece of the economic pie necessitated that one power win a part of that controlled by its hitherto hungrier rivals. Colbert judged that the Protestant powers had demonstrated truly gluttonous appetites during the seventeenth century and were showing no signs of curbing this unsettling habit. These bellicose imperatives, when combined with the gradual development of a world market economy, ensured that state expansionism was gradually externalized to overseas territories during the course of the Old Regime. Colbert may have added nothing new to the basic theoretical tenets of mercantilism. Nevertheless, his vast personal power, his unmatched energy, and his formidable cadre of financiers, all working in conjunction with Louis XIV's thirst for *gloire* and the expanding centralizing sinews of the Bourbon state, conspired to give him the ability to attempt a systematic implementation of his economic beliefs.[17] Earlier proponents of mercantilism were mere intellectuals working in the abstract of political economy. Colbert was a man of action with the power to influence and, at times, dictate state policy. As early as 1664, he was convinced that France's future economic prosperity was dependent on a successful economic campaign against the United Provinces. This strategy increasingly came to revolve around an attempt to undermine Dutch dominance in what he viewed as the most lucrative sector of the world commercial system: the Indian Ocean trade. By 1672, Colbert was convinced that, despite the inherent risks, his cherished economic plans were dependent on the successful prosecution of a conquering foreign policy in Europe and, by extension, the Asian trade.

The desire of France to share in the wealth of the Asian trade had begun long in advance of Colbert's projects. During the reigns of Francis I and Henry III, edicts had been issued exhorting the populace to undertake long ocean voyages, and some enterprising Frenchmen carried out sporadic voyages to the East.[18] In November 1600, the *Compagnie des mers Orientales* was formed by merchants of St-Malo, Laval, and Vitre with a capital pool of eighty thousand écus. Although two ships were sent to the East Indies, this company was soon moribund.[19] On 1 June 1604, Henry IV issued letters patent granting a trading monopoly in Asia to a *Société . . . pour le voyage des Indes Orientales* formed by erstwhile employees of the Dutch Company like Pieter Lijntgens and Girald le Roy, exploiting the connections of the French financier Antoine Godefroy. A promising beginning was soon undermined by a lack of private investment, Portuguese and Dutch opposition, the continued pre-eminence of continental foreign policy aims, and the internal strife of Louis XIII's minority. In vain, the Crown attempted to instill new life into the project in July 1619 by transferring monopoly privileges to a reconstituted concern, the *Compagnie des Moluques*.[20] Richelieu, the *grand maître*, convinced that a strong navy and a well-established trade were necessary preconditions for France's greatness, also tried his hand at creating a viable East India Company. Between 1633 and 1637 several ships were sent to Asia by a *Société dieppoise* and by letters patent of June 1642 monopoly privileges were granted to a *Compagnie d'Orient*. Nevertheless, the Cardinal's scheme to colonize Madagascar (Isle-Dauphiné) eventually bankrupted the company. Private attempts to break into the trade between 1655 and 1662 under the auspices of *Maréchal* de La Meilleraye and Nicolas Fouquet were also a failure.[21]

Until Colbert's time, therefore, French attempts at mercantile expansion to the Indian Ocean were feeble, sporadic, and unsuccessful. This rather unimpressive legacy would be fundamentally altered during the ten years beginning in 1664, when Colbert attempted to align renascent French naval, diplomatic, and economic power behind his quest for Asian riches, a campaign that serves as the basis for this study. The Indian Ocean trade constituted a vital component of the world market economy of the day, so this region was logically one of the principal areas in which a global struggle was waged among the leading European powers as an extension of the warfare that took place on the Continent beginning in 1672. Colbert's form of mercantilism was inherently bellicose, and he was determined to thrust

France to the forefront of this mercantile and imperial struggle. Louis XIV's thirst for *gloire* and the kingdom's formidable wealth afforded him a perfect opportunity to do so in the years before the Dutch War. As we shall see, the methodology, strengths and weaknesses, and resolution of Colbert's initiative were inextricably linked to internal French structures and foreign policy priorities.

The reaction of France's European rivals to this unprecedented quest for Asian trade and wealth was also tied to the priorities that dominated in those societies. In England, the merchants and gentry had won considerable power during the course of the seventeenth century.[22] Accordingly, expanding mercantile interests in Europe, America, Africa, and Asia enjoyed high priority in formulating English foreign policy. London's powerful merchants had received a charter for an East India Company from Elizabeth I in 1600 and established a regular, if somewhat tenuous, trade with India and the Far East in the decades that followed. During the mid-1660s the English Company was at a critical juncture of its history. The first two Dutch Wars had revealed its weakness in the face of the naval power of the VOC and escalating Indian rivalries. At the same time, the leasing of Bombay from Charles II in 1668 provided the London Company with the independent entrepôt that it badly needed to expand and solidify its operations. The actions of Gerald Aungier in the decade that followed served to establish Bombay as a major port on the west coast of India. Colbert's Asian project began in the midst of these advances, posing a twin threat to the English position.

Not only did the appearance of the French Company complicate an already competitive trade, but Colbert, as part of his strategy, would pressure Charles II and Arlington for an alliance against the VOC. The City and the directors of the EIC, as we shall see, would react to these threats in exclusively economic terms. Moreover, the dominance of mercantile priorities in London helped ensure that Charles II would ultimately refuse such overtures. The English king would restrict his anti-Dutch activities solely to the Continental campaign. The EIC, meanwhile, would do everything it could to protect its commercial interests and avoid assisting the French. As Chaudhuri has powerfully argued, the "business constitutionalism" embodied in the structure of the EIC allowed the company to demonstrate a frequent and superior rationality with respect to economic decisions in comparison with other European powers established in the trade over its long history. As this study will show, the response of the EIC directors to Colbert's challenge in the 1660s and 1670s admirably supports this point of view.[23]

In Amsterdam, the center of the "Dutch world entrepôt" of the seventeenth century, mercantile priorities also dominated.[24] By 1650 or so, the Dutch were the dominant global trading power in large part due to a fleet of some 6000 ships totaling at least 600,000 tons.[25] Although van Oldenbarnevelt had originally formed a unified East India Company for economic reasons, political and military considerations soon came to dominate: the Company developed a warlike policy in close cooperation with the States General, lending ships and money to the government in time of need.[26] The States General, in turn, supported the Asian campaign of the VOC, with men like Jan Pieterzoon Coen and Johan Maetsuycker using open warfare and commercial acumen to supplant Portuguese power in the trade by the late 1650s, and established at a series of fortified bases from the Cape of Good Hope to Batavia. This close association between the States General and the company directors, the *Heeren XVII*, was hardly surprising since the two bodies were largely dominated by members of the same merchant oligarchy. VOC profits also played a pivotal role in the commercial greatness of the Dutch republic. Moreover, as Israel has argued, the unique ability to merge the interests of the ruling political oligarchy and those of private enterprise, and above all the ability of this statist model to advance the best interests of the Dutch world entrepôt as a whole, allowed the United Provinces and the VOC to weather many rival challenges during the early modern period.[27]

The States General and the *Heeren XVII* therefore possessed both the motivation and means to protect their lucrative arrangements in Asia, whatever the cost. From the outset of Colbert's campaign, Amsterdam and Batavia formulated a coordinated, well-financed, and forceful response to Colbert's Asian challenge. Even during the disastrous early stages of the 1672 war, the *Heeren XVII*, with the support of the States General, did everything they could to reinforce their Asian holdings, an attitude that stood in marked contrast to that in Paris. The Dutch Asian empire, nevertheless, was also in a transitional phase; the golden age of peak profits was already giving way to rising deficits and a gradual decline, which was exacerbated by wartime expenditures.[28] In much the same way as the Portuguese Asian empire had tottered under the financial and military strains of protecting its widely dispersed possessions against a host of indigenous and European rivals, Batavia was beginning to feel the strain. This shifting state of affairs would afford Colbert's strategy every chance of success.

The late 1660s and early 1670s were also a crucial period in the history of Portuguese Asia. During the course of the seventeenth century, the *Estado da India* had suffered grave losses to the Dutch. By 1670, all that remained of a once lucrative empire was a series of isolated fortresses from Mozambique to Macau. Since the days of Albuquerque, the Portuguese Crown had viewed the *Estado* with a mixture of dynastic, religious, and mercantile motives. The lack of a strong merchant class at home, however, meant that the empire was frequently seen more as a geopolitical extension of the glory and power of the Crown than as a fertile ground for innovative economic ideas and exploitation. Accordingly, the Portuguese had traditionally responded to overt threats to their "monopoly" more often with direct military action and European alliances than with economic and administrative reforms. These long-standing priorities underwent an important change during the early 1670s. The marked shift in Crown policy was partially a result of the palace coup of late 1667 that installed the adroit Prince Regent Pedro in place of his unstable brother Afonso VI. At the same time, this change was linked to Colbert's bold initiative, which forced Lisbon to reexamine its long-standing priorities in Asia. Having learned the disastrous lesson of the 1661 marriage treaty with Charles II, a pact that had promised rehabilitation in Asia based on the support of an outside power, Pedro would ultimately decline Colbert's attractive proposal of an anti-Dutch alliance in Asia. By remaining neutral during the Dutch War, the Portuguese hierarchy would instead be able to initiate a series of long overdue economic, bureaucratic, and religious reforms.[29]

In France, the year 1672 was a great turning point in Louis XIV's reign. Among other things, the decision to attack the United Provinces would ultimately result in the triumph of Louvois over Colbert and in the destruction of the financial reforms of the first decade of Louis's personal rule.[30] What is less commonly appreciated in the historiography is that the Dutch War also constituted a watershed in France's fortunes in the developing world market economy, and particularly in the Indian Ocean component of that system. For the French Crown, dynastic foreign policy priorities on the Continent had long dominated over mercantile concerns, especially in Asia. Henry IV, it is true, granted a monopoly charter to a *Compagnie des Indes Orientales* in 1604, or at about the same time as Elizabeth I was granting a charter to her London merchants for the same purpose and van Oldenbarnevelt was forming the VOC. Nevertheless, the strong preference of the Crown for dynastic and territorial gains in Europe, the political and religious vicissitudes of the first half of the seventeenth century in France, and a relatively weak mercantile class all ensured that up to Colbert's time very little was achieved in the Asian trade. A distinctive feature of Colbert's Asian strategy is that in the years before the Dutch War these traditional dynastic priorities on the continent were joined by mercantile goals in *outre-mer*, and particularly the Indian Ocean. At the outset, this merging of priorities, combined with a novel conjuncture of circumstances in Europe and the East, allowed Colbert to overcome the advantages of the Dutch and English and gave him every advantage in implementing his Asian initiative.

As time went on, however, this juxtaposition of dynastic and mercantile priorities would prove to be a double-edged sword for Colbert. The temporary merging of these priorities between 1668 and 1671 would prove by mid–1673 both tenuous and contradictory. It had not been engendered by any profound societal shift that had fused aristocratic and bourgeois interests nor, for that matter, those of Colbert and Louis XIV; it was merely the result of the circumstances of the late 1660s that made the United Provinces the antagonist to the expansionist designs of Louis on the Continent and those of Colbert in *outre-mer*. There is no question that Louis XIV showed an early interest in Colbert's Asian plans, but no large-scale capital support from the French merchant class would ever develop for the Asian project.[31] It would therefore remain very much a royal enterprise dependent on the king's whim. As long as Colbert retained a dominant voice in the formulation of state policy, particularly of overseas and mercantile policies, as well as Louis's royal favor, this unwelcome economic reality could be overcome. Beginning in early 1671, however, the *Conseil d'en haut* was increasingly forced to weigh the relative importance of dynastic priorities in Europe vis-à-vis mercantile designs in *outre-mer*. This struggle for Louis XIV's favor would increasingly pit the young Louvois, who favored traditional continental foreign policy goals, against Colbert, who continued to press his plans in *outre-mer* and especially Asia. Once the Dutch War began, it became clear that Louis XIV, regardless of his earlier support, was no longer willing to embrace Colbert's mercantile projects at the possible expense of his Continental adventures. Given the gradual reassertion of such priorities, this crucial contest would be resolved in Louvois's favor as the Dutch War progressed, with profound consequences at home and abroad.

I

Paris, 1665

The Birth of a New *Compagnie des Indes Orientales*

> "To what end is it fine that we Pride ourselves to
> be the subjects of the Prime monarch of the Uni-
> verse: If being so we dare not so much as show
> our heads in those places where our neighbours
> have established themselves with power?"
>
> —François Charpentier, *Relation de l'établissement
> de la Compagnie françoise pour le commerce des
> Indes Orientales*

News reached Paris on 10 March 1665 that at long last the first expedition of the *Compagnie royale des Indes Orientales* had sailed. A rainy spring, muddy roads, and the usual diversions had slowed the messengers from Brest. Nonetheless, after several delays, the company ships *St-Paul, Taureau, Vierge de Bon Port,* and *Aigle d'Or* had weighed anchor on 7 March and begun the long and difficult passage to the Indian Ocean via the Cape of Good Hope. The fleet's destination was the island of Madagascar off the southeast coast of Africa, known as the *Isle-Dauphiné* to French mariners of the day. The four ships carried crews totaling 230 men and nearly 300 passengers, a somewhat eclectic mix of adventurers, soldiers, company officials, and would-be colonists. In what would become a rather disturbing habit, the expedition had proven extremely costly to outfit and dispatch. By early March, the ledgers revealed that over 300,000 livres had been spent, a sum the young company could ill afford. These problems were discussed at length at the first stockholders meeting held in the royal apartments of the Louvre on 20 March. Colbert, however, was more than pleased with the news from Brest. As he listened to the appointment of associates like de Faye and Chanlatte to the permanent board of twelve Paris directors, he re-

alized that after more than a year of intense labor his cherished plans to undermine Dutch commercial power in Asia had finally begun. Colbert, to no
one's surprise, was elected "chief and president" of the company as well as
the director representing the king.[1]

Such august positions and titles were becoming increasingly commonplace for Colbert as he neared the height of his personal power and prestige.
It was indeed a remarkable rise, one that would see him become, in the
words of C. W. Cole, "the dominant force in every department of the government save only those of war and foreign affairs."[2] Colbert's career was as
much a product of the sociopolitical dynamics of the early modern state as
the result of the unrivaled bureaucratic energies he displayed in the service
of his early patrons and eventually the Crown. Born in Reims in 1619, the
traditional view has held that his family was solid bourgeois stock in the
midst of rising through the social hierarchy based on the time-honored ex-
pedients of wealth and venality of office. His father, Nicolas, had purchased
the post of payer of *rentes* at the Hotel de Ville in Paris. Odart Colbert,
Colbert's uncle, was a successful merchant banker. Moreover, as recent revi-
sionists like D. Dessert have argued, Colbert's family connections and influence network with the French financial community, especially among leading tax farmers, may have been far more extensive than the traditional view
has held. Utilizing such connections, Colbert had entered the service of
Michel Le Tellier in 1643, soon after the latter had become secretary of
state in charge of military affairs. He served Le Tellier for eight years, gar-
nering the title of *conseiller d'état* in 1649 and arranging a successful marriage with Marie Charon, the daughter of a wealthy financial official, in the
process. This promising foundation was solidified during his apprenticeship
under Mazarin, a mutually advantageous relationship that began in 1651
upon the Cardinal's flight from Paris during the *Fronde* and ended only on
Mazarin's deathbed in 1661. By the end of this decade of opportunity, Colbert had become baron de Seignelay, secretary of the orders of the queen,
intendant general of the affairs of Mazarin, and counselor of the king in all
of his councils, not to mention a very wealthy man. By the early 1660s, he
had also created an apparatus utilizing family and friends that could serve as
the basis for the implementation of his policies.[3]

In this rapid ascent through the labyrinth of French political life, Colbert
had honed the ideas and theories that would shape his policies after 1661,
that notable year in which Louis XIV had begun his personal reign and
Nicholas Fouquet was imprisoned, thus ensuring Colbert's ascent to ministerial pre-eminence. The basic theoretical tenet of French mercantilism, bul-
lionism, encouraging manufactured exports with government support while
hindering such imports with protective tariffs, predated Louis XIV's reign,
in some cases, by half a dozen generations. Colbert was exposed to such
ideas in the Paris of his youth, when the economic traditions of Henry IV
and the theories of the first Bourbon's *contrôleur général du commerce,*

Barthélemy de Laffemas, were still relatively strong. Richelieu was still alive at that time, and Isaac de Laffemas, the cardinal's creature, was in the midst of perpetuating his father's intellectual legacy. Although Colbert never referred to the writings of Montchrétien and Bodin, he was probably familiar with their works. Nevertheless, mercantilism reached its apogee under Colbert not because he was a theorist, but rather because he was a man of action who judged its tenets to be "the only natural and logical" way to achieve his most cherished goal, "a powerful and wealthy France, united under a glorious monarch."[4] By the spring of 1665, Colbert was convinced that a crucial component in attaining this elusive goal was to challenge Dutch pretensions in the lucrative Asian trade, "this great commerce, which is the only considerable one."[5] As the first fleet of the new *Compagnie des Indes Orientales* showed, he was already vested with sufficient power to act upon this belief.

The Indian Ocean campaign of the French company and Crown, which began on that raw March day of 1665, continued for the next decade, frequently dominating the calculations of Louis XIV's great minister. Colbert's anti-Dutch Asian strategy evolved logically from his beliefs on political economy. Foremost among these tenets of mercantilism was the conviction that the volume of world trade was essentially static, and that for France to increase her share meant that the kingdom would have to win part of that controlled by her rivals. In an often quoted *mémoire*, Colbert writes: "The commerce of all Europe is carried on by ships of every size to the number of 20,000, and it is perfectly clear that this number cannot be increased." Commerce caused "perpetual combat in peace and war among the nations of Europe, as to who shall win most of it." His exaggerated estimate on the maritime strength of the major European trading nations competing in this "war" was 15,000 to 16,000 Dutch ships, 3000 to 4000 English ships, and 500 to 600 French ships. Just as importantly, neither the French nor the English could "improve their commerce save by increasing this number, save from the 20,000 . . . and consequently by making inroads on the 15,000 to 16,000 of the Dutch."[6] The bellicosity inherent in such beliefs would in part culminate in the Dutch War of 1672.[7]

In the spring of 1665, Colbert was still convinced that the commercial "war" against the United Provinces could be pursued by using more peaceful, and less expensive, methods. Internal reforms designed to eliminate the endemic abuses and waste of the archaic French financial system were a key component of this campaign. In the wake of Fouquet's fall, the entire fiscal system was in an incredible state of disorder. As Colbert wrote, "It was necessary to disentangle a machine that the cleverest men in the kingdom, who had been involved in it for forty years, had snarled up so as to make it a science that they alone knew, so that they might be essential."[8] The royal revenues for 1661 may have been 31,000,000 livres, but 9,000,000 of this sum was needed merely to meet interest payments! The tax burden was much heavier than the revenues indicated due to inefficiencies and corruption that ensured that less than half of the taxes levied reached the treasury. In November 1661, Colbert had a special court, the *Chambre de justice,* created by royal edict in order to try Fouquet and to investigate financial abuses of the past. Utilizing harsh methods, the *chambre* created a virtual reign of terror among the French financial community. Lists of restitutions for 1662 and 1663 alone contain more than 500 names, totaling 70,000,000 livres.[9] The kingdom's financiers had also suffered when Colbert revised the rate of repayment on the *rentes,* a controversial step that saved the Crown some 8,000,000 livres a year.[10]

Colbert's rather draconian campaign to rationalize the French financial system also included the reorganization of the Council of Finances, opening up tax-farming bidding to increase returns, cutting down on expenditures *de comptant,* and vastly improving the account keeping of the Crown by adopting a *registre de fonds* (anticipated revenues), a *registre de dépenses* (budgeted future expenses), and an *annuel état au vrai* (actual receipts and payments for the year). To increase Crown revenues, Colbert sought to extend the *taille réelle* to the whole kingdom, based on a comprehensive land census or *cadastre.* He was more successful in slashing state expenses in collecting this tax and instead raising the *aides* from their 1661 level of 5,211,000 livres. Revenues from the *grande gabelle* were also increased. Colbert also did his utmost to reform the complex system of internal tariffs and tolls in the realm, an archaic remnant of feudal privilege that did much to hinder French commerce. In September 1664, he was instrumental in forming the Council of Commerce, designed to assist "business men and increasing commerce . . . a symbol of the royal favor that was henceforth to be lavished upon commerce."[11] That same month, the tariff of 1664 was issued. This internal reform was designed to unify the nineteen custom duties then current on goods entering and leaving the Five Great Farms of north-central France into simplified duties collected by the *royal bureau de recette.*[12] To facilitate the movement of goods within the kingdom, Colbert increased expenditures on the roads from 40,000 livres to over 600,000. In the spring of 1665 he was also in midst of resolving the technical difficulties inherent in the greatest of all his transportation projects, the Canal of Languedoc or the Canal of the Two Seas, connecting the Atlantic and the Mediterranean by a water route through France, thus eliminating the long voyage around Iberia and through the Strait of Gibraltar.

What factors motivated Colbert in this reform campaign? What goal sustained him in the face of the outcry his measures provoked in a society still firmly wedded to the vested interests of a feudal past and a vestigial localism that was being challenged by the centralization inherent in the consolidation of the Bourbon state? In large part, Colbert's actions were prompted by a burning desire to enact reforms that would lay the groundwork for France to mount a successful challenge against the entrenched commercial power of the United Provinces, a power that was based largely on Dutch dominance over the European carrying trade as well as the Asian trade. Not surprisingly, increasing foreign and overseas trade was the key doctrinal underpinning of Colbert's form of mercantilism. In a 1664 *mémoire* written for the king, Colbert estimated that nearly half of the vast Dutch merchant fleet was dependent on trade with France for its income. The kingdom may have exported goods worth 12,000,000 to 18,000,000 livres a year, but France derived a net income of only 4,000,000 to 6,000,000 livres since the Dutch gained nearly 13,000,000 livres annually supplying the French with goods from Asia (spices, China goods), the West Indies (sugar), and the Baltic (naval stores). "Their industry and our lack of intelligence . . . have made them masters of all commerce. . . . [S]o far as we can cut down on the profits that the Dutch make from the subjects of the king . . . so far will we increase the power, the grandeur, and the prosperity of the state."[13] As Cole noted half a century ago, "Colbert's whole program . . . was influenced by his desire to make economic gains for France at the expense of Holland."[14]

From the outset, Colbert embraced the campaign against the dour burghers of Amsterdam. He firmly supported the 50-sous-a-ton tax on foreign ships as a means to offset Dutch advantages in shipbuilding and operating costs. The States General protested loudly against this levy. Under the terms of the 1662 treaty of friendship, alliance, and commerce between the two powers, the merchants of the United Provinces succeeded in modifying this levy: henceforth their ships would pay the tax only once a voyage, not upon both entering and leaving a French port as hitherto had been the case. Nevertheless, as Van Breuningen, the Dutch negotiator in Paris, made clear in his correspondence to the States General, further concessions were most unlikely since Colbert was "a true financier and full of the project to increase the navigation of the subjects of the realm."[15] Much to their chagrin, the Dutch were discovering that the halcyon days of Louis XIII, Richelieu, and Mazarin were apparently over. For most of the seventeenth century, the French Crown had been content to strive for traditional dynastic and geopolitical goals on the continent, while allowing the inefficiencies and corruption inherent in the kingdom's financial system to fester. Military victories, not economic ones, were generally judged to be the true gauge of a state's greatness. Even though only half the tax levies ever made it to the royal coffers, a huge population and a rich soil ensured that even that paltry percentage was sufficient to continue the war with the Habsburgs and, from time to time, the bothersome Huguenots. The Dutch could always supply whatever else was needed.

As his actions of the early 1660s reveal, Colbert was determined to initiate a fundamental change in these long-standing priorities. He had no delusions about the crippling economic legacy of Mazarin and Fouquet. Reforms had been needed *internally* before any offensive against the global commercial might of the Dutch could be seriously contemplated, a necessity which explains the insular nature of the reform program of 1661–1664. Colbert's own position in the ruling hierarchy also had to be assured before he could launch the main points in his anti-Dutch crusade, measures that were likely to engender opposition from the king's more traditionally minded advisors, who would neither understand nor support a grand design based on maritime and *outre-mer* priorities. By early 1664, Colbert had largely succeeded in these quests: his personal power was on the rise, his position in the burgeoning bureaucracy was unrivaled, his opinions on most financial matters were virtually unassailable. The initial stage of his reforms, although it had created ill feelings among various sectors of the nobility and the financial community, including perhaps some erstwhile supporters, had nonetheless already begun to yield results. The preparatory work was over. Colbert was therefore able to commence with the next step in his economic strategy: to wage a successful commercial "war" against the United Provinces that would include a strike at the very core of Dutch commercial wealth, the Asian trade. His years of apprenticeship had taught Colbert much about political economy, and one of his fundamental conclusions had been that the Indian Ocean trade was the most lucrative in the world economy, one that yielded the United Provinces 12,000,000 livres annually.[16] To challenge Dutch commercial might mandated a thrust into the Asian heart of Amsterdam's far-flung and lucrative overseas empire.

Colbert turned his attention to this daunting challenge in the early months of 1664. He had received a *mémoire* from a group of Breton merchants the previous year, suggesting the formation of a new East India Company based at Belle-Île. This document convinced him to act on his own long-held desires for such a project.[17] From Henry IV to Richelieu attempts to found a viable *Compagnie des Indes Orientales* had failed due to an overriding preoccupation with internal political and religious problems, the dominance of dynastic continental foreign policy priorities, a chronic lack of private capital investment by the bourgeoisie, and the entrenched position of first the Portuguese and then the Dutch in the trade.[18] The quest for Asian wealth would therefore be far from facile. Colbert, nevertheless, had already begun to lay the groundwork for this project by initiating badly needed reforms in the French navy, the de facto guardian of a renascent company. The royal *marine* had languished under Mazarin's neglect: the number of vessels had been reduced to less than twenty-five; most of these were close to twenty years old, the "best sailors, and an infinity of others [had] gone into foreign service."[19] In 1660, only 300,000 livres had been spent on the navy. Colbert dramatically raised expenditures. By 1662, 2,600,000 livres were spent. His navy budgets would soon come to average close to 10,000,000 livres a year.[20] Nearly every department was reformed. By 1664, tangible results had already been achieved, and he was prepared to begin the arduous task of creating the commercial edifice that would challenge the Dutch East India Company.

Although Colbert's mercantilist doctrines dictated that a large government-protected company enjoying monopoly privileges be established for the exploitation of the Asian trade, his immediate dilemma was deciding on the exact structure of such a company. In the early spring of 1664, he spent long hours poring over the statistics of the VOC. Colbert decided, like every other Frenchman of the seventeenth century who had wrestled with this question, including Richelieu, that the Dutch model was worthy of imitation. After all, a recent inventory of VOC holdings had revealed its property to be worth an estimated 800,000,000 livres.[21] Colbert promptly arranged to receive a copy of the Dutch company charter from agents in the United Provinces, and the quest began to merge the royal patronage inherent in the monarchical state with the nascent capitalism embodied in the joint-stock VOC. One of the primary obstacles he had to overcome was the dubious legacy, both physiological and financial, of earlier French East India companies. Preliminary investigations throughout the country revealed that, with some justification, there was a profound lack of interest on the part of the bourgeoisie, which had traditionally demonstrated a tendency to reinvest its profits in land, *seigneuries,* and other safe investments and generally covet a noble lifestyle. As S. P. Sen noted, "The general public was quite cold to any scheme on the old lines, and for the success of the new enterprise it was necessary to create new circumstances more favorable than in the past, particularly through Royal patronage."[22]

Colbert, nevertheless, was determined to give the impression that the initiative for an East India Company had come from the French merchant community, not from the Crown. In late May 1664, a series of meetings involving businessmen and "persons of quality" were held at the Paris home of the sieur de Faverolles, an important merchant and confidant of the controller general, to discuss the formation of a company. Articles were drawn up along the lines desired by Colbert. On 29 May, representatives of this group, including Pocquelin *père,* Maillet *père,* Le Brun, Cadeau, Sanson, and Jabac, made the journey to Fontainebleau to present the articles to Louis XIV. Colbert recognized from the start that it was vital to have the support of the young king for his project and had effectively argued his case. The king received the financiers and courtiers in a very favorable manner and agreed to consider their document titled "Articles and conditions on which the merchants and business men of the kingdom very humbly beg the king to grant his declaration and the favors therein contained for the establishment of a company for the commerce of the East Indies." After discussing the articles with the Royal Council, he gave them his sanction two days later with only minor modifications.[23]

The main points in the lengthy document that the Royal Council considered furnish valuable insights into Colbert's initial priorities for the Asian project. His desperate need to stimulate private capital investment among both the aristocracy and middle class was reflected in several articles. Anyone who wished to do so could enter the company. Membership would carry no impairment of status for nobles, ecclesiastics, or royal officials. The minimum subscription was set at 1000 livres, larger amounts would only be accepted in multiples of 500 livres to facilitate the calculation of dividends. One-third of this sum was to be paid immediately in cash, the second third after a year, and the last third after two years. Colbert also sought foreign capital: foreigners could enter the company, those investing 10,000 livres or more would be considered French subjects. Louis raised this figure to 20,000 livres. To assure potential investors that their capital would indeed be secure, articles were included that stated that the shares of individuals were not to be seized by the Crown, even if they belonged to the subject of a nation at war with France. The property of the company was not to be seized by the king, even if it owed him money. As a further incentive, persons investing 6000 livres were to enjoy all the rights and privileges of the bourgeoisie in all cities except Bordeaux, Bayonne, and Paris. To enjoy such rights in those cities required the investment of 10,000 livres. The king raised these figures to 8000 and 20,000 livres respectively. Thus the feudal privileges of the past were to be used to stimulate Colbert's foray into the Asian trade.

The forty-eight articles presented to Louis XIV also reflected the huge organizational debt that Colbert owed to the corporate model of the Dutch. The French Company would ideally mirror the successful structure of the VOC. Colbert's desire was to create a company that would encompass merchants, interests, and capital from the entire realm. A "General Chamber of Direction" *(Assemblée générale)* was to be established at Paris with twenty-one directors or syndics. Twelve of these directors would come from Paris, the other nine would be elected by provincial shareholders in proportion to the funds invested by the provincial cities, or as the directors might otherwise decide. Until a final decision was made on this matter, the provincial directors were to be chosen from Rouen, Nantes, Saint-Malo, La Rochelle, Bordeaux, Marseilles, Tours, Lyon, and Dunkirk. If any of these cities demonstrated a lack of interest in the project, its director might be assigned to another city not on the list, or one of the other cities on the list might be awarded two directors. The directors were to be chosen from among merchants who were actively engaged in commerce. Secretaries of the king who had commercial experience might be made directors. Only those shareholders who had invested 10,000 livres would qualify to vote for the directors. In order to serve as a director from Paris it was necessary to have invested 20,000 livres; provincial directors needed to have invested only half that amount. The General Chamber would have the right to establish other Chambers of Direction in such cities as it deemed fit and to issue regulations for the governance of these special chambers. The *Assemblée générale* would also have the right to draw up statutes and regulations for the company, subject of course to royal confirmation. The company was to have a thorough general accounting every six years. No shareholder could retire from the company save by selling his stock to another investor, thus keeping the company's capital the same.

In articles that were no doubt disquieting to France's rivals in the trade, Colbert's bold geopolitical and economic designs in the region were also portended. The king was to grant the company an exclusive privilege to trade in the area from the Cape of Good Hope east to the Strait of Magellan for a term he saw fit. Louis XIV granted this monopoly for a period of fifty years. The bullionist tenets of mercantilism were also to be sacrificed in the quest for Asian riches. The company was to be allowed to send gold and silver to the East Indies in order to assist its commercial operations. The company was to have the right to hold all lands conquered from enemies of the king, all lands it found deserted, and all territory it secured from "barbarians," in full lordship and ownership, including mineral rights and the right to hold slaves. In an attempt to furnish the company with an initial base of operations, Madagascar and its surrounding islands were also to be granted to it, after indemnities were fixed for property already held by French subjects on that island, perhaps the only legacy of Richelieu's ill-fated project. The new company was to be granted all rights of sovereign justice over the lands it held in the East, with judges subject to royal approval. It would also have the right to establish garrisons, build forts, and make cannon, arms, and munitions. The arms of the king would appear on all cannon. The company was to nominate to the king a governor-general, who would have military command in its lands. The right to send ambassadors to the rulers of the Indies and to treat with them for war, peace, and truce would also be granted. In one of the more significant articles, Louis XIV promised to defend the company and protect its commerce against all comers and to provide escorts for its ships, not only off the coast of France but as far as the Indies.

Measures were also taken to stimulate private investment and create favorable economic conditions at home to benefit the trade of the company. The king agreed to advance the company one-fifth of all it spent on ships and cargoes for the first three annual fleets, including an immediate advance of 300,000 livres. After other investors had put up 400,000 livres, Louis would add another 300,000 livres, and so on until the Crown had covered the cost of the first expedition, which would amount to one-fifth the cost of the first three years. The king would supply salt to the company at a reduced price. Goods imported from the East Indies into France that were consumed internally were to pay only one-half the duties of the Five Great Farms, while goods that were reexported were to be free of import and export duties. Any goods that were utilized in the construction, provisioning, and arming of the company's ships were also exempt from import and export duties. When forced to chose between the religious zealotry of the Goan Inquisition and the economically practical de facto freedom of worship favored by the Protestant powers in Asia, Colbert chose to embrace the latter. A young Louis XIV, far less rigid in his religiosity than during the later years of the reign, was willing to accept this decision. A single article touched on the religious duties of the projected company: ecclesiastics were to be established in Madagascar and any other settlements that were taken charged with spreading the faith.

Despite a good degree of organizational homage to the Dutch model, the articles of May 1664 hinted at royal dominance over the Asian project from the outset. The Crown would have de facto control over the company's economic, administrative, judicial, and religious activities. While a symbiotic relationship between Crown and company was eminently predictable given the mercantilist precepts of Colbert and the social and economic structures of seventeenth-century France, it was fundamentally at odds with the true intent and brilliance of the federal VOC charter, which had succeeded in creating the greatest of the early modern joint-stock companies in terms of the number of shareholders, the size of the sales organization at home and abroad, the geographical extent of operations in Asia, and the tonnage of "Europe" and "country" shipping owned. Colbert may have employed much of the language of this document in his own articles, but he assuredly could not create the level of merchant capitalism or, as Holden Furber described it, "the economic and political conditions prevailing in the newly independent northern provinces of the Netherlands" that had allowed the Dutch Company to flourish.[24] He undoubtedly recognized this seminal limitation and sought to compensate as best he could with the wealth and privileges that royal patronage would ensure. The events of May 1664 proved that Louis XIV, when the mood struck him and the goal seemed to complement his thirst for *gloire,* could be a receptive and munificent monarch. To facilitate the continuance of this royal favor, the company was prepared to make every show of devotion to its royal benefactor. It would soon agree to pay homage to the king and to present each new monarch who came to the throne with a crown and scepter of gold weighing one hundred marcs.

Twelve syndics, or temporary directors, were selected on 5 June and an office was opened on the rue Saint-Martin with a black marble plaque above the door inscribed *Compagnie des Indes Orientales.* Throughout the rest of the summer, meetings were held there between the syndics and Colbert to discuss the company's operations. In August, Louis XIV issued a declaration "which gave the articles of the company the force of law, and which thus formed the charter of the new company." The king made some slight modifications in the May document. To reassure investors, no stockholder or director was to be held liable to put into the company more money than his original subscription. No director would be personally responsible for the company's debts. The company would have the right to take prizes in Asia, and the law administered in its territories would be know as the "Custom of

Paris." To encourage French colonization, Louis XIV decreed that the any child of a French man or woman and a native who became Catholic would be recognized as a French subject. At their stern, all company ships would fly the white flag bearing the arms of France. The company's arms were set as a round shield with a golden fleur-de-lys on an azure background enclosed by two branches, one an olive branch, the other a palm frond, meeting at the top and supporting another golden fleur-de-lys with the motto *Florebo quocumque ferar*, "I will blossom whithersoever I am carried." The supporting figures on the shield were Peace on one side and Plenty on the other. Except for goods and naval stores for its own use, the company would pay the 1664 duties, with goods not covered in that tariff assessed at 3 percent. Royal bounties would, nonetheless, aid the company's commerce: 75 livres a ton on all exports, and 50 livres a ton on all imports. To stimulate interest in serving the company, the king declared that artisans who worked in Asia for eight years could return home as masters, while officers, directors, and chief agents would be granted the hereditary status of nobles. The *Parlement* of Paris registered this decree on 1 September 1664, thus formally constituting the *Compagnie Royale des Indes Orientales*.[25]

Once the company was legally constituted, Colbert was confronted with the far more daunting challenge of selling stock and raising the huge amount of capital, nominally 15,000,000 livres, that he and the syndics had decided was necessary in order to compete with the entrenched edifice of the VOC. A good deal of apathy, if not open opposition, had manifested itself throughout France in early 1664 as initial rumors of the project began to circulate. Colbert decided that a concerted propaganda campaign was needed to overcome this latent opposition. He selected a talented member of the Academy, François Charpentier, to write a series of pamphlets designed to accomplish this task. On 1 April 1664, the first of Charpentier's polemics, titled *Discours d'un fidèle sujet du roi touchant l'établissement d'une compagnie françoise pour le commerce des Indes Orientales, adressé à tous les françois* appeared. Early in 1665 his *Relation de l'établissement de la Compagnie françoise pour le commerce des Indes Orientales* was published. These works admirably strove to blunt the most common complaints against the proposed *compagnie* and the legacy of failure surrounding previous French forays into the trade. Charpentier began his *Discours* by arguing for the importance of the Asian trade: "[I]n all the commerce that is carried on in all parts of the world, there is none richer, nor more considerable than that of the East Indies." It was those "prolific countries lying nearer the sun" from which all things "most precious among men," things that contributed most to the "pleasantness of life and to its splendor and magnificence," were derived. The wealth of the Orient had made Portugal great. It had allowed the Dutch to defy the power of the Habsburgs, while paying their stockholders annual dividends of 30 to 35 percent. Even the English and Danes had succeeded in winning a share of the trade. Beseechingly,

Charpentier asked, "To what end is it fine that we Pride ourselves to be the subjects of the Prime Monarch of the Universe; if being so we dare not so much as show our heads in those places where our neighbors have established themselves with power?"[26]

Following Colbert's dictates, Charpentier did his best to convince potential investors and colonists that the French had everything necessary to begin this great enterprise. The way to the Indies was well-known. Moreover, France already possessed "beyond the Cape of Good Hope, the greatest island of all that sea," Madagascar, an island he estimated at 700 leagues in circumference, where the air was so "temperate that one can wear at all times the same clothes that we wear in springtime," and "all things are found in abundance." The French Company would be based on the proven model of the VOC, which had paid dividends totaling 260 percent in the first decade of its existence and by the early 1660s employed 80,000 men. The likely opposition of the Dutch, English, and Portuguese would assuredly be overcome by the firm support of Louis XIV. The king would not only reserve the huge French market for Asian goods for the company, he would protect its commerce and colonies in times of war. Louis's "fortune-bearing influence" would also spread over the company's navigators and "fight for them against the inconstancy of the elements and the malice of men." The young king would offer this assistance in part since the company would provide "an honorable and infallible way for all Frenchmen to acquire some property," while banishing "other infamous ways" of gaining wealth. An "infinite" number of poor would find employment with the company, thus allowing them to abandon the "shameful" ways of beggary and "criminal violence." All in all Charpentier predicted a true panacea for the social ills of the early modern state. He concluded his skillful polemic by urging Frenchmen to banish all doubts and fears and to "sail forth boldly under the banner of the August, the Invincible Louis."[27]

The 1664–1665 campaign to raise funds for the East India Company was notable on several accounts. Cole considered it "the first great, nation-wide, stock-selling campaign of modern history." Dessert and Journet have described the quest to raise the 15,000,000 livres projected by Colbert as perhaps the greatest economic enterprise of the reign.[28] The methods and travails of this campaign also reveal much about the nature, benefits, and limitations of the Bourbon state. In his quest for private capital investment in the enterprise, Colbert had all the weight, power, and prestige of the royal government behind him.[29] He sought to utilize the developing bureaucratic machinery of the French state to facilitate his main task of generating support from a merchant and bourgeois class that had become firmly wedded to the secure returns of investments in property and government office during the preceding decades of Bourbon state-building. How did Colbert seek to "struggle against the lack of enthusiasm among the bourgeoisie and *petite noblesse?*"[30] As early as April 1664 he sent out trusted agents like the Rouen merchant Fermanel to cultivate support in the main port cities of the realm. In June, the campaign began in earnest when Louis XIV, who had "nothing more at heart than the establishment of this Company," wrote letters to the municipal officials of 119 of the chief cities and towns of France, detailing the project's advantages and ordering that the merchants and leading figures of each meet to discuss the company and the methods of raising the largest possible subscription. To assist them, the royal packets also contained the articles of the company, Charpentier's first pamphlet, and a letter from the syndics exhorting investment and heralding the king's unprecedented interest in the company.[31]

The initial thrust of Colbert's carefully planned subscription drive was blunted during the spring and summer of 1664 by the continued indifference of the merchant class and urban bourgeoisie, who employed a predictable series of delaying tactics laced with lamentations of financial difficulties to avoid investing in the project. Events at Poitiers were indicative of the frustrations Colbert encountered from nearly one end of the realm to the other. The council of the *maire* and *échevins* received the king's packets on 23 June. The matter was promptly referred to a meeting of 27 June, "at which the chief bourgeois of the town were to be present to elect a new *maire*." This session in turn decided to refer the matter to the parish assemblies, which would elect delegates to meet at the *hôtel de ville* to learn "the will of the king" and report back to another round of parish meetings. Suffice it to say that by October 1664 not a single subscription had come in, and none appeared to be on the way. The situation was all the more galling to Colbert since his own brother, Colbert de Croissy, was then intendant of Poitou. By early 1665, the situation at Poitiers and elsewhere forced Colbert to utilize more exacting methods to ensure subscriptions: royal officials and clerics throughout the realm sought to utilize the weight of their offices to extract and bully subscriptions from their localities. Significantly, these royal officials, themselves entangled in the sinews of absolutism, also felt increasing pressure to contribute to the cause. Colbert de Croissy, at his brother's urging, personally invested some 12,000 livres. During early 1665 he also "arranged" subscriptions of 20,000 livres from the *Bureau d'élection* at Poitou, 20,000 livres from the *Bureau des trésoriers de France*, and 14,000 livres from the judges of the *présidial* of Poitiers. The city government grudgingly agreed to invest 9000 livres after animated discussions with the intendant in February 1665.[32]

Not all of the towns proved as reluctant as Poitiers. In Lyon, Villeroy, the archbishop, and Charrier, the *prévôt des marchands,* had ties to Colbert and strove to stimulate subscriptions. Villeroy informed Colbert in November 1664 that 1,000,000 livres had been raised. As Charrier wrote, "[T]here is not a subscriber in the city who is not thoroughly persuaded of the success of this glorious plan and who has not great expectations from the protection and attention that you are going to give it."[33] The loyal Fermanel, meanwhile, worked diligently for subscriptions in Rouen throughout late 1664 and early 1665. Despite divided opinions on the benefits of investing in the East India Company vis-à-vis the West India Company, and court decisions that held the *échevins* personally responsible for municipal debts, 200,000 livres were eventually raised. In Bordeaux, the first president of the *parlement*, de Pontac, championed the cause of the East India Company from the start of the campaign. He made sure that, as soon as the *parlement* met, it registered the declaration of the company, and he exhorted the bourgeois of the town to invest lest they lose their hard-won and lucrative privileges. He himself subscribed 6000 livres and convinced four of the presidents of the *parlement* to pledge 3000 livres each. In all, Bordeaux subscribed some 117,000 livres by January 1665.[34]

As the subscription campaign progressed, Colbert's attempt to exploit the machinery of the centralized state became increasingly strident. He wrote letters to Crown officials, the *parlements*, and others promising future advantages if large subscriptions were obtained, while holding out the daunting specter of royal disfavor if unsuitable amounts were raised. Those nobles and bourgeois who were directly dependent on the Crown, "who hoped something from royal favor or feared something from royal wrath," were most effectively pressured. In a December 1664 letter Colbert praised Nicolas Brulart, first president of the *parlement* of Dijon, for his work on behalf of the company, assuring him "that you will profit from an opportunity, in which those who interest themselves will find many other advantages." Brulart replied several weeks later and commended Colbert on his request for a list of those members of the *parlement* who were going to invest and those who would not, a tool that had proven exceedingly effective in generating subsequent subscriptions. Colbert's tactics were generally effective: in Toulouse and Marseilles subscriptions were made out of municipal funds; in Caen the *Bureau des finances* promptly raised its subscription to 31,000 livres after being rebuked by the controller-general; and in Paris, M. Harlay and other members of the *parlement* subscribed after receiving "suitable" advice on the matter.[35]

By March 1665, Charpentier's lucid appeals and Colbert's skillful exploitation of the sinews of royal power had resulted in private subscriptions of nearly 3,500,000 livres in the East India Company, exclusive of the 3,000,000 livres promised by the Crown. These seemingly impressive sums, however, were somewhat deceiving. First, Colbert must have been painfully aware that the combined amount was still far from the 15,000,000 livres envisioned in the articles of September 1664. More perplexing was the clear dominance of the Crown and aristocracy with respect to the capital invested. The hefty sums promised by Louis XIV, while certainly welcomed, also ensured that the wishes and priorities of the king, from the outset of the enterprise, would be difficult to resist in setting *compagnie* policy. Of the private monies pledged before March 1665, an inordinate amount had been promised by the aristocracy, especially the higher nobility of the court and the *noblesse de robe,* groups that embraced the traditional priorities of the king and, like Louis, viewed the Asian campaign as merely an extension of dynastic struggles in Europe. The queen and the dauphin had each promised 60,000 livres. Condé subscribed 30,000 livres, while another half million was pledged by twenty-one dukes and a duchess of the realm. In all, the upper nobility subscribed close to 1,300,000 livres. Another 800,000 livres was obtained from the upper reaches of the Crown's burgeoning bureaucracy. The chancellor, Séguier, promised 40,000 livres, and Le Tellier promised 30,000. Five *receveurs généraux* pledged 100,000 livres. In Brittany, the members of the *parlement* of Brittany promised 90,000 livres, while those of the *Chambre des comptes* pledged another 53,000.[36]

During the winter of 1664–1665 Colbert also discovered that obtaining subscriptions in his new *compagnie* was one thing and collecting on those financial promises quite another, especially when a good portion of these subscriptions had been made for political rather than economic reasons.[37] According to the *compagnie*'s charter, the amounts subscribed were payable in three annual installments. Louis XIV had agreed to contribute his 3,000,000 livres in installments of 300,000 for each 400,000 raised among the stockholders. The first third of initial subscriptions came due in December 1664, with the amount totaling 2,726,000 livres. To Colbert's chagrin, this badly needed capital came in very slowly indeed to *compagnie* coffers, a lethargy on the part of the stockholders that admirably reflected that many of the original subscriptions had been made unwillingly, either in response to veiled threats by Colbert or as insincere gestures designed to curry royal favor. In any case, the Crown machinery, which had done so much to enlist the original subscriptions, was exploited once again by Colbert during the early months of 1665. By March, at the departure of the company's first fleet from Brest, over 1,500,000 livres had been obtained on the first capital payment; eventually some 2,468,000 livres of the 2,726,000 due would be paid in. It is significant that during this formative period in the company's existence the project still enjoyed Louis XIV's strong favor. As a result, the young king was much more willing to live up to his financial obligations to the *compagnie* than were the great majority of the stockholders. The king contributed 2,200,000 livres during these crucial years, and this capital undoubtedly allowed Colbert to overcome many of the problems associated with raising private money for the *compagnie*.[38]

Financial problems, however, were far from being the only obstacles that Colbert had to address during the initial stages of the *compagnie*'s activities. Although the institutional edifice of the *compagnie* had been established and sufficient funding arranged to begin activities, many logistical and strategic questions remained unanswered. Foremost among these questions was formulating a precise strategy for challenging Dutch dominance in the trade. In short, how would it be possible to carve out a substantial share of the vaunted riches of Africa and the Orient in the face of forceful opposition from the VOC? Dutch power, after all, had reduced Portuguese Asia to poverty and confined the English and Danes to marginal participants in the trade during the course of the seventeenth century. These questions would dominate Colbert's calculations for much of the late 1660s and early 1670s. No startling revelations evidently struck him in 1664–1665, since French policy in Asia during this time remained traditional and uninspired. As with the original dilemma of organizing the *compagnie,* Colbert was content to rely largely on Dutch experience and expertise in formulating his first, rather tentative, steps. French agents had been active in the United Provinces since the summer of 1664 buying ships, supplies, naval stores, and information. The comte d'Estrades had paid 1000 livres for a report on the Dutch trade in the East, 500 for a financial statement on the VOC, and lesser sums for information on the construction of Dutch Indiamen and naval expenditures of the States General. Pursuant to Colbert's orders, the ambassador also sought to entice erstwhile employees of the VOC into the service of the French *compagnie.*[39]

The rather exorbitant prices that French agents paid for such reports suggest a dearth of reliable information in Paris at this time to assist Colbert in his initial calculations for undermining the Dutch position. Accordingly, he began his challenge in a conservative manner. Partially out of necessity, the *compagnie's* ships were mainly bought abroad and piloted by foreigners with previous experience in Monsoon Asia. The crews were drawn by and large from the ports of Brittany and Normandy, where many Protestant mariners had either direct or indirect knowledge of the rigors of the Cape route. Logically, Colbert and the syndics resolved to begin the campaign by exploiting the regions beyond the tip of Africa that the French knew best from past experience. It was no accident that the *St-Paul, Taureau, Vierge de Bon Port,* and *Aigle d'Or* made for the island of Madagascar. Earlier French Companies, especially during Richelieu's time, had sought to establish a presence on that great island in the quest for Asian riches. The maritime lessons of the Portuguese and Dutch also demonstrated the necessity of a strategic way station in southeastern Africa on the long ocean passage from Europe to India, and this was undoubtedly Madagascar's chief allure. Before initiating renascent activities on the island, however, it was first necessary to negotiate with the duc de Mazarin regarding his rights to previous developments on Madagascar, inherited from his father, the duc de La Meilleraye. Bellinzani acted as Colbert's intermediary in these talks. The good duke recognized the sudden, and pleasantly unexpected, value of these long dormant claims, and he originally asked for 90,000 livres in cash to settle accounts. In the end, he was content with Colbert's offer of 20,000 livres in *compagnie* stock.[40]

Colbert's initial plan called for the new *compagnie* to compete on its own against the entrenched edifice of the VOC with no royal assistance, save for

Louis's promised investment. During the early months of 1665, as preparations were hastily taking place in Brest for the departure of the *compagnie*'s first fleet, Colbert as yet possessed very imprecise information on the nature of the Asian trade. While this posed few problems with respect to the first fleet, since the choice of resuscitating a presence on Madagascar was clearly mandated by historic as well as practical considerations, the objectives of any future expeditions were more problematic. Lengthy meetings in the *compagnie*'s offices on the rue Saint-Martin increasingly revolved around the question of procuring additional intelligence on the mercantile and maritime realities of the trade, along with an accurate assessment of the strengths and weaknesses of France's rivals, and especially the VOC. In the midst of formulating the specifics of his grand strategy for the *compagnie*, Colbert ordered his minions throughout Europe to redouble their efforts to procure such information and arrange for the services of men with previous Asian experience. Well-weathered pilots from the United Provinces, England, and Iberia, who had plied the waters of the Indian Ocean, were not difficult to find, as these early modern maritime entrepreneurs were frequently willing to sell their services to the highest bidder. Yet Colbert was searching for more than these necessary navigational cogs for the *compagnie:* he was seeking a man of unrivaled knowledge of the Orient and its trade to compensate for his own lack of expertise in these matters. In his social wanderings among the solid bourgeois society of The Hague, d'Estrades discovered such a man. His name was François Caron. His credentials were unrivaled; his ambitions apparently without bounds. For better or worse, this enigmatic merchant-adventurer would dominate the *compagnie*'s early activities.

As Colbert read d'Estrades's reports, he became convinced that the Dutchman's impressive exploits in Asia qualified him for these grand responsibilities. Born in 1600 to French Protestant parents living in Brussels, Caron had entered the service of the VOC in his teens. The Dutch Company dominated his life for the next three decades and established the outlines of his firmly held convictions on the workings of the Asian trade. His was a mercurial career with humble beginnings. In 1618, Caron had arranged passage aboard an Indiaman bound for Hirado as a mere cook's mate. Hirado was the site of the original Dutch factory in Japan, and Caron's initial impressions of the Orient and its complex commercial network were obtained at this locus of the kilns for one of the finest blue and white porcelains produced at the time, the *hiradoyaki*. During the next twenty-two years, he rose gradually through the company's ranks thanks to his ambition, business sense, and fluency in Asian languages. Caron skillfully held various posts in Japan and Formosa between 1627 and 1640, including that of chief of the Dutch factories on those islands. In 1641, he was named a councilor extraordinary in Batavia and the following year won the prestigious appointment of admiral of annual fleet for Europe. In Amsterdam Caron was well received by the directors and returned to the East Indies in 1643 as a councilor ordinary and member of the executive council in Batavia. The Dutch onslaught against the Portuguese *Estado da India* was well underway at this time. Melaka had already fallen, and during the next few years Caron played a notable role in expelling the Portuguese from Ceylon. Accordingly, he was named director-general of the company in 1646, the second-highest position in the VOC. Caron's tenure in the lofty heights of the Dutch hierarchy was, however, short-lived. An acrimonious dispute with the Batavia Council and the *Heeren XVII* over his extensive private trading activities soon led to his downfall. In April 1650 he was relieved of his duties, recalled to Amsterdam, and subsequently dismissed.[41]

During these eventful years with the VOC, Caron had amassed a knowledge of Asian affairs matched by few Europeans of the age. Japan, the South China Sea trade, and Ceylon were of special interest to him and undoubtedly the areas he knew best. He was a man of magisterial appearance, in remarkable health despite his long years in the tropics, and literate. His insightful treatise on the kingdoms of Siam and Japan had, for example, enjoyed an English translation as early as 1663.[42] Caron's career also demonstrated that he was vain, self-centered, extremely jealous of his position, and ruthless in his quest for wealth and power. These less than endearing qualities may have been the logical outgrowths of his humble beginnings and the exacting world he encountered upon reaching Hirado. Nevertheless, they were little appreciated by his colleagues, some of whom described him as extremely vindictive, a man who was incapable of making friends or keeping a friendship, and who would stop at nothing to get his own way.[43] In Colbert's eyes, Caron's expertise in the trade must have initially, and perhaps quite rightly, outweighed these character faults. After his dismissal from the VOC, Caron had settled in The Hague with his wife and children, intent on enjoying the material gains garnered from decades of service and shrewd private trade in Asia.

D'Estrades found Caron in these comfortable circumstances in late 1664 and immediately recognized the worth of this man for the French cause. But the matter of attracting Caron out of his cozy burgher life and into the waiting arms of the new French Company was far from simple. While Caron may have been bored with his somewhat dull bourgeois existence in The Hague after decades of adventurous travels in the Orient, he demurred with the skill of a trained courtesan in an attempt to extract better terms from Paris. With limited success, d'Estrades sought to temper Caron's demands by exploiting the former director-general's resentment toward the VOC. After a good deal of posturing on both sides, a bargain was struck by the spring of 1665. Caron agreed to offer his services to Colbert's *compagnie* in return for a bevy of financial and honorific inducements. These included being naturalized as a French subject in July 1665 with the title of director-general of the French Company at a salary of 18,000 livres a year. The *liste des intéressés* of the company has an entry on 14 March 1665 for the sum of 20,000 livres in Caron's name, although it is not clear whether he himself invested or this sum was invested for him by Colbert as a further inducement. In any event, Caron's wife was also guaranteed a pension from the Crown, his children were presented at court, and Louis XIV even paid a dowry of 20,000 livres for one of his daughters to marry a *gentilhomme qualifié* of Normandy.[44] The extremely favorable terms that Caron extracted, while certainly a testament to his business acumen, also reflected Colbert's firm commitment to the Asian project and his willingness to pay any price to obtain information and individuals that would facilitate the campaign and overcome the difficulties he confronted.

Caron, with his wife and expectant family in tow, soon made the pilgrimage to Paris. While Madame Caron and several of her children amused themselves with the diversions of the capital, Monsieur Caron and his son Johan held a series of consultations with Colbert and the *compagnie* directors. In these meetings, the elder Caron soon impressed the French hierarchy with the wealth of information he possessed on the holdings, infrastructure, and workings of the VOC. His extensive knowledge on the *Estado da India* and the English East India Company were also brilliantly displayed for the benefit of Colbert and his syndics, most of whom had probably never heard of Hirado or Hyderabad. All the same, the mood on rue Saint-Martin was one of confidence. Colbert and his directors were convinced that Caron, despite his overbearing manner and open Protestantism, would yield a respectable return on their significant investment. They pressed the Dutchman for background on the basic structures and products of the trade. The new director-general graciously complied. In graphic detail he described the alternating northeastern and southwestern monsoons that dominated the shipping of the Indian Ocean. He explained that the French would need to develop both a solid trade between Europe and Asia as well as a "country" or inter-Asiatic trade. The latter, if properly conducted, could reduce the need for bullion exports to the East. Not surprisingly, Colbert was especially interested in the specifics of such a trade. Caron listed the principal products that the *compagnie* should seek: the slaves, ivory, and gold of the coast of East Africa, the pepper, cotton piece-goods, saltpeter, and gemstones found in India, the prized cinnamon from Ceylon, the cloves and nutmeg scattered among the islands of Indonesia, and the wide array of "China goods" that would help to fill the *compagnie* coffers.[45]

In these meetings, Caron also set forth general principles on the vexing question of entrenching French power in Asia in the face of strong Dutch opposition. His plan for undermining the VOC was simple.[46] Above all, he urged that Colbert take advantage of the hostility toward the Dutch Company that existed among various indigenous kingdoms. During the 1650s and 1660s the monopolist pretensions of the VOC had resulted in wars with such Asian powers as the rajah of Makassar, the Zamorin of Calicut, and the king of Kandy on Ceylon. These conflicts had strained even Batavia's considerable resources.[47] Caron wanted to exploit this situation. The French could establish fortified settlements near important production centers and a solid trade, with these rulers offering trading and territorial concessions in return for assistance against the Dutch. His years on Ceylon and recent troubles there convinced him that Rajah Sinha II would allow the French access to the lucrative cinnamon trade. Pepper could be obtained on the Malabar Coast of India through an alliance with the Zamorin. The *compagnie* might obtain nutmeg and other spices of the Indonesian archipelago by occupying Ceram. A feasible country trade could also be established: Japan copper and cloves might be traded on the Malabar Coast for pepper, which in turn could be sold in China. Indian cotton piece goods could also be bartered on the African coast and in Indonesia. Caron also urged that the French establish a strong and exclusive trading entrepôt, to rival Goa and Batavia, where subsequent commercial operations could be based.[48] Colbert and the syndics were suitably impressed with Caron's eloquent and rational arguments. A feasible plan for undermining the Dutch pretensions had, it appeared, been found.

By the fall of 1665, Colbert's Asian project was well underway. He had succeeded in the difficult task of interesting the young Louis XIV in his far-reaching plans. Using the successful model of his main and much hated commercial rival, Colbert had established a new French East India Company replete with substantial powers and privileges. François Charpentier's skillful polemics and the controller-general's deft exploitation of the developing machinery of Bourbon France had yielded sufficient capital, despite a lack of enthusiasm on the part of the merchant class, to launch the company's operations. Madagascar, out of both historic and strategic necessity, had been chosen as the site of the *compagnie*'s initial foray into the Indian Ocean trade. In March 1665 the first expedition of the *compagnie* had departed for this great island off the coast of southeastern Africa. At notable expense, Colbert had scoured Europe for experts in the Asian trade who could facilitate his cherished plans to humble the overconfident burghers of the United Provinces. Foremost among these hired mercantile mercenaries was François Caron, who by the autumn of 1665 had provided Colbert with sufficient information to develop a tentative plan of action for the next phase of the Asian campaign. As the controller-general would discover, however, the painstaking planning that went into all of his projects—be it Fouquet's disgrace or the tariff of 1664—could not wholly prepare the *Compagnie royale des Indes Orientales* for the challenges it would face in the ensuing years. Implementing the grandiose plans of the rue Saint-Martin would prove to be a daunting task for the *compagnie*'s servants operating half a world away, in harsh, unknown tropical climes, against experienced and ruthless commercial and military rivals.

II

Surat, 1668

Initial Forays and Difficulties in the Asian Trade

"I am convinced that if there is anything that
our Rivals have made known at the [Mughal]
Court, it is that the French have a very powerful
King, [and] that France is a Warlike and Imperious Nation."

—François Bernier, *Mémoire*

Bernier's detailed *mémoire* of March 1668 was designed to familiarize Colbert with the geopolitical and economic balance of power in the Mughal
Empire, the powerful Muslim state that dominated much of north-central
India, and the relative strength of France's mercantile rivals on the subcontinent. Bernier had compiled this lengthy document in the great Indian entrepôt of Surat on the eve of his departure for Persia. He was one of the earliest French adventurers of the seventeenth century to reach and travel
extensively in the East. His vast experience and acute powers of observation
certainly lent authority to the judgments contained in his report. Beginning
in 1656, Bernier had spent a decade exploring Egypt, Arabia, and much of
India, carefully recording his observations along the way.[1] He had reached
India in early 1659, at a time when the internal situation there could
scarcely have been more volatile. Rivalry for the Peacock throne threatened
to undermine the hegemony of the Mughal Empire. A bloody succession
fight was underway between Shah Jahan's sons, Aurangzeb and Dárá
Shukoh. Aurangzeb had confined his father inside the Agra fort and pro-
claimed himself emperor in August 1658, taking the title of *alam-gir*, "conqueror of the world." In the Deccan and in southern India, the decline of
the once flourishing Hindu empire of Vijayanagar had resulted in a continuing scramble for territory among the sultanates of Bijapur and Golconda as

well as a host of petty principalities. These Muslim sultanates were also involved in periodic warfare with the Mughals. Finally, the Maratha revolt of
Shivaji, although in its initial stages, would ultimately come to pose a threat
to the stability of virtually the entire subcontinent. Bernier soon found himself immersed in these momentous events. On his way to Agra, he encountered the Dárá Shukoh fleeing after the battle of Deora (March 1659). For
a time, he accompanied the Mughal prince as his personal physician, and his
journal offers compelling insights into the final stages of the succession
struggle. After Dárá's execution, Bernier remained for several years at Delhi
and Agra and became well acquainted with the political dynamics of Aurangzeb's court. In early 1665, he traveled with the emperor to Kashmir.
By December of that year he had joined another noted French adventurer,
Jean-Baptiste Tavernier, a Parisian gem merchant with extensive business
experience in Asia. The two headed for Bengal, parting ways at Rajmahal.
Bernier spent the next two years in the rich sultanate of Golconda, acquir-
ing detailed information on trading activities along the Coromandel Coast.
By late 1667, he was back in Surat.[2]

Bernier made several important discoveries upon his return to Gujarat.
First, François Caron and a sizable force of French factors had arrived with
the firm intention of launching the *compagnie*'s activities in India. His conversations with the director-general soon revealed, however, that the early
years of the *compagnie*'s existence had not gone as well as the Dutchman
had hoped. The first expedition from Brest had been marred by acrimonious disputes on the *Aigle Blanc* between the Catholics and Protestants
aboard. Three of the four ships had reached the overgrown, decaying remains of Fort-Dauphin in the summer of 1665, but the French "colonists"
had thereafter demonstrated a singular resolve to avoid the difficult tasks of
staking out claims and clearing the land in favor of a series of fruitless expeditions inland in search of gold and other riches.[3] Colbert, in the meantime,
had sent out two small storeships in July 1665 to help provision the members of the first fleet. One of these ships reached Fort-Dauphin the following February.[4] That same month, French colonists on the island had dispatched a single ship back to France loaded with a rather paltry cargo of
cotton piece goods, a poor return indeed for the 563,306 livres that Colbert and the *compagnie* had spent on the first six ships sent to the East! To
make matters worse, this storeship was captured off the coast of Guernsey
by English privateers in July 1666.[5]

The *compagnie,* nevertheless, continued to reap the bounty of benefits
and privileges that inevitably flowed from firm royal support. It was no accident that the first stockholders meeting of March 1665 had taken place at
the royal apartments of the Louvre under Louis XIV's watchful eye. The
main business transacted that day was the selection of the twelve permanent
Paris directors. Since the balloting was open and took place in Louis's presence, "it is not surprising that what might be called the official slate was

easily elected."[6] Pocquelin *père*, Cadeau, Langlois, Jabach, de Faye, Chan-latte, and Varrenes had all previously served as syndics. Others, like Bache-lier and Herinx, had not. In almost every case, these men had strong ties to Colbert and were expected to do his bidding. In the months that followed, a series of royal decrees was issued on the *compagnie*'s behalf. A royal decla-ration of July empowered the new directors and specified that one director "was to be named by the king as 'perpetual chief' and president of the company and representative of the king, the royal family, and the royal offi-cials." Colbert obtained this post. This decree also changed the name of Madagascar to *Isle-Dauphiné* and encouraged its colonization by promising that any land proprietors who lived there for five years could return to France and enjoy the titles and qualities of those lands. Another decree of July sought to secure debtors as colonists by forbidding the imprisonment for debt of any *compagnie* employee. Le Havre and La Rochelle were made duty-free entrepôts for goods destined for the East Indies. Since Colbert was anxious for the *compagnie* to build its own ships instead of buying them, a decree of September 1665 forbade the collection of duties on ma-terials used by the *compagnie* for such purposes.[7] In early 1666, Colbert se-lected Lorient on the Brittany coast as the maritime base of operations for the *compagnie*. The land was formally obtained in August, and Langlois was dispatched to oversee developments; a shipyard and warehouses were soon established.[8]

Caron, meanwhile, had refined his grand strategy for undermining Dutch pretensions in Asia. He prided himself on his knowledge of the his-tory of the Europeans in the trade and was quick to remind Louis XIV and Colbert that the "Enterprize of our Great Monarch touching the commerce of the East Indies" was "the same Design that Harry the Great [Henri IV] of glorious Memory, had concerted," and to point out that "if it had taken due Effect in those Days," France at present would be "Mistress of those Places, where the Spices are gathered, and which are now in the Possession of the Dutch Company."[9] He pored over maps in meetings with Colbert and the directors, outlining entrepôts near the Cape of Good Hope, on the Malabar Coast of India, and in Indonesia that the French needed to occupy in order to break the VOC stranglehold over the trade. Caron no doubt im-pressed those present with his formidable expertise of the main outlines and minutiae of the trade. This was hardly difficult, of course, since the farthest most of the directors had traveled outside Paris was their country estates.

In these meetings, the director-general let it be known that he was far from impressed with the 1665 expedition. Such fleets could not hope to challenge the maritime might of the Dutch Company nor impress indige-nous potentates with the power of the French Crown: vital preconditions for success in the trade. Therefore, he pressed Colbert for a larger fleet. Caron was not only anxious to return to the scene of the glories of his youth and oversee the operations of the fledgling *compagnie*, he also wanted to return in a style that would impress his erstwhile Dutch colleagues. Colbert began preparations for such an expedition in 1665. The fleet assembled in La Rochelle and was ready to depart by March 1666. In all, there were ten ships, including the *St-Jean-Baptiste* (600 tons, 36 guns), *Marie* (600 tons, 36 guns), *Terron* (300 tons, 24 guns) and *St-Charles* (300 tons, 24 guns). More than 2000 people sailed aboard these ships: officers and crews, four companies of infantry, and several hundred colonists including thirty-two women and even some children. François de Lopis, marquis de Mondevergue, was given formal control over the expedition. His title was fixed as "admiral, lieutenant-general and commander" of all French ships and possessions below the "equinoctial line." The cost of the 1666 fleet upon its departure came to 2,109,457 livres.[10]

Mondevergue's impressive title obscures the fact that he was little more than a watchdog for royal interests in the region, a military man whose main responsibility was to oversee the colonization of Madagascar. On the other hand, Caron fully expected to dominate the *compagnie*'s activities once he reached Fort-Dauphin. Much to his chagrin, Colbert complicated these plans when he decided to send along another director to share in the travails of implementing the carefully planned expansion of the *compagnie*'s activities. Not surprisingly, the man he chose was one of his own minions, M. de Faye. To facilitate the director's task, Colbert embarked over 1,102,400 livres in goods and silver coin and bullion on Mondevergue's ships. This capital was to be used to buy merchandise for prompt shipment back to France, to outfit various trading factories, to pay off local officials whenever necessary, and to meet salary obligations and other operating costs. Colbert's intense interest in the Asian project is clearly reflected in a March 1666 letter to Colbert de Terron, his cousin, who was organizing the expedition: "I am in a state of the greatest imaginable impatience to learn of the departure of the fleet. . . . God grant that by the first dispatches I learn that it has weighed anchor and had a good wind."[11] The wind from La Rochelle may have been fair, but Mondevergue's fleet soon encountered problems. Poor navigating on the run to the Cape of Good Hope firmly ensconced the fleet in the calms of the equatorial zone. The *Terron* began to leak seriously, and a decision was made to head for Brazil. That lush coast offered ample opportunities for exploration, and Mondevergue's fleet remained there from July through November. Fort-Dauphin was only reached in March 1667.

By that time, the situation on Madagascar was close to critical: supplies and specie brought out by the 1665 expedition had long since been squandered, the colonists had spread out haphazardly throughout the huge island in a vain search for the easy wealth that Charpentier's polemic had promised. Most refused to farm. Several powerful Malagasy kingdoms had been alienated and were threatening open warfare. The harsh tropical climate and low-lying location of Fort-Dauphin had exacerbated the spread of disease. In short, Caron found the settlement so deplorable "and the prospect of being able to effect an amelioration so discouraging that he determined . . . to proceed at once to India."[12] His decision was also no doubt engendered by a burning desire to strike out on his own and escape the constraints that Mondevergue and de Faye had exerted over him during the long ocean passage from La Rochelle. Mondevergue, of course, had no such luxury of choice: he was forced to remain on the island and attempt a painful rehabilitation of French fortunes. To his credit, the lieutenant-general did his utmost to turn the place into a viable entrepôt. He directed the construction of fortifications and buildings in Fort-Dauphin, coordinated aid for the settlers in outlying areas, and helped to establish a *Conseil souverain* to oversee the *compagnie*'s operations.

Mondevergue had much less success in dealing with a chronic food shortage that afflicted Fort-Dauphin, a shortage that resulted in part from the colonists' refusal to farm available land. The high rates of debilitation and death that inevitably resulted from the rapid spread of disease were largely out of his control. He also strove without success to improve the strained relations that existed with the neighboring Malagasy tribes. The island's population was a mixture of Indonesian, African, and Arab stock divided into regional tribal kingdoms.[13] Many of these tribal groups had exhibited a long-standing hostility toward any French inland expansion on the island. Even colonists in Richelieu's day had frequently been forced to fight for land and foodstuff. In the years after 1665, this tension was closely related to the food shortage problem. To compensate, the French adopted the policy of pillaging local cattle and cereals. While economically expedient, this policy did little to promote peaceful coexistence on the island. Mondevergue tried to discourage this acrimonious practice, but he met with fierce opposition from the colonists, who generally held the Madagascans in little regard.[14]

Caron remained on Madagascar for over six months. He devoted this time to directing the establishment of a *compagnie* warehouse at Fort-Dauphin and engaging in private trade whenever possible. Caron also strove to dominate the deliberations of the new *Conseil souverain*. At these meetings, he forcefully argued that the *compagnie*'s operations should be established forthwith in India and Indonesia, the locus of the real riches of the Orient. He even offered to bequeath the benefits of his long experience in those regions to the *compagnie* by sailing in person to India to oversee the initial French thrust into that coveted market. De Faye, Mondevergue, and a good number of the French had been put off by Caron's haughty demeanor from the outset. It had been a long voyage from La Rochelle, and by the time of the fleet's arrival in Fort-Dauphin tempers were already frayed. As the months on the island wore on, and the difficulties implicit in their task became clear, frequent quarrels resulted. Exacerbating any latent opposition to Caron was the fact that he was Protestant by birth, a Protes-

tant who, if not fanatical in his beliefs, had assuredly rebuffed Colbert's prudent suggestion that he convert to Catholicism to preclude problems. As
rumors of this rebuff to the "true faith" spread, French priests increasingly
came to encourage the developing anti-Caron faction on the island. By the
early fall of 1667, it was clear that the interests of the *compagnie* and of all
those concerned would be best served by Caron's departure for India.[15]

Accordingly, in October of that year the director-general sailed for Surat
aboard the *St-Jean-Baptiste*. Accompanying him were the storeships *St-
Robert* and *Couronne* and scores of *compagnie* factors, merchants, and
clerks, most undoubtedly anxious to parlay Caron's professed expertise in
the trade into large personal fortunes. Foremost among those sailing with
Caron was Marcara Arachins. Of Armenian origin, Marcara had lived for
some time at Isfahan in Persia. He had traveled extensively in the Near East
and Asia, indulging his passion for dealing in the most prized commodities
of the Orient, especially precious gemstones. Marcara had made at least two
trips through the Levant to Italy to sell his wares. The last of these, in the
early 1660s, had not gone as well as he might have hoped: he had been
cheated by an Italian merchant, lost most of his money, and initiated a futile
lawsuit over the matter. In these depressing circumstances, Marcara heard
of Colbert's project. He traveled to Paris in 1665 anxious to offer his services to the *compagnie* and recoup at least part of his fortune. In meetings
on rue Saint-Martin, Marcara impressed Colbert with his knowledge of the
trade; he was hired, naturalized as a Frenchman, and dispatched to Fort-
Dauphin aboard the *Couronne* in late 1666. His title and salary were to be
finalized on Madagascar. The *Couronne* anchored before Fort-Dauphin in
August 1667. At first, Marcara and Caron got along famously. Acting on
the advice of the Paris directors and their initial impressions, Caron and de
Faye made the Armenian a member of the *Conseil souverain* and a director
of the *compagnie* factories in the Indies. His salary was eventually fixed at
600 livres a month.[16]

Caron's fleet touched at several points along the pepper-rich Malabar
Coast, including Cochin, in late 1667. The director-general appreciated the
importance of procuring a reliable source of this valued product as rapidly as
possible. He was also anxious to send word to the Zamorin of Calicut, the
open enemy of the Dutch on that coast, of his arrival as a prelude to future
negotiations. The French fleet reached Gujarat in February 1668.[17] Surat
was then under the direct control of the Mughal Empire, a great entrepôt
of the Gulf of Cambay region and one of the most active trading centers in
all of India. The city and its environs produced some goods for export:
famed Gujarati cotton piece goods, saltpeter, and indigo. Surat's true prosperity, however, resulted from its strategic location at the crossroads of various trade routes. It was a logical entrepôt for the goods and demands of
Aurangzeb's empire, the Muslim Deccan states, and the interior kingdoms
of the south. Surat was also a logical place of exchange for Malabar pepper,

"up-country" products from Kashmir and Lahore, and Gujarati cotton goods. Notably, the city also served as the starting point for much of the pilgrim or *hajj* traffic to the Islamic holy places, and was frequently referred to as the *Bab ul Makkah* or "gateway" to Mecca. Its wealth and importance had grown throughout the seventeenth century, despite the fact that the city was not located on the gulf proper but was situated on the Tapti River, some four miles upriver from its mouth. The bar of the Tapti prevented ships weighing over eighty tons from proceeding to Surat; large ships were, therefore, forced to anchor at Swally Roads or Hole, an anchorage outside the bar, where their cargoes would be transshipped via smaller native craft to the city.[18]

Surat was a large and cosmopolitan city with Persians, Turks, Arabs, Jews, Armenians, Gujaratis, and Jains all doing business under the watchful eyes of the Mughal authorities. The volume of trade that passed through the city was substantial. The Surat customs duties constituted an important source of revenue for the Mughals. "In 1644 the value of goods passing through the customs house was around Rs. 1,00,00,000. By comparison, the total capital available on 165 ships sent to the east by the English East India Company between 1601 and 1640 amounted to about Rs. 3,00,00,000."[19] In the words of Souchu de Rennefort, Surat was "le magasin des Indes et de l'Asie et la première ville de l'univers pour son commerce."[20] The wealth and strategic benefits of the city attracted not only the leading Muslim and Hindu merchants of the day; the English and Dutch had active trading factories in the town. The Portuguese, meanwhile, still influenced the Cambay trade from their fortified cities of Diu and Daman. Since Albuquerque's day, the Gujarat trade had been highly prized by Lisbon. Even during the twilight years of the *Estado da India,* the famed *cartaz* system was in operation. All indigenous craft were ideally compelled to purchase such passes to avoid confiscation by the yearly Portuguese fleets that cruised the Indian coast and the entrances to the Persian Gulf and Red Sea. As late as the 1660s, the Mughal emperor still purchased such passes in an effort to assure safe passages to Arabia.[21]

French missionaries and travelers had been active in India since the early seventeenth century, and their actions certainly facilitated Colbert's plans. Following well-trod caravan routes through the Levant and Arabia, the Capuchins had founded a religious house in Surat as early as 1639. Adventurers like Thevenot, Bernier, and Tavernier had also traveled extensively in Asia and compiled valuable journals detailing the political, economic, and social structures of the societies they visited.[22] In early 1665, as preparations for outfitting the *compagnie*'s first fleet were underway, Colbert had also dispatched formal French embassies to the Persian and Mughal courts: two royal ambassadors, de Lalain and La Boullaye Le Gouz, were joined by three *compagnie* representatives, Beber, Mariage, and Dupont. Louis's envoys carried special letters from the king designed to assist the work of the *compagnie* in those domains, integrating various suggestions made by Caron. While His Most Christian Majesty was accustomed to diplomatic deference in Europe, he was entering into a region where French power, and his own, was virtually unknown. Louis, for once, was forced to demonstrate a degree of deference of his own. "I have been inform'd to my great Joy, of the Augmentation of your Empire. . . . For me, who tread in the Steps of my Ancestors, Kings of my Kingdoms, ever Glorious Princes, Renown'd throughout the whole World, I have a peculiar inclination to enter into an Acquaintance with your Majesty, who are Famous in all the Parts of the Universe."[23]

The French embassy had reached Isfahan in July 1665. Shah Abbas II soon granted a *farman* that authorized a French trading factory in the kingdom, at Gombroon or Bandar Abbas near the straits of Hurmuz, and promised special customs rates on the export of Shiraz wines.[24] Leaving their colleagues in Persia to act on the provisions of this *farman*, La Boullaye Le Gouz and Beber reached Surat in March 1666. There, they were assisted by the venerable superior of the Capuchins, Ambroise de Preuilly, who had close ties with the local merchant community as well as Mughal administrators in the town. Thanks to his intercession, La Boullaye Le Gouz and Beber were soon able to make for Agra and the "high and sublime court" of Aurangzeb. Although their embassy and presents were indeed modest by Mughal standards, Louis XIV's letter, the envoy's recitation on the relative balance of power in Europe among the Western states trading in the emperor's domains, and the traditional Mughal policy of playing the Europeans against one another, soon resulted in the granting of a *farman* in August 1666. This document allowed the French *compagnie* to import and export commodities with "all manner of graces, favors, and liberties" already conceded to the Dutch and English Companies. Colbert's *compagnie* would pay the same customs duties as its competitors. Its ships could freely anchor at Swally without fear of molestation, their safety would be guaranteed by the Mughal, and they were also allowed to establish a factory in Surat, at a "proper place" of their choosing, to stockpile commodities before shipping them back to Europe.[25] La Boullaye Le Gouz next declared his intention of traveling on to China; he was killed somewhere in Bengal by thieves who mistakenly took his sack of books and documents for a more lucrative treasure-trove. Beber, *farman* in hand, returned to Surat, where he began the work of arranging a suitable site for a factory.[26]

Caron and his entourage from Madagascar had reached Surat in mid-February 1668, determined to build on the promising achievement of La Boullaye Le Gouz and Beber. France's European competitors in the trade, of course, had quite different ideas. Beber's return, Aurangzeb's *farman*, and the arrival of the French in force constituted an unnerving conjuncture of events for the English East India Company and the VOC. As soon as news of Colbert's *compagnie* had reached Asia, English factors had mounted a watchful vigil for the unwelcome French appearance in the trade. In January 1666, the English president and council at Surat still had little to report: "Here hath been a long time a greate noyse, & expectation of a French Comp.a which you advise us they intend to erect in these Parts . . . & how they resolved to send out ships the ensuing Spring, which have been by all these People hourely expected, but as yet none arrived."[27] Reports from subordinate factories like Bantam on Java also revealed anxiety and apprehension: "Great hath bin the expectation of the French but none as yett appeares, their settlement in India must . . . [be] prejudicall to the trade. . . . [I]t will behove those concerned to Endeavor their hindrance, soe the Dutch undoubtedly Intends."[28] Tavernier's exploits were also viewed as a worrying preview of things to come. According to the Surat Council, this "Dutchified frenchman" was both "perfidious, & Ingratefull." He had received many civilities from the English on his journey through the Levant, including free passage from Bandar Abbas to Surat in return for the "performance of soo small a Trust, as was the convaighance of a few letters." Yet, contrary "to all expectation," Tavernier had, according to the Surat Council, delayed embarking in order to travel to the Dutch factory at Gombroon where, "wheather overcoming him with drinke or otherwise by persuasion," the Dutch had taken the original packets and substituted crude forgeries, which the Frenchman had delivered.[29]

After reaching Surat, Caron acted swiftly to establish the French *compagnie* at strategic locations around the littoral perimeter of India and in Indonesia. Aurangzeb's *farman* facilitated the task of finding suitable space in Surat for a factory. A small warehouse to store goods before their shipment to Europe was set up in Swally. Caron also cultivated relations with leading Mughal officials, including the governor and the *shah-bandar* or chief custom official, by lavishing expensive gifts on them. These activities soon entrenched a French presence in Cambay, thus ensuring access to the much desired piece goods of Gujarat. The core of Caron's grand strategy continued to revolve around exploiting indigenous antipathy toward the VOC to establish settlements near the production centers of other leading commodities. Caron's theories on the nature of the trade had been forged during the years between 1620 and 1650, when that commercial interchange still centered on the quest for spices like pepper, cinnamon, and nutmeg, as well as traditional China goods. The director-general continued to embrace these lessons of his youth. This was somewhat unfortunate for Colbert's project, since the trade between Europe and Asia was in the midst of undergoing a profound transformation in the years after 1660, stimulated by a phenomenal rise in demand for hand-woven cotton piece goods. Hitherto, these textiles had had a limited market in Europe. The reigns of Louis XIV and Charles II, however, ushered in an age when these materials would clothe the upper and middle classes in France and England. Moreover, they were in high demand as barter for slaves in Africa to fuel the fires of the increasingly important "country trade" of Asia.[30]

Caron, however, remained largely immune to the strategic implications of these changing realities. He had, after all, spent the crucial period of 1650 to 1664 ensconced in The Hague, removed from the daily workings of Asian interchange. The implementation of his strategy suggests that Caron remained firmly wedded to the traditional priorities and strategies of the trade as it had existed in the days of Albuquerque, Linhares, Coen, or Van Diemen. He was therefore determined to procure a fortified settlement on the Malabar Coast in order to secure a regular supply of pepper. Caron had initiated negotiations on the voyage from Fort-Dauphin with the Zamorin of Calicut, whose domains contained both prime pepper producing regions in the foothills of the Western Ghats and several fine harbors. After reaching Surat, the director-general dispatched a series of letters to the Zamorin professing empathy for his plight at the hands of the Dutch and calling for the granting of a site to the *compagnie* and an entrance into the pepper trade. Eventually, Etienne de Flacourt was to pursue these negotiations and to oversee *compagnie* operations on the Malabar Coast.[31] Caron also wanted the *compagnie* to obtain a share of the rich trade in cinnamon, pearls, and gemstones found on Ceylon. He had fond memories of his days fighting the Portuguese on that lush island and related stories to his underlings involving his personal dealings with Rajah Sinha II, the king of Kandy. Soon after reaching Surat, Caron wrote letters to Portuguese Jesuits and French Capuchins there, seeking the latest information on the balance of power on the island and asking their assistance in initiating negotiations with the indigenous king. Caron expected little difficulty in coming to an understanding with his old friend: Rajah Sinha was then involved in a bloody struggle with the Dutch, who were doing their utmost to extend their power inland.[32]

Much like on Madagascar, however, the *compagnie*'s early work in India was undermined by a daunting series of problems. By late 1668, these difficulties would not only threaten the *compagnie*'s existence and the heavy capital investment of the Crown but also would endanger Colbert's entire project. For a start, French factors throughout the Indian Ocean basin promptly discovered that they suffered from a crippling lack of familiarity with the quality, price structure, and optimum buying seasons for the myriad of products involved in the trade. Local currency and exchange fluctuations were compounded by innumerable differences in weights and measures. French agents dispatched found that it was necessary to master regional variations on such systems for Agra, Bombay, Goa, Calicut, Cochin, the Deccan, and Bantam. Another problem was that Caron, for all his experience with the VOC, was much more in touch with the intricacies of the South China Sea trade than with that of India. His long hiatus in Europe had also weakened his grasp of the changing commercial and political realities in the region. Besides condemning the French to a somewhat outdated strategy, this shortcoming also had more immediate practical considerations: the French frequently overpaid for inferior quality merchandise, as English factors gleefully pointed out to their superiors.[33]

The maritime challenges of the Cape route also posed grave dangers for French mariners long accustomed to rather mundane passages in the Channel, the Baltic, or even in the North Atlantic on runs to the major Iberian ports. Hygiene, sickness, and provisioning problems already endemic on voyages that traditionally lasted only weeks were significantly magnified on six- or eight-month passages, when attrition rates among the crew sometimes reached more than 50 percent.[34] French pilots and sailors also had to become familiar with the sailing routes, anchorages, and seasonal monsoon winds of the Indian Ocean. Colbert had tried to deal with these nautical difficulties by searching for pilots with previous Asian experience, including Frenchmen who had gone into foreign service during Mazarin's years, and by ordering that careful logs, maps, and soundings be kept aboard the *compagnie's* ships. The *journal du pilotage* of the ship *La Force*, which left Port-Louis in March 1668 in the company of the *Aigle d'Or*, affords solid evidence that these orders were carried out whenever possible.[35] Nevertheless, the Portuguese had over 150 years' experience on the Cape route, and the Protestant powers had over half a century each. It was clearly impossible for the French to learn these lessons overnight and without mishaps, as the experience of the *compagnie's* early years would show.[36]

The French were also forced to forge trading links with indigenous Asian powers in the face of implacable opposition from the Dutch, Portuguese, and English. These European rivals had invested considerable time and money to gain trading concessions, including reduced customs duties, from such powers as the Mughal emperor. Quite predictably, they were determined to protect these privileges at all costs. To this end, France's European competitors maintained well-financed envoys at many of the leading Asian courts, including Agra and Hyderabad in the rich Deccan kingdom of Golconda. The time-honored practice of bestowing large, impressive gifts and gratuities to facilitate the awarding of trading concessions was still very much in evidence. Caron hinted at these inherent expenses of doing business in Asia when he compiled a *mémoire* in 1665 on projected embassies to Persia, Japan, and China. "Letters to these Emperors must be writ in Characters of Gold . . . [and] put in a Gold Box set with Diamonds, and the Box inclos'd in a square Purse made of very rich Cloth of Gold, and stich'd together with Gold Wire. put into a Silver Box of the same Form." Initial gifts should include "all sorts of Firearms, even the most curious the Arsenal can afford; of Superfine Cloaths, the most exquisite in their Kinds . . . the best of Serges . . . rich Brocaded Silks." There would also have to be articles that were "rare for their Use, and for their Invention." In this category, the director-general listed "three of the new invented Engines for the extinguishing of Fire. They may be had at Amsterdam, and will be lik'd at Japan, because the Houses there are very subject to Fires."[37]

Once in India, French *compagnie* factors found that it was necessary to make such gifts at virtually every turn in order to compete with their rivals and satisfy the demands of court protocol and politics. Breaking into the most coveted trades on favorable terms could not, it appeared, be accomplished any other way. All the same, Caron relished this part of his duties. After years of service with the relatively parsimonious VOC, he now found himself basking in the heady light of French royal favor. His impressive performances on rue Saint-Martin had won him virtual carte blanche in the *compagnie*'s activities in Asia. Freed from the constraints of de Faye, Mondevergue, and the Fort-Dauphin *conseil*, he enjoyed a free hand in Surat with respect to expenditures he deemed necessary to advance the French cause in India. Nevertheless, while such expenditures were undoubtedly merited, it appears that Caron abused the trust of Colbert and Louis XIV in this regard by making lavish and unnecessary gifts to even minor Mughal officials. A desire to demonstrate his newfound prominence and the seemingly unlimited wealth of his munificent benefactors in Paris played a role in these wasteful displays. Personal vanity and perhaps the desire to redress past slights at the hands of indigenous rulers and erstwhile VOC colleagues alike may also have been at work. Gerald Aungier, the English Company president, described the director-general's presents to one of Aurangzeb's leading retainers on a routine visit to Surat in the following terms: "French Gallantry exceeded all compare, for theire Chiefe Directeur, the Here Caron, made him a present to the vallue of 10,000 in horses, Rich Tapestry, [and] Brasse Guns."[38] Such expenditures, of course, quickly depleted the *compagnie*'s already strained financial resources.

Exacerbating many of these early problems were a series of personality clashes among the French *compagnie* hierarchy, which manifested themselves almost as soon as Caron's small fleet anchored at Swally. This maelstrom revolved around the mercurial director-general. French prelates like Ambroise de Preuilly resented Caron's refusal to convert to the "true faith." The religiosity of Catholic missionaries was no doubt heightened in India, where they were surrounded by millions of Muslims and Hindus. De Preuilly and his colleagues were striving to continue the zealous missionary traditions begun by the Portuguese over a century and a half earlier. Despite the abuses of the Goa Inquisition, which Frenchmen like Dellon and the Capuchin Ephraim de Nevers had experienced firsthand, souls were still being won for the Catholic church. The religious contest in Asia—much like the mercantile struggle there between the European powers—intensified during the 1660s. Rome, in the form of the *Propaganda fide*, was in the process of challenging the erstwhile monopoly of the Portuguese Crown to spread the faith; French, Italian, and Spanish priests were being sent into the fray armed with papal authorization and blessings. In the struggle for power in the Asian trade, the Dutch and English had effectively exploited the excesses of the "popish religion" and especially the Inquisition.[39] De Preuilly and other French priests resented this legacy and were well aware that Caron had used such tactics on Ceylon in the 1640s. The director-general was unrepentant. He continued to embrace Protestantism. He had even advised the Crown that, given the dubious legacy of the Portuguese, a trade could be established in Japan only if Protestants were utilized: "The Trade in Japan should . . . be carried on by Frenchmen of the Reformed Religion. . . . Vessels which go thither, should [also] be free from all Marks and Tokens of the Romish Religion."[40]

The most serious of these personality clashes that undermined the *compagnie*'s early activities was the Caron-Marcara imbroglio. Although the naturalized Frenchmen had gotten along quite well on Madagascar, this state of affairs turned to mutual recriminations soon after they reached Surat. According to Marcara, Caron quickly discovered that he knew virtually nothing of the intricacies of the Indian trade. To compensate, Caron sought to obtain as much information as possible from the Armenian and told him to make himself rich at *compagnie* expense for his trouble. When Marcara refused to betray the *compagnie*, "he brought upon himself Caron's lasting hatred."[41] One of the director-general's foremost priorities in the spring of 1668 was to arrange a cargo for the *St-Jean-Baptiste* and to send it back to France as quickly as possible. This action would not only please Louis XIV, Colbert, and the anxious stockholders, it would also help entrench his personal power and prestige in the *compagnie* hierarchy. Caron was painfully aware that the Crown had invested considerable time and expense to arrange his services and expected a good deal in return. Marcara maintained that in March 1668, while he was directing the factory's activities at Surat and arranging a cargo for the *St-Jean-Baptiste*, Caron was enriching himself at *compagnie* expense. In the course of assembling this cargo, a large sum of money was wasted on worthless indigo. In Marcara's version of events, Caron made this unwise purchase and sought to absolve himself by blaming the Armenian. Matters came to a head in April, when the director-general had Marcara arrested for financial irregularities, put in irons, and sent aboard a small storeship to Fort-Dauphin for a formal hearing on the charges before Mondevergue and the *Conseil souverain*.[42]

By April 1668, therefore, a plethora of problems on Madagascar and in India threatened Colbert's fledgling plans for the Indian Ocean trade. These difficulties were well appreciated by France's European rivals. As Gerald Aungier informed the London directors, "[T]he French have utterly lost their Creditt as well for Merchants as Souldiers by their great debts and indiscreet management of their affaires."[43] The exceedingly efficient VOC intelligence network also ensured that Batavia was well informed on the early problems. Johan Maetsuycker, the Dutch governor-general, summarized the French position in the following terms: "They are doing no business whatever. M. Caron and his first advisor are still quarreling, they even go so far as to indulge in free fights among themselves and partisans."[44] In late April, the *St-Jean-Baptiste* was finally ready to depart. Caron and Marcara had arranged a cargo of pepper, Gujarati piece goods, saltpeter, and indigo that cost the *compagnie* over 279,000 livres. Delays in refitting the ship and arranging this initial cargo of India goods meant that the *St-Jean-Baptiste* had already missed the prime sailing season from the west coast of India to Europe, that is, from late December until late January when the winds associated with the northeast monsoon usually ensured a quick passage to the Cape of Good Hope and allowed ships to avoid the stormy May and June season in those latitudes. In any event, the *St-Jean-Baptiste* also carried other valuable cargo: a series of letters from Bernier and Caron that described the state of affairs in Asia to Colbert and suggested actions that would overcome these early difficulties and ensure the eventual success of the "grand design."[45]

Bernier's *mémoire* predictably betrayed the lessons he had learned on his long travels in Asia and outlined a moderate plan of action to Colbert.[46] France's European rivals, especially the Dutch, had done everything possible to convince the mercurial and zealous Aurangzeb that the entrance of the French into the trade portended nothing but trouble. "I have no doubt that if there is one thing that our Enemies have made known at Court; it is that the French have a very Powerful King, [and] that it is a Warlike and Imperious Nation."[47] While Louis XIV may have relished the news that his *gloire* and military prowess were being made known half a world away—and by his enemies at that—Bernier believed such information was being spread by the Dutch, Portuguese, and English at the imperial court to undermine the *compagnie*'s activities. Among other things, Aurangzeb had been told that the "warlike and imperious" French would never be content with merely peaceful trade. Their king, it was promised, would soon send his fleets to prey upon the innocent shipping that plied the Indian coast, acting little better than pirates. The Mughal emperor was clearly not amused. Bernier's years at Agra convinced him that the French should do everything possible to offset this dangerous propaganda campaign. A formal embassy remained a vital precondition. Nevertheless, such an embassy should speak only *médiocrement* of Louis's power in order not to offend Aurangzeb further. Bernier also urged that the embassy itself be "mediocre": Caron could be sent along with "ten or twelve" men, perhaps two carriages and some horses.[48]

In addition to placating Aurangzeb, this embassy would strive to win over the emperor's powerful grand vizir, Jafer Khan, by dispensing presents to him, his wife, and their children. It was necessary to cultivate powerful connections at the imperial court if the *compagnie* hoped to obtain future *farmans* authorizing the extension of its trading activities throughout Aurangzeb's domains. Bernier urged, for example, that factories be set up in

Patna and Bengal. A skillful agent would also have to remain in Agra to press the French cause, offset the barbs of the Dutch and English Companies, and overcome the likely opposition that would arise among provincial governors with regard to implementing subsequent *farmans* from the emperor in their territories. The decentralized, patrimonial-bureaucratic nature of the empire ensured that these nobles enjoyed considerable local powers. It is hardly surprising that they would resist the implementation of any imperial decree from Agra that may have officially sanctioned the entrance of the French into a particular trade but in fact threatened the traditional commercial and political balance of power in their provinces in the process. As Bernier informed Colbert, experience had shown "that the greatest difficulty in the commerce of the Indies is not in buying or selling merchandise, . . . but in knowing well how to [offset] the '*avanies*' of provincial governors" and their officers.

Bernier also cautioned that the Dutch would jealously guard their dominant position in the trade. Having expelled the Portuguese from their fortresses on Ceylon, in Pulicat and Cochin, the VOC was now "selling spices and pepper at an excessive price, far greater than the Portuguese had ever charged." Dutch justice was justice by the force of arms. They had striven to destroy "by all sorts of artifices," the trade of the *gens du pays* and foreigners alike. To overcome this opposition, the French would not only have to pursue a prudent policy at the Mughal court, they would also have to establish factories in the domains of other major Indian kingdoms. This of course meant more embassies and more expense.[49] Bernier had spent much of the period between 1666 and 1667 in the Qutb Shahi state of Golconda, and his *mémoire* was unequivocal in its praise for the riches of that kingdom. "I am able to inform you that I know very well that the Dutch factory in Golconda is one of the best in all Hindustan, on account of the great quantity of *toilles et gros chite* that they buy there at a good price." His *mémoire* urged that the French *compagnie* send an ambassador to Hyderabad to negotiate for trading activities in Golconda and in particular to make every effort to establish a factory in the key port city of Masulipatnam to exploit the vast potential of this trade. Bernier warned that the Dutch would also do everything possible to undermine French activities in Golconda. He concluded by advising that an ally of sorts might be found in this looming struggle in "Hindustan" in the form of the Portuguese. After all, the Iberians had been rudely expelled from their erstwhile dominance in the trade by the burghers of Amsterdam. Moreover, they alone among the European powers in Asia embraced the Catholic faith like the French. Perhaps an alliance of sorts could be arranged to advance French mercantile interests in the region as well as the "good of Christianity."[50]

Caron also dispatched a long letter aboard the *St-Jean-Baptiste*. In this *mémoire* of April 1668, the director-general refined his overall strategy. Caron remained convinced that a fundamental priority for the *compagnie* was the prompt establishment of a series of fortified trading settlements at crucial points around the rim of the Indian Ocean basin and South China Sea, including several independent entrepôts. Madagascar had clearly not lived up to his 1665 expectations: "Ships that will be sent to the Indies, may readily and plentifully furnish themselves in that Island . . . [and] the Company will reap other Advantages which she promises." In fairness, Caron had warned Colbert and the directors before leaving Paris that Madagascar was in any case "a little remote from the Quarters of the South, to wit, from the Coasts of India, Malabar, Bengall, Surat, Coromandel, and Persia." A more appealing site would clearly have to be found: "[I]t seems to me, that a more proper Place might be found out toward these Quarters of the South, which might be better and the more easily Fortify'd, by reason of its being but a small extent."[51]

At the time of his departure from Brest, Caron had still not decided on a definitive site for this independent French entrepôt. By April 1668 this decision had been made. Caron's choice came down to one of the two large bays on the eastern coast of Ceylon, that is, either Trincomalee or Batticaloa. His preference was communicated via the packets aboard the *St-Jean-Baptiste*. These letters stressed the vital importance of the cinnamon trade, centered on Ceylon, for the commercial prosperity of the *compagnie*. Caron knew the island and the king of Kandy, Sinha II. He had also received reports from Ceylon after arriving in Surat that confirmed his choice. As he pointed out to Colbert, while the Dutch Company maintained a strong presence on the western, northern, and southern portions of the island, they virtually ignored the eastern coast "since this coast did not produce any cinnamon." Nevertheless, the region was one of the "best on the island" with two fine bays located "between 7 and 1/2 and 8 degrees North Latitude, called Trinckemale, and Battekalo." The Portuguese had built fortresses at both of these sites during the heyday of the *Estado da India*. But these strongholds had been taken by the Dutch and subsequently dismantled. Of the two, Caron preferred Batticaloa: it possessed a good anchorage, a fine river emptied into the bay, an ideal site for a fortress existed, and a "cinnamon forest" was located between that coast and the interior kingdom of Kandy. Rajah Sinha II was poor and would be more than willing to sell the *compagnie* this much coveted spice at a reasonable price. He would also no doubt welcome the French as allies to offset a disturbing tendency toward inland expansion that the VOC was beginning to exhibit on the island.[52]

After providing a detailed history of Dutch activities on the island since the 1640s, Caron went on to outline his plan to Colbert. Since it was crucial to avoid alerting the VOC to his designs on Batticaloa and Trincomalee, the director-general had decided to utilize Portuguese clerics and merchants on Ceylon to initiate these "secret" negotiations. He considered the Portuguese ideal intermediaries for this delicate task: not only were they experts on Sinhalese trade and politics by virtue of "their long experience in this land," but most exhibited a profound dislike for the Protestant Dutch, who had dispossessed them of so much in Asia during the course of the seventeenth century. For the leading residents of Goa, the time was at hand to dispossess the dispossessors. "We have found that the Portuguese, who presently are oppressed under the feet of the Dutch are very happy at the coming of the French *compagnie* . . . [and willing] to render assistance." Caron was convinced that the firm desire to exact revenge from the Dutch ensured that he could count on the "good intentions and goodwill" of the Portuguese in these talks on behalf of "their friends," the French. Initial conversations had already taken place with the Kandian court, and Rajah Sinha II had expressed his sincere desire to cultivate better relations with France and to consider appropriate commercial privileges for the *compagnie*.[53]

With the *St-Jean-Baptiste* weighing anchor from Swally Hole in late April 1668, the first tentative steps in the French campaign to break into the Asian trade had been taken. Nevertheless, profound and worrying problems remained. Above all, it was not at all certain that Colbert's initial strategies would allow the French to overcome the plethora of difficulties they faced in this grand design. Serious problems remained on Madagascar. An expensive formal embassy to Agra and a permanent agent there were needed if the *compagnie* hoped to augment its activities in the Mughal Empire. Shah Abbas II was clamoring for even more diplomatic attention in return for his *farman* authorizing the establishment of a *compagnie* factory at Bandar Abbas. It was also necessary to find a way to convince the Zamorin of Calicut and Rajah Sinha II of the wisdom of granting trading concessions on the Malabar Coast and Ceylon. Negotiations had not even begun with the rajah of Bantam toward gaining a base on Caron's preferred entrepôt in Indonesia, the island of Bangka off the north coast of Sumatra. Expeditions to the imperial courts of China and Japan, designed to establish a viable country trade and thus relieve the pressure to export bullion to finance the *compagnie*'s activities, beckoned. Complicating this impressive array of challenges was the fact that the jealousy of the Dutch, English, and, to a degree, the Portuguese had been aroused. Caron and most of the French hierarchy in Asia already recognized that extraordinary measures were necessary if they hoped to overcome these early obstacles, entrench their position, and salvage this cherished project. The director-general's despatches aboard the *St-Jean-Baptiste* were designed to inform Colbert of this irrefutable fact.

Paris, 1669

Shifting Priorities and the
Escalating Anti-Dutch Campaign

"Commerce causes a perpetual combat in peace and war among the nations of Europe, as to who shall win the most of it. . . . The Dutch fight at present, in this war, with 15,000 to 16,000 ships. . . . The English with 3,000 to 4,000. . . . The French with 500 to 600. These last two cannot improve their commerce save by increasing their number of vessels, and cannot increase this number save from the 20,000 which carry on all the commerce and consequently by making inroads on the 15,000 to 16,000 of the Dutch."

—Colbert, *Mémoire*

In early 1669, Colbert's power on the *conseil d'en haut* was in the ascendant. None of Louis XIV's other ministers could rival his degree of influence over such a wide array of governmental functions. Not Lionne. Not the Le Telliers. Although the young king had eschewed a chief minister following Mazarin's death in 1661, Colbert's influence had gradually come to extend over many aspects of the burgeoning French monarchical state. According to Cole's traditional view, "his duties and his interests were more multifarious and pervasive than had been those of either Richelieu or Mazarin. But he was ever conscious that he acted merely as agent of the king."[1] In his capacity as controller-general (1661) and then superintendent-general of commerce (1665), the campaign to reform royal finances had continued. The irksome activities of the *Chambre de justice* toward alleviating financial abuses (until 1665), reforms regarding the *taille, rentes,* and royal accounting procedures, greater supervision over the tax-farming system, and a campaign to regain control over the royal domain yielded favorable results. Despite recent attempts to downplay Colbert's successes during this period, revenues from the tax-farming system increased about 60 percent during the 1660s, from 37,000,000 livres to nearly 60,000,000. The royal estates, which had yielded virtually nothing in 1661, would bring in 5,000,000 livres by the end of the decade. Government intervention in the manufacturing sector also increased, with royal subsidies to private industries totaling over 530,000 livres in 1669. Net Crown revenues easily doubled from the 1661 level of 31,000,000 livres over the next ten years. Income exceeded expenditure regularly, and consequently, a sizable surplus accumulated in the royal treasury.[2]

Appointed superintendent of buildings in 1664, Colbert stove to create a Paris that would rival the grandeur and functions of ancient Rome. He made plans with Blondel for triumphal arches, obelisks, and a wide boulevard encasing the city. The architectural gem of Colbert's new Paris would be a renovated Louvre, ideally creating a fitting residence for France's glorious monarch. Working with Le Pelletier, Colbert also oversaw projects to widen the narrow medieval streets of the city. To help control future urban growth, he enacted zoning regulations and building codes. With La Reynie, the superintendent sought to fight crime in the metropolitan area by creating a lieutenancy of police in 1667 and directing the installation of a street lighting system.[3] Underlying all of these actions was Colbert's conviction that the court and seat of royal administration belonged in Paris, where Louis already possessed "the most superb palace in the world."[4]

His grandiose plans for an imperial Paris, however, were undermined as the 1660s progressed by Louis's growing preference for Versailles, where the king had frolicked in the fabled three-day *fête* of the Enchanted Isle as early as 1664. At first, Colbert did his subtle best to discourage the king's growing fascination with Versailles, which, he informed Louis, "looks toward the pleasure and diversion of Your Majesty rather than to your Glory."[5] Perhaps the most troubling aspect of this fascination was the spiraling level of construction costs. In 1665, he warned Louis that he would be hard pressed to determine what had happened to the 1.5 million livres that had been invested in the palace complex during the preceding two years. By 1669, the cost would approach 2 million livres out of total state budget that averaged approximately 78 million a year for the decade beginning in 1663.[6] Although Colbert's plans for a rebuilt Paris ultimately lost out to the extravagances of Versailles, he successfully lobbied for sufficient funding to continue most of his projects in the city, including the east facade of the Louvre. At the same time, he was the indispensable arbiter over the plans and plethora of detail associated with the Herculean construction project that was unfolding at Versailles. Louis was convinced from the outset that only his driven superintendent, the administrator-bureaucrat-financier *par excellence,* could overcome the true nightmare of logistical and financial headaches inherent in a plan where millions were being expended and an army of twenty to thirty thousand laborers and five to six thousand horses was employed.

For Colbert, the arts and sciences existed in large part "to pay homage to the Grand Monarchy."[7] His efforts during the 1660s ensured that the iconography and the architecture of the Caesars were reproduced more faithfully than during the Renaissance.[8] Specialized services within the superintendency were created to oversee French artistic life. Charles Perrault dispensed commissions to deserving painters and sculptors. Le Brun supervised decoration of the royal palaces as well as the operations of the famed Gobelin tapestry works, which in 1667 had become the "Royal Makers of Furniture to the Crown." André Le Nôtre became the designer of the royal gardens. To teach theory and afford practical training in the arts, Colbert reorganized the Academy of Painting and Sculpture in 1663. The able Le Brun ensured that it maintained a firm grip on the "realm of Beauty" on Louis's behalf. In architecture, Colbert was determined to entrench his preference for classical lines. Le Vau, Claude Perrault, Mansart, and Blondel constituted the nucleus of an able group that would eventually form the basis for an Academy of Architecture. To acquaint promising students with the great ancient and modern works in these fields, Colbert established a French academy in Rome in 1666. An Academy of Music was established in 1669, charged in part with breaking the traditional dependence on Italian opera. In 1666, Colbert brought the *Académie des sciences* under royal protection and held its first meetings in his library.[9] Plans for a royal observatory were soon made and construction on the south side of the city commenced. To immortalize the *gloire* of the reign, Colbert had established an *Académie des inscriptions et des médailles* in 1663, amid a "good deal of art and Latin."[10]

As Roger Mettam's work demonstrates, important historiographical questions remain on defining precisely how glorious, revolutionary, and absolutist the 1660s were in France. Nevertheless, there can be little doubt that during this decade Colbert's priority remained the global commercial struggle against the merchants of Amsterdam, who he believed were unjustly dominating the world market economy and, in doing so, frustrating his quest for the commercial greatness of France. In this field, as opposed perhaps to the areas of administration and social reform, Colbert was a true innovator who, even for Mettam, consistently "saw his own commercial and industrial policies in terms of the French position in the wider world."[11] Bolstered by royal favor and assured of his position in the governing elite, his methods became ever more harsh in this struggle as the 1660s progressed.

One indication of the increasingly bellicose stance Colbert adopted in this struggle with the United Provinces was the superimposition of the tariff of 1667 for the relatively benign provisions of the tariff of 1664. While the 1664 tariff constituted a peaceful internal reform affecting only the Five Great Farms, the edict of 1667 was an aggressive, vigorously protective tariff designed to "injure drastically the trade of other countries." It established new customs borders for virtually the entire kingdom and specified import or export duties on sixty-one key commodities. In essence, it represented an important step in the process of creating a unified customs system for the whole country, an objective that vestigial feudalism, localism, and a plethora of vested interests would undermine until the French Revolution.[12] Although controversial, the escalation of the tariff war against the Dutch was at least marginally successful in the short run: French manufactures were stimulated in response to the effective exclusion of English and Dutch goods, and for a time, a favorable trading balance followed. The merchants of the United Provinces obviously detested this openly protectionist act that sought to undermine the competitive advantages they enjoyed. English merchants trading in the kingdom lamented that the edict had given the French a favorable balance of trade approaching £1,000,000 a year in 1668–1669.[13]

To facilitate this mercantile struggle against the Dutch, Colbert sought to reform the French navy, an inconsequential force at best at Mazarin's death. The good cardinal had cared little for, and knew even less about, the sea and the riches that flowed from possessions or trade in *outre-mer*. "To Colbert the navy was not merely a military instrument, it was a potent weapon by which commerce might be protected, colonies defended, trade extended, the prestige of France increased, and the glory of Louis XIV made yet more resplendent."[14] His task was indeed formidable. In a 1661 *mémoire* to Louis XIV on the condition of the fleet, Colbert reported that "for ten years, not more than two or three French war vessels had been seen on the sea; all the arsenals of the navy completely empty of all things; all the vessels reduced to twenty or twenty-two. . . . [T]he best sailors and an infinity of others [had] gone into foreign service."[15] Of these remaining ships of the line, some were more than twenty years old. The once proud galley fleet had been reduced to six "old hulks," the rest having sunk at Toulon from neglect. At least 6000 French sailors were serving abroad: in 1665 one third of the men in the Dutch fleet under de Ruyter were French, and more than 700 French sailors were said to be employed in the Sicilian fleet that same year. In a well-known episode of 1661, Duquesne was not able to find a single mast in all the naval arsenals of France to replace those given to a dismasted French ship by the duke of York. The naval budget had also been drastically reduced by Mazarin. Budgets between 1656 and 1661 averaged only about 312,000 livres; Richelieu, the *grand maître,* had sometimes spent over 5,000,000 livres a year in the mid-1640s.[16]

The year 1669 marked the culmination of a notable decade of naval reforms by Colbert. One indication of his impact on the *marine* is reflected in a dramatic increase in Crown expenditures during these years: whereas only 300,000 livres had been spent on the navy in 1660, this figure had risen to 2,600,000 livres in 1662; by the end of the decade it would be close to 13,000,000.[17] Colbert strove to reform every department in the *marine*. A primary goal in this campaign was to increase the number of ships in the French navy. To augment the crippled fleet he inherited from Mazarin, both he and the *compagnie* had initially been forced to purchase ships abroad in the 1660s. Three ships had been bought from the centurione of Genoa, nine from Sweden, seventeen from the United Provinces, and others from Denmark and Leghorn.[18] The *St-Jean-Baptiste*, then on the return passage from Surat, had been purchased in Holland. Colbert, however, was determined to establish a formidable shipbuilding industry in France and was preoccupied with procuring adequate timber supplies. Forests with trees suitable for shipbuilding were "a treasure—which we must carefully preserve."[19] His "Ordinance of Waters and Forests" (1669), seven years in the making, rationalized the exploitation of French forests for this purpose.[20] Foreign shipbuilders and carpenters were imported. In February 1669, Colbert informed his cousin, Colbert de Terron, the intendant of the navy at Rochefort, that he was working to arrange the services of a Dutch master carpenter and forty assistants: "[H]e will set a fine example in the economical use of wood, in which the Dutch are always more clever than we." The Dutch master carpenter Gedeon commanded a salary of 22,400 livres a year. Dutch Catholics were encouraged to emigrate and offer their talents to the burgeoning royal shipyards that were established at Brest, Rochefort, and Toulon. By 1669, tangible results had been achieved: the number of ships in the royal *marine* had risen to nearly 120.[21]

Colbert's rise to pre-eminence in the French governing elite is illustrated in the gradual accumulation of de jure titles and de facto dominance he achieved over the royal *marine* during the 1660s. Although he supervised naval affairs from 1661 to 1665, all official acts had to pass through the hands of the secretary of state for foreign affairs, Hughes de Lionne. In recognition for services performed, Colbert, in late 1665, was given official charge of the *marine*. Nevertheless, all orders still had to be countersigned, at least formally, by Lionne. As his personal power and prestige continued to grow, it was inevitable that he would achieve formal royal recognition for his invaluable and multifarious services to the king, including those involving the navy. In a sign of visible support, Louis XIV had "conferred upon his controller-general the additional post of secretary of state for the royal household" on 19 January 1669. On 7 March, the king gave Colbert's secretariat "formal responsibility over the navy in an exchange of functions with the secretary of foreign affairs."[22] These tangible signs of royal favor were indeed significant. At court and among foreign diplomats resident in Paris in early 1669, it was clear that Colbert was foremost among his ministerial equals on the *Conseil d'en haut*. Secure in this knowledge, he was able to become much bolder in his quest to destroy the mercantile power of the Dutch. Not only was France much stronger to engage in this struggle than she had been in 1661, but he was in a much stronger position now than he had been when the decade began. Colbert no longer had to concern himself with the petty squabbles with Lionne and other members of the *conseil* that had sometimes resulted from his policies for the *marine* and his overseas trading companies.

Royal confirmation of Colbert's rise to prominence also served to exacerbate a schism that existed in the governing hierarchy between those who favored traditional, dynastic, land-based geopolitical foreign policy goals in Europe and those who favored mercantile, seaborne priorities in *outre-mer*. Louis XIV, most of his close advisors, such as Le Tellier, Louvois, and Lionne, as well as military grandees such as Condé were land-oriented "men who saw the sea as a hostile, foreign environment, unsuited for French genius."[23] Moreover, as P. W. Bamford points out, the treaties of the Old Regime attest to the frequent willingness on the part of this ruling elite "to sacrifice economic interests at the peace table in favor of dynastic or territorial advantages on the continent of Europe."[24] While this *mentalité* and such actions may have been consistent with the priorities that had long dominated in France, it was fundamentally different from Colbert's maritime and mercantile goals overseas. For most of the 1660s, Colbert had been a "lone voice" on the *Conseil d'en haut* pressing for the incorporation of his "blue water" projects into the mainstream of French foreign policy. He had of course met with a good deal of obstructionism on the part of the king's more traditional-minded advisors. The tendency to denigrate the importance of the *marine* and overseas trade was ingrained in the social and political structures of the Old Regime: feudal legacies ensured the dominance of land over sea warfare, army over navy, and aristocracy over bourgeoisie.[25] As if to confirm this state of affairs, the post-Richelieu period had seen the title of grand master of the navy held by "obstructionists" like the duke of Beaufort. Beaufort, *frondeur* and colorful grandson of Henry IV, was content to head a "decaying fleet of overaged hulks." He resisted civilian control over naval officers, hindered Colbert's intendants, and viewed the navy's function in almost medieval terms.[26] Soon after Colbert received formal control over the *marine* in March 1669, the good duke was killed in a night sortie while defending Candia against the Turks. Louis XIV named his two-year-old bastard son, the comte de Vermandois, grand-admiral of France, to replace him. Thereafter, the title became purely ceremonial. Real power rested with Colbert. Another obstacle to his plans had been removed.

In the meantime, the *St-Jean-Baptiste* had reached Port-Louis in late January 1669 after a difficult nine-month passage from Surat. Its arrival came at an opportune moment. Colbert and the directors had found it increasingly difficult to bolster the flagging interest of private investors in the *com-*

pagnie. The second payment on original subscriptions, due at the end of 1665, had yielded 704,000 livres. Only 24,000 livres had been forthcoming for the third, due initially at the end of 1666, a truly paltry and disturbing sum. This precipitous decline was, in part, due to the fact that many subscriptions pledged during the celebrated drive of 1664–1665 had been made unwillingly as the result of implicit threats to cut off royal favors or patronage. The *compagnie* charter also specified that any stockholder could withdraw without making the final payment, provided he was willing to forfeit the sums he had already paid. "Many elected to do this, rather then throw good money after bad."[27] Another problem, of course, was that until 1669 the early activities of the *compagnie* in Asia had done little to inspire confidence in a mercantile community that had traditionally preferred safe investments in land and royal offices as opposed to the risky business of long-haul overseas trade, a preference that was no doubt enhanced by the debacle of earlier forays into the East India trade. A list compiled on Paris investors who had not paid any of this installment many months after the second subscription was due reveals that this pattern transcended social lines. From the *maison royale*, Condé owed 10,000 livres. Seventy-eight members of *la cour* owed over 300,000 livres. One-hundred-twenty-three members of the *Chambre de compte* had refused to pay in over 69,000 livres. One-hundred-eight *marchands merciers* owed over 70,000 livres, while twenty-eight *marchands drapiers* owed 10,000 livres.[28]

This shortfall in private investment certainly exacerbated what would become chronic financial woes for the *compagnie*. These troubles began in the wake of the huge cash expenditures made on Mondevergue's 1666 fleet. As time passed, Colbert's bold plan to transplant the structures of the VOC for his own *compagnie*'s benefit was undermined in part by the continued apathy of the French mercantile community.[29] While he could transplant the corporate charter of the Dutch Company, he could not immediately transplant the burgher investment, high profits, or other conditions that had attracted such capital and helped fuel the success of the VOC. Dutch power in the trade rested on the sincere, spontaneous desire of merchant capitalists throughout the United Provinces to capture a dominant share of the wealth of Asia. As Israel and others have demonstrated, they had banded together along corporate lines that reflected this reality, entered the trade against heavy odds, and won such great success that the government, in the form of the States General, had forged an alliance with the *Heeren XVII* so the country as a whole might share in the windfall of these victories in Asia.[30] Colbert found no such burning desire in Louis XIV's kingdom among a merchant class that had been weaned from entrepreneurship since the days of Henry IV by lucrative benefits inherent in the venality of offices that was part and parcel of the Bourbon state. The unique and sincere merging of private-mercantile and state-geopolitical and economic interests embodied in the structures of the United Provinces had not been achieved in France.

As a result, the *compagnie* became increasingly dependent on the largesse and whims of a munificent monarch. Deprived of bourgeois support, Colbert's Asian project would, as time passed, become merely another sinew in the matrix of the early modern monarchical state, "financed largely from royal fund, . . . organized largely through government initiative, and . . . kept going largely by government support."[31]

On the afternoon of 15 December 1668, the second stockholders meeting of the *compagnie* took place at the Tuileries. The young king was present, ensconced in a large armchair behind a velvet-covered table. Colbert began by offering a detailed report on the state of the *compagnie*'s finances and early activities. He informed the stockholders that nineteen ships had already been dispatched to the East. To date, however, only the storeships *St-Paul* and *St-Robert* had returned to Brest, the former in June 1667, the latter in August 1668. Both had arrived loaded with less than impressive cargoes. Due to "extraordinary misfortune," Mondevergue's large expedition had been forced to make for the coast of Brazil, where it had remained for three months. Nevertheless, brief reports by Caron and Mondevergue from Fort-Dauphin gave him cause "for hoping that this enterprise would have the success that His Majesty hoped for." He concluded his remarks by stating that success was assured, since Louis had helped to form the *compagnie,* had "seen to its execution, and given it financial aid." At that point in the proceedings, the king himself addressed the gathering. He began by reiterating his firm interest in the project and his resolve to assist it. On the thorny issue of unpaid subscriptions, Louis adopted a more menacing tone. He declared that he had personally scrutinized the list of those who had already given up their stock merely because they were afraid "to risk some little sum" on this momentous project that was so dear to him. While he would prefer not to remember the names of these individuals, "his memory was too good to forget them." The *compagnie* ledgers revealed that to date over 6,284,000 livres had been paid in, including 2,680,000 livres from the king. Louis promised to subscribe another 1,500,000 livres. The final order of business was the election of new directors to replace three who had resigned. Messrs Gueston, Picquar, and Desmartins, all nominated by Colbert, were chosen. The minutes of this meeting were signed in Louis's own hand.[32]

As 1669 began, therefore, Colbert was confident of both the continued support of the king and of his own position within the cauldron of the High Council. Louis's generous support—although it carried a price that he could scarcely appreciate at the time—allowed him to overcome the feeble private investment in the *compagnie* that had been forthcoming. To give these recalcitrant stockholders additional time to live up to their obligations, he had already pushed back the dates when the second and third installments were due until November 1668 and January 1669 respectively. Colbert was also no doubt cheered by the impressive work accomplished by

Langlois and others at Lorient, granted to the *compagnie* in August 1666. As with the royal *marine*, one of his main priorities for the *compagnie* was to end the practice of buying vessels abroad by establishing a viable ship-building industry in France. By early 1667, two frigates and a small store-ship had been constructed and launched by the *compagnie* at Lorient. Emboldened by this early success, Colbert and his directors decided to attempt a more challenging project: work was well underway on a thousand-ton vessel, the *Soleil d'Orient*, a ship designed to afford the huge cargo space characteristic of the famed carracks of the *Carreira da India*, but with superior handling capabilities.[33]

In Paris, meanwhile, Colbert's most disturbing problem remained a crippling dearth of information from Fort-Dauphin and Surat, a state of affairs that effectively prevented him from taking decisive actions to remedy many of the *compagnie*'s early problems. A mere trickle of information reached the capital between 1665 and 1668. The sketchy despatches written by Caron, Mondevergue, and de Faye soon after their arrival on Madagascar had, it was true, reached him in 1667 and 1668. Moreover, he had done his utmost in his reports to the king and at the stockholders meeting of December 1668 to view these despatches in the most positive manner possible; setbacks were either rationalized or glossed over, and marginal successes were exaggerated. In truth, these early reports told Colbert virtually nothing about the implementation of the major points in his strategy. In January 1669, he remained almost totally in the dark regarding the success or failure of the initial phase of the campaign. While he longed to pursue his goal of undermining Dutch pretensions in the trade, nothing significant could be decided or done until he received firm reports from Asia. As the most recent meeting at the Tuileries revealed, many shareholders were growing increasingly impatient to see a return on their investment in the form of the arrival of a rich cargo of India goods in France. These fundamental considerations of course gave pivotal importance to the rather modest cargo of the *St-Jean-Baptiste*. Future strategic imperatives were dependent on the information contained in the despatches of Caron, Bernier, and others, while future private investment depended on the cargo contained in that Dutch-built hull.

News of the arrival of the *St-Jean-Baptiste* at Port-Louis reached Paris during the first week of February. Louis XIV and Colbert were delighted with the news that the ship had made the voyage successfully from India, that it was carrying a rich cargo, and that a number of despatches were also aboard. The directors were promptly summoned to the Tuileries and given the good news. According to the ship's manifest, the pepper, indigo, and cotton goods aboard the *St-Jean-Baptiste* had been purchased for just over 279,000 livres. Colbert of course expected them to fetch much more at auction in France. Confident of this fact, the directors decided to begin immediate payment of a dividend that Louis had ordered in the fall of 1668: 6 percent was paid to stockholders in good standing, that is, who had completed all payments on their original subscriptions. Over 113,000 livres were soon distributed.[34] Colbert was content to allow his minions to carry out these duties. He was absorbed in devouring the information contained in Caron and Bernier's despatches and was developing a plan of action that would allow him to solve the early problems of the *compagnie,* to salvage his cherished plans in Asia, to once and for all entrench France as a power in that trade, and in doing so to destroy the pretensions of the Dutch. Such were his powers of concentration and devotion to this task that it took him merely a month to digest all of this information and formulate plan of action designed to accomplish these tasks. By March 1669, nearly everything was decided.

In this difficult process, at least two important sources of information complemented the advice of Bernier and Caron. The first of these was a *mémoire* of 1666 from La Boullaye Le Gouz. The royal envoy began by offering judicious advice on matters relating to *compagnie* organization and operations: a chief agent should be appointed for each factory with sufficient power and "honorific titles" to prevent dissension, regular communications should be established through the Levant, a school of Oriental languages might also be set up for young Frenchmen to learn Turkish, Arabian, Persian, and Malaysian, thus facilitating trade throughout the East. La Boullaye Le Gouz proffered very definite ideas on mastering the geopolitical situation confronting the French. Above all, it was "necessary to dispatch men-of-war of the king" to make his power known, "sparing neither powder, nor cannonballs," in order to combat "the pride of the Dutch." To facilitate their plans, the French should also seek to ferment warfare between the English and the Dutch, "always supporting the weakest of the two." In his view, it was impossible for the *compagnie* to establish a trade without a series of territorial bases. These fortified entrepôts, with "a good port and good air," could easily be taken by Louis's maritime forces, since none of the Asian potentates possessed a navy. Alternatively, the French might purchase Chaul from the Portuguese or Bombay from the English "in order to control the Gulf of Cambay and the Gulf of Ormuz" or Tranquebar from the Danes "to dominate the Gulf of Bengal."[35] It may be an exaggeration to state that La Boullaye Le Gouz advised Louis XIV and Colbert to launch a concerted campaign to conquer the Indies, but he certainly called for a much more aggressive campaign than had hitherto been contemplated in Paris.

Other crucial advice that Colbert received at this time came from the Portuguese Jesuit Damião Vieira. Vieira had served in the *Estado da India* for over twenty years, including long periods in Agra, and possessed a good deal of valued information on the trade. The cleric had returned to Europe via the overland route, arriving in December 1668, and then proceeded to Paris. There he met with Colbert and compiled various reports for the Crown on the vexing question of how the French could best break into the trade. In his reports, Vieira argued that there were three keys to establishing a viable French presence in Asia. First, it was necessary to impress the local rulers with *la réputation des forces* of Louis XIV, and particularly French maritime strength. Next, it was necessary to prepare for the opposition of the VOC. Vieria informed Louis XIV that the Dutch would not "resist the designs of Your Majesty openly," as "past experience, and the examples they have given in identical conduct against the English and the Portuguese" had shown that they would use *leurs ruses ordinaires* to undermine the French *compagnie*. One way to guard against this Dutch opposition was to form alliances with indigenous powers. Yet, the soundest means of avoiding problems with the Dutch, in his view, was to conclude a firm alliance with Portugal. Vieira informed Colbert that such an alliance would aid the French immensely by offering them the political and economic benefits of Portugal's long experience and connections in the region, together with the military strength of their remaining fortresses. Moreover, the Portuguese Crown, given "the present and pressing need" in the *Estado,* was likely to respond favorably to such an offer from the French.[36]

Colbert devoted considerable time and energy during the months of February and March 1669 toward developing a revised strategy to overcome the early problems that were undermining his Asian project. He pored over the reports of Caron and Bernier, pondered their advice, and sought to reconcile their recommendations with those of La Boullaye Le Gouz and Vieira. Given his limited knowledge of the region, the distances involved, the exotic and little-known rulers the French had encountered, unfamiliar languages and customs, and the conflicting advice he received, this had been a difficult task. The first fruits of these labors appeared on 8 March with his *Mémoire sur l'Éstat présent de la compagnie Oriente de france dans l'Isle Dauphiné et dans les Indes.*[37] The details of his revised strategy would continue to appear without pause until the end of the year. By December 1669, the Crown, the *Conseil d'en haut,* the *compagnie* directors, most of the maritime community in France, as well as the governments of England, Portugal, the United Provinces, and elsewhere, would be aware of his solution for this dilemma. His plans would capture the imaginations of mariners and merchants throughout Europe and come to effect the calculations of monarchs, governments, and diplomats from London and Lisbon to Agra, Batavia, Hyderabad, and Kandy.

The *mémoire* of March 1669 began by acknowledging that mistakes had been made. In Paris, the directors had erred in dispatching fleets that were too large and costly without possessing adequate information on what awaited them in Asia. Reflecting increased dependence on royal favor, the *mémoire* admitted that "[t]hese great expenses of the first fleets would have been capable of completely ruining the *compagnie,* if it had not been sustained not only by the protection, but also by the great sums of state revenues that the king liberally gave it."[38] His review of the letters from Asia convinced him that the problems at Fort-Dauphin and Surat were "grandes et considérables." Colbert estimated that well over 470,000 livres had been squandered since 1665, a sum that threatened the very existence of the *compagnie*. His practical solutions to these worrying problems were well reasoned. In the future, the Paris directors were ordered to send out only two or three ships a year until such time as firm markets and suppliers had been assured. Expenditures would be monitored much more closely in an effort to stem the fiscal waste that had characterized the *compagnie*'s early years. The directors were instructed to do their best to sell any returning merchandise in prime buying seasons in order to maximize profits. As for Madagascar, these early reports forced Colbert to modify the traditional French stance; henceforth the island would "be considered as an entrepôt of convenience and not of necessity." He encouraged French settlers to farm the island in order to become self-sufficient in foodstuffs, thus relieving a drain on *compagnie* resources and perhaps improving relations with *les naturels*. He deferred a definitive decision on the location of Caron's main entrepôt for the "universal intercourse of all the factories that are established in the Indies." In the interim, Surat would serve that function. He concluded by stating that the Crown was searching for an *homme de guerre* who would help resolve the problems of the *compagnie*.[39]

This *mémoire* is the earliest piece of documentary evidence indicating a significant shift in tactics regarding the seminal question of entrenching French mercantile and military power in Asia. Hitherto Colbert had been willing to allow his *compagnie* to compete on its own, albeit with an abundance of cash from royal coffers, against its European and Asian competitors. Early setbacks, the worrying reports from Asia, the developing anti-Dutch campaign in Europe, and the pressure to show a return for initial Crown investments all compelled Colbert to embrace a more aggressive Asian strategy in the early months of 1669. Such a strategy would allow him to solidify the existing holdings of the *compagnie,* to facilitate the execution of his more grandiose plans in the trade, to salvage his sizable investments, and, somewhat ironically, to assist Louis XIV's profound thirst for *revanche* against the upstart Dutch on the Continent. Colbert's cryptic reference in his March *mémoire* to an *homme de guerre* who would help solve the *compagnie*'s problems signified that he had chosen to embrace La Boullaye Le Gouz's militaristic advice. By the end of the glorious decade of the 1660s, the peaceful reformer of Reims had decided that the only instrument capable of resuscitating the flagging fortunes of the *compagnie* and ensuring the success of his cherished plans in Asia was a large and powerful royal fleet, equipped with a detailed plan of operations and the firepower, if necessary, to cower or batter France's rivals into submission.

The warlike preparations of 1669 certainly facilitated Colbert's nascent plans of sending a costly royal fleet to Asia by allowing him, at least temporarily, to overcome the inherent bias against such *outre-mer* projects on the part of the French ruling elite. It has traditionally been assumed that Colbert's blue water projects never found a "responsive chord in the heart of his king."[40] Nevertheless, there is strong evidence that in the spring of 1669 he was indeed able to interest Louis XIV in his Asian project and the idea of dispatching a grand royal fleet to the East Indies. Colbert's power was formidable at this time. Louvois was not yet a serious threat. Moreover, it was he, not the young Le Tellier, who had reformed the financial chaos of the kingdom and filled the royal coffers. Louis XIV had already recognized this ministerial pre-eminence by showering him with a plethora of offices and other signs of royal favor. The young king, who was also impatient for *gloire* and anxious to revenge the humiliation of the War of Devolution, recognized that Colbert had the ability to provide the substantial sums his projected campaign against the Dutch would entail.[41]

It was in this setting of proven performance and the promise of future services that Colbert, in early March 1669, presented his plans for the escalation of the Asian campaign to the king. Louis XIV was evidently taken with the idea of demonstrating his military prowess and *gloire* in a region long famed for its riches and wealth that had hitherto resisted French ambitions. Not even his illustrious grandfather, Henry IV, had been able to accomplish such a feat. The king expressed his wish to establish regular relations with great potentates like the emperors of Hindustan, China, Persia, and Japan at least in part, since lesser European states had long-standing ties with these rulers. While French fleets fighting in European waters may have been commonplace and unexciting for the king, the thought of his men-of-war making his power known in exotic kingdoms was not. Colbert's plan also complemented his anti-Dutch Continental campaign to an impressive degree, offering, for example, the possibility of shutting off a valuable source of revenue to the burghers of Amsterdam and thus undermining their ability to resist the French onslaught when it would come. For these reasons, Louis XIV sanctioned Colbert's plan and, in its initial phases, took an active and sincere interest in it.[42]

Bolstered by this support, Colbert wrote to Colbert de Terron in May 1669, informing him of the king's firm intention to send a strong royal fleet to the Indian Ocean together with three *compagnie* ships that were expected to sail from Port-Louis around the New Year.[43] Originally, Colbert estimated that a fleet of six men-of-war and at least two storeships would be necessary for the mission he envisioned. Heeding La Boullaye Le Gouz's advice, he specified that these vessels would have to be "de la qualité nécessaire por bien faire connoître la grandeur et la dignité de nostre Maître dans ces pays si esloignez."[44] Colbert prided himself on an intimate knowledge of the ships in the burgeoning fleet, and he originally proposed that the men-of-war *Navarre, Trident, Fleuron, Infante, St-Charles,* and *Tigre* serve as the nucleus of the fleet. Since several of these vessels were then at sea, and refitting problems would undoubtedly delay the departure of the expedition, he soon revised this list to men-of-war already in port including the *Navarre, Triomphe, Jules, Bayonnais,* and *Rouen.*[45] Colbert de Terron was instructed to prepare a detailed *état* on the projected cost of the mission and admonished to assemble the squadron with as much secrecy as possible, it being "important and very necessary" to keep the design from the Dutch.[46]

De Terron's reaction upon receiving these instructions can be easily imagined. To be sure, he was a capable man and one of his cousin's most important aides in naval matters.[47] Nevertheless, the intendant was already overwhelmed with problems relating to the massive expansion of the royal shipyards and arsenal at Rochefort. In 1661 there had been little more than an old fortress there; by 1663 a city had been laid out, and by the end of the decade the town had well over 5000 inhabitants, a large arsenal, a foundry, a shipyard, and storehouses. Colbert wanted Rochefort to rival the great Dutch naval base at Saardam, and great strides had been made. De Terron, already pressed by the demands of his post and his cousin's incessant demands for more progress, the construction of more ships, and the outfitting of several fleets at once, could not execute his orders as diligently as he perhaps would have liked during the summer and fall of 1669. In the difficult task of raising crews and supplies, he drew largely from the ports of Brittany and Normandy. Two men-of-war for the expedition, the *Rouen* and the *Flamand,* were nonetheless outfitted under the auspices of M. Dumas at Le Havre. In September, Colbert was clearly worried about the lack of progress on the project and was forced to issue explicit orders to his intendants in Rochefort and Le Havre to work "without stop" toward assembling the fleet so that it could depart by January and profit from favorable winds on its voyage.[48] Portuguese carracks had traditionally left Lisbon by March in order to exploit the winds of the southwest monsoon that would ideally take them to the Indian coast by the following September. Colbert, aware of this priority due in part to Vieira's reports, was determined that his squadron would do the same, with time for a short stopover on Madagascar. By November 1669, several key officers had not reached Rochefort and there were still serious difficulties in raising the crews. He was forced to admit "Je suis en peine de l'Escadre pour les Indes Orientales."[49]

The *homme de guerre* chosen to lead this important expedition was Jacob Blanquet de La Haye. The scion of an old aristocratic family, La Haye was the veteran of a distinguished military career that included commanding the fortress of Aimeries, serving as a colonel in the regiment of La Fere, and finally attaining the rank of lieutenant-general of the armies of the king.[50] Louis XIV's formal powers assigned to La Haye gave him the title of "Lieutenant-general of the king on the islands of Dauphiné, and Bourbon, and other islands and lands that are obedient to us in the East Indies." He was authorized to appoint governors and other officials that were deemed necessary in any lands he might occupy, "on the islands, or *terre firma* in Africa and Asia from the Strait of Gibraltar to the Indies."[51] As was frequently the case for aristocratic commanders of European naval expeditions of the age, La Haye's expertise was grounded in Continental strategy, siege warfare, and cavalry charges. His appointment had been secured thanks to a noble lineage, persuasive connections at court, and demonstrated prowess in the martial arts of the army. He knew virtually nothing of the sea or maritime warfare and probably cared even less for such matters. Like Louis XIV, he had also probably never undertaken a long ocean passage. To compensate, technical command over the voyage was entrusted to a skilled naval officer, the *chef d'escadre,* M. de Turelle. Although a controversy would develop over La Haye's behavior soon after his leaving port, it appears that he was an honorable man determined to serve his king and country to the utmost of his abilities. His exploits before 1669 had at least earned him a reputation as an intelligent and brave, if somewhat arrogant, officer.[52]

Colbert's instructions to La Haye of December 1669 outlined the purpose and plan of action for the expedition. The squadron was to be gone for at least three years and charged with founding several considerable, fortified establishments to ensure the commerce of the *compagnie* and the power of France in the region. In a passage that was destined to have vital importance, La Haye was told to cooperate with and, in fact, to follow the wishes of the *compagnie* directors in Asia, especially Caron, who was said to have a "profound" knowledge of everything that could and should be done for the "greatest advantage" of the *compagnie.* As Colbert wrote, "Even when the sieur de La Haye knows that it would do harm, after having represented his views, [the king] desires that he follow their opinions exactly."[53] La Haye was also ordered to reconnoiter sites near the Cape of Good Hope that might serve as an entrepôt to replace the unhealthy Fort-Dauphin. The lieutenant-general was instructed to take possession of Madagascar in the king's name, an act that was designed to bolster the *compagnie*'s shaky financial situation by cutting what had been significant expenditures on the island. Although the island's importance was already diminished in Colbert's eyes, La Haye was ordered to do everything he could that would lead to the "advantage and conservation" of the fledgling French colony there.

Since the squadron would be the first royal French fleet to sail in Indian Ocean waters, La Haye was to make every effort to impress the indigenous populations with the "beauty, strength, and artillery" of his men-of-war. The lieutenant-general was instructed to exchange compliments with the indigenous rulers he encountered and to inform them that Louis XIV, the most powerful of European monarchs, would soon send an even larger squadron with proper embassies to their courts. These sections betray the impact that the *mémoires* of Bernier and La Boullaye Le Gouz had made on Colbert's calculations. The main tenets of Caron's strategy, as summarized in his letters from Surat, were also embodied in La Haye's formal written

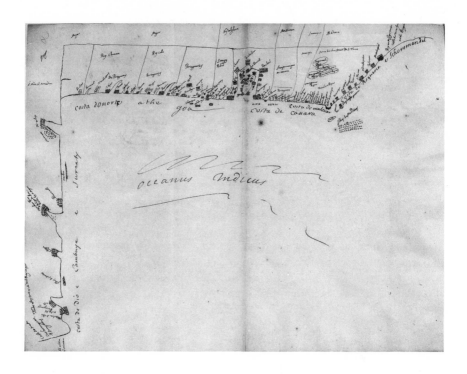

"India Oriental," Damiao Vieira, c. 1668
(Bibliotheque Nationale, Paris, Melanges de Colbert, 31, fol. 299)

instructions. In Colbert's words, there was nothing of "greater importance" for the good and advantage of the *compagnie* than a considerable establishment on Ceylon. Restating Caron's analysis of the balance of power on that island, he told La Haye that "as the Dutch at present only occupy the western and southern portions of the island in strength," it would be easy to found an establishment at Trincomalee or Batticaloa on the eastern shore, which would "be very important and which [would] give the cinnamon trade to the *compagnie*." The other establishment that had always been "deemed necessary and very advantageous" was one on the island of Bangka, off Sumatra, which was "capable of becoming more important than that of Batavia." La Haye was ordered to devote all his energies to founding these establishments and told that this service was the "greatest and most important that he [could] render to His Majesty."[54]

Although Colbert dismissed the English as "weak" and embraced Vieira's advice that the Dutch would "not openly oppose the execution of His Majesty's designs," he did his utmost to guard against "surprises on their part" by making his Asian squadron one of the most powerful European fleets to sail to the Indian Ocean up to that time.[55] Throughout late

1669 he strove to ensure that the expedition, which had come to be called the *escadre de Perse* to divert attention from its true destination, was furnished with everything deemed necessary for success, including "a thousand good men to put ashore in case of necessity." Of these, 600 would come from the ship's crews, while the remainder would be experienced and well-trained soldiers from his new *régiment royal de la marine,* well suited for garrisoning any forts that La Haye founded.[56] Colbert de Terron's *état* on expenditures reveals that over 1,000,000 livres would be spent outfitting the fleet.[57] This was an impressive sum, especially considering the rising financial demands of Lionne's Continental diplomacy, the monetary drain of Louis and Louvois's policy of expanding the army, and a host of other projects associated with preparation for the Dutch War. An *Extrait de l'Éstat des munitions embarquées sur les vaisseaux de l'escadre de Perse* details the truly formidable array of weapons and ammunition embarked on the royal men-of-war.[58] To facilitate the work of establishing fortified settlements throughout the East Indies, Colbert and his minions also recruited qualified engineers and craftsmen to sail with La Haye, and Colbert de Terron embarked large quantities of building materials and tools aboard the royal vessels.[59]

Colbert was not content, however, with merely overseeing the outfitting of his grand Asian fleet during the last half of 1669. His private conversations with the king and the formal discussions of the *Conseil d'en haut* convinced him not only that his Eastern campaign complemented the traditional dynastic designs of Louis and others, but that he could exploit this connection for the benefit of his project. Above all, Lionne's negotiations toward destroying the Triple Alliance, that irksome instrument that had frustrated Louis XIV's initial foray into the Spanish Netherlands, afforded him a perfect opportunity to press his own negotiations in Europe toward an anti-Dutch alliance in Asia. The aim of such an alliance would be to offset the much vaunted power of the VOC, to provide much needed assistance to La Haye in his demanding task, and finally to help ensure the entrenchment of French power in Asia. As Colbert scanned the diplomatic landscape of Europe in 1669, he recognized at a glance that France's other rivals in the Asian trade, the English and Portuguese, were prime targets of Lionne's machinations. England had become the Protestant brother-in-arms of the United Provinces in the successful quest to halt Louis's armies in the Low Countries in 1668. Portugal was the natural enemy of the Spanish Habsburgs, the titular rulers of the disputed territory to the north. This realization, when coupled with the advice of Caron and Vieira, prompted Colbert to undertake negotiations in London and Lisbon beginning in the spring of 1669 toward arranging an anti-Dutch triple alliance in Asia, a diplomatic initiative with great import for La Haye's expedition, French ambitions in *les Indes Orientales,* the financial reforms of the previous decade, and Colbert's entire economic edifice.

IV

London and Lisbon, 1670

Enemies or Allies in Europe and Asia?

"France being Most Intent upon improving its
Commerce . . . is endeavouring by all imaginable
means to draw the English & Portuguese into a
Triple League . . . beyond the Line, thereby to
become Masters of the Commerce."

—William Perwich to Lord Arlington

By early 1670 Henry Bennet, baron of Arlington, had established himself as
the pre-eminent minister at the court of Charles II in the wake of the fall of
the king's erstwhile favorite Edward Hyde, the earl of Clarendon. Arlington
attended the sessions of Parliament, the Privy Council, and "the Committee
'for Foreign Affairs' (the 'inner ring' of advisors) more assiduously than any
other." Foreign ambassadors, the plethora of men seeking posts during the
initial decade of the renascent Stuart power, as well as corporate groups
such as the East India Company, all courted his favor while fearing his opposition. As secretary of state, he had striven to entrench his minions in "every important foreign embassy and a string of prestigious domestic posts."
He had initially demonstrated his considerable diplomatic skills—and won
considerable royal favor—by orchestrating the end of the Second Anglo-
Dutch War and the formation of the Triple Alliance against Louis XIV in
late 1667 and early 1668. The cabal ministry of Clifford, Arlington, Buckingham, Ashley, and Lauderdale was dominated by Bennet. Much like Colbert, however, Arlington was still a creature of his king, who himself was responsible for many of the most important initiatives of the era.[1]

During the late 1660s, Charles II had pursued a cautious and pragmatic
policy that sought to regain prestige aboard and to "ensure himself the
widest possible freedom of action, with wholly subservient ministers" at
home, including Arlington.[2] To be sure, the king still ruled over a divided

realm. The Cavalier Parliament was also little impressed by Arlington's diplomatic successes abroad. The Commons rejected Charles's call for religious comprehension and were instead clamoring for the renewal of the Conventicle Act (1664) aimed at the Dissenters. Rather than praise the king and his Secretary of State for their adroit volte-face ending the Second Dutch War and forming the Triple Alliance against Louis XIV, Parliament demanded an investigation into miscarriages relating to the prosecution of the campaign. Of particular interest was an exact accounting of how their substantial war subsidies had actually been spent. Although the war may have ended rather better than most MPs had expected, the three-year struggle with the United Provinces had resulted in "the breakdown of Charles's finances, the paralysis of his war machine, military humiliation, and a treaty by which his country secured none of the objectives for which it had fought."[3] Clarendon paid the immediate price for these galling setbacks punctuated by the June 1667 disaster at Chatham. His fall, however, did not suffice to still parliamentary opposition.

Even in these difficult times, Charles sought to extend his power. While it is an exaggeration to refer to his actions as a renascent drive for Stuart absolutism, the English king certainly adopted many of the methods of his French cousin in this campaign. As Louis had eschewed a prime or chief minister following Mazarin's death, Charles allowed England's greatest governmental post, lord chancellor, to remain vacant in the wake of Clarendon's fall. The king sought to increase his personal control over the administration by having commissions, and not favored grandees, carry out the weighty duties of the posts of lord treasurer, lord privy seal, and treasurer of the navy in 1668–1669. When the kingdom's most important military post, that of captain-general, fell vacant in 1670, Charles simply did not appoint a successor, perhaps even bettering Louis's gambit of naming his two-year-old bastard, the comte de Vermandois, grand admiral of France the previous year. Ministers who crossed the king's will, such as Coventry, Anglesey, and Ormonde, were promptly dismissed. Charles also strove to ensure himself the greatest possible freedom of action in his personal life. He adeptly juggled a bevy of mistresses in the years between the Second and Third Dutch Wars: Barbara, duchess of Cleveland, Moll Davis, Winifred Wells, Jane Roberts, the countess of Kildare, and Nell Gwyn among others.[4] It is not entirely clear, however, if affairs of state taught Charles how to deal with the varying demands of his mistresses or if the travails of his love life yielded valuable lessons for ruling England.

Chronic financial difficulties remained a problem, one that Parliament sought to exploit at every turn. The war of 1664–1667 had resulted in an enormous debt of £2,500,000 that Charles and Arlington were hard pressed to address, as royal revenues were usually insufficient to cover even regular expenditures. In 1667, regular revenues to the Crown were less than £900,000, while optimistic estimates on expenditures yielded a figure of £1,200,000. In the summer of 1668, a committee of the Privy Council had produced a plan to balance royal income and expenditures, but that fall the king's Treasury Commission concluded the plan was unworkable. While a rapprochement with the United Provinces was achieved in early 1668, any threat to go to war against Louis XIV as part of this diplomatic coup was pure bluff. Charles was broke, the Parliament was not inclined to provide additional war taxation, and Spain had not been forthcoming with any cash to help outfit an English fleet. In May 1668, after a long and acrimonious debate, Parliament finally voted for a levy of a mere £300,000. This amount was perhaps enough to launch a small fleet, but hardly enough to begin a war, and in any event only two-thirds of the amount had been raised by Easter 1670. Although the English economy improved marginally between 1668 and 1670, and regular Crown revenue increased to a level in the financial year 1669–1670 to cover current expenses, "there seemed little hope of reducing the accumulated debt." In October 1670 this interest-bearing debt was estimated at close to £2,000,000.[5]

These grave economic problems undermined Charles's quest to free himself from dependence on Parliament. Unless he could arrange other sources of funding, the king remained tied to the largesse of the Lords and Commons. In the session of 1669–1670, Charles did his best to cultivate Parliament by consenting to a new Conventicle Act, among other things, and this royal groveling resulted in a grant of £400,000. Like the £300,000 levy of 1668 on wine, brandy, and linen, this increase was directed against French imports, no doubt in part as retaliation for Colbert's tariff of 1667, which had hurt English exports across the Channel.[6] The Crown's fiscal woes also made the king and Arlington much more sensitive to pressure from the much vaunted mercantile class of London, entrenched in its bastions of the City and the East India House on Leadenhall Street. For much of the seventeenth century, English foreign policy had responded to priorities set by these merchant capitalists and their escalating global struggle with the United Provinces. This intense rivalry between the Protestant powers had resulted in the Dutch Wars of the 1650s and 1660s, struggles fought by the emerging Atlantic economies in part for the spoils of the decaying imperial carcass of the Habsburgs. This mercantile rivalry with the Dutch and the king's financial predicament made a military alliance with a rich and seemingly munificent Louis XIV an exceedingly attractive idea.

Charles had been stung by his royal cousin's dismissive treatment during 1667 and 1668, as his letters to his sister Henrietta, or Madame, who had married the duke of Orleans in 1661, demonstrate.[7] It has been argued that the English king embraced Arlington's Triple Alliance as a means to convince Louis that it was worth having and paying for England's friendship. Charles nevertheless made a feeble attempt to convince Louis that his rapprochement with the Dutch was the surest method of arranging a settlement between Spain and France on the latter's terms: "I have chosen that

which I thought most comfortable to what I owe to the repose of Christendom, and have joined the States General . . . to bring a peace between you
and the Catholic King . . . in which I believe I have not done a disagreeable
thing to you."[8] The French king was not amused, however, and his foreign
policy after 1668 revolved around destroying the Triple Alliance as a prelude to another attack into the Low Countries in search of *gloire*, wealth,
revanche, and the inheritance in Flanders conceded by the January 1668
pact with the emperor. Despite Arlington's attempts to breathe life into the
Alliance, ideally by extending it to include Denmark, the empire, and German states such as Saxony and Brandenburg, Louis and Lionne had little
doubt that this ramshackle pact could be broken. Indeed, cracks appeared
from the outset. Mercantile rivalry overseas was an intractable problem: negotiations to settle such disputes were undermined by the refusal of the EIC
and the VOC to make any concessions. Spain had refused to pay Sweden
the subsidies that had been promised as the price for Sweden's joining the
Alliance. Buckingham and Clifford strove to undermine the deal with de
Witt. In the years after 1668, the only question was whether Louis would
destroy Arlington's work by detaching the Dutch or Charles from the pact.[9]

In early 1668, the decision had been made to dispatch a new ambassador
to London to encourage Charles's pro-French sentiments and to convince
him of the benefits of a firm alliance with Louis. Colbert was anxious to
have a hand in these negotiations since such an alliance would be directed at
the Dutch. His rising power on the *Conseil d'en haut* had the desired effect:
the new ambassador would be his younger brother, Charles Colbert, marquis de Croissy. Colbert de Croissy, like most of the family, owed his newfound prominence to the power of his older brother at court. Like Jean-
Baptiste, he had begun his career in the office of Le Tellier. In 1656 he
purchased a counsellorship at the parlement at Metz. Two years later, he
was appointed intendant of Alsace and did much to reorganize that recently
annexed territory. His diplomatic career began with a series of missions in
Germany and Italy between 1659 and 1661. The title of marquis and the
post of *président à mortier* had come in 1662 in recognition of these services. After intendancies at Soissons, Amiens, and Paris (1665–1667), he returned definitively to diplomacy. Colbert de Croissy had represented Louis
at Aix-la-Chapelle and was a signatory to that treaty. In August 1668, he
left for London with instructions from Louis and his brother to detach
Charles from the Triple Alliance and to replace it with an offensive and defensive alliance between England and France.[10]

Charles's letters to Madame suggest that he was more than willing to discuss the matter. "I am very glad to find, by your letters as well as Trevor's
relations, the inclinations there is to meet with the constant desire I have always had to make a stricter alliance with France than there has hitherto
been . . . and when Monsieur de Colbert comes, I hope that he will have
those powers as will finish what we all desire. . . . [H]e shall find nothing

wanting on my part."[11] The new ambassador arrived on 6 (16) August. He made his public entry into London and held his first formal audience with Charles late that month with much fanfare: "[On] 19 [29] August I saw the magnificent Entrie of the Fr: Ambassador Colbert received in the Banqueting house: I had never seene a richer Coach than what he came in to Whitehall." Colbert de Croissy promptly leased Leicester House from the Sidney family and began the tedious business of ingratiating himself into the powerful court clique that frequented the entertainments hosted by the king and Arlington in London, Newmarket, and Euston.[12] He soon discovered that although Charles wanted such an alliance, especially if it were aimed at the Dutch, he was determined to protect England's commercial and naval interests. In a letter of September 1668, the king informed Madame that while he was indeed "satisfied with Monsieur Colbert" and his "inclinations [were] still the same," there were two chief "impediments" against "an entire union." The most important of these was "the great application there is at this time in France to establish trade, and to be very considerable at sea, which is so jealous a point to us here, who can be only considerable by our trade and power by sea." Charles made it clear that "any steps that France makes that way must continue a jealousy between the two Nations, which will upon all occasions, be a great hindrance to an entire friendship. . . . [I]t must be dangerous to me at home to make an entire league till first the great and principal interest of this nation be secure which is trade."[13]

There were other formidable obstacles to overcome in reaching such an alliance. In his instructions to de Croissy of August 1669, Louis XIV made it clear that Arlington, as the architect of the Triple Alliance, would be an opponent of any firm pact between the two Crowns: "[I]f the affairs of England were today in other hands than those of the said lord . . . the close alliance between their majesties . . . would be very easy to arrange, and would almost conclude itself." Since English ministers "scarcely ever felt any scruples about taking French money," de Croissy was to offer Arlington a lump sum of £25,000 and a pension of £2,500 a year to overcome his opposition. Louis was not sure that this tactic would succeed, given the secretary of state's "aversion for this Crown and his commitments to Spain and Holland," but de Croissy was to make the offer.[14] Arlington, however, proved both incorruptible and opposed to the alliance. While Charles may not have believed that French aggrandizement on the Continent was a significant danger to England, his secretary of state most certainly did. Arlington was extremely wary of Louis's military power and his demonstrated territorial ambitions directed at the weak cornerstone of his own European diplomatic system, Habsburg Spain. Since Louis's money, for once, had failed to achieve its objective, de Croissy was forced to embrace the disadvantageous policy of seeking to undermine Arlington's position at court by discrediting him at every opportunity with his king. As Ralph Montagu, the English ambassador in Paris, informed Arlington, "[T]he French Ambassador does do

you all the ill offices that can be here, and says, if it were not for you, France
and England would join."[15] Louis and his *Conseil d'en haut* in vain hoped
that Bennet would lose favor and be replaced by the more manageable and
pro-French duke of Buckingham. But, as Louis admitted in December
1668, Arlington remained "absolute master of English affairs."[16] French artifices over the next two years did nothing to alter this state of affairs.

Another intractable source of opposition to the alliance was the powerful
merchant class of England. English merchants and businessmen were extremely anti-French at that time, "owing to [their] belief that the current
balance of Anglo-French trade was very unfavorable to England; its attitude
hardened by Colbert's protective tariff of 1667, which raised duties on foreign manufactured goods about 100 percent." Although much has been
made of Colbert's mercantile struggle with the United Provinces, the escalation of his economic campaign against the Dutch also had notable effects
on commercial relations with England: France was the only major European
market during the 1660s in which the value of English exports declined.
Merchants in Parliament responded to Colbert's aggressive 1667 tariff with
a motion to raise duties on French imports, and the levies of £700,000 between 1668 and 1670 were to be raised largely on duties falling on traditional French imports.[17] Perhaps chief among the mercantile opponents to a
league with France were the twenty-four members of the Court of Committees of the East India Company, the corporate entity most threatened by
Colbert's developing Asian strategy. The power and political influence of
the EIC directors was growing as the Company's shaky operations stabi-
lized and expanded in the years after the Second Dutch War.

English mercantile power in Asia had been less than impressive for much
of the seventeenth century. In terms of trading volume, profits, dividends
paid to investors, and factories held, the London Company had been badly
outstripped by the VOC. The exploits of early captain-adventurers such as
James Lancaster, Henry Middleton, and Thomas Roe and the administrative skills of men such as William Methhold had resulted in the foundation
of factories from Bandar Abbas in Persia to Bantam on the island of Java.
Effectively excluded from the Indonesian trade by Jan Pieterszoon Coen's
ruthless quest for a monopoly on these spice-producing islands, the English
had increasingly concentrated their trading activities in India. By 1653, the
London Company possessed a string of littoral trading factories in India, including posts at Surat, Masulipatnam, Madras, Balasore, and Hugli in the
rich Mughal province of Bengal. Problems, however, persisted. "During the
second quarter of the century the directors faced one crisis after another in
trying to keep the company afloat." Adherence to the initial and archaic system of successive joint stocks terminable at short intervals ensured that the
"problem of liquidity was always with them." The political and military
"disruptions" caused by the Thirty Years' War, the policies of Charles I,
which included chartering a rival East India Company in December 1635,

and the dissolution inherent in the civil war "all adversely affected the fortunes of the Company."[18]

A partial rehabilitation began with Cromwell's charter of October 1657. This document did much to unify and solidify the company's operations by establishing a permanent "joint stock," based on the Dutch model, in place of the traditional system of successive joint stocks terminable at short intervals. The desire to promote the East India trade continued during the initial stages of the Restoration. In April 1661, Charles II issued a charter that reiterated the main points of Cromwell's declaration: the company would finance its operations based on a permanent joint stock, it might declare war and make peace with indigenous Asian powers, it could dispense civil and criminal justice in the territories it controlled, and interlopers could be repatriated. Although parliamentary confirmation proved elusive, Charles rather haphazardly provided a boon to English pretensions in the trade by procuring a vital independent entrepôt for the Crown, and eventually the company, by the terms of his 1661 marriage treaty with Catherine of Braganza. On paper, the alliance with Portugal stipulated a quid pro quo between the Crowns, with the English providing protection for the *Estado da India* against the continuing ravages of the VOC and receiving Bombay, Tangiers, and a good deal of cash in return. A prolonged and acrimonious dispute involving the transfer of Bombay between 1661 and 1665, a series of lawsuits by dispossessed Portuguese landowners in the vicinity, as well as the high cost of maintaining a royal garrison, quickly convinced Charles to lease this Indian headache to a reluctant company in 1668.[19]

For the company, this was indeed fortunate timing since events of the 1660s had revealed its continuing vulnerability on both land and sea to Asian and European rivals. In 1664, Shivaji had sacked Surat, instilling fear and apprehension in the hearts of rulers and merchants from Agra to London. While the able George Oxenden had managed to defend the English factory during the attack, this violent foray by the Maratha leader into Aurangzeb's domains was a clear demonstration of the company's continued feebleness on land in the face of the superior forces of the indigenous powers. More disturbing to the merchant capitalists of Leadenhall Street was the fact that the Mughal emperor had not been able to provide the protection inherent in his *farmans* that were, of course, vital for continued trading operations in Gujarat. The Second Dutch War, while gaining New Amsterdam for England, had nevertheless exposed the continuing weakness of the East India Company vis-a-vis the naval power of the VOC. Porakad and Karawar, small, but significant, English factories on the Malabar Coast, were captured by the Dutch during the initial stages of the war. The remaining factories in India were also judged to be vulnerable to attack. As Oxenden informed the London directors, "[Y]ou must expect nothing there [in Malabar] and in a short time nowhere else."[20] Gerald Aungier, Oxenden's successor as president in 1669, sought to remedy these problems

by beginning the process of turning Bombay into an exclusive, fortified entrepôt for the company's activities, a bastion of English power on the Indian coast, ideally immune to the political and military machinations of her
enemies. The small, unhealthy community he inherited would soon be
transformed into a thriving town of over 50,000 inhabitants.[21]

Aungier's accession to power, his far-reaching reforms in Bombay, and
the welcome 1667 peace with the United Provinces ushered in a period of
notable expansion in the company's activities. Between 1668 and 1669, free
from concern of predatory Dutch fleets in both Indian Ocean and Atlantic
waters, the English Company exported goods worth over £202,000 to Asia
and imported commodities worth £432,869. By 1670, the proceeds from
the company's sales of imports into their docks and warehouses on the
Thames at Blackwall and Poplar were running at about £1,000,000 a year.[22]
In light of these events, the men who sat in the Court of Committees on
Leadenhall Street, like their merchant brethren in the City, had no desire to
jeopardize these hard-won advances in another encounter with the Dutch
and their much vaunted military might in Asia. The merchant class as a
whole had generally supported the second Dutch War "in the hope that it
would be as profitable as the first." It had been a disappointment. "There
had been no economic expansion; there was no reason to believe that a
third war would differ from the second." Arlington "was well aware of the
shifting currents of mercantile opinion," especially regarding the East India
Company. The Bombay agreement of 1668 was emblematic of the close
ties that existed between the Crown and the company. The secretary of
state had business and social ties with various directors and was willing to
fight for their interests, in particular when it concerned commercial rivalry
with France.[23]

The Leadenhall directors and their agents in Paris and Asia had followed
Colbert's strenuous efforts to establish France as a major power in the trade
with intense interest and apprehension. The initial setbacks of the French
compagnie fleets and the rather mindless concentration on Madagascar offered some encouragement. From the outset, however, London made it
clear that it was "not in our Interest, to encourage them in the trade."[24]
Not until the spring of 1668 did news of Caron's arrival in Surat and the
early disputes of the French hierarchy in Asia reach London. While the English saw this as rather typical French behavior and were no doubt heart-
ened by it, there were worrying, if not ominous, signs from Paris. Foremost
among these, according to the company's friends in the French capital, was
Louis XIV's disturbing and uncharacteristic interest in Colbert's efforts in
outre-mer: "[T]he French King doth soe much encourage the Comp. & fur-
nisheth them with money, desiring to bring the trade of India to his kingdome, that there hath been 3 or 4 ships preparing this season [1668]. . . .
[W]ee believe they will go on in that trade & therefore expect they will
stand in competition with us in the future."[25] While peace still existed

between the powers in Europe, the English Company's response to this implicit threat, in true capitalist fashion, was to call for more efficient business practices on the part of its servants. In a letter of March 1668, Oxenden was ordered to manage all his affairs "with great frugality": goods were to be bought "cheap," cargoes were to be dispatched as quickly as possible to Europe, and expenditures were to be cut wherever and whenever possible. The following February, the directors noted in response to Colbert's threat that "[a]s to the French, the more they engage in the India trade, the more carefull you must be, in the manadgment of ours."[26]

The relative unease of the Court of Committees was exacerbated in 1669 by reports relating to the escalation of Colbert's project in the wake of the *St-Jean-Baptiste*'s arrival. Hitherto, the French *compagnie* had been content to concentrate on peaceful mercantile competition with their Dutch and English counterparts, a rivalry in which the Protestant powers by virtue of experience and financial backing at home enjoyed every advantage. Beginning in the summer of 1669, it became apparent that Colbert had lost patience with such a strategy and was considering a militant reformation of his Asian project. This was hardly welcomed news in the warehouses along the Thames. In letters of December 1669 and January 1670 to Arlington, Perwich warned that Colbert was violently stirring about the "propagation of Commerce" and that "it may bee feared that the French will have Such considerable forces in both the Indies according to the great marine preparacons they are now making" that upon the "first noyse of a breach" the French would be able to act "& find the World in those parts unprepared to receive them."[27] Francis Vernon, Montagu's private secretary in Paris, informed London in November 1669 that Colbert was assembling a powerful fleet of at least six men-of-war "to go to India," adding that Louis XIV supported the project and "Resolves by all means to Establish a trade in India."[28] In the months that followed, Montagu, Perwich, and Vernon detailed Colbert's preparations for his grand Asian fleet in their despatches to Arlington. The secretary of state in turn wasted little time in informing his friend on Leadenhall Street of this worrying turn of events. Based on this information, as early as 1669 the directors were able to warn Aungier of a "considerable fleet of 7 or 8 great ships" that Colbert would be sending and ordered that all necessary precautions be taken.[29] Needless to say, the directors also expected their good friend Henry Bennet to use his considerable power and influence to undermine any French diplomatic initiative that would either directly or indirectly facilitate Colbert's plans in the Indian Ocean trade.

In the midst of these geopolitical and economic machinations relating to the Asian trade, Charles II had decided to break the diplomatic stalemate regarding the alliance with France by proffering an offensive and defensive pact to Louis, highlighted by "what was to become the notorious offer to declare himself a Catholic, if Louis gave him £200,000 with which to secure his position." He devised this plan of action with his sister in December 1668, announced his intentions to James, duke of York, Arlington, Clifford, and Lord Arundell of Wardour at a meeting of 25 January 1669, and dispatched the trusted Arundell with his proposal to Paris in March 1669.[30] The political, religious, and economic pitfalls inherent for Charles in any rapprochement with Louis XIV ensured highly secretive and poorly documented negotiations over the next thirteen months. These rather murky discussions ultimately yielded the so-called secret Treaty of Dover of 22 May/1 June 1670, as well as two sham treaties of December 1670 and February 1672, concessions to the Machiavellian nature of kingship in Restoration England and the political and religious divisions in the cabal. According to the provisions of the treaty signed at Dover, Charles agreed to declare himself a Catholic at a moment convenient for himself and then to join Louis in waging war on the United Provinces at a time of the latter's choosing. Since a public declaration of Catholicism would undoubtedly create problems with his subjects, he would be assisted by Louis with 2,000,000 livres and, if necessary, troops. Neither king would be able to make peace with the Dutch without the other's consent. For his trouble, Charles would receive Sluys, Walcheren, and Cadasand and be paid 3,000,000 livres annually during the war. Louis would bear the expenses of land forces, except for the promised 6,000 English infantrymen, and he would add thirty of Colbert's men-of-war to Charles's fifty.[31]

Much has traditionally been made of the fact that Arlington, Colbert, and de Croissy were excluded, in one fashion or another, from the initial stages of these negotiations. Arlington, of course, was highly suspicious of Louis's territorial ambitions on the continent at the likely expense of Habsburg Spain. He was also "appalled" by Charles's Catholicity scheme. Yet the secretary of state was also "the one man in England whose acquiescence in the French alliance was absolutely indispensable."[32] Out of political and personal expediency, Arlington did acquiesce. As he later told de Croissy, he had done so merely "pour éviter sa perte."[33] It is clear, however, that he was also swayed by the arguments contained in an April 1669 letter from Montagu, in which the ambassador informed him that the French were so determined to have an alliance that they would offer terms that Charles would be unable to refuse. As Montagu advised, "[W]hatever is done, I would have your Lordship have the doing it."[34] Bennet heeded this sound advice. He swiftly acted to mend his strained credit with Madame, to insinuate himself into the negotiations, and to give the appearance that he genuinely favored the alliance.

Although he had decided to play along with Charles's distasteful diplomatic gambit in an effort to retain his influence at court, Arlington in fact did his best during the next year to undermine the talks with Paris. In revived public discussions toward a commercial treaty in the summer of 1669 he made blatantly unreasonable demands, including a call for the elimination of Colbert's 1667 tariff with no corresponding reduction in English tariffs, both to prevent any Anglo-French understanding and to win further favor with London's merchant community. This strategy was thwarted by Charles's willingness to let the commercial treaty die a merciful death, while continuing with secret political and military discussions with the French. As the king's sister pointed out with a seemingly irrefutable logic that Charles was all too willing to embrace, the soundest way to expand English commercial power was to destroy the Dutch.[35] After being brought into the political discussions with de Croissy in the fall of 1669, Arlington adopted similar tactics. His draft of demands presented to the French ambassador in December of that year called, among other things, for French assistance for the English conquest of all Spanish America. By all accounts, this document left the younger Colbert speechless. Once it became clear that such tactics could not succeed, the secretary of state sought to win the most favorable terms possible for his king, while holding out hope that the timing for the public declaration associated with the Catholicity scheme and thus the timetable for any attack on the Dutch would allow the Crown to avoid another costly war with the United Provinces.[36]

It has generally been assumed that Colbert was excluded from the very early stages of the negotiations initiated by Arundell's March 1669 mission to Paris.[37] If this was indeed the case, it probably reflected a realization on Louis XIV's part that his controller-general's mercantile and *outre-mer* priorities were at odds with the commercial concerns and demands of the English and would thus complicate any negotiations with Charles. The restored Stuart had, after all, stated in his correspondence with Madame that Colbert's "great application" toward trade and sea power was the most important impediment to an "entire union" between the powers, and that future French steps in that direction would "continue a jealousy between the 2 Nations which will upon all occasions be a great hindrance to an entire friendship."[38] Colbert is usually considered to have been let in on the secret talks in mid-June, at about the time when both Charles and Louis demonstrated their serious intentions to pursue the discussions. At that time, Louis's foreign policy goals on the continent had conspired to confront the young king and his ministers with a difficult choice between fighting another war with Spain or a war directed against the Dutch. Upon hearing of Arundell's offer, Colbert immediately began to press, along with Lionne, for the acceptance of the English proposal and a war with his main commercial rival.[39] It is not entirely clear, however, if Colbert was left out of the negotiations until mid-June. His letters to de Croissy from late March on suggest that he may have been aware of Charles's offer. From that point on Colbert pressed his brother, who after all had been sent to England to detach Charles from the Triple Alliance and to arrange an anti-Dutch treaty, to work toward the extension of any alliance to include a joint offensive in Asia against the Dutch and thus facilitate the lofty mission of the large royal fleet he was then outfitting at Rochefort.

On 20 March, Colbert ordered his brother to work toward such an alliance with the English but with great circumspection so that the Dutch would not discover his plans: "It is very certain that the extreme avarice and the tyrannical manner" with which the Dutch conducted themselves in trade created animosity toward them, a situation which the French might exploit. Ten days later, he advised de Croissy to use the complaints of the English Company against the VOC to his advantage: "[I]t is always necessary to profit from all the complaints that you have on this matter to advance your negotiations." On 20 April he reminded his brother that the principal difference between the Protestant powers consisted in the liberty of trade that the English Company was claiming in Asia against the monopolistic pretensions of the VOC. Colbert instructed de Croissy to remind Charles II "that if he unites with the King," the two powers could take joint action against the Dutch and break their stranglehold over the trade in the East Indies.[40] On 18 April 1669, following a conversation with the English monarch on the subject of the Asian trade and Colbert's desire to unite with the English to challenge the commercial and military power of the VOC, de Croissy informed his brother that Charles had demonstrated very little interest in such an arrangement. A little more than a week later, Colbert acknowledged this disappointing news but nevertheless instructed de Croissy not to lose any "favorable occasions" to make Charles realize the advantages that he could obtain by extending any alliance with Louis XIV to the Indian Ocean as well.[41]

The best efforts of the French ambassador over the next year were all in vain. Charles and Arlington recognized the power and influence of the London merchant community in general and the members of the Court of Committees of the East India Company in particular. The recently restored Crown had little desire to antagonize such interests by embracing any offer from Colbert and his brother that would either directly or indirectly assist French commerce. Therefore, any attempt to extend the treaty signed at Dover in the spring of 1670 to include clauses for a joint offensive in Asia against the Dutch Company was a priori doomed to failure, as the Colberts discovered. Charles and, less enthusiastically, Arlington were willing to accede to a deal in Europe since Louis's armies would seek to destroy the United Provinces on land, and French booty from a successful campaign would, for the most part, be restricted to the dynastic territory the young French king claimed to the north. The provisions of Dover, as favorably interpreted by the English Crown, seemingly guaranteed it prizes that would translate into increased trade. While Charles and Arlington thus believed they could sell the Anglo-French treaty in all of its permutations to a hostile Parliament and the merchants of London under such circumstances, they could not hope to do so if such an alliance, secret or not, called for English assistance for establishing a powerful French presence in the most lucrative trading system in the world and one in which the London Company itself enjoyed, at best, a marginal position. French assistance toward extending English trade and empire may have been acceptable, as Arlington's semi-serious clause on Spanish America reflected, but Charles and his clever ministers recognized that the day an English fleet fought to extend French trade and empire was a day not far removed from another Naseby. William Langhorn, the English chief at Madras, later provided words that aptly summarize Colbert's negotiations with London: "[T]he French desire no better than to have us to joyne with them. . . . [W]e will never be drawne to doe a thing so much against our Interest and our inclinations."[42]

Colbert's diplomatic efforts to assist the escalation of his Asian project therefore seemed to be an utter failure as the year 1670 wore on. Despite the successful conclusion of an anti-Dutch European pact at Dover in June of that year, there seemed to be little hope that de Croissy's lamentations could overcome the powerful vested interests at work in the English capital. His brother's disappointing despatches beginning as early as the spring of 1669 in this regard convinced Colbert to turn his attention increasingly to the third partner in his envisioned grand Asian alliance: Portugal. While London was rife with obstructionist elements opposed to an Anglo-French accommodation in the East Indies aimed at the VOC, Lisbon seemingly held the promise of the type of convenient quid pro quo directed at the Dutch Company that Colbert was seeking. In short, fifty years of abuse at the hands of the Dutch gave him every reason to hope that his efforts would enjoy greater success than at the court of the Stuarts. By 1663, the VOC had succeeded in depriving the *Estado da India* of a sizable share of it Asian wealth as well as a good part of its territorial holdings. Authoritative, not to mention impassioned, voices in Lisbon and Goa were calling for revenge, and revenge was precisely what Colbert was willing to offer the Portuguese Crown in the spring of 1669, as Louis XIV's armies continued to grow, the royal treasury continued to fill, and the grand royal fleet destined for Asian waters began to assemble. Richelieu and Mazarin had both sought to exploit Portugal to forward the Continental and dynastic goals of Bourbon France. Colbert was merely seeking to use a similar strategy to complement his mercantile aims in *outre-mer*.[43]

The ducal house of Braganza headed by the capable João IV (1640–1656) had ended sixty years of "captivity" at the hands of the Habsburgs and their Continental and imperial foibles with the revolution of December 1640. This act, in conjunction with the Catalan revolt of the same year, demonstrated the feebleness of Spanish absolutism, ensured the failure of Olivares's stratagem, and signaled the impending defeat at the hands of France. For much of the next thirty years, the Portuguese were forced to acquiesce in the role of a convenient diplomatic and geopolitical counterweight to Spain in the final stages of the Franco-Habsburg struggle. João IV, his widow Dona Luisa de Gusmão (regent until 1661), their son,

Afonso VI, as well as his dominating minister, the count of Castelo-Melhor, all sought to arrange a solid league with France as the best means to ensure success in the war for independence that raged from 1640 to 1668 and thus obtain a final formal recognition by Madrid and the rest of Europe of the renascent Portuguese state.[44]

These negotiations were tedious. For Portugal, the military situation was desperate for much of this period: a continental struggle centered in the Alentejo raged on against successive Spanish invasion forces, while the war in the *imperio* with the Dutch continued in Brazil, Africa, and throughout the Indian Ocean. João IV and his successors were determined to arrange French support to facilitate the successful completion of this daunting martial challenge. On the other hand, Mazarin was largely content to use the Portuguese card in order to leverage a better deal with Madrid. He continually refused to consider a league unless the Portuguese invaded Spain, exacerbating the troubled times for his Habsburg enemy, a demand that first João and then his widow found nearly impossible to meet without first obtaining meaningful support from France. During the mid-1650s the negotiations had revolved around a league that would be cemented by the possible marriage of Louis XIV to the Infanta, Catherine of Braganza. Mazarin broached such talk with the 1655 mission of the chevalier de Jant to Lisbon. The dowry of the young Portuguese princess would include a good deal of cash, the cession of the North African city of Tangier, and perhaps even one of the fortresses of the *Estado da India*. In the end Mazarin and the young king resolved on the peace with Spain formalized at the Treaty of the Pyrenees of November 1659. Dom João da Costa, upon his arrival in Paris early that year, much to his chagrin learned the true French estimation of the alliance with Portugal: Louis would not marry the Portuguese infanta and embrace a league with the House of Braganza, but rather would wed the Spanish infanta, Marie Thérèse, and at long last conclude peace with the Habsburgs. A secret article of the peace required France to break off relations with Portugal so that "the affairs of Portugal shall be placed in the state they were in previous to the revolution."[45]

Despite the rather stinging rebuke of the Peace of the Pyrenees, Queen Regent Luisa and her advisors had little choice but to continue the quest for a French alliance: the exigencies of the military situation at home and abroad necessitated it. At last freed from the onerous demands of the longstanding war with France, Philip IV could concentrate his efforts on once again uniting Iberia under a single crown. The king's son, Don Juan José, commanded the invasion force of 1662 and 1663 that captured Borba and, in the greatest victory of the war for Spain, the second city of the Portuguese realm, Evora. This stunning victory, a reverse that ignited riots in the streets of Lisbon, was destined to be short-lived. The wily Mazarin had authorized sub rosa assistance for Portugal to ease the pain of the 1659 pact, and da Costa had raised some 600 men in France under the Anglo-

German count of Schomberg, who accompanied the Portuguese envoy back to the Alentejo and set about completely reforming the Portuguese army with a good deal of success. Schomberg's efforts were a notable factor in the Portuguese victories that followed: Ameixial (1663), the retaking of Evora (1663), and Montes Claros (1665). By late 1667, Philip IV was dead, and his wife's regency for their sickly infant son was marred by a power struggle with Don Juan de Austria. In these circumstances, the queen regent announced her willingness to recognize Afonso as king of Portugal. The Continental struggle had been won.[46]

In the meantime, Dona Luisa de Gusmão had done her utmost to arrange assistance for Portugal in her overseas struggle with the Dutch. While Mazarin and the young Louis had shunned the offer of Catherine of Braganza's hand and what was expected to be a sizable dowry, in London Charles II, constantly in need of ready money, proved to be a much more interested suitor. In June of 1661 Francisco de Melo, later the marquis de Sande, concluded the famed league and marriage treaty with the English Crown. On paper, the alliance was a classic quid pro quo: Charles would receive a dowry of 2 million cruzados, the cession of Tangier and Bombay, and the right for English merchants to trade in Portuguese colonies; in return the English promised to defend Portugal and her colonies from the depredations of the Spanish and Dutch "as if it were England itself."[47] Catherine sailed from Lisbon to Falmouth in April 1662 to begin her travails as the wife of the philandering Charles and the "barren" queen of England. While Charles indeed dispatched some land forces that helped to arrest the offensive of Don Juan José, the English quite simply refused to honor the clauses in the treaty that called for them to protect Portuguese colonies against attacks by the Dutch. This became painfully clear as early as 1662. The English fleet under the earl of Marlborough, which was transporting the new Portuguese viceroy, Antonio de Mello de Castro, to Goa to facilitate the transference of Bombay, declined to engage the Dutch fleet—then on the Malabar Coast under Rijkloff Van Goens—that was in the process of capturing Cochin, Cannanore, and Cranganore, the last Portuguese strongholds on that coast. In turn, Mello de Castro refused to hand over Bombay. Since the English had failed to live up to their end of the bargain, the viceroy argued, why should he honor the provisions of the pact? The imbroglio that ensued over the transference of Bombay lasted over two years. Only a stern warning from Afonso VI and his Overseas Council in the end convinced Mello de Castro to turn the island over to the English in 1665.[48]

As early as 1662, Turenne proposed that French influence be assured in Lisbon by marrying both Afonso and his younger brother Pedro to French princesses. After all, a renewed campaign against the Spanish Habsburgs remained a likely possibility. Louis XIV had not only sanctioned the match between Charles II and Catherine but actually encouraged it. In 1663 the

English king and his bride returned the favor by consenting to Sande's trip to Paris to negotiate the twin marriages to the royal brothers, talks that were much to the liking of Castelo-Melhor, a traditional supporter of reviving a league with Paris. Afonso was betrothed to Marie-Françoise-Isabelle of Savoy, with the marriage contract being signed at Paris in February 1666. The ambitious Pedro, an implacable foe of Castelo-Melhor, refused the match made for him, declaring he would not marry, a declaration he would soon retract in a spectacular manner. Afonso VI was one of the more tragic figures in Portuguese history. He was the second son of João IV and Luisa de Gusmão, his elder brother, Teodosio, had died in 1653 at the age of nineteen. A childhood affliction had resulted in the partial paralysis of Afonso's right arm and leg, as well as slightly affecting his powers of concentration. The king had nonetheless learned to read and write. His passions, however, were riding, coursing bulls, and frequenting dog and cock fights. Marie-Françoise and her Jesuit confessor, Fr. Verjus, arrived in Lisbon in August 1666 for the formal marriage ceremony, intent on extending French influence at court. Afonso was less than enthralled with the festivities. Bored with the ceremony, he left early to dine alone in bed. The young king was also unable to consummate the marriage. His ambitious new queen, disappointed in the royal bed, swiftly succeeded in gaining admission to the Council of State meetings, in having Schomberg named commander-in-chief, in challenging the powers of Castelo-Melhor, and in beginning an affair with the king's brother Pedro.[49]

Louis XIV's agents in Lisbon were less successful in preventing the much-desired peace between Portugal and Spain. The marquis de Saint-Romain was dispatched to Lisbon in 1666 to undermine these negotiations, which would deprive France of the traditional Portuguese card in a renewed war with the Habsburgs. In March 1667 an offensive and defensive league between France and Portugal was at last signed in part to persuade Castelo-Melhor to abandon his talks with Madrid, in part to lay the groundwork for Louis's foray into the Spanish Netherlands. The clever Castelo-Melhor—perhaps not realizing the precariousness of his situation in light of the cabal forming against him led by the queen, the infante, and the powerful duke of Cadaval—was not content with this diplomatic triumph. Although the treaty was ideally to be kept secret until such time as Louis was ready to invade Flanders, he sought to exploit the French alliance to force Madrid to terms, a strategy that succeeded. Before Castelo-Melhor could enjoy the fruits of these talks, however, the complicated maneuverings involved ensured his downfall. At the urging of the queen and the French faction at court, Afonso dismissed the count in September 1667. This step proved fatal for the unfortunate Afonso, as he was now isolated and deprived of the advice and support of the skillful Castelo-Melhor. In a palace coup of late 1667, Pedro and his supporters made short work of the reign. By March 1668, Afonso had been deposed and imprisoned, Pedro ruled with the title of prince regent bestowed on him by a grateful Cortes, a scandalous suit of nullity had been pursued and an annulment of the royal marriage obtained, and Pedro and Marie-Françoise had promptly married. While it appeared that French influence had scaled new heights at this volatile Iberian court, Louis and Colbert would discover that Pedro was not easily dominated by his wife. The prince regent refused to continue the war with Spain as specified by the secret treaty of March 1667 with France, and in February of the following year he sanctioned the treaty with Spain signed at the convent of St. Eloi.[50]

In the spring of 1669, Colbert was undoubtedly hoping that the new prince regent would prove more accommodating toward an alliance with France in the Indian Ocean directed against the Dutch than he had been in honoring the Continental pact directed against Spain. This hope proved to be in vain. Pedro, Cadaval, and the rest of the Portuguese ruling hierarchy ushered into power by the palace coup of late 1667 would reveal that they were pre-eminently determined to protect and resuscitate what remained of the once glorious *Estado da India*, while seeking to rehabilitate the Continental prestige of Portugal. Therefore, the generous concessions in the *outre-mer* that Mazarin had been humbly offered by Dona Luisa and her advisors in the mid-1650s, Colbert and his agents would be forced to grovel for in the late 1660s. On one level, this dramatic volte-face demonstrates the changing priorities of the French Crown that were ushered in by Colbert's rise to ministerial prominence in the mid-1660s. Mazarin, like Louis and the Le Telliers, was exceedingly traditional in his conception of power and wealth; he had little or no interest in overseas trade or possessions, as the dismal state of the French marine in 1661 eloquently demonstrates. Such priorities were of course a seminal part of Colbert's theories on political economy, but the offers of the 1650s from Lisbon were unfortunately no longer available a decade later. For one thing, the Portuguese were not nearly as desperate in 1669 as they had been in 1659: peace had been achieved (at a price) with both Spain on the Continent and with the United Provinces in the *outre-mer*. Pedro had already begun to turn his attention to stabilizing the realm at home and reviving what remained of the empire abroad. The prince regent and his advisors had little interest in jeopardizing this important work in renewed warfare with either Spain or the United Provinces, the logical end of any renewed Franco-Portuguese alliance. This was the state of affairs in Lisbon as Colbert and Saint-Romain began their quest for an Asian alliance in the spring of 1669.[51]

In March, Colbert dispatched formal instructions on the negotiations to his ambassador in the Portuguese capital. He began by reminding Saint-Romain of the "pains" that Louis XIV had taken to form the East India Company, "of the great sums of money" that he had given it from the royal treasury and would continue to give until the directors then in Asia had established a solid trade and overcome the difficulties that awaited "at the outset all enterprises of this nature." Colbert reminded the ambassador that of the four European nations trading in Asia—France, England, the United Provinces, and Portugal—the Portuguese had the longest experience and for many years had dominated the commerce and "all the islands of Asia, and established diverse places and considerable posts on the coasts of Africa, Persia, the Indies, China, and Japan," noting "that this great power had been notably diminished after the Dutch had introduced their commerce in these same countries, and at present find themselves reduced only to the places of Goa, Diu, and several other less considerable ones on the Coromandel coast." In terms that anticipated the thrust of Saint-Romain's arguments to the Portuguese Crown, Colbert contrasted the great wealth (the annual Dutch fleets "transport merchandise to the value of 10–12 million livres") and power (the VOC possesses "more than 150 ships in the Indies . . . land armies of 10,000 to 12,000 men, and at sea 40 to 50 warships") of the Dutch Company with the poverty and weakness of the *Estado* ("on the contrary the Portuguese have neither warships or troops"). According to Colbert, this "prodigious difference" between the powers and the insatiable desire on the part of the Dutch to augment their position and entirely exclude the Portuguese from the trade necessitated a "powerful and effective remedy," namely, the formation of a commercial and military *"société"* with a nation with similar interests, not only to combat the nefarious designs of the VOC but also "to take back from them a part of the commerce and of the places that they have usurped by force." In Colbert's view "only the French" were capable of procuring this great advantage for the Portuguese. Saint-Romain was therefore instructed to turn the 1667 treaty into a full-fledged commercial union in Asia based on reciprocal trading rights and, following the advice of Caron, the granting of at least one fortified post in the *Estado* to the French.[52]

Saint-Romain presented the French case to Pedro in April 1669 and continued talks well into the new year. In the course of his negotiations he logically attempted to exploit the influence of the French faction at court, most visibly in the form of Marie-Françoise, as well as the religious affinity of the two Crowns. Following Colbert's advice, he also sought to utilize the thirst for revenge against the Dutch that was virtually endemic in Lisbon at the time and to stress the admittedly poor performance of the English as allies and saviors for the tottering *Estado* in the years following the marriage treaty between Charles II and Catherine of Branganza. The French offer was made at a crucial stage in the history of Portuguese Asia. Erected by da Gama and Albuquerque, the *Estado* was based on a series of fortified settlements along the rim of the Indian Ocean basin from Mozambique to Macao that sought to enforce a monopoly on the spice trade by in part shutting off the traditional caravan trade through the Levant. Huge profits had resulted for the Crown during the early sixteenth century. By the 1660s, however, all this had changed. The Levant trade began to revive as early as the 1530s, and by 1600 the Crown managed to import "little more than 12,000 quintals, most of which was relatively low-priced pepper" via the Cape.[53] These commercial difficulties were exacerbated by military setbacks in Asia: Hurmuz was lost to an English-Persian attack in 1622; Melaka fell to a Dutch blockade in 1641; Ceylon had been lost to the VOC by 1658; and finally the Malabar Coast possessions had been captured by Van Goens's fleet in 1662–1663.[54]

One of the more pressing questions confronting Pedro and his claque following the ouster of Afonso was how to reverse this alarming trend and rehabilitate the *Estado*. Should the Crown, as in 1661, embrace a foreign alliance as the basis for this turnaround, or should peaceful internal reforms be adopted? As Saint-Romain pursued his negotiations, Pedro was in the process of resolving this Asian dilemma, a resolution that was no doubt accelerated by the aggressive demands inherent in Colbert's instructions. In late 1669 the decision was made to appoint a new viceroy for the Asian possessions, a decision that offered little evidence of how the prince regent would resolve this dilemma. Luis de Mendonça e Albuquerque was the nominee. The royal fleet charged with carrying him to Goa began to prepare in the Tagus in early 1670. While Saint-Romain was evidently convinced that a grand design was afoot in Lisbon regarding the *Estado*, it was not clear whether the *restorador de Ceilão*, as Mendonça Furtado was styled, would achieve this laudable end by violent or peaceful means. Beginning in January 1670 the French ambassador therefore held a series of meetings with the new viceroy in an attempt to discover the answer to this vital question, while hopefully generating support for the proposed alliance. Mendonça Furtado came from an aristocratic family that had gained much by the 1640 revolution. His father, Pedro de Mendonça, was one of the principal supporters of João IV in December of that year and shared in the largesse of his grateful monarch. In typical fashion Luis had begun his career in the war against the Spanish in the Alentejo. He had then launched a notable career in the *Estado*. Mendonça Furtado had served as *capitão-mor* of the ships of the *Carreira da India* on successful voyages between Lisbon and Goa in the 1650s; had commanded the armada that on three occasions in 1658 attempted to break the Dutch blockade of Goa and relieve Jaffnapatnam, the last Portuguese outpost in Ceylon; and finally had served as co-governor-general of the *Estado* in 1661–1662. In Asia, Mendonça Furtado forged a reputation for military prowess, financial acumen, and a strong dislike of the Dutch. He possessed one of the most impressive physiques of all the Portuguese in Asia, and his successful individual combat against a mounted Bijapuri cavalry commander near Margão in 1658 had become a legend. Wise investments in private trade had also made him rich. He returned to the *reino* in 1663 and gracefully integrated himself in the faction around Pedro that would soon overthrow Afonso. Mendonça Furtado had tried to dissuade Pedro from marrying Marie-Françoise, even offering to repay her dowry long since spent, an act that created a temporary rift between the two that was formally healed by his appointment as viceroy with the title of count of Lavradio.[55]

In his talks with Mendonça Furtado, Saint-Romain received mixed signals. As he informed Colbert and Louis XIV in letters of January and February 1670, the viceroy evidenced "a great desire to take some action against the Dutch there," especially action aimed at the reduction of Batavia, which was the "only good place that they had there and the basis of their power." Moreover, he "does not believe that one can diminish the commerce of the Dutch in the Indies without waging war on them there."[56] Drawing on decades of fighting the Hollanders in Asia, Mendonça Furtado was also willing to furnish Saint-Romain with various stratagems for waging a war with the VOC, including plans to exploit indigenous assistance, to wage "une simple guerre de Pirates" using small ships designed to ruin Dutch commerce, and to establish a strong, fortified French settlement near the Strait of Melaka, near the center of Dutch power. Nevertheless, he refrained from revealing the exact nature of his instructions from Pedro and continually stopped short of embracing the proposed league with France as the soundest means for restoring the *Estado* to its former glory. As the French ambassador discussed the matter with members of the Council of State such as Cadaval, the marquis of Fronteira, and the marquis of Tavora and the members of the Overseas Council such as Salvador Correia de Sá e Benavides, the profound division among Pedro's advisors on the issue became clear.

Nearly all members of the ruling hierarchy saw that a Franco-Dutch conflict in Europe was inevitable.[57] On this point there was little debate. Rather, the dispute raged around the question of how best to exploit this impending struggle for the benefit of the realm in general and the *Estado* in particular. The opinions of Pedro's councilors contained in a document titled *Instrucção da Secretaria do Estado e pareceres sobre a liga de Franca e Inglaterra* offer valuable insights into the divergent views on this question. The pro-French faction at court, championed by Marie-Françoise and Fronteira, argued that such an opportunity could be exploited "to regain a part of the places they had lost in the Indies."[58] In Fronteira's words, Colbert's proposal offered "the most opportune and desired opportunity that the kingdom could have to restore itself to the most important and glorious of all the conquests, which is the *Estado da India*." In terms that reflected the mixture of dynastic glory, mercantile benefits, and religious zeal that had long characterized the Portuguese presence in Asia, he concluded: "[W]ithout conquests one cannot have capital, [and] it is without doubt true that in order to have a kingdom one has to have conquests, and in India, Your Majesty pledges himself to the honor of God, the glory of the nation, [and] the interest and remedy of your vassals."[59] The opposing faction led by the duke of Cadaval was not convinced that the proposed league was the best way to rehabilitate the *Estado,* since external dependence had failed in 1661 with the English and any league with France would also result in renewed war with Spain in Europe as well as with the Dutch in Asia. In arguing against an external alliance, Cadaval maintained there was "great doubt of the recovery of India according to the treaty celebrated between Your Majesty and the king of England [and] if Your Majesty recovers India with the arms of France, that king will want the profit of his expense."[60]

The first official word that Saint-Romain received on the proposal came as early as August 1669 in a *consulta* of the Overseas Council. After summarizing Colbert's offer, this document merely called for a strict adherence to the provisions of the 1667 treaty but little else. Thus, while Portuguese commanders throughout the *Estado* were instructed to assist French ships in need, it recommended to Pedro that Colbert's *compagnie* not be allowed to establish trading factories in the port cities of the *Estado,* nor should Lisbon grant one of her fortresses to the French, as Caron and others had suggested and Saint-Romain requested.[61] This news could not have been totally unexpected for the French ambassador, since his despatches to Colbert throughout the spring and summer of that year suggest that Pedro was being gradually won over by the Cadaval faction with regard to the alliance. Colbert was more irked by this initial rebuff from Lisbon than by the news in his brother's despatches from London. Perhaps he had taken the advice of Damião Vieria to heart on the willingness of the Portuguese Crown to embrace his offer, "given its current and pressing need." In any event, his impatience at what he believed was an ill-conceived response emerges from his letters to Saint-Romain, in which he constantly chastises Pedro and his advisors for being "blind" to the grim reality of their situation in Asia. "The Portuguese can not see clearly what to me appears perfectly obvious, [that] it is impossible for them to exist in the Indies, and resist the power of the Dutch if they do not align with another European power." Despite his disappointment, Colbert ordered Saint-Romain to continue to press for the league or, failing that, the incorporation of pro-French clauses into the official orders or *regimento* of Mendonça Furtado, as well as permission to establish a French naval magazine on the banks of the Tagus.[62]

For the remainder of 1669 and all of 1670 Saint-Romain continued his talks with the Portuguese hierarchy to little avail. In December 1669 he discussed the matter with Marie-Françoise, who informed him that Schomberg had also raised the issue of granting one of the remaining *fortalezas* to France, a concession that she believed her husband was unlikely to make.[63] Although the ambassador tried to hold out hope of an eventual agreement, it became increasingly clear that Pedro had been definitively won over by Cadaval's arguments on the issue. Nevertheless, Saint-Romain informed Colbert that he believed his efforts could help contribute to the naming of Tavora as the next viceroy when Mendonça Furtado's three-year tenure expired in 1674, an appointment that would bode well for France's ambitions in that region. In the meantime, he argued, the hatred toward the Dutch was such in many areas of the *Estado* that most Portuguese there would offer to assist the French royal fleet then forming "even without orders from this court."[64] This of course remained to be seen. The Portuguese made precious few concessions beyond the recommendations of the August 1669 *consulta* of the Overseas Council. Pedro rejected Saint-Romain's call to include pro-French clauses in Mendonça Furtado's formal *regimento*. He did, however, write letters to Portuguese commanders in Brazil and the *Estado* instructing them to favorably receive French ships in their ports. The prince regent also acceded to Colbert's demand that a French naval magazine be establish on the Tagus, something that would prove of utility to the French navy in the ensuing Continental struggle. Pedro's request that Mendonça Furtado's fleet be allowed to sail to India in the company of Colbert's grand fleet was rejected in November 1669, as soon as it became clear that the Portuguese would in all likelihood reject the comprehensive league in Asia that the French were seeking.[65]

Throughout the course of these discussions, English and Dutch diplomats resident in Lisbon were extremely apprehensive about Saint-Romain's efforts. Francis Parry, the English envoy, informed Arlington in August 1669 that he had broached the topic of the French ambassador's orders regarding the India trade with the Dutch resident and was told that the "States [General] had now Sent him expresse Command to be vigilant in this business, and by all Arts imaginable to hinder its taking effect."[66] France's rivals were especially wary of the close relationship that apparently existed between Saint-Romain and Marie-Françoise and made much of the prominent role the French ambassador played at the baptism of the royal couple's first child, Dona Isabel Luisa Josefa, in 1669. As Parry advised Arlington in two letters dated November 1670, these early fears were unfounded. In the first he wrote: "There has been a Rumour some time about Towne of a League that is making between the French king and this Crowne . . . to make a joint warre on the Hollander in the Indies. But there is a Person living in the french Ambassadors house, and very well acquainted with all his actions, who assures me that nothing is yet concluded." A week later, he was able to inform the secretary of state: "[I] now have it from a good hand that the French Ambassador, notwithstanding all his persuasions cannot prevail with these people to engage in any Acts of hostility against the Hollander."[67] Cadaval's arguments on the dubious nature of recovering any Asian territory based on the arms of either England and France, the sincere desire of the populace for continued peace at least with Spain, and the simple judgment on the part of the Council of State that the French—despite all of Colbert's efforts—were still no match for the Dutch in an open test of strength in Asia evidently decided the issue. Instead of embracing the admittedly timely and attractive French offer for quick revenge against the Dutch, Pedro and his advisors instead decided to remain as neutral as possible in the threatening conflict and to utilize any war that might develop among their rivals in the Asian trade to instead initiate badly needed reforms in the *Estado.*

Colbert's campaign, beginning in March 1669, to facilitate the escalation of his Asian project by arranging an alliance with the English and Portuguese was therefore doomed to failure. In London, the power and influence of the mercantile community and the directors of the EIC were more than sufficient to undermine any negotiations designed to forward French commercial interests in Asia. In Lisbon, Colbert's enticing proposal had the misfortune of reaching a de facto king and his Council of State intent on reforming a once glorious monarchy that had been gravely reduced in power and stature by decades of foreign domination, limited demographic and economic resources, and a worldwide empire to be defended against increasingly effective enemies. French policy had helped to bring Pedro to power in 1667 with the full expectation that he would prove sympathetic to the desires of Louis XIV and, by extension, Colbert. The prince regent, once safely ensconced on the throne, proved to be a bitter disappointment to Paris by pursuing policies that he believed were in the best interest of his realm, not those that would conveniently complement the dynastic or *outre-mer* priorities of France. During the course of Saint-Romain's negotiations, Colbert must have mused that Afonso and Castelo-Melhor might have proven more receptive to his offer. Nevertheless, while de Croissy and Saint-Romain were doing his diplomatic bidding in London and Lisbon, Colbert was immersed in assembling and dispatching the instrument that he hoped would ensure the success of his cherished Asian campaign. What diplomacy had failed to obtain, an effective demonstration of maritime force along with a carefully laid plan of action might yet achieve.

V

Surat, 1671

Advance and Indecision on the Eve of the Dutch War

> " The French have 12 shipps arrived, whereof 7
> men of Warr, 2 Victuallers, & 3 Merchant Shipps
> belonging to their Company, the menn of Warr
> are commanded by Mons. La haye called Vice Roy
> of S. Lourenco. . . . [H]e anchored at the river's
> mouth the 21st September [O.S.], giving no
> Small allarum to the towne."
>
> —Gerald Aungier and Council in Surat to
> London Directors

Among those at Swally Hole to greet La Haye and his grand fleet were several French *compagnie* clerks from the makeshift warehouse recently erected near the mouth of the Tapti. These men promptly sent word of the expedition's arrival to the factory in Surat. Among those receiving this welcome news was François Baron, by far the ablest of the three new Asian directors Colbert had seen fit to appoint in late 1670, both as a response to early complaints from the East on Caron's "damaging" behavior and in an effort to expand the *compagnie* hierarchy to keep pace with its expanding field of operations.[1] Baron had first demonstrated useful administrative abilities for the Crown in the late 1650s after the French consul in Cairo had been hastily recalled to Paris. In recognition for these services, he had been named consul for the rich caravan entrepôt of Aleppo in 1661, a post he held for the next decade until news reached him of his appointment as a *compagnie* director. Baron had then followed the traditional overland route across Persia to the port of Bandar Abbas where he obtained passage to Gujarat on the English ship *Loyall Oxiden*. As John Child, the English factor in that Persian port, noted, "Barron the some time Consull at Aleppo for the French Nation . . . is to be director for the French East India's whole affaires, he hath with him brought from Aleppo his Nephew, a Chiriugon, & servingman trumptor, & cooke."[2] The *Loyall Oxiden* with the new director and his rather eclectic entourage aboard reached Swally in May 1671. On 8 October, Baron went aboard the French flagship and spent much of the night in conversation with La Haye, learning the particulars of the voyage to that point. As the newly styled Viceroy related, the news was decidedly mixed.[3]

Early outfitting delays in Rochefort and Le Havre had continued into the first months of 1670, ultimately causing the fleet, as Colbert most feared, to miss the monsoon winds that would have allowed it to reach India by the fall of that year. The most serious setback had been the loss in January 1670 of the newly built, 850-ton man-of-war *Rouen* with sixty guns, originally designated as La Haye's flagship. Dumas, the marine intendant in Le Havre, had received orders in September 1669 informing him that this new warship would join the *escadre de Perse*. Although he worked diligently to ensure that the *Rouen* and *Flamand* left Le Havre by early December in order to make the rendezvous with the rest of the squadron at Belle-Île, his efforts yielded less than desirable results. Dumas and M. Le Magnou, the captain of the *Rouen,* had great difficulties in raising a crew for the new man-of-war and were frequently chastised in letters from Colbert.[4] It appears that Le Magnou never took his duties very seriously, perhaps he was less than excited about the prospect of a long voyage to the East Indies, a voyage famed in contemporary folklore for its inherent dangers. In any case, matters went from bad to worse when the *Rouen* was lost in a fierce squall in Le Havre in mid-January 1670. William Perwich wrote cheerfully in a report to London that the ship was lost "by a strange and wonderfull accident of a great gust of wind."[5] The French Crown, however, did not take the loss of its man-of-war so lightly. Louis XIV promptly issued orders for Le Magnou's arrest, citing his negligence in sleeping ashore during a "dangerous time" of the year and delegating authority to an inexperienced ensign as the primary factors for the ship's loss. Le Magnou had wisely fled and was still on the run when the expedition finally departed.[6]

The *Rouen* disaster was emblematic of the outfitting problems that plagued the expedition from the outset. During early 1670 long *mémoires* were written by Louis and Colbert exhorting de Terron to complete preparations so that the squadron could depart. To compensate for the loss of the *Rouen,* Colbert added the frigate *Diligente* and the storeship *Europe* to the fleet. The fleet's officers gradually made their way to Rochefort, and the huge array of munitions and provisions were slowly loaded. The most pressing problem, that of raising the crews, was solved in January 1670 when Louis XIV issued orders assigning 600 *matelots* of the *enrôlement général* of Brittany to the fleet. Louis also sanctioned the embarkation of 400 well-trained soldiers and 30 officers from Colbert's recently formed *régiment royal de la marine* on La Haye's ships. By February 1670, four of the men-of-war were nearly ready at Rochefort, and the fifth, the *Flamand,* had started the voyage south from Le Havre. Colbert's anxiety over losing the favorable monsoon winds of the summer of 1670 heightened when a series of last-minute delays conspired to keep the fleet in port. It was not until the final days of March 1670 that the squadron was able to depart. The ships, crews, firepower, and other relevant information relating to the Persian squadron are given in table 1, figures that adequately reflect both the success of Colbert's naval reforms and construction campaign of the 1660s and his commitment to the success of the Asian venture.[7]

TABLE 1:   The Persian Squadron of 1670

SHIP	TYPE	BUILT	TONS	DATE	GUNS	MEN	COMMANDER
Navarre	Man of War	Rochefort	1000	1666	56	400	de Turelle
Triomphe	MW	Rochefort	800	1661	38	350	Forrand
Jules	MW	Toulon	700	1661	36	262	de Luche
Flamand	MW	Dunderque	650	1664	36	302	Dumayne
Bayonnais	MW	Bayonne	550	1667	34	252	La Houssaye
Diligente	Frigate	Brest	——	1663	14	241	Desmarets
Sultane	Flute	Brest	500	1669	16	——	Beaulieu
Europe	Flute	Brest	500	1669	16	443	Desprey
Indienne	Flute	LaRochelle	500	1668	12	——	de la Clide
Totals					258	2250	

The royal squadron had departed from Rochefort on 29 March and anchored two days later off Belle-Île where the rendezvous with the company ships *Vautour, Phoenix,* and *Dauphin* was to take place. The outfitting efficiency of the *compagnie,* however, was no better than that of Colbert's intendants, and these vessels were unable to sail from Port-Louis until mid-April. La Haye spent a frustrating week at Belle-Île taking on more provisions, sending off a copy of his journal to Louis XIV, and dispatching letters to Port-Louis that outlined his intended ports of call and rendezvous points: first at Cape Verde, second at the Bay of Saldanha on the South African coast, and finally at Fort-Dauphin. After the royal fleet set sail once again on 11 April, problems developed almost immediately. Five days out of Belle-Île, the *Sultane* made for repairs in Lisbon. In early May, the vice-admiral *Triomphe* broke her rudder and also limped toward Lisbon accompanied by the *Indienne.* As Saint-Romain later informed Colbert, these two vessels reached the Tagus six days later: "M. Foran has entered . . . this river in order to repair his rudder. . . . [O]ne of the flutes has put into port with him, it was taking on a lot of water and had lost one of its masts." Saint-

Romain hoped that the ships could be repaired and put to sea within two weeks, with ample time to make the rendezvous at Cape Verde. The *Sultane* reached the Portuguese capital with great difficulty on 14 May.[8]

La Haye's diminished squadron had thereafter made provisioning stops at Madeira and Cape Verde before heading out into the mid-Atlantic to take advantage of the prevailing westerlies on the voyage toward the Cape of Good Hope. It was not until late August that the French ships made landfall near the Bay of Saldanha, some sixty miles north of the Cape, in a demonstration of competent ocean navigation that must have pleased Colbert when he learned of it. The two-and-a-half month passage across the equator and South Atlantic had nevertheless taken its toll. Many of the poorly fed seamen and infantry troops aboard the cramped, filthy ships were suffering from scurvy and a variety of other afflictions. The lieutenant-general landed as many men as possible at Saldanha in the hope that it might improve their condition. He then spent the next six weeks careening his ships, waiting for the six straggling vessels to appear, and reconnoitering the area for a site for a fortified settlement. This exploration was one of the main points contained in his instructions, as Colbert was anxious to establish as many fortified way stations as possible near the Cape to facilitate the difficult passage between Europe and India. La Haye carried out this important task with diligence and vigor. In the first of many subsequent meetings with armed representatives of the VOC, he even drove off a small Dutch detachment that tried to interrupt his exploration of the coast from Table Bay. The lieutenant-general soon found a suitable site for the post Colbert desired on the West African coast near the Bay of St. Martin; a flag was promptly raised on the highest point overlooking this fine natural harbor, claiming it for the French *compagnie* much to the consternation of the Dutch.[9]

In early October, the royal expedition had departed from Saldanha to confront perhaps the most dangerous part of the passage: rounding the Cape of Good Hope. This feat was only accomplished with some difficulty as the stormy weather common at that time of the year dispersed the fleet. The *Navarre*, with La Haye aboard, anchored at Fort-Dauphin on 23 November. In the weeks that followed the rest of the ships made their way in various states of disrepair into that harbor. On 4 December, the lieutenant-general formally took possession of the island in the name of Louis XIV. This was probably done at Colbert's request, in order to spare the *compagnie* what had become the burdensome expenditures of the fledgling colony. Mondevergue relinquished control and M. Champmargou, one of the leading planters on the island, was named the first royal governor of Madagascar. To celebrate the transference, a Te Deum was sung in the town's church, and public festivities followed in the streets. These celebrations were short-lived, however, as La Haye soon found himself plunged into a morass of problems that prolonged the stay of the royal fleet far longer than the four to six weeks foreseen in Colbert's instructions. First, the lieutenant-general was charged with resuscitating the *compagnie*'s sagging fortunes on the island. Second, the assumption of royal control also mandated that the indigenous population be brought under an increased level of centralized control, a less than realistic goal. Third, La Haye was expected to deal with the internal strife that had done so much to hinder the *compagnie*'s early operations and was also expected to explore alternative sites for a *compagnie* entrepôt in the region, while awaiting the three royal stragglers that had made for Lisbon as well as the three ships sailing from Port-Louis.[10]

The traditionally strained relations between the French colonists and neighboring Malagasy tribes were exacerbated at about the time of the fleet's arrival by intertribal warfare that invited French intervention in a quest for increased power. This state of affairs was heightened further by the aggressive policies La Haye adopted from the outset, policies that ultimately resulted in open warfare between the Europeans and several of the indigenous tribes. The lieutenant-general resolved to deal with the colony's problems in a very forceful manner. Above all, he was anxious to demonstrate the power of his fleet and of his grand monarch to *les naturels*. Colbert's instructions, after all, had been quite explicit on this point. Soon after the ceremonies of late November, La Haye toured the environs of Fort-Dauphin and the major French plantations in the southern half of the island, not an especially difficult task since these establishments—the most expansive of which belonged to Champmargou—numbered less than a dozen. As the lieutenant-general discovered, French authority in the countryside was tenuous at best, with local chieftains exercising effective control. Cattle and other livestock were relatively plentiful, but the Europeans frequently had to fight for them. True to the laws of the marketplace, the Malagasy chieftains had also raised the price of the dietary staple of rice to unprecedented levels in response to increased demand in the form of the more than 2000 men who had recently arrived aboard Louis XIV's ships. During his travels in the interior, La Haye sought to obtain formal homage to Crown authority and to discourage opposition to the expansion of French influence on the island. While several chieftains, including Dian Mananque, who since Richelieu's time had fought against various French projects on Madagascar, went to Fort-Dauphin and rendered at least formal allegiance to the Crown, Dian Ramousett or Ramosa, another *grand du pays,* had openly declared himself against the expansionist designs of the French Crown.[11]

Unable to bear this affront, La Haye began an ill-advised campaign against Ramousett: "There is news from Fort-Dauphin that Mr. l'Admiral with his troops have attacked Ramousett, *grand du pays,* who refuses to come to Fort-Dauphin to render his homage."[12] In early January 1671, La Haye had marched boldly into the interior of the island with 700 of his best troops and nearly 600 native retainers in search of Ramousett. This expedition, the lieutenant-general's first major operation in the Indian Ocean, proved to be a colossal embarrassment for the French, who became involved in an ugly guerrilla war that they were ill-prepared for and had little chance of winning. Ramousett "took great pleasure in drawing [the] general and his fine army across a hundred dangerous rivers, among rocks, deserts, and mountains." After campaigning for several months, La Haye had "gained nothing but a dangerous illness for himself which was almost fatal."[13] Although the lieutenant-general eventually recovered from the colic and fever that afflicted him, a score of officers and several hundred men were wasted in this peripheral affair. More importantly, La Haye squandered precious provisions and munitions that would be needed for the fleet's operations in India, Ceylon, and Indonesia once the formal campaign against the Dutch was underway. In any event, his galling setback against Ramousett convinced La Haye that the periodic hostility of the Malagasy tribes and the travails of Fort-Dauphin's lowland climate made the place unsuitable for permanent settlement. He therefore sought with renewed vigor to find a suitable alternative for the *compagnie*'s main entrepôt in the region.[14]

In early April, the ships *Jules* and *Diligente* were ordered to reconnoiter the Bay of St. Augustin on the southwestern coast of the island. On 11 April La Haye sailed from Fort-Dauphin with the *Navarre* and five other ships of the fleet for the nearby island of Mascarenhas or Île Bourbon, a destination that was reached on 27 April. Two days later, the *Indienne* was sent out to explore the Bay of Antongil and the island of St. Marie in northeastern Madagascar. Much to his delight, La Haye found the situation on Bourbon entirely different from that in southeastern Madagascar: while Fort-Dauphin appeared to be a moribund colony beset with insurmountable problems, Bourbon had all the attributes of a flourishing settlement. As the lieutenant-general judged the situation, the climate was much healthier than at Fort-Dauphin, cultivation was progressing rapidly, and the major towns of St. Denis and St. Paul were being constantly augmented by colonists disenchanted with the rigors of life on Madagascar. La Haye promptly concluded that Bourbon should serve as the locus for *compagnie* operations in the region. Here was the convenient and accommodating entrepôt that Colbert was searching for to compete with the Cape settlement of the Dutch. On 6 May, at St. Denis, he officially took possession of the island in the name of the king, declaring himself "viceroy, admiral, and lieutenant-general" of French holdings in the East Indies. M. de La Hure, an able lieutenant of the fleet, was named royal governor. After a brief call at St. Paul, the French ships sailed for Fort-Dauphin, dropping anchor in the harbor in late June 1671.[15]

Another reason for La Haye's long stay in southeastern Africa was the necessity of regrouping his dispersed fleet before continuing on to Surat and the main points contained in Colbert's instructions. It was preferable to fulfill his difficult mission with as large and powerful a force as possible, and this required waiting for the *Triomphe, Indienne, Sultane, Dauphin, Vau-*

tour, and *Phoenix* to appear. During the course of La Haye's campaign against Ramousett and his voyage to Bourbon, most of these ships gradually rejoined the fleet. All sailing in the Indian Ocean is dictated by the winds of the alternating monsoons, and centuries of experience had shown that the southwest monsoon furnished favorable conditions for the passage from southeastern Africa to India between July and September. To reach Surat and profit fully from these conditions therefore necessitated that La Haye and his fleet depart from Fort-Dauphin by mid-August at the latest. Once the initial delays in port and the slow initial stage of the voyage had conspired to deprive the squadron of the monsoon of 1670, it was forced to *invernar,* as the Portuguese called it, or winter at Madagascar until the next favorable season.[16]

As La Haye later discovered, the royal ships *Triomphe, Indienne,* and *Sultane* had all anchored in the Tagus in May 1670. M. Du Trembley, the *commissaire d'escadre,* and M. Forrand, captain of the *Triomphe,* had immediately written to Colbert, explaining their predicament and asking for additional orders.[17] During their two-month stay in Lisbon these officers held a series of meetings with Saint-Romain, who was then in the midst of his negotiations with Pedro and the Council of State on the matter of an Asian alliance. Among other things, the ambassador was able to provide Du Trembley and Forrand with letters from the prince regent pursuant to the Overseas Council's *consulta* of August 1669 that supported the right of French ships in need to receive aid in the ports of the Portuguese empire. As Saint-Romain informed Louis XIV, "I will give M. Forran copies of the letter of recommendation from the prince of Portugal in favor of the vessels of the king, for the ports of Brazil and for Angola and Guinea."[18] Saint-Romain also discussed the value of the so-called Rios de Cuama region of Mozambique with La Haye's officers. All of the European powers involved in the Asian trade had found that it was nearly impossible to trade their wares in sufficient quantities to cover the cost of the spices and other Eastern commodities they sought. This unwelcome reality had traditionally mandated that large quantities of bullion had to be sent out from Lisbon, Amsterdam, and London to cover the difference. In the age of mercantilism, every effort had been made to reduce the amount of bullion dispatched from Europe by developing a "country" trade, that is, an inter-Asiatic trade, to finance the purchase of Eastern goods. Nevertheless, as late as 1670, gold and silver, in terms of value, still formed a significant portion of the outgoing cargoes of ships headed from Europe to Asia, as Colbert had discovered beginning in 1664.

One of Pedro's main priorities in his campaign for the internal regeneration of the *Estado da India* was to develop Mozambique and the Rios de Cuama region, roughly corresponding to the Zambezi River basin, to compensate for the losses to the Dutch that had culminated in the early 1660s and as a valued source of the gold and silver that was said to exist in that

region. Antonio Alvares Pereira had reiterated the need to exploit the precious metals in the Rios in a letter of 1661. Antonio de Mello de Castro,
viceroy at that time, declared: "There is no doubt the region of the Rios is a
great and important thing." Yet, more pressing needs in the *Estado* and very
limited resources in Goa ensured that matters remained much the same in
the Rios until the late 1660s when, ironically, it was the work of Colbert's
compagnie in nearby Madagascar and the departure of La Haye's squadron
that prompted Pedro and his ministers to take a much more active interest
in exploiting this region.[19] The astute Saint-Romain did not fail to inform
Colbert of the potential benefits of the Rios. In a letter of February 1670,
he advised: "The Portuguese have always believed they have rich and abun-
dant gold mines . . . where the Cuama river flows." Since the Portuguese
did not "have a settlement within 60 leagues of the mouth of this river,"
the *compagnie* might easily accomplish something; it appeared that Pedro
was already convinced that the French intended to "establish themselves
there and make themselves masters of this river and the rich mines." With
an eye toward a future reconnaissance by La Haye, he concluded: "[T]he
mouth of the Cuama river is on the coast of Africa opposite from the isle
Dauphine between 22 degrees of latitude and the Tropic of Capricorn."[20]

Through de Terron, La Haye had received information on the Rios even
before his departure from Rochefort. Given the bullionist tenets of his theories on political economy, Colbert was undoubtedly intrigued by these reports.[21] Any plan that might help avert the flow of bullion from the coffers
of the royal treasury merited, especially with the specter of another of Louis
XIV's wars looming, careful consideration. Yet there is every indication that
Colbert resolved to pursue the matter with the utmost care, since perhaps
his fondest wish at this time was to arrange an immediate Asian league
against the Dutch, an instrument that he viewed as a key component in La
Haye's mission and a valued weapon in the larger campaign against the
mercantile might of the United Provinces. Any overt actions in Mozambique would assuredly alienate the Portuguese Crown and effectively kill
any chance for the success of Saint-Romain's negotiations. There was also
the danger that such a move could upset Lionne's diplomatic strategy by re-
moving Madrid's traditional distraction with a Franco-Portuguese alliance.
Saint-Romain, however, furnished additional information on the matter for
La Haye in letters that were carried by Forrand Du Trembley and de La
Clide upon their departure from Lisbon in early July 1670. The *Triomphe,
Sultane,* and *Indienne* had parted company near Cape Verde. The *Indienne*
made for Saldanha where her crew saved the *Phoenix* from sure destruction.
The two ships managed to reach Fort-Dauphin in February of the following
year. Forrand and Du Trembley, perhaps anxious to test the value of Pe-
dro's letters, ignored La Haye's sailing orders and took the *Triomphe* and
Sultane to the Brazilian coast for well over a month, time that was spent
buying provisions and trading for sugar and tobacco, a New World crop

that was becoming increasingly important in Asian markets. These royal ships had also reached Madagascar in February 1671.[22]

Forrand and Du Trembley had unexpectantly come upon the *compagnie* ship *Dauphin* anchored at Bahia during their Brazilian sojourn. Based on his talks with Saint-Romain, Forrand may have instructed her captain to reconnoiter Mozambique and the mouth of the Zambezi, since this large, well-armed storeship spent several months on that coast before rejoining the main body of the fleet in Fort-Dauphin. Soon after taking power in Goa, Luis de Mendonça Furtado warned Lisbon about the threat posed to the *Estado* by Colbert's Asian project: "Your Highness and his ministers should be aware of the care and diligence with which the king of France establishes himself in these parts; this matter demands the utmost attention both at home in Lisbon, and from the Viceroys of the State of India."[23] The new viceroy had earlier received a report from João de Sousa Freire, the governor of Mozambique, on the stay of the *Dauphin*. While the arrival of the French ship had caused "great fear" among the inhabitants, Sousa Freire had restored order and "made the French believe the place had more troops than in truth it had."[24] Although no direct evidence of the visit to Mozambique by the *Dauphin* has survived, the failure to find any compelling proof of the mineral riches of the region in conjunction with the apparent strength of the Portuguese garrisons along the coast—a state of affairs that seemingly contradicted the information provided by Saint-Romain—may explain why La Haye did not pursue the matter further. Another factor was certainly that the lieutenant-general was anxious to avoid any actions that would alienate the Goa hierarchy while the possibility of direct anti-Dutch talks with Mendonça Furtado remained. Until he could meet personally with the Portuguese viceroy, La Haye was determined to treat this potential ally with every consideration.

By July 1671, La Haye was at last able to prepare for his belated departure from Madagascar. The sailing season for the west coast of India and Surat was at hand, his once dispersed fleet had gathered at Fort-Dauphin, and the reconnaissance of southeastern Africa and its adjoining islands was complete. Before setting sail, however, two tasks remained. The first involved reestablishing control over the unruly officer corps of the squadron. Forrand's disregard for his sailing orders was indicative of a more general challenge to La Haye's authority that had developed on the voyage to Fort-Dauphin. The first despatches to reach Paris from the officers of the fleet made it clear, in the words of C. W. Cole, "that La Haye's haughty and stubborn character had caused him to be hated by all of his subordinates."[25] Some of the malcontents, including *chef d'escadre* de Turelle, had even addressed an official protest about the lieutenant-general's behavior to Louis XIV and Colbert. The Crown eventually responded to these letters by reprimanding all those involved in this challenge to La Haye's authority. Du Trembley was instructed to inform his fellow officers that the king would never tolerate open disagreement with the expedition's commanders.[26] In the meantime, La Haye had restored control long before these letters reached him. Forrand was arrested and charged with disobeying orders and disclosing secret information concerning the squadron in Lisbon and Brazil. The rest of the disgruntled officers were either forced to reconcile themselves to La Haye's command or to resign their commissions. Most of the latter group returned to France aboard the *compagnie* ship *L'Aigle d'Or,* then in Fort-Dauphin on the return leg of her voyage from the East Indies via Surat.[27]

Prior to his departure, La Haye also compiled several long despatches for Colbert. The most important was dated aboard the flagship *Navarre* on 1 August 1671. In it, the lieutenant-general proposed that a permanent establishment be created at the Bay of St. Martin which could serve as a way station for French vessels on the Cape route. Next, La Haye conveyed his firm belief that the island of Bourbon should be developed as the main *compagnie* entrepôt in the region of southeastern Africa; everything he had witnessed on that island convinced him of its suitability for that function. He assured Colbert that work was already well underway toward cultivating and fortifying the place. As for Madagascar, La Haye argued that Fort-Dauphin should be abandoned and the French presence on the great island restricted to a small post on the Bay of Antongil, a site that could easily be put in regular communication with Bourbon. If his plans were acceptable to the Crown, he would continue the task of putting them into effect at all of these places on his return trip from the Indies. The eventful nine-month stay on Madagascar finally at an end, La Haye had sailed for Surat on 11 August. His formidable command included the powerful, brass-gunned men-of-war *Navarre, Triomphe, Jules, Flamand,* and *Bayonnais,* the well-armed storeships *Europe* and *Sultane,* and two *compagnie* storeships.[28] Following a brief provisioning stop at one of the Comoro islands, the squadron traversed the Arabian Sea in less than a month and dropped anchor at Swally on 1 October.

While the astute and calculating Baron probably listened to La Haye's recitation with great interest, he may also have noted several of the more glaring mistakes that had been made during the course of the expedition, particularly the waste of men and supplies resulting from the ill-conceived campaign against Ramousett. Nonetheless, these errors in judgment were more than compensated for by the impressive and reassuring sight of Colbert's grand fleet lying calmly at anchor in Swally Hole. Flags and pendants flying, brass guns gleaming, it was one of the greatest concentrations of European firepower yet assembled in Asian waters, and titularly it was entirely at the disposal of the *compagnie.* The Abbé Carré, a French prelate charged with carrying royal despatches overland to La Haye, may have exaggerated slightly when he later claimed that the fleet's appearance "struck terror all over the Indies."[29] There can be little doubt, however, that in a trade long dominated by poorly armed, rather ungainly merchantmen, Louis XIV's men-of-war inspired respect and apprehension among all of France's European and Asian rivals. Aurangzeb was sufficiently impressed by the reports of his underlings on La Haye's arrival that he immediately dispatched a new governor and 2000 well-trained cavalry troops to Surat out of concern that the infidel fleet would attempt to capture the town.[30] Aungier, his council, as well as Dutch agents in Gujarat began an intricate game of diplomacy designed to divine the purpose and ultimate destination of the fleet. In October 1671, both of France's main competitors in the trade feared the worse, assuming that the squadron had either been "Sent by the French king to Joyne with the Portuguese for retaking Cochin and Zeilon from the Dutch," or some other aggressive project that might even include Bombay.[31]

During lengthy discussions aboard the *Navarre* in early October, La Haye was also no doubt anxious to hear news of the *compagnie*'s affairs. After all, he had received only sketchy reports at Fort-Dauphin from the officers of the *Aigle d'Or* on the *compagnie*'s operations. The viceroy may also have wondered why it was that Caron, the initiator of the project and the man most trusted by Colbert to bring his grand design to fruition, was not on hand to greet him properly and discuss the important business at hand, that is, how to best utilize the fleet that he had clamored for to destroy Dutch pretensions in the trade. Baron could offer La Haye relatively little comfort on both accounts. After reaching Surat in May 1671, he had taken stock of the *compagnie*'s financial and geopolitical situation in Asia and was less than impressed. In a long letter to Colbert he had outlined the "great confusion of affairs" that had greeted him upon his arrival. Caron had left the previous month with three ships on a voyage to Java in the hopes of gaining permission from the rajah of Bantam to establish a factory in his domains. In his wake, Baron found the *compagnie*'s finances in ruins: the coffers in Surat were nearly empty thanks largely to internal graft and the grandiose gifts Caron had made to Aurangzeb's officials in the town and to other potentates. The irregular traffic with Paris and Port-Louis from 1668 to 1671 had deprived the *conseil* of necessary capital with which to conduct daily operations. Consequently, loans had been taken out with local moneylenders at a relatively high rate of interest that had gone unpaid. The *compagnie*'s credit had predictably suffered, and as time went on it had become increasingly difficult to arrange additional funds. Complicating matters was a good deal of internal bickering that did much to undermine the *compagnie*'s operations.[32]

The continuing Caron-Marcara imbroglio was indicative of the these disputes. After dispatching the hapless Armenian to Fort-Dauphin in chains in early 1668, the director-general mistakenly assumed that his rival was vanquished. In fact, Mondevergue and de Faye, little enamored of Caron, had cleared Marcara of all charges and restored him to his former rank and salary. In October 1668 de Faye, also disenchanted with the deteriorating situation at Fort-Dauphin, had decided to proceed to India with the ships *Aigle d'Or, Marie,* and *Force.* Marcara and François Martin, a young *compagnie* clerk at the outset of a brilliant career, traveled in his entourage. This small fleet had called at Ceylon, Cochin, and Calicut before anchoring at Swally Hole in March 1669.[33] Caron thereupon feigned friendship for the Armenian, who was soon sent to the Muslim Deccan state of Golconda to negotiate for the establishment of a factory in that rich kingdom renowned for its cotton piece goods and gemstones. Marcara performed this task admirably in light of the fierce opposition at court of the English and Dutch, who were already established on the Coromandel Coast at Madras and Pulicat, towns within Qutb Shahi dominion. By December 1669, he had obtained a *farman* authorizing a factory at Masulipatnam, the leading port of the kingdom. Before he could begin trading operations there, however, Caron had him arrested once again and dispatched back to France to answer charges of misusing *compagnie* funds.[34] In Surat, Caron's haughty character and de Faye's open support for Marcara engendered a brief, but acrimonious, power struggle between the directors that only ended with de Faye's sudden demise in late April 1669. In the years that followed, Caron found himself immersed in similar disputes with various rivals on the Surat Council, who "found fault with the fact that he styled himself 'general,' that he appeared with a bodyguard, and that he made great expenditures." The Capuchin fathers, led by Ambroise de Preuilly, continued to detest and oppose him for his staunch refusal to abandon Protestantism and embrace the Catholic faith.[35] These personality disputes did much to undermine the *compagnie*'s formative years, as English and Dutch officials in Asia pointed out with obvious relish to their superiors in Europe.[36]

La Haye probably listened to this news with little enthusiasm since he was charged with healing such rifts, establishing a unified chain of command in Asia, and above all defining Caron's precise role within that hierarchy. This would prove to be difficult since Colbert himself was in the midst of revising his own views on this crucial question. Between 1665 and early 1670, he had little choice but to throw all of his considerable support behind the former Dutch director: Caron alone was deemed to have the requisite knowledge of the Asian trade, long-standing ties to various indigenous rulers, and impressive linguistic skills to ensure the success of the *compagnie.* Colbert had made a substantial financial investment to recruit the Dutchman and was determined to reap a sizable return for his money. Caron was also responsible for many of the ideas that had culminated in the escalation of the Asian project in 1669 and the formation of La Haye's fleet. It is not surprising, therefore, that during the *compagnie*'s early years Colbert supported Caron at every turn. In March 1669, upon receipt of the letters aboard the *St-Jean-Baptiste,* Colbert had ordered de Faye to stop giving aid to Marcara and to place all his trust in Caron. That same month, Louis

XIV rebuked Mondevergue for reversing the judgment against the Armenian. According to the king, Caron had become a French subject, his family was residing in the kingdom, and on his "experience and ability . . . rested the sole hope of the success of the *compagnie*."[37] La Haye's instructions of December 1669 reiterated this same confidence in the Dutchman. According to Colbert, Caron alone had the "profound knowledge . . . of everything that can and should be done in the Indies for the greatest advantage of the *compagnie*."[38] As late as December of the following year, he wrote to La Haye: "[A]s you will find in the Indies a great division between the French . . . and the sieur Caron . . . I order you above all to support and contribute toward giving all the authority to the said Caron." In this revealing letter from the king, Louis even supported Caron against the harsh criticism of the Capuchins in order to forward the *economic* interest of the *compagnie* and his kingdom: "I will be grateful if they are able to convert him; but I wish that, without considering his unpleasant religion, they follow his sentiments completely on economic matters."[39]

Caron's fortunes at court, however, took a turn for the worse at about this time. Nearly every despatch that reached Colbert's hands beginning in 1669 heaped criticism on his favorite, information that he may have preferred to dismiss as jealous gossip but that prudence dictated he consider in formulating his plans. M. Joubert, a harsh critic of Caron, had only recently returned to the capital, and in his conversations with the Paris directors and Colbert he outlined in graphic detail the mismanagement and disorder at Surat, which he claimed were the direct result of the Dutchman's policies. From the outset, Colbert had only wanted to utilize foreign experts until sufficient Frenchmen could be trained in the particulars of the trade, since mercantilism was essentially a nationalist economic creed. Careful logs were to be kept on early passages to be used by subsequent French pilots. Heeding Saint-Romain's advice, Colbert took concrete steps to entice the many Frenchmen who had gone into the employ of foreign powers back to the service of the Crown. As French merchants, pilots, and seamen obtained an acceptable level of financial and navigational expertise in the realities of the Asian trade, foreign mercantile mercenaries like Caron became increasingly expendable. Although this point had certainly not been reached by late 1671, Colbert was evidently prepared to temper his earlier support for Caron. The appointment of three new French directors to help direct the day-to-day operations in Asia was the first sign of this shift in strategy. For these positions, Colbert selected Baron, a Lyon merchant named Blot, who had passable political connections but no experience in the trade, and a somewhat shadowy figure named Gueston. Blot traveled to Surat aboard the *St-Jean-Baptiste* on its second outward passage, reaching Swally in October 1671, while Gueston evidently reached Gujarat late in the year.[40]

The six- to eight-month delay in receiving despatches from Paris ensured that Caron remained blissfully unaware of his shifting fortunes at court in the early months of 1671. Ironically, this delay meant that at almost the time when Colbert was originally questioning his decision to vest nearly absolute power in the Dutchman's hands, Caron was basking in the royal favor embodied in the 1669 letters from Louis and Colbert that had only then reached Fort-Dauphin and Gujarat. This royal reaffirmation of faith in the director caused the *Conseil souverain* to reverse its initial judgment in favor of Marcara. Bolstered by this support, Caron also began a campaign to rid himself of all sources of potential opposition: Marcara, who refused to render an account of his activities in Golconda, was arrested and sent back to France in irons, outspoken critics in Surat like Martin and Goujon were sent to languish in the remote factory at Masulipatnam, while the director's minions were appointed to the *conseil* and other key positions.[41] By early 1671, Caron felt secure enough to leave Surat and to begin work on his long-range plans for the establishment of French commercial power in Asia. During his long tenure with the VOC, he had spent a good deal of time in Indonesia, and the strategy he outlined to Colbert contained several projects in that archipelago. Upon his arrival in Surat, the director had initiated negotiations with the rajah of Bantam, or Banten, on Java for a French factory in that kingdom to challenge the trade centered on the nearby Dutch stronghold of Batavia, as well as for permission from that potentate to set up a fortified settlement on the strategic island of Bangka off the northern coast of Sumatra, a post that would allow the *compagnie* to influence the considerable mercantile traffic passing through the Straits of Melaka. Caron knew from past experience and recent reports that the rajah was ill disposed toward the increasingly territorially minded Dutch and would welcome any quid pro quo that would offer French assistance against the zealous burghers of Batavia in return for territorial and trading concessions in Bantam and on Bangka.[42]

No doubt anxious to offer further evidence of his services to the *compagnie* and the Crown before departing on his extended voyage east, Caron rather dilatorily oversaw the loading and dispatching of the *Aigle d'Or* at Swally. The voyage of this ship exemplifies many of the problems that beset the *compagnie*'s early operations. Having sailed from Port-Louis in March 1668, this 300-ton flute ushered in the year 1671 by lying idly at anchor at the mouth of the Tapti. Absorbed with internal political struggles, hindered by a lack of capital and bad credit, opposed by jealous European and Asian competitors, and much more interested in his more grandiose designs, Caron demonstrated little enthusiasm for the difficult task of assembling a cargo for this vessel. As Gerald Aungier informed London, by late January the French director had put together a "poor lading" of the traditional products of saltpeter, some cotton piece goods, indigo, and spices aboard the *Aigle d'Or*, which began the return voyage on the twenty-second of that month.[43] Caron probably judged that Colbert and the directors, desperately awaiting the appearance of any East India goods, would greet the arrival of even this pro forma cargo with much fanfare. In contrast to the slow, threadbare preparations relating to the *Aigle d'Or*, the director spared little expense or time in assembling his expedition for Bantam. These preparations were assisted by the timely arrival in February of the *compagnie* ship *Vautour* with a £30,000 cargo and "newse of 12 saile more of menn of warr than Merchantman expectede in September next which hath much raysede their Reputation here."[44] Borrowing heavily from indigenous moneylenders, based largely on collateral afforded by this stock, Caron finished outfitting the *St-Paul* and *François* and then sailed for Indonesia with these "great shipps," the *Vautour,* and £20,000 of goods in April.[45]

Although Caron's subsequent despatches contain little detail on his voyage to Indonesia, the evidence afforded by the letters of the English factors on Java at the time, Henry and John Dacres, helps us to overcome this dearth of information. The director, whose personal vanity and ambition are adequately documented in all the contemporary sources, arrived in the archipelago anxious to demonstrate his newfound power to his erstwhile colleagues in the Dutch Company, especially old rivals such as Governor-general Johan Maetsuycker. Caron's flotilla reached Bantam in early July, and no expense in cash or shot was spared in an attempt to impress the rajah and Europeans at court with the seriousness of the French king and his *compagnie* to establish a trade in those parts. Facilitated by suitable "gifts" and the promise of French support against further Dutch encroachments, the business was soon concluded. A *farman* of late August gave the French the right to establish a factory in Bantam. According to the Dacres, the French would "pay 1000 per anno for every Ship small or great that Comes from Suratt, the Coast of Bengall, or those parts, 500 for each ship that Comes from Euroape, or elsewhere, besides Custome of pepper & other Commodityes laden here, & 1000 per anno for ground roome." The matter of Bangka was more difficult, since the VOC exerted nominal control over it according to a 1668 treaty with Rajah Samprou in which the Dutch were acknowledged as lord protectors of the island, the rajah promised to pay a yearly tribute in produce, and the rajah also agreed not to admit any other foreigners without the express permission of Batavia. Caron nonetheless obtained tacit approval to establish operations there from the rajah, who no doubt hoped that the long-awaited arrival of French ships in his ports portended a relative shift in power among the Europeans involved in the trade more to his liking than had hitherto existed.[46]

After obtaining these formal concessions, Caron lost little time locating a suitable site for the factory and beginning the work of trading the European wares aboard the *Vautour* for the much-coveted spices produced on Java and the goods from the rest of Indonesia as well as China and Japan available in its markets. The director-general must have reveled in this return to the site of the professional triumphs of his youth. Unlike Surat, he now found himself in a culture he professed to understand, speaking various dialects that he had mastered as a young man, trading for products that he knew well, that had once made him rich enough to arouse the jealousy of his colleagues in Batavia, and that, after being unceremoniously banished from the VOC, had financed a comfortable life in The Hague. The hold of the *Vautour* was soon filled to a respectable level with "Pepper, course Benjamem, Tortise shell, and other goods."[47] The Batavia council, however, was little amused by the return of their fallen director in the vanguard of what was perceived as a disturbing escalation of the French presence in the trade. The initial posturings of Colbert's *compagnie* on Madagascar and in Gujarat, while certainly a nuisance, were not viewed as particularly disturbing since the Dutch Company traditionally had little interest in those regions. The arrival of Caron at Java, negotiating for factories at choice locations in the heart of Batavia's area of operations, with three ships already in evidence and reliable reports of the impending arrival of many more, was an entirely different matter. Maetsuycker promptly dispatched a small fleet to watch the movements of the French flotilla and to prepare to capture it as soon as news of rumored war in Europe reached Asia. Caron resolved to avoid this possibility at all costs. Leaving "3 Merch.ts here, & about 6 sould.ers with aboute 400 Bales of goods, & purpose to bee here againe, about [next] May," his fleet began the return voyage to Surat in early September.[48]

Following La Haye's initial discussions with Baron, life aboard the French fleet anchored at Swally evolved into a boring and unpleasant routine aboard the overcrowded ships lying at anchor in the hot Indian sun. The only excitement for the crews related to Louis XIV's dictum that all ships encountered in Asian waters should strike to his flag, an order that La Haye was determined to uphold. This matter of maritime etiquette had much more significance than might appear. Indigenous rulers and merchants alike were sensitive to the relative power of the Europeans they traded with and were apt to interpret any sign of subservience at sea in Asia as a reliable indicator of the relative strength of these nations in Europe. Concessions on local duties and lucrative trading connections usually shifted in response to such indicators. As English Company officials complained to London, La Haye first by threats and then by "compliments would faine have prevailede with your President to strike to his flag, being a King's flag, and he representing the French king's person." But Aungier, "so Sensible of the great dishonour [that] would accrue to your affaires and to the nation . . . should we tamely strike to the French," resolved not to strike to their "King's Admirall but only Salut him as our Shipps Passed by him and when he came into the Hole." The English and Dutch also avoided problems by flying pendants instead of flags.[49] La Haye first set foot on Indian soil on 18 October. On 5 November 1671 he received Aungier aboard the *Navarre,* and a week later the viceroy was in the midst of being entertained at the English house in Swally when he received word that Caron had anchored in the Hole aboard the *Vautour.* On the return voyage from Bantam, the director had made a brief stop at Calicut to negotiate with the Zamorin, leaving the *St-Paul* and *François* to take on a rich cargo of pepper in that port before heading north.[50]

La Haye and Caron thereupon began a series of conferences on the crucial question of the squadron's future actions. The director had three sites in mind for the first major fortified *compagnie* entrepôt: the Coromandel Coast town of San Thomé, the island of Bangka, and one of the major bays on the northeastern coast of Ceylon. As Caron had already pointed out in his letters to Colbert, San Thomé was ideally located with respect to the large textile trade of that region. The Portuguese had held the town for many years, only to be expelled by the king of Golconda in the early 1660s. Although Marcara had tried and failed to extend his 1669 *farman* from that ruler to include a factory at San Thomé, Caron believed his negotiating skills in conjunction with Louis XIV's men-of-war might change the king's mind. The rajah of Bantam had proven to be extremely accommodating on Caron's recent voyage and would welcome an increased French presence on Java and Bangka as a needed counterweight to the bothersome Dutch. Nevertheless, Dutch power was far more formidable in Indonesia than anywhere else in Asia, something that Caron knew from past experience and that had been demonstrated to him once again the previous summer. This fact probably convinced him to postpone his plans for Bangka for the moment in favor of beginning operations on the island of Ceylon. Locus of the lucrative cinnamon trade and strategically located on Indian Ocean trade routes, Ceylon had been controlled by the dominant European powers in the trade since the days of Albuquerque. Caron wanted to continue this trend by entrenching French power there to herald rising French ambitions in Asia and as a needed steppingstone to eventual dominance over the European share of the trade, the logical culmination of Colbert's project. The director-general had years of experience on Ceylon and had enjoyed relatively cordial relations with the king of Kandy, Rajah Sinha II. As he informed La Haye, negotiations had already begun with Sinha II, who had become increasingly disenchanted with the actions of the Dutch, through Capuchin and Portuguese intermediaries.[51]

The resolution taken by La Haye and Caron to begin operations on Ceylon was simple in comparison to the problems that had to be overcome in Surat in the quest to implement this plan. Blot had come out from France with zealous opinions on solving the *compagnie*'s ills. As a conservative member of the mercantile community of Lyon, he believed that the financial strains of extending commercial operations from Madagascar to Java within eight years' time were too much for the young *compagnie* to sustain. Blot recommended a more cautious course of action; he was vehement in his opposition to the creation of any more factories, arguing that the *compagnie* should abandon most of those it already possessed. He even suggested that the Surat settlement should be forsaken in favor of a commercial post at the Portuguese city of Chaul. Blot was also convinced "that the state of things at Surat was hopelessly rotten, that every servant of the Company there was thoroughly dishonest and untrustworthy, and that he was the only person who could set matters right."[52] The cause of these problems was not difficult to divine: Caron was to blame. Blot mistrusted the director-general's motives and openly stated that he could never work with him. Caron may have been "the oldest and most experienced man in the business; but he was extremely jealous of his supreme position and rank, and aspired to a preeminence that M. Blot could not concede to him."[53] Blot also quarreled with La Haye in late 1671 over the question of reprovisioning the royal fleet with *compagnie* resources, maintaining that the *compagnie* was under no obligation to aid the king's ships with resources that could be better spent paying off existing debts. The director told La Haye that he should return to France with the royal fleet, which in his view was "inutille" and in fact damaging to the *compagnie*'s interests. Although Blot claimed to be operating in this manner based on secret instructions from the Crown, there is no documentary evidence to support this contention.[54]

The viceroy described his considerable frustration in attempting to resolve this dispute in letters to Louis XIV and Colbert of late 1671. He began his letter to Louis by lamenting the poor communication between Paris and Asia, which had done much to complicate his mission. As he informed the king, the last royal dispatch he had received was dated December 1670, and it had reached him via the Capuchins in the Levant! La Haye then tried to explain the less-than-impressive results he had obtained regarding the prime directive in his instructions, the foundation of fortified settlements for the *compagnie*. Predictably, he attempted to blame divisions among the directors for his problems. Had he found a "good correspondence" among the directors at Surat, he would have already begun this work. Blot's arrival, however, had disrupted everything, as this director seemed to have come "seullement pour retirer les effets de la compagnie et abandonner les Indes." La Haye rejected the notion that Blot was acting on secret Crown instructions and stated that, even if such orders existed, they would be harmful "au service de Vostre Majesté et Ennemis du bien et de l'advantage de la *compagnie*." He was especially critical of clauses in his instructions that ordered him to follow the opinions of the directors, even when he believed they were mistaken. This ill-considered decision had mired the fleet in a quagmire of internal *compagnie* politics that now threatened the success of the entire enterprise. La Haye's advice on avoiding such problems in the future was simple: give absolute authority to the viceroy. Although he agreed with Caron's plans—"it is with pleasure that I embrace and will execute them," he wrote—he was already running short of funds. The 100,000 livres he had been entrusted with at Rochefort for victuals were nearly depleted. His crews and troops had only been paid until September 1671, and no additional funds had been forthcoming. He was therefore forced to consider the less than palatable option of temporarily paying these salaries out of his own private funds.[55]

In his letters to Colbert, La Haye furnished additional details on the situation at Surat. The large royal men-of-war had greatly impressed the merchant community of the town as well as the Mughal authorities. The Indians may have been accustomed to fleets of European merchantmen sailing in their waters, but Louis XIV's ornate, well-armed fighting ships were quite another matter. Their appearance had done much to raise the reputation and credit of the French on that coast. The reports of local Mughal officials, which voiced fears of an attack on Surat, had prompted Aurangzeb not only to send a new governor and 2000 cavalry troops to reinforce the place but also to issue orders preventing the sale of provisions to the fleet in an attempt to prompt an early departure. Regarding the acrimonious dispute between the directors, La Haye wrote that while Baron was originally prepared to support "nostre dessein," he had been turned against the plan by the pleadings of Blot. As a result, both men wanted to use the 50,000 écus he had brought for the *compagnie* to pay off debts rather than to outfit ships to accompany the royal squadron on its mission. La Haye informed Colbert that he would do his utmost to achieve his primary goal: "new establishments for the service and good of the Company, the advancement of the nation, and the *gloire* of our monarch." But Blot, "fort chaud et sans sens," was opposed to everything necessary for attaining this objective. In contrast, La Haye described Caron at this point as judicious and well-intentioned, an opinion he would have good reason to modify as the expedition continued. In the end, La Haye had been forced to nearly overstep his authority in order to pressure Blot and Baron to accept a compromise in which the *compagnie* would outfit the ships *Phoenix* and *St-Jean-Baptiste* to join the squadron. Given Aurangzeb's directive, supplies remained a problem. In a painful lesson in the laws of supply and demand, the English and Dutch had agreed to sell provisions at a premium price. Nevertheless, Caron had advised that they stock provisions for a year, and it had only been possible to purchase quantities sufficient for half that time.[56]

In light of the compromise reached with Baron and Blot, final preparations for the departure took place at Swally throughout the Christmas season of 1671–1672. On 9 January, after more than three months at anchor at the mouth of the Tapti, the French fleet lifted anchor and began its voyage south. As usual La Haye sailed aboard his flagship, the *Navarre,* accompanied by the men-of-war *Triomphe, Jules,* and *Flamand;* the royal flutes *Sultane, Indienne,* and *Europe;* the king's frigate *Diligente;* the *compagnie* vessels *St-Jean-Baptiste* (with Caron aboard), *Phoenix* and *St-Louis;* and several small barks to help reconnoiter the coast. The man-of-war *Bayonnais,* leaking badly, was disarmed and left behind. As January began the customary sailing season from the west coast of India for Africa and Europe, the *Dauphin* began the long passage back to Port-Louis carrying a respectable cargo of pepper, saltpeter, and benjamin along with despatches from La Haye, Caron, Baron, and Blot for the *compagnie* and the Crown. The *Vautour* also departed from Swally at this time on a passage to the fledgling factory at Bantam.[57] The destination of La Haye's grand fleet, and implicitly the main objectives of Colbert's plans, engendered a good deal of postulating and apprehension on the part of France's rivals in the trade. Upon the squadron's arrival at Swally, Aungier had written that he expected the fleet to join with the Portuguese in order to recapture Cochin and Ceylon from the Dutch. Nothing had happened in the intervening months to alter this generally held opinion. After the fleet's departure, London was informed that La Haye's ships had "shaped their course for Goa; where tis believed Mouns. La Hay will stay some time to treat with the Viceroy of Goa about some private designes between them and also to supply the fleet with provitions which he much wants." As the French viceroy had loaded his ships with bricks and "a great quantity of timber for platformes for a fort & sparrs for pallizades," it was believed he intended to erect various fortifications, "but where is not yet discovered; some fancy it to be on the Malabar coast near Cocheen, others the Island of Banca."[58] As both Europe and Asia prepared diplomatically and militarily for the renewed French onslaught against the United Provinces in the winter of 1671–1672, the definitive answers to these perplexing questions would not be long in coming.

VI

Batavia and the Malabar Coast, 1672

Frustrated Alliances and a Frustrating Start to the Anti-Dutch Crusade

> "The Portuguese at Goa had in October last received a great relief from Lisbon. . . . [F]rom their great sea preparations and other signs we have long been of the opinion that they intend to join with the French ships arrived at Surat, Jointly to fall upon us at Malabar or Ceylon."
>
> —Maetsuycker and Batavia Council
> to *Heeren XVII*

The arrival of La Haye's squadron at Surat had been anything but a surprise to Johan Maetsuycker and the members of his council *(Raad van Indie)* at Batavia. Dutch agents in Paris had kept the *Heeren XVII,* the seventeen men who directed the vast operations of the United Dutch East India Company, well informed on virtually every phase of Colbert's expedition from the outset. In May 1670, the Seventeen had informed Batavia, "[T]he fleet equipped at Rochelle has sailed for the East Indies. She consists of five large men of war carrying some 60, others no less than 40 guns . . . 12 or 13 in all with 1500 soldiers." Since these ships carried large quantities of stone, the fleet's objective was likely "to raise a fortress at once on the place where they will disembark, which we are informed will not be Madagascar." The merchants in Amsterdam and The Hague could not resist adding that "the merchantmen have a lading of Scarlett cloth, some silver, amber, [and] red corral."[1] By September of that year, the Seventeen were already feeling the mounting pressure of the warlike preparations that characterized Franco-Dutch relations during this period, as Louis XIV, Louvois, and Lionne continued their careful military and diplomatic preparations, which would culminate in the spring campaign of 1672. The Dutch directors were clearly taking no chances: "The Prospect becomes daily more certain that our State will again be involved in war, we have resolved to augment the number of men which we intended to send out to India." In light of these rather ominous developments, the governor-general was admonished to "take every necessary precaution" and to "be quite prepared for the event and in the meantime [to] secure the possession of all those islands which produce clover and spices."[2]

In many ways, Maetsuycker was a most unlikely man to hold the lofty position of governor-general at this crucial time in the company's history. By birth a Roman Catholic, he had studied law at Louvain. In 1635, as the Seventeen searched for a qualified legal expert to assist the expanding activities of the court of justice at Batavia, Maetsuycker had offered his services, promising to profess the reformed religion as practiced in the Dutch East Indies. This flexibility would serve him well during the ensuing years, particularly during the Third Dutch War. Arriving on Java in 1636, Maetsuycker spent the next six years compiling the Statutes of Batavia, the legal code that served as the basis for the legal system in Dutch colonial possessions in Asia for the next two centuries. Following a trip to Amsterdam in 1643, he had returned to Batavia as commander of the Ninth Fleet the following year, with strict orders from the Seventeen to belatedly put the truce ratified in Europe between the United Provinces and Portugal in November 1641 into effect. Although hard-liners in Batavia led by crusading Governor-general Anthony van Diemen (1636–1645) favored the continuation of the successful campaign against the crumbling *Estado da India,* Maetsuycker had followed his instructions and made his hesitant colleagues adhere to the truce until it expired in 1652. In recognition of his obvious talents and no doubt his willingness to follow orders, Maetsuycker was appointed governor-general in 1653. He would hold this position for the next twenty-five years, the longest term in the company's history. His first success was not long in coming. In 1655, Maetsuycker dispatched a fleet of fourteen ships and 1200 men under Gerald Hulft to Ceylon: Colombo was taken in May 1656, and by July 1658 the Portuguese had been expelled from the island.[3]

By early 1672, the expulsion of the Portuguese from Ceylon afforded Maetsuycker little comfort, given the serious problems he then confronted. An interpretation that has recently held great attraction for scholars in the field holds that in the competition for Asian trade during the seventeenth century, the entrepreneurial structures of the Protestant trading companies of the Dutch and English gave them inherent and insurmountable advantages in their struggle with the monarchical monopolism of the Portuguese Crown. The "revolution" in the Asian trade resulting from the entrance of these companies into the fray was in part characterized by the development of efficient, centralized bureaucracies, permanent joint stocks, and the ability to internalize protection costs. Heralding this so-called revolution was the destruction in 1622 by a combined Anglo-Persian force of the Portuguese *fortaleza* at Hurmuz, which for a century had dominated the Persian Gulf trade. This act ushered in a basic reorientation of Euro-Asian commercial interchange by facilitating the drastic reduction of the significant "peddler" overland trade through the Levant, a trade that the inefficient monarchical monopolism of the Iberians could never achieve but that was part and parcel of the protocapitalism implicit in the activities of the Dutch and English Companies.[4] This attempt to portray the VOC as a vanguard for pristine protocapitalist structures is certainly attractive. It also offers a pat explanation for why the Portuguese ultimately proved to be no match for their Protestant rivals during the course of the seventeenth century. Nevertheless, one problem with the strict dichotomy of protocapitalist vis-á-vis monarchical monopolism that essentially lies at the base of this model for examining the commercial struggle between the Atlantic economies (and Asian companies) of the Dutch and English and the Portuguese *Estado da India* is that it assumes largely static and unchanging structures and priorities for these combatants during the course of the seventeenth century. This was far from the case, as Dutch policies in Indonesia, India, and on Ceylon during the middle decades of that century well illustrate.[5]

At the time of the amalgamation by the States General of the hitherto competing Dutch Companies into a single United Netherlands Chartered East India Company in 1602, there was general agreement that this new entity should at all cost avoid what was perceived as the fatal error of the Portuguese in Asia, unnecessary and prohibitively expensive territorial expansion, in favor of pursuing a profitable trade that would shun burdensome military expenditures. From the time of Jan Pieterszoon Coen onward, however, this pristine entrepreneurialism had been undermined by a competing desire to obtain the much-coveted monopoly over three of the principal spices found in the Indonesian archipelago—cloves, nutmeg, and mace—precisely by embracing extended effective control over the spice-producing regions. Warfare was virtually endemic with the indigenous sultanates of Indonesia for the remainder of the seventeenth century, a struggle that was exacerbated by a renascent Islamization in the region that fostered the pride of local rulers in their own identity and made them all the more resentful of European intrusion into their domains. At the same time, conflicts among the chief Indonesian states, beginning in mid-century, only invited Dutch intervention and expansion, especially when these local potentates frequently appealed to Batavia for support. On the Moluccas, the Dutch were forced to fight a bloody struggle with the sultan of Ternate from 1650 to 1655. The king of Makassar, the most powerful Muslim ruler on Celebes, fought a continuing campaign against Batavia from the early 1650s until 1668 that did much to drain Maetsuycker's resources. The destruction of the powerful sultanate of Acheh on Sumatra, while yielding access to the tin mines of Perak and suzerainty over Bangka and Billiton, was also obtained only at a high price. In west Java, the power of the sultan of Bantam, Abulfatah Agung, continued to grow. His plans to expand his domains eastward into Mataram and to ultimately surround Batavia had already led him to make concessions to Caron and the French Company.[6]

On Ceylon, the foremost proponent of territorial expansion inland, as part of a strategy designed to obtain an effective monopoly over the lucrative cinnamon trade, was Rijkloff Van Goens. Born in 1619, Van Goens had sailed to Batavia with his father in 1628. Orphaned soon thereafter, he had been placed in the household of the Dutch governor at Pulicat where he learned much about the company's trade in India and demonstrated considerable business acumen and a ruthless efficiency in diplomacy. The years 1654 to 1663 established his reputation as one of the most formidable military commanders in the Indian Ocean. His capture of five well-armed Portuguese carracks in 1654 certainly helped earn him the powerful position of "Commissioner, Superintendent, Admiral, and General by land and by sea on the coasts of India, Coromandel, Surat, Ceylon, Bengal, and Melaka" three years later. Establishing his headquarters at Colombo, Van Goens directed the final stages of the onslaught against the *Estado da India* on the Malabar Coast. These victories, while obtained in part due to the refusal of James Ley, the earl of Marlborough, to honor the provisions of the 1661 Anglo-Portuguese alliance, nonetheless deprived the Portuguese of their last major settlements on that pepper-producing coast. As governor of Ceylon from 1662, Van Goens's expansionist plans were frustrated until 1664 by the traditional fear on the part of some members of the Seventeen and the Batavia Council of incurring burdensome expenditures at a time when warfare was still raging in Indonesia and the shrewd and capable Rajah Sinha II seemed to retain considerable military prowess.[7]

Maetsuycker had initially favored a cautious policy on Ceylon. The warfare with European and indigenous enemies alike may have caused him to lose his faith in the 1651 "Instruction to Batavia" from the Seventeen, which called for the extension of "peaceful trade through the Indies." Given mounting problems and military costs in *Achter-Indie*, he was ill disposed to any plan that would have further divided his available forces and funds. During the mid-1660s, the increasing threat from European competitors forced the governor-general to reverse his views on the advisability of Van Goens's designs on the island. The appearance of the ship *Anne* on the Sinhalese coast in 1660 signaled renascent English activities on the island that fueled apprehension in Batavia and Amsterdam alike. As Maetsuycker wrote in 1666, the English were determined "to induce Rajah Sinha to make common cause against us and secure for themselves free trading in Ceylon. This is a serious matter."[8] The rajah, still seeking to play the Europeans against one another to his greatest advantage, had asked for Dutch protection over the bays of Batticaloa and Trincomalee. Van Goens had proposed taking them outright, "so that we could exclude any other nation from the island." News that a palace coup in Kandy had temporarily rendered Rajah Sinha militarily impotent decided the issue. As the governor-general and council informed the Seventeen, "We have after due consideration given orders for the execution of [Van Goens's] plan."[9] Van Goens exploited the situation with ease; Batticaloa and Trincomalee were quickly taken and fortified, and the Dutch began to expand to inland areas that they had hitherto avoided. Batavia was delighted with these initial reports, and the council was soon convinced that perhaps it would be advisable to conquer the entire island and make Dutch power on Ceylon comparable to what it was in Indonesia.[10]

The financial and military strain of this expansionist policy soon became painfully evident in Batavia and Colombo. Van Goens's troops may have occupied new inland territories, but underlying this facade of early success was that the governor had committed the company to a policy that its resources simply could not sustain. Maetsuycker registered his "great uneasiness" with the military situation on Ceylon as early as October 1668, when he informed the Seventeen that "our posts are now extended so far in the interior and spread so far apart that by any sinister design of Rajah Sinha they are entirely at his mercy."[11] This able king had promptly restored order in Kandy and in early 1670 launched the type of counteroffensive that the Batavia Council feared: Van Goens's men suffered heavy losses in the initial fighting and had soon retreated to their pre-1665 positions. This warfare continued in the lush littoral landscape of the island for the next two years. For Maetsuycker, the cost could not be denied: in the late 1660s the company deficit on Ceylon was already averaging 250,000 guilders, the figure would soon reach 730,000 guilders! Van Goens's expansionist desires also facilitated Colbert's wish to share in the much-vaunted cinnamon trade of the island. Faced with a continuing campaign against the Dutch, Rajah Sinha was exceedingly receptive to Caron's diplomatic feelers through Capuchin and Portuguese intermediaries that called for the establishment of French trading operations on the island and the granting of either Batticaloa or Trincomalee to the *compagnie*.[12]

Much the same situation existed for the Dutch Company on the Malabar Coast. Open warfare had begun between the VOC and the powerful Zamorin in the mid-1660s, following that potentate's unpolitic decision to raise the price of pepper, largely in response to the arrival of the French and the increased demand for that prized spice. At times, the fighting had been particularly vicious. John Petit, the English factor in Calicut, described in graphic detail one incident in which Dutch Company troops launched a surprise attack on the Zamorin's camp. After overcoming the guards "whome they killed with little trouble . . . they came upon where the king's wife and other women of quality were lodged," and shot and killed several of them, including "the king's daughter into the thigh & his wife into the eye."[13] Although Van Goens and Van Rheede, governor of Cranganore, were eventually able to field a force of over 1000 men, mostly indigenous retainers, in this struggle, doing so necessitated leaving Cochin and the remaining Dutch possessions on that coast virtually undefended. As Petit informed Aungier, "Cochin was left with but 30 men, in Cranganore 20; & in Palliapor but 2; soe that it had been an easy matter to have surprised either of those places."[14] The Zamorin badly needed assistance to prosecute this war and exact revenge for the outrages of Van Goens's troops. Caron and M. Flacourt, the *compagnie* chief for Malabar, had already begun negotiations toward procuring trading privileges and land to erect factories in his domains. The local ruler had proven receptive. In 1670 as a sign of good will, he had granted the *compagnie* the small coastal village of Alicot, located at the southern limits of his domains. He had also allowed the *St-Paul* and *François* to buy and load pepper on their return journey from Bantam in late 1671.[15] Commenting on the gravity of the problems then confronting him, Maetsuycker lamented: "What a fearfull charge doth Ceylon and Malabar draw after it, and how many years hath this continued in hopes of a profitable issue. . . . God in mercy put an end to these bad times and cause them to issue for the best."[16]

By the early months of the fateful year of 1672, the Seventeen in Amsterdam and the governor-general in Batavia therefore confronted a complex and potentially very dangerous conjuncture of events. The appearance of La Haye's royal squadron in Asian waters, periodic warfare with indigenous rulers in Indonesia and elsewhere, Louis XIV's warlike preparations in Europe, Caron's already fruitful negotiations in Bantam, Kandy, and Calicut, as well as justifiable fears over a triple alliance directed against them "beyond the line," all conspired to put the VOC in a very vulnerable position. To be sure, the financial and military power of the Dutch Company remained formidable: the 1670 annual fleet had returned home with 9.2 million pounds of black pepper and 134,000 pounds of white pepper, the largest amount to reach Europe during the entire century, while a fleet of approximately sixty-five fighting ships remained at Maetsuycker's disposal in Asia.[17] Nevertheless, the extant sources suggest that in much the same way as Van Goens's policies overextended the company on Ceylon, the far-flung empire created by Coen and Van Diemen was on the verge of overextending the resources of the Amsterdam directors and Batavia as they prepared to defend their widely dispersed possessions against Asian and European rivals who were either bent on revenge like the reforming *Estado da India,* firmly committed to winning a larger share of the trade like the French and English, or merely defending themselves against Dutch territorial intrusions like Rajah Sinha II. Rather than avoiding the costly mistakes of the Portuguese, the Dutch had indeed come to embrace them: overextension, huge military and administrative costs, almost constant warfare against a plethora of enemies, an obsessive desire to monopolize key commodities in the trade, and a growing primacy of imperial geopolitical priorities over sound mercantile practices. The risk to the Dutch Asian empire from Colbert's project, a strategy that sought to combine a solid seaborne coalition in the Indian Ocean assisted by Louis's armies and any useful alliance that might be arranged with indigenous powers, was correspondingly great.

The Seventeen were well aware of this threat, and their rising anxiety is well reflected in the official correspondence with Maetsuycker. As late as 1669, the main preoccupation of the *Heeren* remained the quest for monopoly over Indonesian spices for geopolitical as well as economic reasons. "We are pleased to hear that Banca and Billiton have placed themselves under the protection of the company. This promises well, not so much on account of the profits we may expect from their products but because it will keep these islands from the possessions of other nations."[18] In 1670, as the threat from Louis XIV loomed larger, the directors had ordered Maetsuycker to take every precaution to prepare for the onslaught and secure the main spice-producing islands.[19] The departure of La Haye's fleet in March of that year had only exacerbated their fears: "We are very anxious to know more of their proceedings in India. . . . [W]e hear that their destination was Banca, which seems much more probable [than Ceylon] as they have for some time had an eye on that island." Colbert's negotiations in London and Lisbon had also come to the attention of the directors and afforded little comfort, especially operating in conjunction with Louis's bellicose attitude and Lionne's diplomacy. "Our State is very uneasy about the warlike preparations France is making. . . . Neither are we on the best terms with England. Besides there is a rumor of a treaty between France, Portugal, and England."[20] The Seventeen recognized that their ability to reinforce Batavia and conserve their Asian trade depended principally on the outcome of any war in Europe: "[W]e must keep ourselves on the defensive, ready for any emergency, which will greatly depend on the failure or success of our armies in Europe."[21] Colbert also recognized this fact and would thus support Louis's planned invasion. If successful, such a campaign would afford him the swiftest means possible to attain his goal of destroying Dutch commercial power both in Europe and the Indian Ocean trade.

After discussions with his council, the governor-general decided on a series of measures to meet this threat. Maetsuycker devoted most of his energies to reinforcing possessions in Indonesia, since holdings in the archipelago were the most valued part of the empire. Reports on Caron's machinations relating to Bangka caused him to erect a fortified post on that island: "The Dutch have sent men-of-war, sloopes, and other craft loaded with wood, stores, lyme, & iron . . . to build a castle there."[22] Fleets were organized to patrol the waters around Java and Bangka and to guard the sea-lanes to the north, since "the trouble . . . caused by the French force at

Sea, with which we have been threatened for some time," had interrupted the valued "navigation for Japan."[23] Possessions on the Malabar Coast and Ceylon were judged to be in the most immediate danger. Maetsuycker accordingly took steps to improve the company's position in those places. To stem the flow of needed men and money into the continuing campaign with Calicut, the Dutch pressed hard to conclude a peace with the Zamorin, even offering him twenty-six brass cannon to move along the negotiations.[24] To safeguard shipping on that coast, Adriaen Roothaes was dispatched with a fleet of twenty ships to convoy merchantmen to Surat and Persia. Van Goens left Colombo with a fleet of twelve ships to monitor La Haye's fleet on that coast and to protect Ceylon.[25] As William Langhorn, the English governor at Madras, noted: Maetsuycker omitted "noe dilligence in Zeilon; Negapatam & all along [the Coromandel Coast] to provide for the worse, sufficiently alarmed at the appearance of so unruly a people."[26] John Petit nonetheless continued to believe that Ceylon was vulnerable and that Van Goens was hard pressed to prepare for the French fleet.

The Dutch were not the only Europeans established in Asia who were apprehensive about the approach of La Haye's squadron. Considerable time was devoted in Bombay and Goa to discussing a suitable reception for the most visible demonstration of Colbert's resolution to challenge for a meaningful share of the trade. The arrival of the viceroy's fleet at Swally had complicated the significant series of reforms that had been initiated by Gerald Aungier following his appointment as company president in Surat in 1669. More than any other of the London Company's servants, Aungier was responsible for recognizing the true potential of Bombay. The new president shunned the traditional seat of operations in Surat and instead spent most of the next seven years in Bombay. Above all, Aungier wanted to create a strong, fortified, independent entrepôt there, one that could withstand the military threat of Aurangzeb, Shivaji, and European rivals alike, while serving as a valued economic center for the company's expanding activities on the west coast of India. He would establish the company's first regular military force. A small militia, commanded by officers drawn from the company factors and made up of Indian companies of infantry, was also set up. To protect Bombay and its fine harbor from the ravages of the Mughal fleet commanded by the Sidi of Janjira, Shivaji's growing navy, the famed Malabar "pirates," as well as the Dutch or French, Aungier maintained a small permanent force of company ships in the area. Proper fortifications were begun. He advised the Court of Committees that once these preparations were complete, the company headquarters on that coast should be formally transferred to Bombay.[27]

Aungier would also oversee a remarkable period of population and economic growth in the town. Marshes were drained, a hospital was founded, courts of judicature were set up, and an assembly of landowners convened to regulate local taxes and other sources of revenue ideally on an equitable basis. Since indigenous capital was vital for successful commercial operations in Asia, the president also did his best to attract rich Hindu, Jain, Muslim, and Parsi merchants to Bombay. A particularly effective strategy for accomplishing this goal was to afford a freedom of religion of sorts within the confines of English-held territory, a practice that Aungier adopted despite the admonishments of the more zealous members of the Court of Committees. This policy attracted large numbers of Hindu merchants from the neighboring "Province of the North" of the Portuguese *Estado,* where the excesses of the Goa Inquisition were allowed to manifest themselves at will. As the *gentio* merchants of Bassein pointed out in a June 1671 petition to Mendonça Furtado, these abuses, especially the practice of taking and forcibly converting Hindu orphans, had led to such an influx into Bombay from the "Norte" that the tax-farming receipts on tobacco alone had increased sixfold in less than six years.[28] To ensure English control over the island's resources, Aungier allowed the appropriation of Portuguese estates and *fazendas* to continue at a rather alarming rate. This practice dated from the time of his immediate royal (Henry Gary) and company (Oxinden) predecessors and predictably engendered loud protests locally and in Europe.[29] All of Aungier's plans, however, seemed temporarily at risk in 1672 as La Haye's fleet approached.

After departing from Swally in early January, the squadron had leisurely made its way down the west coast of India. As would soon become apparent to La Haye and Caron, the acrimonious delay at Surat had given all of France's rivals in the trade an opportunity to prepare. "The noise they have made hath so awakened all who have the least Jealously of them that they cannot but be well prepared to receive them."[30] The fleet anchored first before the strategic Portuguese stronghold of Daman.[31] By mid-January, the French fleet had anchored off the small Portuguese fort at Vissava on the island of Salsete, close to Bombay. Caron was keen to explore this vicinity for a suitable factory site, while Aungier took every precaution to discourage this work. After spending "great quantityes of Powder" in an effort to impress local Mughal authorities (and overawe the English), La Haye had "sent a Shallope with 80 men by way of Mahim and Bandora" to Bombay with a request to buy provisions. Aungier ascribed more nefarious motives to this request. After landing a lieutenant to purchase supplies, the shallop had "put into the Bay and went for the Island of Caringa, Sounding the Bay as [it] went." The town, however, was well-prepared. As Aungier wrote, the lieutenant could "not faile to give Mons. La Haye an account in what a posture he found the Government and the Guards being doubled manned and the Militia in armes." London was promptly notified that these preparations had undermined the French "design": the fleet had sailed on for Goa without incident, while for the moment, at least, the president could return to the business of entrenching a solid trade.[32]

The fleet carrying Luis de Mendonça Furtado to the Portuguese Asian capital of Goa had anchored in the Mandovi in May 1671. Mendonça Furtado had taken formal possession of the government of the *Estado* on the twenty-second of that month and then proceeded upriver to his palace, a renovated residence of the kings of Bijapur, in "Velha Goa."[33] He had been absent from the Asian possessions for nearly a decade. In that time the problems confronting the Crown had increased dramatically from 1662 when Antonio de Mello de Castro had written upon his arrival that "the needs of the *Estado* are so many and so great . . . and there is not even a single penny to help meet necessary expenses."[34] While Pedro and his Overseas Council had resolved to undertake a concerted reform program in the *Estado* as early as 1668, that campaign was barely under way upon Mendonça Furtado's arrival. Only after reaching Goa, meeting with his councils of state and finance, and perusing the despatches that awaited him from the outlying parts of the empire, could the new viceroy truly appreciate the challenge that confronted him. Besides being financially distressed, the *Estado* faced a host of commercial and military adversaries. Militarily, reforms were needed in the wage and quartering system. A regular maritime correspondence with Lisbon through the so-called *Carreira da India* had to be reestablished. Finally, the plethora of abuses by the various religious orders entrenched in the *Estado* had to be addressed and corrected.[35]

In the midst of this daunting array of problems, Mendonça Furtado was confronted with the imminent arrival of La Haye's squadron and the likely offer of an anti-Dutch alliance that would be proffered by Louis XIV's viceroy and Caron. Baron had already written an intriguing letter to the Portuguese viceroy in December 1671. This despatch offered an extremely biased version of the latest news from Europe, including a rumor that France and Portugal would soon be declaring war on the Dutch in India and that Louis XIV's armies were already in Flanders. On a more realistic note, Mendonça Furtado was informed that the French royal squadron would soon be leaving Swally and that La Haye badly wanted to hold direct talks in Goa.[36] In his earlier discussions with Saint-Romain in Lisbon, the Portuguese viceroy dismissed the French as mere dilettantes in the trade, believing that, while Colbert might have been serious in his efforts, the French could not hope to achieve anything of consequence in Asia without the firm support of Louis, an unlikely proposition at best. All the same, Mendonça Furtado recognized that the French were convenient dilettantes, for Saint-Romain's initiative for an alliance against the Dutch Company, especially when such talk involved a military attack, was a strategy worth encouraging, since it unwittingly complemented the desires of Pedro and Mendonça Furtado for internal reform. As long as the French, Dutch, and perhaps even the English were busy warring against one another in Europe and Asia, Lisbon would be free to pursue reform in the *Estado* without opposition. Any setbacks the Dutch suffered in a renewed war with Louis would of course be an unexpected boon. Mendonça Furtado had therefore encouraged the French ambassador during their conversations, offering military stratagems to be used against the VOC, while reiterating his firm conviction that "one can not diminish the commerce of the Dutch in the Indies without making war on them there."[37]

The Portuguese viceroy's perspective on Colbert's campaign to establish the French in the trade, however, had altered somewhat since late 1669, in light of his stopover at Mozambique and the information contained in initial dispatches from the rest of his *fortalezas*. This new evidence convinced him that the French Company and especially Louis XIV's continuing support, most visible in the form of La Haye's fleet, could not be dismissed so lightly. He had already seen the disquieting reports on the escalating presence of French factors throughout littoral India and the rest of the Indian Ocean basin, efforts that had yielded favorable commercial *farmans* from Aurangzeb, the king of Golconda, the Zamorin of Calicut, and the sultan of Bantam. The price of pepper had already risen in Kanara and along the rest of the Malabar Coast as a result, complicating his task of loading and reembarking the remaining four ships of his fleet on their return voyage to Lisbon.[38] Caron's negotiations with Rajah Sinha II on Ceylon, made known to him through Portuguese Jesuits, were also upsetting. João de Sousa Freire's letters from Mozambique detailing French activities on Madagascar, activities that threatened the Crown's renascent plans for the Rios de Cuama and the stay of the *Dauphin* on that coast, were yet another cause for concern. In October 1671, the viceroy evidenced a notably different opinion on the expanding French presence in the trade in a letter to Pedro that warned him of the great threat Colbert's actions then constituted to the *Estado*.[39] Although French intentions were not clear to him, Mendonça Furtado proved to be a man of his word. That fall, he reinforced the forts of Diu, Daman, and Bassein. Immediately following the Christmas festivities of 1672, he issued orders for the men at the outlying inland forts scattered throughout the Old Provinces of Goa, Bardes, and Salsette to report to the coastal fortresses that guarded the mouth of the Mandovi. As he informed Lisbon, "I tried to reinforce all the *fortalezas* and forts of this city, and those of the Province of the North as well as was possible with men and munitions."[40]

While the Portuguese viceroy frantically undertook defensive measures in the *Estado*, the French squadron was approaching. By late January, the fleet finally neared Goa. Still unsure of his reception there, La Haye sent the *Flamand* ahead to seek permission to provision his ships from Panjim and its environs. The officers of this man-of-war were well-received, and on 25 January 1672 the rest of the fleet anchored near the mouth of the Mandovi, between the forts of Aguada and Nossa Senhora do Cabo.[41] At first, La Haye and Mendonça Furtado stood on ceremony and refused to meet each other formally. Despite their other qualities, both men were extremely vain, jealous of their rank, and obsessed with matters of protocol. Mendonça

Furtado was particularly irked that the Frenchman styled himself "viceroy," a title reserved exclusively for the titular head of the *Estado* from the time of Albuquerque's immediate successors onward. He also had no explicit instructions from Lisbon on how to receive the French, regarding both matters of substance and etiquette, aside from vague warnings from the Overseas Council to show suitable caution. As the Portuguese viceroy wrote, "One finds at present in this bar of Goa, 11 French warships. . . . [T]he intercourse that one has with that Nation is with great affability and correspondence among friends but always with the necessary caution, vigilance and care that Your Majesty has ordered." At last, an acceptable compromise was arranged that circumvented the potential pitfalls of a formal meeting: "Finding myself without clear orders of Your Majesty on the correct manner in which to receive them, above all I resolved to meet [La Haye] on the quay of the fortress of Aguada, not allowing him to enter the fort or any other *praca*."[42]

Although La Haye and Caron disembarked on both 27 and 28 January, it appears they were able to hold talks with Mendonça Furtado only on the first day. This meeting on the public quay at Aguada embodied the last serious attempt to arrange a Franco-Portuguese Asian alliance against the VOC, a campaign launched in Lisbon more than two years earlier, and one which portended much for the eventual resolution of Colbert's project. The timing of this meeting could hardly have been better for French purposes. At that very moment the annual Portuguese fleets for Cambay, Kanara, and the Persian Gulf, charged with intercepting interlopers in the Crown monopoly trade, were preparing to sail. This fact did not escape the attention of Dutch and English agents resident in Goa, whose apprehensive was reflected in reports to London and Amsterdam. As Aungier wrote, "The Portugall fleet is ready consisting of 12 Small frigatts and two Ships . . . but whether those two fleets are to Joyne or no or what either of their designe is, as yet Wee cannot certainly inform you."[43] Maetsuycker and the Batavia Council had come to a more pessimistic conclusion: "We have long been of the opinion that they intend to join with the French ships arrived at Surat, Jointly to fall upon us at Malabar or Ceylon."[44] In their quest for an alliance, however, La Haye and Caron were destined to enjoy no more success than Saint-Romain's considerable efforts had yielded in the Portuguese capital.

The exact details of what transpired at this crucial meeting and, in particular, why Mendonça Furtado rejected La Haye's overtures are difficult to discern from the available evidence. La Haye's despatches from the Malabar Coast are bereft of any insights and merely suggest that the "jealousy" he encountered in Goa precluded the possibility of any deal. None of Mendonça Furtado's ciphered letters for early 1672 apparently have survived, and it is almost certain that he would have discussed such matters only in code. His extant letters for this period are dominated by mundane descriptions of the stay of the French fleet and matters of protocol regarding the question of how to receive La Haye.[45] There can, however, be little doubt that the French viceroy and Caron pressed Mendonça Furtado for an alliance in their discussions and that these entreaties were firmly rebuffed. Several factors were involved in the Portuguese viceroy's actions. First, as a close confidant of Pedro, he was clearly not willing to break with official Crown policy on the proposed alliance, which had been set as early as the August 1669 *consulta* of the Overseas Council. Next, Mendonça Furtado had grown much more anxious and jealous of rising French ambitions in the trade since his initial talks with Saint-Romain in Lisbon and was determined to do nothing that would further advance Colbert's plans. Third, he recognized that he could exploit a neutral stance during the looming struggle with the Dutch to begin badly needed reforms in the *Estado*. Finally, as a veteran of many wars in Asia involving both European and indigenous powers, the viceroy had evaluated the combatants of the 1672 conflict and judged that the chances for a French victory in an open struggle with the VOC, even with his support, were at best slim. As he later informed Pedro in a coded letter, "[T]here is no doubt Majesty that the French do not have the power in India to oppose the Dutch, who are extremely powerful."[46] Therefore, Mendonça Furtado resolved to adopt a stance that would fulfill the stipulations of the 1667 agreement, including offering La Haye the right to reprovision his fleet in Goa, without going far enough to incur Dutch reprisals. After making this known to La Haye on the quay of Aguada, the viceroys "retired, one to his Castle, & the other to his fleet."[47]

Though stung by this diplomatic rebuff, La Haye and Caron could console themselves with the prospect of some supplies and the varied diversions afforded by the Portuguese Asian capital, a town "as large as Rouen." For the next week, foodstuff was periodically loaded aboard the French ships anchored off Aguada in an attempt to offset the shortfall from Surat.[48] A limited number of officers and crewmen were also allowed to disembark, men who eagerly sought out the pleasures of life in the cosmopolitan metropolis of seventeenth-century Goa. The squadron was also augmented by the timely arrival of reinforcements from France. Three vessels joined the fleet near the mouth of the Mandovi: the man-of-war *Breton* (fifty-six guns), one of Louis XIV's finest fighting ships, under Régnier du Clos with a crew of 270 and 100 infantrymen, as well as the flutes *Guillot* and *Barbaut*. Colbert had decided to dispatch this flotilla at about the same time he had made the decision to form the Persian squadron. The cost of outfitting du Clos's fleet was over 100,000 livres, and the captain carried another 100,000 livres to help La Haye pay salaries—already in arrears—and for victuals. Colbert's plan was to keep the viceroy constantly reinforced with royal money, ships, and men. As long as the finance minister and his project continued to bask in the light of royal favor, this strategy was feasible. As du Clos's instructions reveal, that support was still firm in 1670–1671: "His

Majesty has resolved to reinforce the said squadron and every year to send it everything that will be necessary to maintain it in the Indies." The small fleet had left La Rochelle in March 1671; the *Guillot* had called at Bourbon and then made directly for the Malabar Coast, while the *Breton* and *Barbaut* had stopped at Bourbon and Ceylon before anchoring off Mormugão in late January. The arrival of these reinforcements from France largely offset the notable number of desertions that took place in Goa and put La Haye's fleet in a virtually unassailable position to carry out its instructions as it prepared to head south in early February.[49]

On the second of that month the French squadron, much to Mendonça Furtado's relief, weighed anchor and shaped a course toward Calicut and the heart of the pepper-producing regions of India. Despite the careful preparations of Maetsuycker and Van Goens, news of its approach still had a notable effect in VOC enclaves such as Cochin, where Petit noted: "The Dutch Topasses . . . are all run away from them."[50] One week later, Tellicherry was reached. De Flacourt, *compagnie* chief at the small factory there, informed La Haye and Caron that the Zamorin was still anxious to arrange a formal alliance. This local ruler was then at the town of Ponnai, some ten leagues to the south, observing a religious festival. On 12 February, the squadron anchored off Ponnai, and two days later serious negotiations began when the Zamorin's heir and several leading nobles went aboard the *Navarre* for talks. These envoys proposed a simple quid pro quo alliance that offered various trading concessions in return for military assistance against the Dutch. Although La Haye and Caron originally demurred by stating that France was not yet at war with the United Provinces, at the end of this four-hour conference a tentative agreement was reached. The Zamorin technically received what he most wanted: assistance in his struggle with the VOC. Henceforth, La Haye and Caron promised, his domains would be placed under the protection of His Most Christian Majesty. The Dutch would not dare to attack. In return, Colbert's *compagnie* would be allowed to begin extensive trading operations within the Zamorin's kingdom. The indigenous potentate also promised to provide a steady supply of competitively priced pepper and agreed to reconfirm the ceding of Alicot to the *compagnie*. Caron landed at Ponnai on 16 February and formally ratified this alliance.[51]

Alicot was a small coastal village situated in the midst of a rich, spice-growing region that had originally been granted to de Flacourt in 1670. Significantly, it was located at the southern extreme of the Zamorin's domains, directly across a river from the Dutch fort at Cranganore. The Zamorin's initial grant had been made in an effort to create an effective buffer between his kingdom and VOC-held territory, with an eye toward exacerbating the hard feelings that already existed among the Europeans, perhaps even escalating this rivalry into an armed conflict that would relieve the pressure on his beleaguered forces. As such, this strategy at least initially failed: de Flacourt was pitifully short of money and manpower, and until the arrival of La Haye's fleet no large-scale military operations against the Dutch could be contemplated. Recognizing this fact—and jealous of a French outpost so close to their own—the Dutch had quickly expelled de Flacourt and still maintained a small garrison at Alicot. On 17 February 1672, the French squadron anchored off the village, determined to restore Colbert's *compagnie* to its "lawful" possession of the place. La Haye promptly sent envoys to discuss the matter with the Dutch governor of Cranganore, Van Rheede. In response to complaints about the unjust occupation of Alicot and a request to remove his troops forthwith, Van Rheede declared that his troops would remain and that he had standing orders from Batavia to prevent the French from landing in company territory. At last confronted with a familiar European enemy acting in an all too familiar manner, La Haye responded to this bluff with force. He landed a sizable detachment from the *régiment royal de la marine* with orders to expel Van Rheede's men. Vastly outnumbered, the Dutch chose the prudent course of retreating across the river to Cranganore in disarray. As Maetsuycker later related to the Seventeen, La Haye's troops had driven "away our guards from Alycott," burnt the "house of the Corps de Guards," and, most galling of all, "[p]lanted their King's Standard there, with this pretence that they had been incited thither by the Zamorin."[52] The spoils of the victory were indeed paltry: Alicot consisted of little more than the gutted guardhouse and a stone wall. Nevertheless, La Haye landed de Flacourt with 6000 livres, munitions, and orders to fortify the place properly.[53]

Flushed with the "victory" at Alicot, the Persian squadron sailed south on its course for one of the prime objectives in Caron's strategy, the island of Ceylon. Meanwhile, Van Goens and his fleet of twelve ships had spent much of early 1672 cruising the waters from Colombo north to Cochin in what had proven to be a vain effort to make contact with Colbert's squadron. On 21 February, the two rival fleets finally sighted one another off Cape Comorin, resulting in one of the expedition's most controversial and highly debated moments. At a hastily arranged conference aboard the flagship *Navarre*, La Haye and nearly all his officers argued that the French should attack. Political, military, and strategic factors all seemed to dictate this course of action. War with the United Provinces might have already begun in Europe. If not, it could not be long postponed. La Haye believed that this unexpected and highly advantageous occasion should be exploited. The VOC was the main obstacle to the expansion of French trade in Asia, and the main objective of his fleet was precisely to forward the interests of the *compagnie*. As he pointed out, the positions of the fleets, the prevailing wind, and force of arms were all favoring the French. Reports from de Flacourt and others indicated that Van Goens's vessels were poorly armed merchantmen, ill prepared to engage Louis XIV's men-of-war equipped with brass-guns. The Dutch fleet, moreover, found itself caught between the

French ships and the Indian coast. Even though the two nations were not yet officially at war, this had not constrained the French at Alicot. A pretext involving Louis's orders on striking to his flag could easily be arranged. What better way was there to forward the *compagnie*'s plans on Ceylon than to engage and defeat the Dutch fleet charged with protecting Batavia's interests on that island?

At this critical moment, however, Caron forcefully opposed this course of action. In his lengthy reply to La Haye and his officers, the director-general put forth three main arguments. First, he pointed out the obvious: France and the United Provinces were not yet at war. While military force had been used at Alicot, the entire incident constituted nothing more than a skirmish, hardly worth noting in his next despatch to Colbert. Attacking Van Goens's fleet, on the other hand, would be quite another matter, a significant and clear violation of the tenuous peace that still existed between the two countries. Caron also enunciated one of his pet theories on Dutch power in Asia, namely, that it was "hydra-headed" in nature. In his view, destroying Van Goens's fleet would accomplish little more than ensuring that Maetsuycker would send a larger and more powerful fleet from Batavia to exact revenge from the French and, if necessary, yet another after that. Dutch maritime might in eastern seas could, it appeared, not be openly challenged by Louis's grand fleet. Finally, he cautioned that whatever the outcome of the proposed engagement, the squadron would suffer irreparable losses that would critically undermine its ability to complete the main points contained in Colbert's instructions regarding Ceylon and Bangka.

La Haye and his officers must have been shocked by the striking shift in Caron's views embodied in these almost defeatist arguments. Nonetheless, they had very little choice in the matter given the clauses in the viceroy's instructions of December 1669 from Colbert that outlined his relationship with the *compagnie* directors. These standing orders, which were still in effect, in essence subjugated him to the will of the *compagnie*'s chief resident in Asia. As Colbert had written, "[E]ven when the sieur de La Haye knows that it would do harm, after having represented his views, [the king] desires that he follow their opinions exactly." Because of these instructions, Caron eventually won this crucial discussion off Cape Comorin. Orders were reluctantly given by La Haye ensuring that the lead ships in the French line would maneuver to avoid a possible confrontation with Van Goens's vessels. Having gauged the strength of the French fleet, the Dutch governor was all too willing to avoid a battle on that day, having resolved to exploit the hesitancy exhibited by his rivals politically and to wait for a more favorable opportunity to attack Colbert's squadron. The two fleets therefore passed peacefully by one another on that February morning, one bound for Cochin to examine what destruction, if any, had been wrought on Dutch possessions on that coast by the French, the other intent on reaching Ceylon now that it was clear that that island, at least for a time, would be relatively un-defended.[54]

There were several short-term implications of this important nonengage-ment off Cape Comorin. Van Goens did not fail to exploit the incident for the advantage of the VOC. Through skillful propaganda, Dutch factors soon turned "this encounter into a tribute to their own glory and the dis-honor of the French." Reports were circulated throughout the port cities of India that Louis XIV's "fine and powerful fleet" had fled from Van Goens's ships and "had not dared to insist on their giving salute." Any ill will that already existed between the director-general and the French officer corps was also exacerbated by the events off Cape Comorin. According to the Abbé Carré, Caron's action "caused much discontent and murmuring from most of the captains and officers of our fleet who said openly that express orders of His Majesty had been ignored."[55] La Haye might have been able to console himself with the knowledge that the final decision was not his and that this was indeed one of the occasions Colbert had envisioned when "harm" would be caused by acquiescing to the opinions of the directors or, in this case, a single director. Nevertheless, it is at this point in the expedi-tion that the relations between the two men, which in Surat and at Goa had been so harmonious, began to deteriorate. Caron's rather inexplicable deci-sion off the southern tip of India caused La Haye, for the first time, to question the director's motivations and loyalty, surely a less than desirable state of affairs as the squadron neared Ceylon and the specter of implement-ing Colbert's designs in the face of Van Goens's still intact fleet.[56] Events in Europe, meanwhile, were already conspiring to deprive Caron of one of the most forceful arguments he had used in the conference off Cape Comorin, namely, that the French and Dutch were still technically at peace. The onset of the Third Dutch War in the spring of 1672 would indeed have a seminal impact on all aspects of Colbert's Asian strategy, including the fate of the Persian squadron and the quest to establish the East India Company as a major power in the Indian Ocean trade.

Paris, the Low Countries, and Trincomalee, 1672

Gloire in Europe, an Enigmatic Defeat on Ceylon

> "Our Letters dated April 5 and 12 last informed
> you of the unjust War declared against our State
> by the Kings of England and France, in which we
> commanded you to treat these nations with hostil-
> ity. We hope you received our letters in good time
> and that you have been fortunate enough to gain
> some advantage over our Enemies."
>
> —*Heeren XVII* to Batavia Council

In the early spring of 1672, it appeared that Louis XIV and Colbert would soon achieve every success in their joint campaign against the United Provinces. Determined to win *gloire* for his person, his reign, and his realm, the young king left Paris on 27 March to join the army that Louvois had gathered at Charleroi, troops that Louis personally intended to lead to a re-sounding victory over the Dutch ingrates. The king decided that, for the moment, no formal declaration of war was needed, he merely had notices posted in the realm that declared that he had gone off to chastise the Hol-landers, since they had failed to give him "satisfaction." The military re-forms and careful preparatory work of Louis and Louvois since 1668 had indeed yielded impressive results: the French king had over 120,000 men at his disposal for the impending land campaign. This force would be com-manded by some of the finest military minds of the age including Condé, Turenne, Luxembourg, and Vauban. Charles II had even made good on his promise to contribute a brigade to the cause. In April, the duke of Mon-mouth, his bastard son, had delivered two English regiments, two Irish, and one Scottish to the French muster. At sea, the English fleet under the duke of York and the earl of Sandwich and the French fleet under d'Estrées would join at Spithead under the eyes of the Stuart king in May and total more than ninety fighting ships. Complementing this array of military fire-power was the skillful diplomacy of Louis and Hugues de Lionne (until his death in September 1671). These efforts deprived the Dutch of their erst-while allies in the Triple Alliance, England (1670) and Sweden (1672). Moreover, the Habsburg emperor, Leopold I, preoccupied with a continu-ing threat from the Ottoman Turks and the unruly Magyars, had signed a secret pact of neutrality in late 1671. In Germany, the elector of the free imperial city of Cologne and the bishop of Münster also came to an under-standing with the French king and his money.[1]

The United Provinces were hard pressed to meet this formidable threat, especially on land. Since 1668, the States General had demonstrated an un-canny ability to disregard the blatant signs portending Louis's encore march into Flanders. Only the September 1670 movements of French troops near the frontier town of Peronne, preparing for the invasion of Lorraine, goaded Jan de Witt, the councilor pensionary, to propose the addition of six cavalry regiments and ten infantry regiments to the States of Holland. While de Witt may have recognized the need to be strong in light of Louis's ambi-tions, he underestimated "the difficulties in creating an adequate force for doing the job." Above all, he did not "realize that the army as well as the navy needed preparation and training well in advance of war." Money was not his problem: 8.7 million guilders were spent on the army and navy in 1671 alone.[2] Yet, at the end of that year the army was still composed of lit-tle more than "30,000 ill-fed and ill-clothed men . . . rotting away in dilapi-dated fortresses."[3] In early 1672, more radical measures were taken in a des-perate, last-minute effort to prepare for the French onslaught: William III of Orange, over de Witt's opposition, was named captain and admiral gen-eral in February; a decision was also made to conscript another 20,000 men as well as 10,000 *waardgelders* (city militia). On the eve of Louis's attack de Witt could report that on paper the number of infantry regiments had in-creased from 569 at the end of 1671 to 709 and the number of cavalry regi-ments from 89 to 161. As the dominant maritime power of the seventeenth century, the Dutch were much better prepared to meet the Anglo-French threat at sea. The only question confronting de Witt and William was the whether the gifted de Ruyter and the victorious fleet of Chatham could be reassembled and put to sea in time to prevent the squadrons of the duke of York and d'Estrées before they had joined and, failing that, to catch them while they were still preparing in the Thames.[4]

The Third Dutch War began in late March in an entirely fitting manner. Charles and Arlington, anxious to get money from the campaign to liberate themselves from an overbearing Parliament, while appealing to the mercan-tile class of London, chose to initiate hostilities with a surprise attack on the Dutch Smyrna fleet. Sir Robert Holmes, the conqueror of New Amsterdam, intercepted this fleet returning from the Levant as it entered the Channel, and before news of a formal declaration of war could reach it. Holmes, however, could not repeat his spectacular voyage at the start of the Second Anglo-Dutch War, as his fleet was repelled by the Dutch conveyors in an action of late March. Holmes captured few Dutch merchant ships and suffered heavy damage to his ships for his effort.[5] After the formal declaration of war on the twenty-ninth the results for the allies remained decidedly mixed at sea. Although de Ruyter, with a fleet of about eighty-five sail, was unable to follow de Witt's suggestions and repeat the great 1667 raid up the Thames, he was able to catch the combined Anglo-French fleet at anchor in Sole Bay on the Suffolk coast in early June. Although the two-day battle that followed was indecisive, as both sides suffered heavy losses, "the honors and the substantial advantages all belonged to the Dutch, or rather to De Ruyter." The allied fleet was "miserably shattered" and spent more than a month refitting in the Thames. Thereafter, a naval stalemate developed for the remainder of 1672, in which de Ruyter fought a defensive campaign along the Dutch coast, exploiting its dangerous shoals, to frustrate Charles's plan to summon towns, harass merchant shipping, and land an expeditionary force under Prince Rupert that would attack Zeeland. James's quest to capture the returning East India fleet in mid-July was also a failure.[6]

On land, the situation was another story, as Louis XIV's huge army made staggering early advances against the ineffective opposition offered by the Dutch. Departing from Charleroi and Sedan, the French army marched down the Meuse as if on maneuvers, temporarily bypassing the formidable obstacle of Maastricht. After passing through the allied electorate of Cologne and Düsseldorf, the army proceeded down the Rhine: Turenne's corps on the left bank, that of Condé on the right, as Luxembourg's corps closed from Westphalia toward the Dutch defenses along the Ijssel and Groningen. William of Orange had left The Hague in mid-April to take command of the republic's army at Doesburg, but with less than 20,000 troops, he found himself unable to meet the force of this powerful attack. The Rhine fortresses were all enveloped by early June and posed few problems for the siege mastery of Sebastien Le Prestre de Vauban. Louis and Louvois, meanwhile, thoroughly enjoyed themselves, conducting sieges of as many as four of these strongholds at a time. On 8 June, de Witt harangued the States of Holland about the need to prepare for the defense of that province, calling for the establishment of a "place of security" for the country and its government around Amsterdam. Four days later, Louis and his army made its fabled passage of the Rhine at Tolhuis and advanced into the Betuwe. Only the wounding of Condé and the death of Longueville tarnished the *gloire* of the first weeks of the campaign. Countless Dutch towns had already capitulated, and Louis's armies occupied most of the country.[7]

The astute Condé, recognizing that the moment for the *coup de grâce* was at hand, advised that a cavalry attack be made on Amsterdam to finish the matter. Louvois, however, was too absorbed with the pleasures of witnessing the great victories being won by the military machine he had helped create to sanction any plan that might end these festivities prematurely. Elevated by the start of the Continental campaign to the status of royal favorite and confidant, the younger Le Tellier instead advised that Nijmwegen and other places first be reduced before heading into the provinces of Utrecht and Holland, the heart of the Dutch republic. At this crucial juncture, Louis XIV supported his war minister, "and there is no doubt that in doing so he made a terrible mistake."[8] The victories, nevertheless, continued for a time. The count of Rochefort took Amersfort and nearly captured Muiden. On his return to the main army, the count captured Utrecht on 23 June, and the Dutch Catholics gave a "fervent welcome" to Louis, who treated them graciously in return. Upon hearing news of the fall of Utrecht, the count d'Estrades, former ambassador to the Dutch, informed Louis that the republic itself could be "abolished" if the monarch so desired. The young king, in a munificent mood, issued a proclamation on that day which promised to confirm the privileges and freedom of conscience to towns that surrendered to his armies; those that resisted would be burned to the ground.[9]

From the outset the strategy of de Witt and William had been to withstand the overwhelming first assault by the French and their allies until long-term factors judged to be in their favor could impact the struggle. These factors included such geographic obstacles to the French advance as the Zuider Zee and the polder region west of Utrecht, the great wealth and commercial power of the area around Amsterdam, the tenuousness of Louis's alliance, and the latent fears in Europe of the Bourbon king's quest for Continental power. Unable to blunt the initial French advance, de Witt and the States General had been forced to send envoys to Louis's camp to find out what price would have to be paid in order to halt the hostilities. In late June, meetings were held at Doesburg and Rhenen between the Dutch delegation led by de Groot and Louis's underlings, including both Louvois and Pomponne. After much discussion, the envoys from the United Netherlands offered all land south of the Meuse, Maastricht, all the towns that the French had captured, and ten million guilders in cash. This offer, born of desperation, would have given Louis the ability to overrun the Spanish Netherlands at his leisure. Pomponne argued that the proposal contained nearly everything that the French had hoped to achieve and should be accepted. Louvois, however, euphoric with the easy victories already obtained, maintained that much more could be extracted. In the midst of his glorious campaign, it should come as no surprise that Louis once again chose to embrace the opinion of his young war minister. The offer was rejected. Emboldened by Louvois's assurances, Louis demanded more land, more money, more *gloire,* more of the true faith, and, at Colbert's behest, more trading privileges. De Groot thereupon returned to The Hague. Negotiations were at an end.[10]

In the midst of these talks, the Dutch had stumbled on the artifice that saved them from almost certain destruction. Muiden, on the Zuider Zee, was located at the junction of several rivers and canals and was the key to main dikes by which the process of inundating the approaches to Amsterdam and the province of Holland might begin. The sluices were opened there on 23 June, Amsterdam followed suit two days later, and the famed flooding of the country began. By the end of the month the waters had risen to a level sufficient to protect both Amsterdam and The Hague from Louis's invading armies; one of the most impressive land offensives of the entire seventeenth century had miraculously been transformed into a naval campaign within the span of a week. The young king's war, which had promised nothing but swift total victory in its initial stages, now became much more complex, as the long-term factors judged by de Witt and William to be in the United Provinces' favor began to materialize. Luxembourg's advance was soon halted before Groningen. The favorable diplomatic situation also began to take a turn for the worse. Louis's victories engendered predictable apprehension on the part of his European rivals. By the end of the summer, the elector Frederick William of Brandenburg, Leopold, Charles IV of Lorraine, and the electorate of Mainz had already decided to aid the beleaguered Dutch: an imperial army under Montecucculi and a Hohenzollern force advanced on the Rhine and Turenne. The alliance with England was also far from assured, the war was far from popular, and Charles's Declaration of Indulgence had further exacerbated religious friction with Parliament. The grim specter of confronting Parliament in the autumn without a "glorious victory" to appease its probable doubts forced the king and Arlington to postpone reassembly until the following February. In The Hague, de Witt paid for the disastrous early stages of the war with his life in August, a bloody footnote to the accession of William as stadholder the previous month. The young prince of Orange would prove to be more than a worthy nemesis for Louis XIV's Continental designs. While the Bourbon king had returned home to bask in his triumph, declaring that the remaining Dutch strongholds were not "worth his presence," the changing nature of the war was amply demonstrated to him in September 1672, when William launched a bold attack on Charleroi.[11]

In Paris, Colbert had viewed the events of the early spring with obvious glee. As Louis's armies advanced into the heartland of the Dutch republic in early June, he could hardly contain his excitement at the unlimited economic possibilities offered by what appeared to be a total victory over this hated commercial enemy. Colbert flooded the king's camp with a series of congratulatory letters on his amazing successes, assuring him that matters in the capital and at Versailles were proceeding well. He had supported the decision to attack the United Provinces for reasons of political economy as well as *realpolitik:* French commercial power in Europe and the *outre-mer* could only be achieved at the expense of the dominant power in those trades, the

Dutch. The Hollanders were mortal enemies "who would go to any lengths to ruin the French." As Adam Smith argued long ago, the mercantile warfare of the 1660s logically culminated in the military warfare of the 1670s. Colbert's internal reforms and increasingly aggressive tariffs of the first decade of Louis's personal reign had been largely ineffective in the quest to wrest a share of the trade from the United Provinces. By 1669, he had decided that bolder measures were needed to destroy the commercial might of the Dutch in Europe and Asia. Uncharacteristically, he therefore supported the decision of Louis XIV, the Le Telliers, and Turenne to wage war against the Dutch. For the only time in the reign the economic priorities of Colbert and the dynastic priorities of Louis briefly appeared to be symbiotic.[12]

Like most of the members of the *Conseil d'en haut,* Colbert favored a swift, decisive campaign to humble the Dutch. A short war would allow him to achieve his economic goals while avoiding the more daunting outgrowths of a long campaign, such as burdensome expenditures that would jeopardize the hard-won fiscal reforms of the preceding decade, the likelihood of the formation of another anti-French coalition to check Louis's ambitious Continental designs, and the breakup of the tenuous alliance system put together by Louis and Lionne thanks largely to generous subsidies from the royal treasury. If successful, the economic rewards of such a campaign would be indeed be formidable. Antwerp might be taken, the Scheldt reopened, and France might dominate the renascent trade of that region. Finally, the East India Company would supplant the VOC as the dominant European power in the Indian Ocean trade. It is therefore misleading to suggest that Colbert made no long-term plans between 1668 and 1670 to exploit the economic potentialities of the impending Continental campaign. The formation, at considerable royal expense, of the Persian squadron and the seriousness of his commitment to La Haye's mission offer ample evidence that Colbert was determined to exploit the economic "potentialities" afforded by the king's thirst for *revanche* against the United Netherlands.[13] In May and June 1672, Colbert's gamble on the war option seemed to have paid off, as Louis's armies embarked on their inexorable march toward Amsterdam. While he ran the expanding administration of the Bourbon state in the king's absence, French armies seemed on the verge of utterly destroying his mercantile rivals and thrusting their incredible wealth into his lap. In these heady circumstances, Colbert was more than happy to contribute his ideas to any peace proposals made of de Groot: retaliatory Dutch tariffs would be lifted, the VOC would be gutted, its trade assumed by his own *compagnie.* What more could be asked?[14]

As Colbert and his directors well knew, the *compagnie* could use all the help that Louis's armies, as well as his treasury, could afford it. Despite his formidable exertions, a regular trade had still not been established with Asian markets. Between 1668 and 1672, only eight of the twenty-eight *compagnie* ships that had been dispatched to Fort-Dauphin and Surat returned successfully. Six of these came from India carrying cargoes of pepper, in-digo, cotton piece goods, and saltpeter. While the sale of these goods at auction yielded a respectable profit over invoice, most of the ships had not been fully laden. It was also difficult for the directors to contemplate paying dividends to their already dubious shareholders on six cargoes over a five-year period when millions of livres had been expended from the *compagnie*'s dwindling resources to obtain such meager results. Colbert hardly needed to be reminded that in 1670 alone the returning fleet from Batavia had car-ried over 9 million pounds of pepper or that the Portuguese had equaled the French record in terms of the number of ships and far surpassed it in terms of cargoes in this same period.[15] His effort to mirror the successful in-frastructure of the Dutch Company had also proven to be less than success-ful: all of the provincial chambers, except Lyon, were miserable failures and only existed on paper. The disappointing results of the subscription cam-paign continued to haunt the *compagnie*. Colbert's heavy-handed threats to extract promised sums from members of the aristocracy and the *haute bour-geoisie* yielded little more than vocal protests to Louis about the excesses of the minister and his agents. Of the 15 million livres that were projected in the articles of September 1664, only 8,179,885 had been raised, "with mer-chants a feeble minority of the shareholders—a sharp contrast to the En-glish and Dutch Companies." In Paris, only 650,000 livres were forthcom-ing from a loosely defined merchant community, half of them from the twelve syndics themselves.[16]

Colbert had learned a difficult lesson between 1664 and 1672. While this inveterate *mémoire* writer might have emulated the Dutch Company model on paper, he could not create the bourgeois support, the entrepreneurial spirit, or the true merging of interests between company and state that ex-isted in the United Provinces and had helped make the VOC the dominant commercial power during the seventeenth century. The French quest to win a sizable share of the Asian trade, unlike the earlier campaigns of the Dutch and English, would thus not be based on solid support from the kingdom's merchant class. With its entrepreneurial spirit dulled by venality of office and other safe investments at home, this important group possessed neither the inclination nor the economic desire to invest in such risky overseas ven-tures, as the subscription campaign of 1664–1665 amply demonstrates. As a result, Colbert's quest would be dependent from the outset on investment and support from a Crown and aristocracy that, despite his best efforts, con-tinued to view the campaign as merely a very minor extension of the more important dynastic struggles in Europe. The significance of this dependence on royal favor can hardly be overstated. As Colbert would discover during the Dutch War, the seemingly symbiotic nature of the joint economic and dynastic campaign against the United Provinces would prove to be a dou-ble-edged sword. Before the spring of 1672, he had been able to exploit the anti-Dutch nature of his Asian project to garner a bounty of royal interest and favor. The king's initial support allowed him to overcome the lack of merchant investment and to finance the *compagnie*'s early operations. This royal largesse had also facilitated the escalation of the campaign in 1669, encouraged his negotiations toward an anti-Dutch Asian league, and allowed the dispatching of La Haye's grand fleet and du Clos's reinforcements. Louis XIV's early enthusiasm, continuing negotiations in Lisbon and London, and his own formidable power in the *Conseil d'en haut* had also allowed Colbert to receive the king's blessing for a system to reinforce the fleet frequently with royal ships, men, money, and munitions. This is revealed by the Crown's instructions of September 1670 to du Clos, as well as letters from Louis and Colbert to La Haye that same month.[17] The reinforcement plan was further delineated in Louis XIV's letter to La Haye of 27 December 1670, in which the king promised to send at least two men-of-war a year to Asia, expecting a similar number to return to Europe. "My intention being that during all the time you remain in the Indies you will always have six good men-of-war, with several storeships."[18]

In early 1672, as the land campaign approached, Colbert probably began to suspect that the crucial ties he had forged between his own mercantile plans in Asia and the geopolitical campaign in the Low Countries had a decidedly negative side as well. As Louis's interest returned to traditional dynastic priorities on the Continent once again, and as it became clear that no military alliance could be arranged with the Portuguese and English in Asia, the ambitious reinforcement plan originally outlined—and acted upon—between early 1670 and late 1671 was curtailed, and the importance of Colbert's project began to diminish in the eyes of the king. Colbert found himself snared by the artifice of attempting to exploit the king's Continental campaign for the benefit of his own *outre-mer* priorities. In stark contrast to this harsh reality in Paris, the hierarchies in London and Amsterdam would demonstrate solid support for the VOC and EIC throughout the Dutch War, and support for Asian trade priorities would remain a vital component of both war aims and strategy. Two letters from Louis XIV to La Haye trace the initial stage of this shift in royal opinion in Paris. The first, dated 11 February 1672, was written while negotiations were still underway with Charles II and Pedro. La Haye was informed that France and England would be declaring war on the United Provinces the following April. In the king's opinion, there were three possible choices of conduct: La Haye could make war and do the best he could with his limited resources; he could go on the defensive and wait for the Dutch to declare war and attack; or he could negotiate a truce with Batavia that would avoid hostilities in Asia. For Louis's *gloire*, the first choice was obviously the most desirable: "It would be much more to my satisfaction and more glorious for me to declare war on them and wage it against them as strongly and powerfully in the Indies as I will wage it in Europe." However, given the circumstances, the viceroy was instructed to avoid rash moves and to make his decision only in conjunction with the directors. Whatever his decision, La Haye was ordered to fortify the positions he had already taken. A company ship would bring him

200,000 livres to help with expenses, but priorities in Europe had convinced Louis not to send the two men-of-war originally promised.[19]

This change in royal attitude was further defined in Louis's letter to La Haye of 15 March, compiled after the proposal for a joint Anglo-French naval campaign in Asia had been definitively rejected in London. The king stated that Croissy had pressed hard for such an alliance with Charles II "in order to combat our enemies there and to give, at the same time, the necessary orders to our subjects in those countries to act in concert to attack them, to ruin their commerce and enrich our subjects." The English king had originally replied that he would like to send a naval force to act in concert with La Haye, and Louis did not doubt that there would be little difficulty in achieving their goals, because the Dutch could not hope to resist the combined forces of the "two most powerful nations in the world." In the end, however, Charles had refused the offer, arguing that he was short of funds and, in any event, did not believe that the VOC could be defeated given their power "par mer et par terre dans lesd. Indes." Consequently, La Haye was ordered to fortify the places he had captured and then to send back the greatest number of ships possible to help in the Continental campaign. Louis estimated that the viceroy needed only two men-of-war to defend his posts by sea. He concluded by stating that it was simply unnecessary to have a large number of royal vessels in Asia given the "impossibilité d'attaquer les hollandois."[20]

For the moment, La Haye and Caron remained blissfully unaware of these shifting priorities in Paris. After the chance encounter with Van Goens's fleet off Cape Comorin, the squadron had continued on its course for Ceylon. The fleet reconnoitered the coastline of the island, reaching the Bay of Batticaloa, halfway up the eastern shore, on 20 March. In his previous letters to Colbert, Caron had noted that Batticaloa and Trincomalee both had much to recommend them as sites for a *compagnie* entrepôt. A brief reconnaissance of the bay, however, revealed the presence of several Dutch ships anchored before the rebuilt Portuguese fort overlooking the principal anchorage, which evidently convinced La Haye and Caron to make for Trincomalee the following morning. On 22 March, the French fleet anchored in Trincomalee: "[L]e sujet du départ de cette escadre de France, & le secret qui fait tant de bruit en Europe & même aux Indes."[22] Trincomalee was made up of two bays: the larger expanse of Kutiari and a smaller inner bay referred to as the "bay of the sun" by the French. The following day, de Turelle and a party were landed to search for provisions and soon returned with five emissaries from Rajah Sinha II. These Sinhalese nobles were entertained aboard the *Navarre*, and negotiations were begun toward concluding an alliance that would include a formal grant of the bay to the *compagnie* by Sinha II in return for French military assistance in his campaign against the Dutch. La Haye promptly reconnoitered the bay and drew up a fortification plan designed to convert Trincomalee into a bastion of French power in Asia. This plan centered on three key positions that dominated the entrance to the inner bay. Substantial batteries were begun on the two islets there, the *Île du soleil* and the *Île de Caron*, as well as on a point that jutted into the bay from its eastern shore, Breton Point. La Haye estimated that, when completed, the deadly crossfire that would result could resist the strongest men-of-war then in Asian waters.[23]

Meanwhile, Aungier and Mendonça Furtado were confounded by the apparent ease with which the French had been able to occupy and fortify Trincomalee under the very nose of the VOC and on one of its most prized possessions. The English and Portuguese had both long dreamed of establishing (or reestablishing) commercial operations on the island but had been dissuaded from doing so largely by the vaunted military power of Batavia. La Haye's seemingly rapid success on Ceylon was a blow to the myth of Dutch military invincibility in Asia. As the president wrote, "The newse of the French settlement at Zeloan is of noe mean concern, they have met with notable and unexpected success; & if they follow up wisely, they will not only advance the Interest of their Nacion; but give a great shock to the Dutch State of India."[24] Aungier was quick to appreciate the larger implications of La Haye's actions, which evidently exposed the hollowness of Batavia's declared monopoly. As he informed the Court of Committees, "We see no reason but your Hons. may also, when you judge it a conven. time appoint factoryes to be settled on the same Island . . . at lesse charge, and to as great advantage as either of them."[25] Mendonça Furtado, no doubt jealous of his rival's notable success, was more curt. He merely informed Pedro that the French had "put into the *Bahia dos Arcos,* that is also called Trinquimale (the first port that the Dutch captured) on the island of Ceylon, placing artillery at its entrance." Based on his years of fighting the Dutch on that island and the Malabar Coast, the viceroy went on to state that La Haye would have a difficult time solidifying his gain unless substantial reinforcements reached him from home. Suspicious of French intentions, especially if their efforts at Trincomalee should be frustrated, Mendonça Furtado also warned Pedro that "as this Nation has entered India with great expenditures in cash and not being able to become masters of any Dutch post, they may intend one of those of Your Majesty." At the very least, the specter of future French aggressions allowed him to complain of "insufficient manpower" and ask that "capable subjects trained in warfare" be dispatched posthaste to Goa.[26]

Although in de facto control of Trincomalee, La Haye and Caron badly wanted to secure formal recognition of this fact from Rajah Sinha II to legitimize their claims and to rebuff the anticipated complaints of the VOC. The French leadership also recognized that the king could provide assistance through additional supplies and manpower to expedite the construction of fortifications. On 26 March La Haye sent a formal embassy to Kandy, led by a *brigadier des gardes* named Boisfontaine. His instructions specified that Boisfontaine was to seek an alliance based on a simple quid pro quo. The French would place Kandy under the "protection" of Louis XIV, and its commerce to Bengal, Bantam, Malabar, and Persia would be "immune" from harassment by the Dutch, provided its ships carried French passports purchased at a minimal price, a device perfected by the Portuguese a century and a half earlier. In return, La Haye and Caron expected an outright grant of Trincomalee and Kutiari and substantial assistance in fortifying the area. The envoy was also instructed to get French merchants formally admitted into the island's trade, to obtain detailed information on the price structure and transportation network utilized to ship cinnamon to the coast, and to find qualified masons and carpenters to assist with erecting the fortifications at Trincomalee. On 2 May, M. de Orgeret, a member of this embassy, returned with news that Boisfontaine had been well received by Rajah Sinha and that three envoys from the king were waiting ashore to meet with the viceroy. La Haye and Caron entertained these nobles several times over the next week.[27]

At these conferences a thorny stalemate developed, which lasted for the remainder of the spring. La Haye and Caron continually pressed for adequate provisions for feeding the more than 1500 men still with the expedition, for indigenous laborers to assist with the debilitating work of erecting fortifications under the hot tropical sun, and for a formal grant of Kutiari and its dependencies. Although Rajah Sinha II's envoys made frequent promises of supplies and hinted time and again that hundreds of laborers were on their way to Trincomalee, this aid was extremely slow in coming as long as the French leadership refused to accede to the king's main demand. As early as 7 May, his envoys had raised the subject of direct military assistance against the troops of the VOC. While such a request was logically what Rajah Sinha expected as part of any meaningful alliance, La Haye and Caron avoided a firm commitment, asserting that the French were not yet at war with the United Provinces. On 17 May, M. de Beauregard returned from the inland capital with a formal grant of Kutiari, Trincomalee, and their dependencies, a document that Rajah Sinha knew was worth very little unless the French took forceful measures against the Dutch to entrench themselves at those sites and thus complement his own campaign. De Beauregard was accompanied by seventy Sinhalese troops to help with the fortifications, a sign of good will on the part of the king, and news that a thousand more might be on their way from Batticaloa. Still, La Haye and Caron refused to break openly with the VOC, rejecting a request the next day to assist the Sinhalese in ambushing a Dutch column. This rather inexplicable decision to avoid open hostilities with Van Goens did more than anything else to undermine the alliance with Kandy, to sabotage the extremely favorable circumstances that greeted the fleet upon its arrival at Trincomalee, and to deprive the French of any early advantage they might have enjoyed in the Asian campaign.[28]

Caron, and perhaps even La Haye, originally believed that the strength of the squadron alone would be sufficient to overawe the Dutch and to win a secure position on Ceylon. The viceroy's instructions to Boisfontaine did not even mention the possibility of joint military action against the VOC. The overall tone of this document suggests that the French leadership had decided that, once Rajah Sinha's domains and commerce were placed under the protection of "la Majesté Impérialle de nostre souverain et Invincible Monarque des Françoise," the Dutch would not dare to interfere.[29] This incredibly naive conviction dominated French policy on the island, and there was therefore no open break with the VOC. As a result, the flow of supplies from the hinterland of Kutiari to Trincomalee slowed as the spring wore on, creating a major dilemma for La Haye and Caron. The fleet had left Surat ill provided for the voyage ahead due to the internal bickering among the directors there. While some provisions had indeed been taken on in Goa, these were not sufficient to make up for the original shortfall and the continuing demands of the squadron. La Haye had evidently been assured that he could obtain everything he needed on Ceylon and had thus not taken full advantage of the stops along the Malabar Coast, including the Portuguese Asian capital.[30] By April, crucial foodstuffs such as rice were already running low. The combination of a poor diet, bad hygiene, the travails of the hot monsoon climate, and the rigors of constructing La Haye's fortifications began to take a heavy toll, and disease spread rapidly through the expedition. A makeshift hospital was established near the mouth of the Kandy River. Several chief officers of the fleet, including the *chef d'escadre*, de Turelle, fell victim to conditions at Trincomalee. The mortality rate among the common seamen and infantry troops was predictably even higher, with five or six perishing in a single day.[31] As early as 8 April, these food shortages had prompted La Haye to dispatch the ships *Phoenix, Europe,* and *St-Louis* to the Coromandel Coast of India for supplies.[32]

The viceroy's provisioning problems were exacerbated in mid-May, when Van Goens's fleet at last appeared at the entrance of the bay. After reinforcing Cochin, the Dutch governor and admiral had returned to Ceylon after receiving word that Caron and the French fleet were entrenching themselves at Trincomalee. The Dutch Company was convinced that the occupation of Kutiari was merely the first stage of a grand plan concocted in Paris to rob them of the trade. As Maetsuycker informed the Seventeen, the French had seized the bay "with 9 stout ships," with La Haye and Caron "having doubtless the sole conduct of that design and pretending to have been by express letter invited and solicited to it by the king of Kandy." Batavia had no doubt that the French had begun "to fortify themselves upon a ground which is unquestionably our Company's property." Still, the governor-general and his admiral were in a delicate position. As Maetsuycker admitted, "[I]t would have been more convenient and easy" had the combined fleets of Roothaes and Van Goens intercepted Colbert's squadron and kept it "out of the Bay" than now face the need "by force to expell them."[33] Louis XIV's men-of-war equipped with brass-guns, even with the ravages of the voyage, were still a far cry from the lumbering *naos* of the Portuguese that the Dutch had been able to ravage for most of the seventeenth century. La Haye's fortifications were well underway, further complicating the strategic difficulties already confronting Van Goens. "Attacking them with our forces in the Inner Bay . . . was a thing judged by us esteemed of danger, which might cost us many ships and men, besides that in doing so, we should appear the aggressor and begun the war."[34]

After a series of conferences with his officers aboard the flagship *Tulpenburgh*, Van Goens resolved on a plan that called for a strict blockade of the bay by land and sea, the gradual expulsion of the French from their land positions, and ultimately the forced withdrawal of the entire fleet due to a lack of provisions. The Dutch governor decided to avoid an all-out attack, and its inherent risks, unless French reinforcements arrived and initiated hostilities. In an extraordinary session of the Batavia council held in July "about affairs relating to the island of Ceylon, and the naval force of the French," Maetsuycker and his councilors fully supported Van Goens's decision "to drive the French at Trinquemale from the mainland and to interrupt and deny them all manner and provision." As the *Heeren XVII* were informed, the strategy consisted of remaining "masters at land . . . to annoy and tire out the enemy . . . and then by our Fleet lying without that bay, to hinder the approach of any provision to them and thereby reduce them to extremities." Since word of the war in Europe had not reached Batavia, open hostilities would be sanctioned by the council only if the French attacked "on the coast of Malabar, or on the other side of Ceylon, or anywhere else." In this case, Batavia was prepared to "annoy them, everywhere to the utmost of our power, by destroying their ships in the Bay of Trincomalee or in other places."[35] Even before this extraordinary meeting, Maetsuycker had demonstrated that he was clearly taking no chances with the French threat on Ceylon: in April two ships originally intended for the Coromandel Coast were instead sent to reinforce Van Goens, while orders were sent out to Pulicat and Surat that resulted in the appearance of three additional ships at Kutiari.[36]

Van Goens's arrival with twelve ships on 15 May prompted La Haye to send out de Beauregard with his compliments and a polite warning to the Dutch not to enter the bay in force. This envoy was rudely received by the perplexed governor, who handed de Beauregard an official protest that asserted Dutch sovereignty over Trincomalee, which had "been by our Govern. in the name of our Sovereign Committee [given] to our trust, to keep and defend the same, against all and everyone that shall attempt to invade or prejudice our sovereign jurisdiction." Since La Haye's proceedings "in no way" agreed with "right and equity" and thus had to be "looked upon as hostile," a violation of the reputation of the Seventeen, injurious to the "subjects of the Company" and "contrary of the law of Nations," Van Goens found himself "obliged to desire [La Haye] in the most friendly and serious manner" to withdraw from Trincomalee. If this was done, the Dutch governor graciously offered to "assist [him] with what shall be in our power."[37] In his reply, the French viceroy complained bitterly about the ill-treatment he had received at the hands of the Dutch Company during his voyage, noting that official protests against these actions had been sent to Paris and Amsterdam. He then made his case for legal French possession of Trincomalee in forceful terms: "We are in this Bay which your Excellency doth not possess, but which belongs to the king of Ceylon and which he hath yielded to us, allowing us to stay there, and assuring us of the possession by good patents and by several of his Grandees . . . with his assurance . . . he hath not given nor allowed you." In terms that defied the policy that he and Caron would in fact pursue, La Haye threatened to defend the bay with all the forces at his disposal, especially if the rumors of war in Europe proved to be true. In strangely prophetic words, he concluded: "If after all this caution & care on our part . . . your Excellency . . . abuse[s] the law of Nations . . . [we] shall by all manner of means make it appear, how advantageous the Peace and Protection of France hath been to you, & how pernicious a thing war is to those who wrongfully undertake it."[38]

Van Goens obviously found "little satisfaction" in this reply. On 20 May, he responded in a letter that needlessly stated the obvious: French actions betrayed "a premeditated and firm resolution to affront our State Company and to ruin and annoy the same." He promised to deal with this grave threat by force of arms, "which God and our Principalls have put into our hands." As if additional justification for his impending blockade were necessary, he concluded with a lengthy list of La Haye's transgressions on his voyage: driving off a small Dutch force at Saldanha, forcing Dutch ships at Swally to salute Louis XIV's flag against local custom, holding "secret" negotiations with Mendonça Furtado in Goa, and taking Alicot by storm. With a flair for understatement, Van Goens described these actions as "highly suspicious to our State." He then reiterated his belief that both powers would be best served if the French abandoned the bay as quickly as possible.[39] La Haye's final letter to the Dutch governor, written on 22 May, sought to refute Van Goens's charges regarding Saldanha, Swally, Goa, and Alicot. He further advised Van Goens, although how seriously is not altogether clear, "not to be always so suspicious, and also to believe that the Portuguese . . . or any other nation shall be capable of making us violate the rights of Nations." He was bound to uphold such rights and treaties, "as we also have been commanded expressly to do in all the orders and instructions received from His Majesty." La Haye was resolute in defending his right to occupy Trincomalee. He also challenged the monopolistic pretensions of the VOC in India and Ceylon by asserting that the French might occupy any place not explicitly granted to the Dutch Company by local rulers. Regarding sites like Alicot, Trincomalee, and "divers other places which you appropriate to yourselves," the viceroy noted, "I have not heard of anybody, the Great Mogul, the Portuguese, the Sevagy, the Samorin, or any other powers that are of your opinion."[40]

Van Goens recognized that the time for decisive action was at hand and implemented his strategy with vigor and skill. The French responded to this challenge in feeble fashion. Caron merely embraced his dictum of no open aggression more tightly than at Cape Comorin. Shackled to the director's will by his instructions and still unsure whether war had been declared in Europe, La Haye—with two exceptions—acquiesced in this policy. On land, Van Goens's troops soon cut off provisions to Kutiari from the surrounding countryside, mortality rates climbed, and a series of raids began against positions in the inner bay, which yielded a sizable number of French prisoners and forced them to abandon Breton Point. Still, Caron and La Haye would not join Rajah Sinha II's war. Only on 9 June did the viceroy temporarily break with the director and send in the troops of the *régiment royal de la marine* to recapture Breton Point from a Dutch force that had stormed that strategic post the previous night.[41] Van Goens's sea blockade proved equally effective: the *Phoenix, Europe,* and *St-Louis* were all intercepted as they returned from the Coromandel Coast with supplies. The actions of their captains did little to improve the reputation of French arms in Asia. The *Phoenix's* commander, M. de La Melinière, after frustrating Van Goens's attempt to board his ship on 31 May, did not make for the inner bay but instead anchored in Kutiari, where his ship was captured by three longboats sent from the Dutch anchorage. There has long been a suspicion that, on 5 June, M. Dupré and the officers of the *Europe* capitulated to Van Goens as part of a pre-arranged deal struck at the Dutch factory at Negapatam. As Carré wrote, "[I]t would appear that this coup was arranged . . . [since] as soon as she saw the Dutch fleet she went straight towards it to surrender."[42] On these occasions, Caron held to his policy, La Haye deferred to his authority, and nothing was done to intervene. As the *St-Louis* approached on 13 June, the viceroy finally broke with Caron and sent the men-of-war *Triomphe, Breton,* and *Jules* to engage Van Goens's ships then in the midst of intercepting the French storeship. The firepower exhibited by Louis XIV's fighting ships in the melee that followed caused the Dutch ships to retreat to their anchorage. Nevertheless, M. Chanlatte tacked and returned to Madras rather than face the dangers waiting at Trincomalee.[43]

By mid-June, the situation was critical: victuals were dangerously low, more than 300 Frenchmen were ill, another 300 were judged unfit to fight, Van Goens had become increasingly aggressive in his tactics, and Rajah Sinha had become totally disenchanted with the French as allies. At this critical juncture, the inexplicable policies of Caron and La Haye were compounded by the equally bizarre decision to leave Trincomalee with most of the squadron in order to seek provisions en masse on the Coromandel Coast. Caron was responsible for this decision. He argued that it was vital for the French to regain their strength by resupplying on the Indian Coast before continuing with the campaign. Such a maneuver offered the surest means to break the Dutch naval blockade, since Van Goens would not oppose the departure of Louis XIV's fleet from the inner bay. A garrison could be left behind to defend French claims at Kutiari. After reprovisioning, the squadron would return and continue its work before heading for Bangka. How the French fleet would enter the bay on its return was a question that Caron never adequately explained. This plan was fundamentally flawed, of course, since it avoided the seminal issue then confronting the expedition: whether to begin concerted hostilities with the Dutch. Van Goens and Maetsuycker were also likely to interpret the squadron's departure as a sign of weakness, if not open retreat. There was also very little likelihood that any garrison that Caron left behind would be able to withstand the aggressive blockade of the Dutch governor, a strategy whose effectiveness, in conjunction with Caron's policies, had already reduced the entire royal squadron to such extremities that it was necessary to consider the rash actions that were discussed in early June. Despite all these flaws, Caron still held the supreme command over matters concerning the expedition, and, as it had done off Cape Comorin, his opinion held sway. Orders were given to prepare for the voyage to southern India.[44]

Once the decision to depart had been made, La Haye spent the remainder of the month making arrangements for the garrison to be left behind at Trincomalee. An infantry captain, M. Lesboris, who had displayed loyalty and determination on the voyage, was named "governor" of the French settlement with jurisdiction over all the territories contained in Rajah Sinha's grant. Lesboris's garrison included four lieutenants, two ensigns, a clerk, two surgeons, three gunners, sixteen skilled workmen, two infantry companies totaling ninety men, thirty Sinhalese Christians, and three companies of indigenous troops totaling approximately three hundred men. The company ship *St-Jean-Baptiste* would also be left behind to augment the defenses of the inner bay and serve as a storehouse until a proper magazine was completed.[45] Despite shortages, La Haye did his best to provide this garrison with adequate supplies until October, by which time he indicated the squadron would return. Caron, however, apparently favored a quick passage to Bangka and Bantam before returning to Ceylon.[46] On 7 July 1672, the viceroy held a final meeting with Lesboris and dispatched an envoy to Kandy to inform Rajah Sinha that the fleet was heading for the Coromandel Coast in search of provisions and would be back within three months' time.[47] Two days later, the men-of-war *Navarre, Triomphe, Jules, Flamand,* and *Breton,* the frigate *Diligente,* the flute *Sultane,* and the storeship *Barbaut* sailed out of Kutiari. After passing by Van Goens's anchorage without incident, the squadron shaped a course toward the north and the east coast of India. The *Barbaut* parted company soon thereafter, bound for France with valued despatches from Caron and La Haye in the trusted hands of M. de Beauregard, who was ordered to report to Colbert personally on the fleet's activities and to do his utmost to arrange additional reinforcements.[48]

The fate of Lesboris's garrison and the French settlement at Trincomalee was a swift defeat at Van Goens's hands. The Dutch governor was anxious to launch an attack before French fortifications were complete and any substantial aid from Rajah Sinha II arrived. On 12 July, the Dutch fleet entered Kutiari in force. Four days later Breton Point fell. Van Goens then landed several hundred troops on the larger islet in the "Bay of the Sun." The morale among Lesboris's men was decidedly poor, and, badly outnumbered, they promptly surrendered. All that remained were the main French batteries on the smaller islet supported by the guns of the *St-Jean-Baptiste*. On the night of 18 July, the Dutch stormed and captured the *compagnie* ship. In an untenable position, Lesboris opened negotiations, and formal articles of capitulation were soon worked out. Since Van Goens had judged the French naval "attack" of 13 June to constitute a flagrant breech of the peace, the French troops were taken prisoners of war along with their colleagues from the *Phoenix* and the *Europe*. These men were eventually sent to Batavia. Lesboris was also compelled to acknowledge that La Haye had acted "unjustly" when he had occupied Trincomalee, as Kutiari and its dependencies "rightfully" belonged to the VOC. Van Goens subsequently utilized the Sinhalese retainers of the garrison as forced labor to complete the fortifications in the inner bay. He prepared carefully for any potential counterattack by La Haye's fleet by mounting over one hundred guns on these defensive works and stockpiling large quantities of munitions that had been captured from Lesboris's command.[49]

So, rather ingloriously, ended the Ceylon enterprise of Colbert's grand fleet, arguably at one of the expedition's most crucial moments. The conditions that had greeted the French on their arrival at Trincomalee could hardly have been more promising. Recently reinforced at Goa with the flotilla of du Clos, the *escadre* was nearly at its apex in terms of ships, men, and firepower. In contrast, Dutch resources during the spring of 1672 were strained by fighting continuing wars against the Zamorin of Calicut and Rajah Sinha II in an attempt to meet a French challenge that Maetsuycker believed would enjoy Portuguese and English support. La Haye and Caron had also found a willing ally in the king of Kandy, who granted them territory and would likely have firmly supported them in every way had they openly broken with the Dutch. Yet this extremely promising set of circumstances was squandered within four months' time on the very eve of receiving word of the outbreak of hostilities in Europe by the ill-advised policy of refusing to break openly with the Dutch. A debate has long raged over the genesis of the essentially passive stance of the royal French squadron in the spring of 1672 and *inter alia* the decision to depart en masse from Ceylon in July of that year. Since both La Haye and Caron sought to legitimize their positions in self-serving letters to the Crown in the months that followed, it has been somewhat difficult to affix responsibility for this policy.

In a letter to Louis XIV of September 1672, which has served as the basis for the orthodox view, the viceroy maintained that Caron was to blame for the lost opportunities off Cape Comorin and Trincomalee. His standing orders from the Crown on deferring to the director's decisions had, he told the king, made it impossible for him to attack Van Goens in February, even though a glorious victory seemed assured. The viceroy argued that a Dutch defeat off the Cape would have allowed him to occupy Ceylon at will. Such a victory, combined with Rajah Sinha's serious support at Trincomalee, would have meant that "we could have defended ourselves against all the forces the Dutch Company possesses." Van Goens's blatant acts of hostility at Kutiari, acts that hardly seemed to bother Caron although they were an obvious insult to Louis's reputation, had finally convinced him "to attack [them] both with the fleet of Your Majesty and onshore with 50 soldiers and experienced officers leading the troops of the king of Ceylon." But Caron had continually blocked this strategy and instead forced him to sail to the Coromandel Coast, instead of settling the matter with the Dutch by force of arms at Trincomalee.[50] It should be noted that La Haye's letter was written after he had received letters from Paris on the Indian coast informing him that war in Europe was imminent, information that no doubt colored his version of events on Ceylon. Nevertheless, the viceroy's narrative is, on the whole, convincing and conforms in most respects to the evidence available in other extant sources.

Caron's version of events during this crucial phase of the project was given in a letter to Colbert of July 1672.[51] Since news of the war in Europe had still not reached Asia, the director-general went to greater lengths than perhaps he would have done otherwise to take credit for the policy of nonaggression. He boasted: "I can assure you that the Viceroy has maintained the union and peace between France and the Dutch notwithstanding several rude and uncivil encounters on their part which could have easily been remedied with the power of the squadron . . . but by his consideration and my opinion he has not used violence." Caron justified his decision to depart by giving Colbert a particularly dismal view of the situation on the island. In a passage with great import, he noted, "[N]otwithstanding the diminution of our forces and weaknesses of our people. . . . Mr le Viceroy has several times evidenced to me on the rude behavior of the Dutch, his opinion to go with the squadron and attack [them]." Caron then admitted that he had prevented an attack, arguing that the chances for success were small given the "diminished" state of the fleet. La Haye's desire to initiate open hostilities involved a "great risk: that this important squadron could be ruined forever by the worthless Dutch to the great scorn of the Majesty of rance in all the Indies." He also reiterated his pat argument on the "hydra-headed" nature of Dutch power in Asia for Colbert's benefit, a line of reasoning he had assuredly avoided in his long after-dinner conversations in Paris during the winter of 1665–1666. He declared that even if La Haye had gotten his way off Cape Comorin and defeated Van Goens's fleet, Maetsuycker would have only sent a more powerful one that "would ruin the precious squadron of the king entirely." He concluded by pointing out that neither he nor La Haye had yet received orders to declare war on the Dutch.

It appears certain, therefore, that while La Haye was prepared to begin concerted hostilities as early as Cape Comorin, he was prevented from doing so by Caron's contrary opinion and his own instructions that shackled him to the director's will. Caron's logic on this important question was at best obtuse. He knew from long personal experience that Batavia would oppose French entrenchment on Ceylon with all of the resources at its disposal, as the actions of Van Goens and Maetsuycker in the spring of 1672 demonstrated. Forceful Dutch resistance was also certain to materialize on Bangka or anywhere else the Dutch Company hierarchy judged its interests to be threatened. If the sentiments Caron expressed in his letters to Colbert between 1668 and 1671 regarding fortified settlements on Ceylon and in Indonesia were indeed sincere, then the director-general should have been willing to use all the forces at his disposal to implement these designs. To expect to occupy Trincomalee without a fight was not only unrealistic, it also ignored seven decades of historical precedent set by the VOC, a glorious period in the history of the United Provinces that Caron had done a good deal to forward. His unwillingness to accept a reality that to him of all people should have been self-evident suggests that he had either experienced a profound change of heart since returning to Surat from Bantam or was deliberately misleading Colbert and La Haye. The fleet he had pressed for so diligently, and that had been formed at such expense, was evidently not to be used to forward the interest of the *compagnie*, but was merely a glorious reflection of his own vanity that he intended to parade around the leading ports of Asia as a testament to his own personal greatness. La Haye, however, was not totally blameless in this grand opera. The viceroy recognized that the Dutch would never allow the French to establish themselves without a fight, but he did nothing to break with the director's unwise policy and act upon this conviction.

There has nevertheless been a tendency to overstate the magnitude of the French setback at Trincomalee. The events off Cape Comorin and on Ceylon in the spring of 1672 constituted more of a missed opportunity than a crushing defeat for La Haye's mission and Colbert's ambitions in the trade. As La Haye and the main body of the fleet sailed toward the Coromandel Coast in early July, Lesboris's garrison still maintained a tenuous French foothold on the island. The Persian squadron also remained essentially intact: with five royal men-of-war armed with brass-guns, a frigate, supporting (albeit nearly empty) storeships, and crews and infantry troops totaling well over 1200 men, it remained the most powerful naval force then operating in the Indian Ocean, more than capable of executing the main points in Colbert's instructions. Two things were needed to exploit the favorable conjuncture of events for Colbert's ambitions in Asia that existed in the summer of 1672: the French leadership had to abandon the policy of nonaggression dictated by Caron and the regular reinforcements promised by Louis XIV and Colbert had to appear. Although La Haye and Caron did not know it at the time, the war had of course already begun in Europe; news to that effect was making its way both by the Cape and Levant routes to Surat and ultimately to the squadron. This news would furnish the viceroy with the weapon he needed to liberate himself from Caron's overbearing personality and increasingly inexplicable policy decisions. The question of reinforcements would prove to be more fickle. Much depended on the Crown's reaction to the despatches from Trincomalee that de Beauregard carried aboard the *Barbaut,* the course of the king's continental campaign, and Colbert's ability to maintain royal favor and influence the royal decisions in the midst of the escalating demands of the war. As La Haye would discover, these factors that would all exert a profound influence on his fleet and the Asian campaign were all essentially out of his hands after parting company with the *Barbaut* off Kutiari. The fate of Colbert's Asian project would be decided as much on the fields of Flanders as on the decks of La Haye's warships.

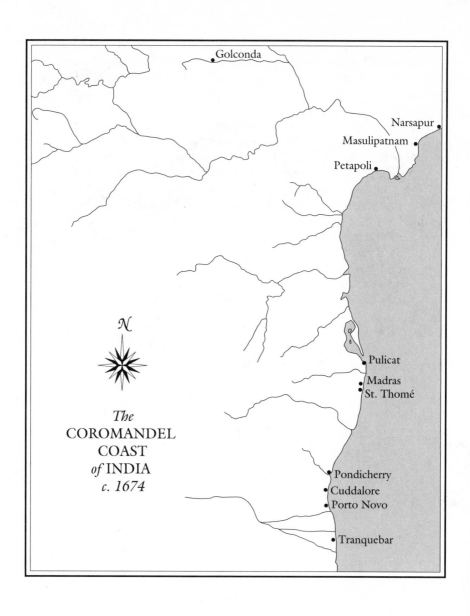

Golconda

Narsapur
Masulipatnam
Petapoli

N

Pulicat
Madras
St. Thomé

The
COROMANDEL
COAST
of INDIA
c. 1674

Pondicherry
Cuddalore
Porto Novo

Tranquebar

The Coromandel Coast, Paris, and Flanders, 1673

Escalating Difficulties in Europe and Asia

"If I had 20 well-equipped men-of-war here with
sufficient money, Your Majesty could be Master of
a kingdom as rich and as great as France."

—La Haye to Louis XIV

Louis's Asian viceroy penned these intriguing words on the Coromandel
coast of India at the end of a rigorous eight-month siege, from August
1672 until March 1673, in which the French successfully defended the
town of San Thomé from the armies of the Qutb Shahi king of Golconda,
Abul Hasan. La Haye's sojourn on the east coast of India had begun the
previous July, when his squadron had anchored before the Danish settlement of Tranquebar in search of provisions and naval stores, after enduring
the reverses inflicted on it at Trincomalee by Van Goens. Although the
Danish Crown had rejected Colbert's rather callous overtures to purchase
Tranquebar in 1669, the town's governor, M. Egger, received the French
graciously, promptly sending out some cows, pigs, fowl, and rice to their
ships. The Danes, however, could not provide sufficient naval stores to repair the deteriorating royal vessels. Egger could only advise that La Haye
head north to Madras, as rumor had it that five English ships had recently
put into that port from Europe carrying large quantities of naval stores.[1]

At Tranquebar, La Haye also received a packet of despatches from
France, which included an important letter from Louis XIV dated 20 June
1671. These packets had reached Surat in early February 1672, not long after the squadron had departed from Swally, but a series of mishaps on the
Malabar Coast had delayed them in reaching the viceroy's hands.[2] The traditional view laments this delay and further holds that the letter at last freed

La Haye from Caron's machinations and allowed him to exploit the full military potential of the squadron, but this interpretation is somewhat misleading. In the letter, Louis began by complaining about the lack of information that had reached Paris and ordered La Haye to send more frequent reports via the Capuchins in the Levant or aboard returning ships. He then moved on to his main point: "I have deemed it necessary to advise you that in case during the execution of my orders you have taken some posts in the Indies, you will place them in a state of defense." Why? As the king explained, his subjects were eagerly awaiting secure factories in the Indies as a refuge for their commerce, and since "it was doubtful" whether he could long suffer "the bad conduct and Ingratitude" of the Dutch, he would soon let them feel the full effects of his "Indignation." As the Indies were the only place where the Dutch could "harm my subjects," all necessary defensive precautions were to be taken.[3] Although La Haye later argued that his actions off Cape Comorin and Ceylon would have been much different had he received this letter sooner, the fact remains that this June 1671 despatch did not explicitly order the viceroy to initiate hostilities. Not even a letter from the king written in February 1672 on the eve of the war in Europe mandated this course of action.[4]

The French fleet had anchored before San Thomé on 20 July 1672.[5] The lure of south Coromandel textiles had long drawn European traders to this region. The Portuguese, attracted by the legend that the apostle St. Thomas was buried at Mylapore, began to settle at San Thomé de Mylapore in 1517. By 1600, San Thomé was a town of "riches, pride, and luxury . . . second to none in India."[6] Seven decades later, it remained a marginally important trading center. For many years, the Portuguese lived relatively peacefully at San Thomé under the aegis of Vijayanagar. The advances of the Muslim Deccan sultanates of Bijapur and Golconda at the expense of this great southern Hindu empire, however, resulted in rapid changes. Mir Jumla eventually claimed suzerainty over the place for the king of Golconda, Abdullah Qutb Shah, in 1646. Increased European competition on the Coromandel Coast during the 1650s and 1660s, with the English established at nearby Madras and the Dutch at Pulicat, eventually resulted in the expulsion of the Iberians in May 1662 following a Qutb Shahi siege directed by Neknam Khan and assisted by a Dutch naval blockade. While the Portuguese sought revenge, Neknam Khan turned San Thomé into a well-fortified garrison town; a strong wall with four bastions was built on the eastern or sea side to guard against naval attacks, and a massive gate was erected in the middle of the western wall.[7] Since the late 1660s, the French had considered San Thomé a potentially valuable possession for the *compagnie*. Although Marcara failed in his quest to extend the terms of Abdullah's *farman* to include the town, he was able to transact some business there: "[T]he French . . . make much show and spend much money. They have an agent, an Armenian by birth, who buys for them, mostly fine muslins for

France."[8] San Thomé also figured in La Haye's initial discussions with Caron in Surat, and the town had been mentioned by the director on Ceylon as a likely site to reprovision. The question of whether the fleet anchored before San Thomé with the firm intention of capturing it is much less certain.[9]

There is no doubt that the arrival of Colbert's fleet on the Coromandel Coast fueled the imaginations and fears of all the powers involved in the trade. The few French Company agents and clerics on that coast at the time, including François Martin and the superior of the Capuchins, Ephraim de Nevers, viewed the squadron as the instrument that could at last elevate France to its rightful position as a leading power in Asia. These men waited impatiently for La Haye and Caron to exploit the resources at their disposal for the glory of their king and his East India Company. Though nominally allied to Louis XIV's anti-Dutch campaign by the actions of Charles II, English factors on the Coromandel Coast foresaw only troublesome times ahead for their trade upon the arrival of the French in force. As William Langhorn, the ex-Cromwellian governor of Madras, lamented, "So we are like to have our Share of troubles. . . . [T]he bare report of them . . . has already caused all sort of callecoes [up] the country [to rise] about 3%; besides the distemper their proceedings cause; bringing a kind of feavor."[10] For Maetsuycker and the council in Batavia, reports of La Haye's arrival on the Coromandel Coast—while not unexpected given events at Trincomalee—nevertheless exacerbated the already dangerous and complex set of circumstances confronting the VOC in the midst of the Third Dutch War. Abul Hasan was initially cheered by the appearance of yet another European power that could serve as a convenient pawn in regional geopolitical struggles, while increasing custom revenues were levied at ports like Masulipatnam, money that would prove useful in the looming campaign against the zealous and ambitious Aurangzeb.[11]

Frustrated by Caron's policy and emboldened by the news contained in Louis's despatches, La Haye wasted little time in involving the squadron in a bloody campaign at San Thomé. Ironically, his actions were not directed against France's declared enemy, but rather at the Qutb Shahi garrison of the town. On 21 and 22 July, the viceroy's envoys were "rudely" received by the acting commander of San Thomé on the sandy beach below the town's bastions. This officer refused to sell any provisions to the fleet and haughtily informed the Frenchmen that standing orders from Hyderabad proscribed that no Christians could enter the town. To exact suitable retribution for this "insolence" and any insult to Louis XIV's honor, the royal men-of-war launched a blistering bombardment of the town on the twenty-third, complemented by a landing party under La Haye that easily bested a Qutb Shahi force on the beach. At a council meeting aboard the *Navarre* the following day, a decision was made to storm San Thomé. Several factors contributed to this bellicose resolution. Caron obviously coveted San

Thomé for its commercial advantages. La Haye had judged the town to be a worthwhile prize as early as the afternoon of the twenty-third, and he received advice from other quarters that also urged him to attack. Ephraim de Nevers, who had spent many years in India, proffered his opinion in a letter to La Haye. The Capuchin urged that the French force take San Thomé, maintaining that they would "never find a better occasion than the present for this feat," since there had been no governor for several months, nor even anyone of "sufficient position to undertake a defense of the place." According to de Nevers there was "no time to lose, as the Moor general was at Poonamalle, only half a day away by road and could send troops, if once warned of the design to take the town." Portuguese clerics and merchants alike, anxious that the property they had lost in 1662 be restored to them, also did their best to convince La Haye of the advantages of the place and the ease with which it could be taken from the "infidels," who had indeed made a poor showing on the twenty-third.[12]

The successful attack on San Thomé on 25 July was the first significant French military victory in Asia. On that day, under the blazing East Indian sun, La Haye admirably demonstrated his skill in the art of warfare by overcoming the town's imposing defensive works and large garrison thanks to a classic *ruse de guerre*. On the twenty-fourth, the viceroy landed four field pieces and 400 troops, including most of the *régiment royal de la marine*. He concentrated his command on the southern side of the town, hoping to create the impression that the force of his attack would be directed at that point. A fierce bombardment on the morning of the twenty-fifth from the royal men-of-war at anchor offshore in conjunction with the firing of the landing party succeeded in drawing the Qutb Shahi defenders to the southern and eastern walls, leaving the low northern wall virtually unprotected. At the opportune moment, La Haye ordered one of his infantry captains, de Rebrey, to storm this wall with some 200 men, utilizing long ladders that had been hidden at the base of the wall the previous night. De Rebrey's detachment scaled the wall unopposed, achieved a nearly complete surprise attack on the garrison, and opened the gate on the southern side of the town, allowing the rest of the French force to enter. A rout soon ensued in which many of the Qutb Shahi troops fled from the town, many jumping from the bastions to avoid capture. La Haye had a white fleur-de-lys raised from a seaside bastion to halt the naval bombardment and began counting the dead. The Qutb Shahi garrison had numbered about 750 before the attack. Of this number, 80 were killed, 350 were thought to have escaped by the main gate, which had been thrown open in the panic, another 200 had escaped by leaping off the walls, and 120 men had been captured. To celebrate this glorious victory a Te Deum was sung in the town's old cathedral dedicated to St. Thomas. In a gracious mood, La Haye also promised to restore the properties of the Portuguese clerics and laymen who flocked to San Thomé from Madras after the attack, provided they agreed to support him.[13]

Although the capture of San Thomé undoubtedly presented attractive commercial advantages to the *compagnie* and afforded a great deal of *gloire* for the arms of Louis XIV, the decision to storm the town was ill advised with respect to the political and military situation on the Coromandel Coast. It would have profound implications for the fate of the squadron and Colbert's entire project. First, this act effectively alienated English and Portuguese authorities in India and precluded the possibility of any meaningful support from Goa or Madras. Langhorn and the English Company merchants at Fort-St. George were greatly alarmed at the prospect of a substantial French factory only three miles from their own. The economic realities of the Asian trade were clearly preponderant over the temporary alliances that their misguided king and his ministers had concluded in Europe. On 27 July, a special council was held in Madras to discuss "whither the French taking St. Thomé and Rumours of warrs in Europe will oblige us to any Provision, for the safety of the Townfort Treasure and c.a interest of the Hon. Company, the danger of the French being now much greater than even of the Hollanders."[14] Mendonça Furtado and his Council of State in Goa still considered San Thomé to be rightfully a part of the *Estado* and expected La Haye to restore it to their possession. The Portuguese viceroy advised Pedro to seek a diplomatic solution in Europe that would ensure this result. His immediate problem was to ensure that the long-suffering Portuguese community in Madras did not rush to San Thomé to accept La Haye's offer, thus implicitly recognizing French sovereignty over the place. João Pereira de Faria, one of the viceroy's agents on the Coromandel Coast had warned him of such an exodus in a letter from Madras in late July. Mendonça Furtado responded by ordering João Coelho, a leading Portuguese merchant on that coast, to forestall a mass exodus to San Thomé and any armed support for the French.[15]

Much more worrisome for La Haye than the loss of the already dubious support of the English and Portuguese was that San Thomé, unlike Alicot and Trincomalee, had not been granted to the French by the local ruler who exercised titular jurisdiction over that place. In fact, La Haye had captured the city from that very potentate. In itself, this was not a serious problem, as the Portuguese and Dutch had demonstrated time and again. Unfortunately, La Haye and Caron made the mistake of affronting one of the largest states in India at that time: the Qutb Shahi kingdom of Golconda. The sultanate of Golconda dated from the early sixteenth century; it was a conquest state ruled by a Turco-Persian dynasty, dominated by a Muslim elite exploiting a military fief system, and grounded on the labor of indigenous Telugu-speaking Hindus. By the mid-seventeenth century, the sultanate had expanded to include most of the territory contained in the modern state of Andhra Pradesh. Golconda was a wealthy kingdom; traditional income from landed property had been gradually supplemented by the development of the most important market for large diamonds in the world and, thanks to the investment of the Dutch and English Companies, a steady increase in exports like textiles, indigo, foodstuffs, saltpeter, and iron. Since the early 1630s, the sultanate's foreign policy had been dictated by the need to keep the Mughal menace at bay. Although Shah Jahan had allowed the sultanate to survive during his Deccan campaign of 1635 in return for a yearly tribute and other signs of fealty, there had traditionally been an expansionist party in Agra, championed by Aurangzeb, that favored outright annexation. Abdullah weathered a 1656 invasion that sacked Hyderabad and nearly captured the Golconda fort, but the Mughal threat only increased after Aurangzeb seized the Peacock throne two years later. To meet this challenge, Abdullah raised at least "30,000 and perhaps as many as 80,000 horsemen for his standing army," complemented by an artillery park manned by well-trained European gunners who had fled from places like Goa in search of the riches to be won fighting *for* rather than *against* Asian kings.[16]

La Haye and Caron had therefore offended an indigenous state with sufficient military power to exact retribution. Like most powerful Asian dynasties, the Qutb Shahis had traditionally dismissed the Europeans who had come to their domains in search of profit as unworthy of serious attention. They could remain so long as they sent suitable gifts to court, paid yearly rents for their factories, and adhered to the commercial terms set forth in their *farmans*. Otherwise they would be expelled, as the Portuguese had discovered in 1662. News of the fall of San Thomé to the French was apparently without precedent in the military history of the sultanate and therefore invited a forceful response. Exacerbating the gathering troubles for La Haye and Caron was that the venerable Abdullah had died in April 1672 and been succeeded by his son-in-law, Abul Hasan. The young king was acutely aware of the continuing Mughal threat and also anxious to demonstrate his power to any potential rivals, to his vassals, and to Aurangzeb, who might interpret French actions at San Thomé as a further sign of decay in Hyderabad as well as an open invitation to invasion. Abul Hasan and his chief minister, Sayyid Muzaffer, thus wasted little time in preparing to retake the town. Exploiting the military obligations of his nobles, a large force of heavy Persian and Turkish cavalry was soon raised, supported by artillery pieces ranging from 18-pounders to a giant 120-pounder and a large infantry detachment. Baba Sahib was given command of this army along with the generals Mandala Naik and Bouzoura Trimbak Raju. Carré estimated the size of the Qutb Shahi force as 50,000 men, but this estimate was badly exaggerated. The actual number was close to Langhorn's figure of 16,000. In any case, the army Abul Hasan formed for the task of retaking San Thomé vastly outnumbered the diminished ranks of Colbert's fleet, which numbered between 800 and 900 men and 1000 indigenous retainers at this point.[17]

Baba Sahib's army had reached the environs of the town in early August.

Mandala Naik's contingent of 1500 cavalry originally occupied the most advanced position at a village called Kudumbaukum, about four miles west of San Thomé. This heavy cavalry, made up largely of Persians and Turks riding imported, armored horses, had long enjoyed superiority over the lighter-armed and mounted Telegu and Maratha warriors of the Deccan. Mandala Naik deployed this fine and experienced force along the main roads leading to San Thomé, with orders to intercept all manner of refreshment destined for the French garrison.[18] Baba Sahib soon resolved to concentrate his efforts on the western wall of the town. Local laborers promptly began the tedious process of constructing the trenches and earthworks that would allow Qutb Shahi artillery to move gradually closer in preparation for the barrage that, in the end, would breach the wall and expose the place to a general assault. Throughout the fall of 1672 this work had continued with as many as 3000 men being employed in the endeavor. As the entrenchments progressed, Qutb Shahi infantry occupied abandoned buildings in the western suburbs, and Baba Sahib's siege guns began a periodic bombardment of the western wall and its massive gate, called Porte Royale by the garrison.[19]

La Haye did everything he could to prepare for this onslaught. A special commissioner compiled a detailed list of all of the town's resources, foodstuff was stockpiled, a central market was established where goods were sold at fixed prices, and decrees were issued to prevent internal disorder. No doubt relishing the challenge, the viceroy did his best to put San Thomé in a strong defensive posture. The town's walls and bastions were repaired and several advanced redoubts constructed. To augment the firepower of these positions, La Haye had thirty-eight brass guns of the vice-admiral *Triomphe* allocated among the town's bastions. Large quantities of powder and shot were disembarked from the royal men-of-war. Envoys were dispatched to indigenous rulers along the Coromandel Coast who had expressed a willingness to assist the French cause.[20] After the siege began, the viceroy exhibited great personal courage, leading various sorties against the advancing Qutb Shahi positions.[21] In October 1672, La Haye ordered the *Breton, Navarre, Diligente, Flamand,* and *Sultane* south along the coast to buy foodstuff in light of the general effectiveness of Mandala Naik's men. A month later he received word that Sher Khan Lodi, the provincial governor of the Cuddalore region of Bijapur, would grant the French a settlement in his domains. La Haye promptly dispatched one of his most trusted aides, Bellanger de Lespinay, to Valikandapuran. A *farman* was soon obtained granting Pondicherry to the French. By February 1673, Bellanger de Lespinay was sending foodstuff to San Thomé.[22] Even with these supplies, the provisioning situation worsened, and the viceroy was compelled to confiscate the cargoes of at least five ships passing San Thomé; two of these were English, one was Danish, one belonged to a Portuguese resident in Madras, and the fifth was a Muslim vessel from Bengal. These actions did little to endear the French to the authorities in Goa, Tranquebar, and Madras.[23]

English actions in nearby Fort-St. George were especially damaging to the French cause. The governor there, William Langhorn, was the son of a prominent East India merchant. Admitted to the Inner Temple in 1664, he had inherited his father's business interests soon thereafter and by 1668 had been created a baron. A shrewd businessman, Langhorn had been appointed by the Court of Committees in 1670 to investigate the charges of financial irregularities made against Edward Winter in the wake of that governor's earlier mutiny in Madras. Langhorn's administrative skills resulted in his prompt appointment as governor of that settlement, while his financial acumen was best revealed in the extensive private trade he soon developed, which would yield him more than £7000 a year.[24] Langhorn, like many agents of the London Company, attached very little importance to Charles II's temporary European alliance with Louis XIV; maintaining the company's trade and his own private dealings in light of the uncertainties of the war were his paramount concerns. A French factory at San Thomé, moreover, was clearly antithetical to these English trading interests on the Coromandel Coast. As the governor noted, "The extreme Prejudice their Neighbourhood is to you, and all of us . . . is argument enough how I stand affected." Langhorn resolved to do whatever he could, albeit with diplomatic correctness, to undermine La Haye's position. Criticized by some of his councilors for periodically allowing supplies to be "carryed hence by stealth to the French," he informed London that the French had sufficient quantities of ammunition and meat, "so as to appear against them in their refreshments only, were but to breed ill blood to no purpose."[25] In his letters to Hyderabad, Langhorn continually sought to pressure Abul Hasan to expel the French: "[I]f the French continue at St. Thoma it will be no good Staying for us here . . . for so near such an unquiet people as we know them to be, it will be neither convenient nor safe for us." The English governor continually rebuffed La Haye's entreaties for military assistance, arguing that he could not afford to offend Hyderabad, while simultaneously rejecting the Qutb Shahi demands to break with the French, since he did not have "our king's order for it."[26]

By late 1672, the situation had become critical for the French. Provisions were dwindling, Baba Sahib's entrenchments had moved to within musket range of the western wall, and the Qutb Shahi siege guns, including the 120-pounder, were brought to bear with notable effect. La Haye decided that only a major attack would halt this dangerous advance. On 5 November, he led his personal guards, 150 French infantry troops, 350 local retainers, and 150 armed *matelots* out of the town an hour before dawn. In the engagement that followed, the French delivered a nearly complete surprise attack. They were able to rout the enemy forces in the most advanced trenches, as well as to repel a cavalry charge from the main Golcondan camp, thanks in part to a lively bombardment from the town's bastions. La Haye's men spent the next week destroying these impressive works, fighting off frequent attacks by Baba Sahib's horsemen. As the viceroy informed Louis XIV, "We remained . . . until all their entrenchments were razed to the ground, which was not a *petit travail* given the height and thickness of their works, there were [also] constant attacks in which the Muslims were always badly beaten."[27] This "victory" was, however, destined to be short-lived. By early December the besiegers had once again advanced to their previous positions. A general assault was forestalled only by frequent barrages from the town's bastions and the fortified outer redoubts, which formed an unbroken chain around San Thomé. In a series of attacks on these redoubts during the final week of the year, Baba Sahib's much-vaunted cavalry suffered heavy losses. François Martin, usually a reliable source, wrote that 200 enemy troops were killed, while La Haye's journal doubled that number.[28]

In any event, the unexpected tenacity of the French garrison gave rise to an antiwar party in Hyderabad and abortive peace talks at San Thomé during early 1673. Sayyid Muzzafer headed the peace party at court, arguing that the French were proving to be a much more difficult foe than originally anticipated. Rather than squandering additional money and troops, he advised Abul Hasan to enter into talks that would allow La Haye to retain the town, provided a suitable "gratuity" and a yearly rent could be arranged. To bolster his case, the chief minister cited rumors of sizable reinforcements supposedly on the way from France that would further complicate the successful completion of the siege. Sidi Musa Khan, the nawab of the Carnatic, then involved in a fierce political feud with Muzzafer, championed the war party. The nawab, who stood to lose sizable revenue if the French remained in San Thomé, maintained that the siege should be continued and cited reports from Mandala Naik and Trimbak Bussora Raju stating that the French were near capitulation to bolster his case. Although Abul Hasan ultimately sided with Sidi Musa Khan and ordered that additional resources be committed to prosecute the siege, reinforcements were extremely slow in materializing, as the sultanate's coffers were drained at about this time by demands from Aurangzeb for his annual tribute of 800,000 silver rupees and a large sum that was also paid to Shivaji to avert an attack by the Marathas.[29] In the meantime, Baba Sahib began formal talks with La Haye in January over the disposition of the town. As the viceroy informed Louis XIV, the French could "retain Saint-Thomé and its dependencies independently if I pay about 4000 livres each year and nearly 20,000 livres [now]."[30] La Haye rejected this offer in early February in part because he simply lacked the funds to meet these terms. He had also been assured by Langhorn that a fleet of twenty ships was on the way from Europe to reinforce him, news that made the viceroy all the more willing to reject Hyderabad's terms, to the English governor's delight. The siege began anew.[31]

Langhorn's steadfast refusal to provide assistance had convinced La Haye by early 1673 that his only hope for meaningful aid rested with the Crown's pledge to dispatch regular reinforcements to Asia.[32] Caron had exploited this reality as early as August 1672 in an attempt to return home. Chaffing under the military exigencies of the situation that had deprived him of his earlier pre-eminence, he pressured La Haye for leave to return to Paris, ideally to press Louis XIV and Colbert for reinforcements. Underlying this laudable goal, of course, was his desperate desire to reach France as quickly as possible to defend himself against mounting charges of misconduct and to justify the less than spectacular results of the expedition. There is also the possibility that Caron may also have wished to desert the squadron once he had helped involve it in a messy war of attrition on the Coromandel Coast. La Haye, who had become increasingly suspicious of the director's motives and was anxious to be rid of him, sanctioned Caron's return to France aboard the man-of-war *Jules* in September 1672. The viceroy also resolved to send the *St-Louis* to Surat to seek support from Baron and the other directors there.[33] Caron had loaded the bulk of his private treasure aboard the royal vessel and departed with his son Johan in early October. The director's son Balthazar departed that same day from San Thomé aboard the *St-Louis* with the family's silver plate, planning to continue the family's commercial operations in Gujarat. Unfortunately both for Caron's reputation and historians of the *compagnie*, this man, who was so instrumental in Colbert's Asian project, never reached France. Reaching the mouth of the Tagus in late March 1673, the *Jules* ran aground near Cascais and floundered. As d'Aubeville, Saint-Romain's replacement in the Portuguese capital, informed Colbert, Johan Caron, most of the crew, and La Haye's letters were saved. But Caron and thirty-one others drowned. The director's personal goods, valued at over 250,000 livres were also lost.[34] Exacerbating these troublesome times for the Caron family was that the *St-Louis* had earlier been captured off Ceylon by Van Goens, who was said to have remarked that Caron's silver plate was a gracious gift from one old employee of the Dutch Company to another.[35]

During the course of February 1673, Baba Sahib's main battery did a credible job of reducing the western wall of San Thomé to rubble, and a final assault appeared imminent. La Haye, however, once again demonstrated his considerable military skills in two engagements that ultimately succeeded in lifting this siege against such heavy odds. On 23 February, a surprise night attack directed by the viceroy captured the main Qutb Shahi battery, and all of its guns, save the 120-pounder, were spiked. According to Carré's colorful account, the muzzle of this piece was loaded with powder; "[T]he powder was then fired, and the gun blew up with such force that the whole adjoining earth was shaken, and the noise was like a terrible clap of thunder."[36] This sortie badly undermined the morale of the Qutb Shahi troops, who had already become somewhat unreliable because their pay was several months in arrears. As Langhorn noted, "[A]ll this ill successe comes onely by Babba's not paying the soldiers as he ought for which reason most of the best desert the service."[37] The decisive engagement of the siege took place on 9 March when La Haye ordered a general French attack, in which most of the Qutb Shahi trenches were captured, Mandala Naik killed, and Trimbak Bussora Raju badly wounded. These reverses prompted an immediate volte-face in Hyderabad. Sidi Musa Khan was thoroughly discredited in Abul Hasan's eyes and fell from royal favor. The king had tired of this loathsome matter and issued orders for his army to retire to a distance of seven miles from San Thomé, lifting the siege. Congratulations soon reached La Haye from rulers along the Coromandel Coast and Langhorn praising his notable success.[38]

La Haye's ability to withstand the eight-month siege at San Thomé was a noteworthy accomplishment. Far from home, vastly outnumbered, blockaded on three sides, and abandoned by their English allies, the French had acted with skill and courage to best Abul Hasan's army and win a good deal of *gloire* for the arms of Louis XIV. La Haye's initial impressions of India's great wealth and fickle geopolitical situation, combined with this easy victory over the powerful Qutb Shahi dynasty, convinced him that great things could be accomplished in Asia. In September 1672, he boldly declared that with twenty ships and four thousand men he could make Louis "master of both the Malabar and Coromandel coasts."[39] He reiterated this belief in February 1673 letters that lauded the benefits of San Thomé for the *compagnie*. The viceroy vowed to do everything possible to retain this town and continue his campaign but noted that the Muslims, Dutch, and English were all intent on preventing the entrenchment of French power in India. By the spring of 1673 it was clear that the precondition for the successful continuation of the Asian project was the arrival of significant monetary and military aid from France.[40] In a despatch compiled after the siege was lifted in March, the viceroy lamented that no reinforcements had reached him since January 1672; his most recent instructions dated from March of that year. "However, I hope that God will give us the time to await the orders of Your Majesty and the reinforcements that will be sent to us." This lack of timely support had retarded his ambitions and prevented him from exploiting the favorable conditions he had encountered on his arrival in India. Although the French had clearly bettered their enemies, the fleet's dwindling strength had forced La Haye to conclude that peace might be a more advantageous strategy than war, at least until he had "sufficient troops to wage it properly." If such reinforcements would arrive, the spoils would amaze Louis's rivals: "a kingdom as rich and as great as France."[41] This alluring possibility hinged, as it turned out, on the king's continued willingness to embrace Colbert's *outre-mer* projects in the face of mounting setbacks in the European campaign.

In Paris, Colbert had watched with great apprehension as the Continental

campaign degenerated. He had willingly embraced the gamble of open warfare with the United Provinces for reasons of political economy. As Louis's
armies raced toward Amsterdam and Dutch strongholds fell one after another, Colbert had become caught up in the euphoria of the moment. By
late June, it appeared that everything he had worked and hoped for in his
mercantile struggle with the Hollanders would be achieved with ease by the
force of Louis's arms. "If the king conquers all the provinces subject to and
forming part of the States of the United Provinces of the Netherlands, their
commerce becoming commerce of the subjects of the king, there would be
nothing more to desire." With these words, Colbert began a *mémoire* of 8
July, written in the midst of de Witt's desperate effort to negotiate a settlement, which detailed his economic peace proposals. It would be a simple
matter to cut "down a part of that of the Dutch so as to transfer it into the
hands of the French." Colbert argued that Louis should oblige the Dutch to
revoke their prohibition of French wines, brandies, and other goods and to
recognize his right to charge whatever taxes he saw fit on Dutch ships and
goods entering France. To obtain a dominant position in the lucrative Levant trade, the king would forbid Dutch ships from entering the Mediterranean and force them to withdraw their agents from Constantinople and
other ports in the Near East. The granting of the islands of Curaçao, Saint
Eustatius, and Tobago and of a fort in Guinea would help the French supplant Dutch power in the West Indies and West Africa. As for the East Indies, Louis would demand an island of his choice in the Moluccas, and one
or two fortresses on the Malabar Coast from among those the VOC had captured from the Portuguese, say, Cochin and Cannanore. With these advantages, the position of the *compagnie* would be secure and annual profits of 5
to 6 million livres might be expected.[42]

Colbert's lofty ambitions and euphoria were shattered over the next year
and a half, as the Dutch withstood Louis's initial onslaught and began to
construct a European coalition against the increasingly bewildered French
king. The opening of the sluices at Muyden, Louis's failure to capture Amsterdam, the election of William of Orange as stadholder on the very day
that Colbert was writing his peace terms, the inability of the combined Anglo-French fleet to defeat de Ruyter, William's unexpected siege of
Charleroi, and Luxembourg's futile winter offensive constituted a mere prelude to the frustrations of the next six years. Louis had returned to Saint-
Germain on 1 August 1672, long before the usual campaigning season had
ended, convinced that the few remaining Dutch strongholds were not worthy of his royal attention. William's attack on Charleroi perhaps convinced
him otherwise, rather rudely interrupting revelries at court and drawing
Louis up the Oise valley to Compiègne, where he exchanged views with
Louvois on the advisability of attacking the Habsburgs in Flanders. After returning to Saint-Germain, the king spent most of the rest of the winter asking Condé, Turenne, and Vauban for their recommendations on how to de-

ploy the army for the offensive the following spring. In late January, Louis decided to array his forces according to the advice of Turenne: 48,000 in Holland and 30,000 each in Germany and Flanders.[43] Louis was determined to outdo the glorious campaign of the previous year and to execute "big plans that would succeed on all fronts." As the king later explained the strategy of the 1673 campaign, Turenne was charged with observing "the army of the emperor and his allies," and Condé was sent into Holland "to keep my enemies occupied and I decided to lead my own army . . . [and] to attack Maastricht."[44]

The crucial campaign of 1673, much like the fabled advance of the previous spring, began gloriously enough. On 1 May, Louis left Saint-Germain with his queen, Marie-Thérèse, and two mistresses, Mlle. de La Valliere and the marquise de Montespan, in tow and joined his troops at the northern frontier. As Pomponne noted, "Never was there a more splendid army." Passing through the Spanish Netherlands in a *transitus innoxious*, the army marched along the banks of the Scheldt, making feints against Ghent and Brussels in an attempt to hide the army's prime objective. Soon some 40,000 men had engulfed the environs of the formidable citadel of Maastricht, including the duke of Monmouth, John Churchill, and the famed musketeer d'Artagnan. Louis's cavalry and infantry promptly secured the countryside, and Vauban's engineers began the serious work of the siege, which took place largely in muddy, decidedly unglamorous trenches that were skillfully planned and opened. Early on the morning of 30 June word reached Louis XIV that the Dutch garrison was prepared to surrender. A task that had taken Frederick Henry three months to achieve in 1632 and that had daunted the duke of Parma for more than four in 1579 had been achieved by Louis's army in less than four weeks' time.[45] News of the capture of Maastricht produced great rejoicing in Paris. As Colbert informed the king on 4 July, "Paris has never been so jubilant. On Sunday evening, the bourgeois, on their own initiative, without being ordered, lit bonfires of joy."[46]

This rejoicing was to be decidedly short-lived as the war, which had begun as a concerted offensive against an isolated opponent, the United Provinces, had evolved by 1673 into a dangerous European struggle that tempered Louis's early victories and threatened him with defeat. The French, to be sure, enjoyed some successes: Frederick William by the Treaty of Vossem (June 1673) temporarily abandoned the war, and Alsace, Lorraine, and the electorate of Trier were all occupied. But these actions were more than offset by military and diplomatic setbacks during the course of the year. In the Schooveldt channel in May and at Texel in August, de Ruyter again held off the combined Anglo-French fleet under the command of Prince Rupert. In September, William was able to retake Naarden from the French, while the imperial army under Montecucculi outmaneuvered Turenne along the Main. After Louis's return to Saint-Germain in mid-

October, the military situation deteriorated further: by the end of that month orders had gone out to Luxembourg to evacuate nearly all of the French-held territory in the United Netherlands, a bitter commentary on the fleeting nature of the victories of 1672. The fall of Bonn to Montecuc-culi and William in early November not only shattered the myth of French invincibility but also portended continuing troubles for Louis in Germany which would culminate—at least symbolically—the following May with the declaration of a *reichskrieg* against the French by the German diet. Diplo-matically, things were no better. By the Alliance of The Hague of late Au-gust, Louis was confronted by a coalition of the Dutch Republic, the duke of Lorraine, as well as the Austrian and Spanish Habsburgs. War was for-mally declared on Spain in late October.[47] Perhaps more worrisome were the unmistakable signs from London that the secret alliance of 1670 was under severe strain. De Croissy's letters made it clear that the general un-popularity of the French alliance, the imbroglio surrounding Charles's Dec-laration of Indulgence and Parliament's retaliatory Test Act, as well as the lackluster results of the naval campaign, would soon compel the English Crown to seek a separate peace. The Treaty of Westminster in February 1674 would confirm these fears and deprive Louis of his principal ally in the struggle.[48]

The unwelcome prolongation of the Dutch War had at least three major effects on Colbert and his policies: it threatened his position as the king's pre-eminent minister, it undermined his careful economic reforms of the 1660s, and it helped to ensure the failure of his project to win a sizable share of the Asian trade. The debate over the relative power of Louis's min-isters on the *Conseil d'en haut,* though it has long fueled research in the French foreign affairs archives, is bound to be ultimately inconclusive, given the secret sessions of that body and the consequent dearth of sources.[49] Nevertheless, there can be little doubt that the onset of the Dutch War ele-vated Louvois to a position of royal favor that he had hitherto not enjoyed. The young Le Tellier shared the traditional dynastic priorities on the Conti-nent that Louis himself found so attractive. The pair had thoroughly en-joyed the process of reforming the army in preparation for the campaign against the Dutch and had reveled in the highly stylized sieges of the war. In contrast, Colbert, the rather humorless bureaucrat, remained behind in Paris to oversee financial and administrative matters. These circumstances ensured the accession of Louvois to royal favor, a process that was underway even before 1672. The war certainly accelerated this process, and together Louis and Louvois increasingly monopolized the direction of war and diplo-macy, as Ekberg notes, "to the exclusion of the other ministers of state."[50] It would be a mistake, however, to judge that Colbert's power was eclipsed by that of Louvois during the Dutch War. Louis realized that large sums of cash were needed to fight the type of campaign he envisioned, and Colbert had demonstrated an unequaled ability to augment state revenues and raise extraordinary funds. While the king may have threatened to find someone else who could raise the 34 million for military expenditures over and above the 6 million for foreign treaties when Colbert had initially balked at these figures while preparing the budget for 1672, there is very scant evidence to suggest that this threat was anything more than mere hyperbole.[51] As late as 1679, when Louis dispensed royal "gratification" in consideration of services, Colbert received 400,000 livres and Louvois only 300,000.[52] Colbert's projects, not his personal position among the chief ministers, were destined to suffer most by the escalation of the Dutch War.

As most French schoolchildren know, the Dutch War definitively upset Colbert's careful economic reforms of the 1660s, reforms that had perhaps doubled the king's net income between 1661 and 1671 and resulted in a sizable surplus in the royal coffers.[53] Despite this rather miraculous shift in Crown finances, Colbert recognized the fragile nature of his success. Intendant reports from 1670 reveal that an economic slowdown of sorts may have been underway in the countryside.[54] Moreover, it was obvious that unless the campaign against the Hollanders was swift, his gamble in embracing the war would fail and all his work would be threatened. By the spring of 1673, he already feared the worst and was willing to temper the economic goals of the Continental campaign in order to achieve a settlement. In his April *mémoire*, the terms to be discussed at the Cologne Conference were far more modest than his euphoric demands of the previous July. The Dutch should be made to pay for the damage they had done to French trade, especially in the East Indies; the Franco-Dutch tariff treaty of 1662 should be revoked and a new one postponed; and, provided no concessions were demanded in return, the Hollanders should abolish their prohibition of French wines and brandies.[55] Louis's incessant demands for funds were deeply disturbing. In a letter of August to the king, Colbert contrasted such demands and the consequent need to fix the *taille* for 1674 with the "misery" and "extreme scarcity of money" in the provinces.[56] Louis's demand for 34 million for the campaign of 1672 and 60 million for 1673 destroyed any hope for continued financial stability and compelled him to renounce his earlier efficiencies and embrace time-honored "extraordinary measures," including raising old taxes, enacting new ones, and selling offices and parts of the royal estates to feed Louis's growing appetite for money. The deficit, which hovered around 8 million in 1672, doubled to nearly 16 million in 1673 and would reach 24 million by 1676. The economic "miracle" of the 1660s was over.[57]

Colbert had originally been able to gain substantial royal support for his *Compagnie des Indes Orientales* and the Persian squadron because Louis, in addition to a vague awareness of the economic benefits that might result for his subjects, recognized that the Asian campaign conveniently complemented his anti-Dutch preparations in Europe. The inherent contradictions in this novel juxtaposition of priorities would only be exposed during the

Dutch War, when the relative importance of dynastic vis-à-vis mercantile priorities would be resoundingly resolved in favor of the former. From early 1669 to late 1673, Colbert discovered that the anti-Dutch connection between his Asian project and the king's campaign in Europe could yield mixed blessings. At first, this connection allowed him to receive the king's approval for sizable expenditures on the *compagnie* and La Haye's squadron and the promise of regular royal reinforcements. As the military and diplomatic situation in Europe deteriorated in late 1672 and into 1673, Louis's early enthusiasm for the Asian project dwindled, and Colbert's plans were allowed to atrophy. Perhaps nothing illustrates the reassertion of traditional foreign policy aims at this time better than the lack of support La Haye received from home between 1672 and 1674. On the eve of open hostilities with the United Provinces, Louis reneged on his December 1670 promise to reinforce the squadron with two men-of-war and 200 troops a year.[58] By mid-March 1672, Louis had concluded that an attack against the VOC was impossible. As a result, no royal ships, money, or men were sent to Asia during 1672, at a time when they were needed most.[59] The triumph of dynastic over mercantile priorities culminated in 1673, when mounting setbacks in Europe caused Louis to abandon Colbert's Asian initiative in favor of the Pyrrhic *gloire* of the Flanders campaign. In February 1673, Louis informed his viceroy that the primacy of the Continental campaign meant that he would have to return to Europe forthwith with all his remaining men-of-war.[60] This decision constituted a virtual death knell for Colbert's Asian strategy.

Since the beginning of the war, Colbert had been frantic to learn details of the expedition's progress so that he might dispatch the most appropriate assistance to his Asian fleet. La Haye, however, had failed to demonstrate the same ardor for sending regular despatches to Paris as he had for the taste of battle with Abul Hasan's forces. Louis XIV had chastised his viceroy for this dearth of information in letters of June 1671 and February 1672, and ordered that more frequent despatches be sent either via the Capuchin fathers established in the Levant or aboard any returning ships.[61] For most of 1672 and early 1673, Colbert had been forced to rely on the tenuous, and at times distorted, reports he received from his brother in London, information obtained at best from Arlington and his friends on the Court of Committees and at worst gleaned from the gossip of returning seamen at the company's docks along the Thames at Blackwall and Poplar.[62] It was only in February 1673, the very month when Louis had issued orders for La Haye to return home with all his remaining ships, that the *Barbaut* reached La Rochelle with news of the occupation of Trincomalee. In early May, immediately following the departure of Louis and his entourage for the northern frontier, word of La Haye's exploits on the Coromandel Coast began to reach Paris via the survivors of the *Jules* and in a series of reports on the disaster from d'Aubeville.[63] Colbert was overjoyed with these much desired, if somewhat belated, returns on his sizable investment in the *compagnie* and the Persian squadron. Predictably, he wasted little time in attempting to exploit these successes in his quest to reverse the shift in royal priorities that was inexorably undermining his Asian project.

By 8 May, Colbert had compiled a *mémoire* on the subject for Louis.[64] He began by detailing the unfortunate loss of the *Jules* in the Tagus, a mishap which he blamed on the ineptitude of the Portuguese pilots charged with bringing the man-of-war upriver to Restelo. Colbert did not lament Caron's untimely death. He had already concluded that the enigmatic director-general, if not secretly in the employ of the VOC, was in any case expendable. Caron's duties could be carried out by Baron and the other French directors, whose loyalties were more certain and who lacked the Dutchman's unrivaled expertise for exploiting company funds to bolster his personal reputation and fortune. The previous June, he had informed La Haye that in case the other directors "of a common consent, estimate it appropriate to do something to oppose the ill effects of the conduct of the said Caron. . . . His Majesty wishes you to support [them] totally."[65] The loss of Régnier du Clos and 30 others was more troubling. Nevertheless, 104 crewmen had been saved along with the packets from La Haye. As he advised Louis, "[O]ne learns from Lisbon by the principal [surviving] officers of the crew of this vessel, and by some of the letters from the said de La Haye that he has taken the city of St. Thomé on the Coromandel coast . . . [that] had been for 150 years under the domination of the Portuguese, and retaken from them by the Muslim inhabitants of the country, subjects of the king of Golconda." Colbert went to great lengths to impress the king with the *gloire* that had been won by storming an ancient Indian city "as large as La Rochelle" and with the economic worth of the city: "[I]t can serve as a very important post for the commerce of the East India Company." He then proceeded to the crux of the problem. It would be, he argued, "difficult for the said de La Haye to hold out against the inhabitants of the country if he does not receive additional assistance." Colbert concluded by noting the contradictory reports he had received on Trincomalee: "[S]ome say that the garrison has revolted against the Sr. de Lesboris, others that the Dutch had retaken it, but no definite word has yet arrived." To bolster his call for additional reinforcements, he had the Capuchin Denis, one of the survivors of the *Jules* and a committed supporter of French ambitions in Asia, accompany his despatches north into Flanders.[66]

Colbert's *mémoire* reached Louis's itinerant court at an opportune moment. The king was in a buoyant mood following his personal and military triumphs of June 1673. On the sixteenth of that month, the marquise de Montespan, the fertile object of Louis's carnal passions, presented him with their fourth bastard child in five years, Louise-Françoise de Bourbon. On the thirtieth, Maastricht had formally capitulated, with the vainglorious king entering the citadel and performing a suitable ceremony two days later in what "must have been one of the great moments in the life of a king who longed to be a great captain like his grandfather Henry IV."[67] Despite this seemingly fortuitous timing, Colbert discovered that it was exceedingly difficult to interest the king in a significant reescalation of the Asian campaign, a campaign that had been relegated to the backwaters of policy priorities by Louis and Louvois in early 1672. The king, it appeared, wished to embrace only the traditional priorities that had dominated during the time of his illustrious grandfather. Although the swift capture of Maastricht confronted Louis and his war minister with the necessity of concocting a strategy for the remainder of the campaigning season, the pair remained embedded in the morass of diplomatic and military minutiae associated with the Continental campaign for the rest of the summer, with neither the time nor the inclination to devote serious attention to the potentialities of the anti-Dutch campaign in Asia. Louis may have perused Colbert's report and received Denis before departing from the environs of Maastricht on 12 July on his march south toward Lorraine, but he did not see fit to congratulate La Haye until the end of August. Only at Breisach, when the cities of Alsace submitted to his demands, did Louis XIV write to his Asian viceroy. While the king was impressed by La Haye's ability to capture and hold San Thomé against such heavy odds, both he and the young Le Tellier viewed such victories merely as an extension of their dynastic goals in Europe, not in relation to their economic implications for the *compagnie* or Colbert's overall plans. As Louis informed La Haye, "I have read with great pleasure and satisfaction everything you have done in the Indies . . . [especially] the capture of St. Thomé . . . a post . . . through which I can make my power known."[68]

Colbert, all the same, achieved a degree of success with his May *mémoire*. As a passing fancy engendered by the temporary successes of early summer, Louis sanctioned limited reinforcements to retain his new Asian prizes. Although events in Europe would soon cause Louis to forget his promise for even limited support, Colbert did his utmost in difficult circumstances to exploit this unexpected opportunity. Relishing the challenge, he compiled a slew of *mémoires,* following the arrival of the *Barbaut* in late February, designed to consolidate the advances made by La Haye's expedition and salvage the Eastern project. Uncertain of the fate of Lesboris's garrison at Trincomalee, Colbert had summoned de Beauregard in early March and informed him that he would be returning to the East Indies as soon as a royal ship could be outfitted. De Beauregard was instructed to call first at the *Île Bourbon,* where he would deposit sixteen women to assist with the colonization of that island. He was then expected to proceed with all possible haste to Ceylon. At Trincomalee, de Beauregard would present Lesboris with letters from Louis and Colbert that exhorted the governor to hold the place at all costs and promised one or two small ships a year for its defense.[69] Due in part to the demands of the Continental campaign, the only ship deemed available for this mission was the *Barbaut*. Renamed the *Dunkerquoise*, this well-traveled flute departed from La Rochelle in late May. By November 1673, the news of the previous spring had allowed Colbert to prepare a ship for the relief of San Thomé. The royal flute *Éléphant*, with 100 infantry troops and 100,000 livres aboard to assist La Haye with his campaign, departed late that month from Rochefort bound for San Thomé. Tragically, this ship was lost in a gale soon after leaving port.[70]

Because Colbert recognized that in all probability the material reinforcements he had dispatched were not sufficient for the task at hand, he strove in the fall of 1673 to resurrect his quest for an anti-Dutch alliance in the Indian Ocean with England. On 13 September, he instructed his brother to raise the matter anew with Charles, Arlington, and the directors on Leadenhall Street, "to aid and mutually protect trade, by sharing necessary resources, be it provisions, munitions, or even men, in order to resist our common enemy, which is the Dutch, and even by attacking them, if this is judged necessary." Colbert lamented to de Croissy that he was at great pains to see the conclusion of such an alliance, "be it to defend ourselves or attack." He would arrange the necessary powers from Louis XIV if Charles or his ministers should demonstrate even the slightest interest.[71] Despite the worrisome setbacks of the previous year, Colbert was therefore willing to embrace the military option against the United Provinces as late as the fall of 1673 to achieve his economic objectives, evidence that refutes the recent revisionist assertion that from the outset he was cowed against his will into supporting the Dutch War by an overbearing Louis XIV.[72] In any event, de Croissy's efforts were again a failure. While Arlington wrote to the directors on Charles's behalf, urging that the company assist the French, and the men of Leadenhall Street composed letters to their servants in the East to this effect, nothing ever came of this contrived plea.[73] More damaging to Colbert's last-ditch efforts to salvage his Indian Ocean project, however, was that the meager military reinforcements he had indeed arranged were most probably a matter of too little, too late. The crucial period from April 1671 to May 1673, when traditional aims on the Continent had originally reasserted themselves and no royal assistance had been sent to Asia, apparently proved decisive. In 1674, the combination of escalating difficulties at home, Louis's lack of firm support, and events transpiring in the European "capitals" of Asia would decide the fate of Colbert's grand squadron and his grandoise strategy for Asian wealth.

Les Indes Orientales and Paris, 1674

Reconfirming Traditional Priorities in Europe; Establishing the Basis for the Postwar Trade in Asia

> "The Portuguese doe with noe meane difficulty keepe [a] footing in India. . . . But the Prudence of this Viceroy hath raised them much. . . . The Dutch are rich and powerfull, possessing the most advantageous places of India; but as they gained them by their sword and violence; soe they must maintayne them by the same meanes which will force them to a continuall vast expence of men and treasure. . . . The French carry themselves very high, but surely cannot boast of any gaine hitherto . . . though tis probable their ambitions may carry them further in time, according as they succeed in their Warr with Holland. . . . But the English [countrie]under your Honours happy management serves as a Plant watered by Divine Providence."
>
> —Gerald Aungier to London Directors

In early 1674, the president of the English Company could indulge in such insightful, albeit self-serving, judgments on the relative strength of the European powers established in the Indian Ocean trade. After all, as Aungier reported, it appeared that the rather tenuous holdings of the London Company would indeed survive the inherent dangers of yet another war against the maritime might of the United Provinces. The president had little taste or use for this latest war against the Hollanders.[1] Dividing his time between Surat and Bombay, Aungier was continuing his reform program that would transform the rather ramshackle island outpost obtained from Charles II in

1668 into a thriving city that would serve as the locus for the company's future prosperity on the west coast of India. Since his accession to power in 1669, he had not wavered from the policies he judged essential for the creation of an independent, fortified entrepôt that the company so badly needed. Despite loud protests locally and in Europe, the expropriation of erstwhile Portuguese estates had continued apace. Although precise figures are difficult to ascertain, a Portuguese document valued property "usurped without justification" by the English between 1666 and 1668 alone under royal administration at well over 150,000 xerafins.[2] Aungier's policy of de facto religious toleration to encourage rich Hindu, Jain, and Parsi merchants to abandon the nearby holdings of the Portuguese in favor of Bombay also yielded impressive results.[3]

As Aungier also pointed out, the Dutch Company had won their dominant position in the trade thanks largely to the ruthless and effective use of military force, "their sword and violence," by men like Coen, Van Diemen, and Van Goens. Superior entrepreneurial structures may have allowed the Dutch to outfit their fleets and thereafter exploit the spoils, but brilliant naval blockades and decisive victories at sea and on land had actually yielded control over many of the spice-producing islands of Indonesia, as well as Batavia, Melaka, Ceylon, and Cochin. For much of this same period, England had been ravaged by the societal uncertainties and struggles associated with the Revolution, Civil War, and Restoration. Under such circumstances, the enfeebled London Company could not hope to compete on an equal footing with the VOC. This unwelcome fact had been painfully clear since the initial reverses in Indonesia at the hands of Coen, following the breakdown of the accord of 1619, losses that forced the Court of Committees to reorient their trade toward India in the 1630s and 1640s. The first two Dutch Wars only served to reinforce the belief on Leadenhall Street that open warfare against Batavia was far from the wisest policy to pursue in the quest for an increased share of the trade. For the members of the Court of Committees, renewed warfare with the Dutch in 1672 had therefore been judged as both unwanted and unnecessary. More galling was the misguided and murky alliance that had been secretly forged with His Most Christian Majesty at Dover, a Stuart alliance that was frankly unpalatable to many of the directors as well as their supporters and friends in Parliament and the City.[4]

The London directors had responded to the outbreak of the war by developing a strategy consistent with the business constitutionalism and "impersonal character of the East India Company's commercial operations," as outlined by Chaudhuri among others, that was designed to maintain a stable trade in the face of the economic dislocation engendered by the conflict.[5] The formation of the French Company had already prompted the Court of Committees to issue precise instructions to Oxenden and Aungier, calling for more efficient business practices to offset this increased competition in Asia.[6] Since many of the directors evidently believed that the unpopular alliance with Louis XIV could not be maintained for long, a conservative plan was fashioned whereby sustained warfare with the VOC, a state of affairs that would expose company possessions to the ravages of Maetsuycker's fleet, would be avoided if at all possible. English ships would sail to and from the Indies in large, well-armed convoys to discourage Dutch attacks, and English factories would be placed in a defensive posture.[7] Leadenhall Street hoped that three factors would allow it to weather this latest showdown with the Dutch until such time as Charles would come to his senses and seek a peace or would be forced to do so by a recalcitrant Cavalier Parliament. There was reason to believe that Maetsuycker would be so preoccupied with the threat from La Haye's fleet that he would all but ignore English positions in littoral India and elsewhere. As Aungier noted in a 1673 letter, he hoped the French would "keepe the Dutch so well employed that they will not have leasure to disturbe our Shipps."[8] The Court of Committees was also convinced that its relatively harmonious relations with indigenous princes would afford the company protection from Dutch advances, at least on land. As the directors informed Langhorn in late 1673, "Wee therefore require, that you exercise such Caution and prudence, as not to give, any European just occasion of af-fronte, But in a more especial manner that you provoke not the Natives," since a good relationship with indigenous kings ensured that no European could attack without risking open warfare with that potentate.[9] London, moreover, was confident that the early news on the European campaign would dissuade Maetsuycker from taking an aggressive stance. A letter of May 1674 from Langhorn seemed to confirm this belief: "[T]he Dutch . . . truly . . . seem to be in s[uch] great consternation on their sad news from Europe that they know not which way to turn."[10]

During the course of the war, there were only two occasions when it ap-peared that the English might become involved in large-scale hostilities in Asia. The first occurred in early 1673 and related to a French relief force from Surat seeking shelter in Bombay. Soon after capturing San Thomé, La Haye had sent letters to the Surat *conseil* requesting that Baron proceed to the Coromandel Coast with as many men and as much money as possible. Before an expedition could be outfitted, however, M. de l'Estoille, the *com-pagnie* chief in Persia, reached Gujarat and informed the *conseil* that its trade in that kingdom was threatened because a proper embassy had not been sent to the Safavid court to renegotiate Shah Abbas II's 1666 *farman*. Gueston thereupon decided to lead an embassy to Isfahan, thus jeopardiz-ing Baron's mission, since it was believed the cost of outfitting two expedi-tions simultaneously would be prohibitive. There was also talk of sending an embassy to Agra to present Aurangzeb with gifts from Louis XIV, including a richly decorated coach that La Haye's fleet had brought and that had been sitting in the *compagnie*'s warehouse ever since. In the end, the *conseil* had authorized all of these missions, but at diminished levels. Baron's contingent had sailed from Swally in February 1673 and included the refurbished man-of-war *Bayonnais,* the royal flute *Guillot,* and the *compagnie* storeship *St-Denis.* Van Goens had deployed a fleet of twenty ships along the Malabar Coast to intercept this relief force. Baron's small squadron had encountered Van Goens's ships near Bombay and put into that harbor on 21 February. There they were "rec.d with much friendship" by Aungier, who undoubtedly feared a Dutch attack. To forestall such an attack, the English president and Baron "advised togeather touching the more convenient laying [of] the French Shipps with ours in a line close under the Command of Our Guns." While Van Goens's fleet probably could have stormed Bombay, the Dutch admiral left the English enclave unmolested. In doing so, he was evidently deterred not by the military power of this ramshackle Anglo-French alliance but by the fear that an attack might unwittingly create the type of firm anti-Dutch Asian alliance that Colbert's ambassadors had failed to achieve in years of negotiations. After more than a week in Bombay, Baron's ships sailed south and reached San Thomé in early May.[11]

The second incident that threatened to upset London's careful policy was the Anglo-Dutch naval engagement of September 1673, fought some twenty leagues south of Masulipatnam, off the town of Petapoli. This battle, the largest naval encounter of the Third Dutch War in Asia, pitted an English Company fleet of ten ships under William Basse against a VOC fleet of eighteen to twenty ships titularly under Van Goens's power but in fact commanded by Cornelius van Quaelbergen. Basse's fleet had reached the Coromandel Coast the previous spring and spent several months sailing along that coast avoiding the Dutch. On the first of September, the two fleets had finally met. Emboldened by reports from William Langhorn stating that the VOC ships were poorly armed, thinly manned, and already weakened from periodic encounters with the French, Basse had offered battle to van Quaelbergen's larger squadron. Although the English fleet was probably superior in terms of seamanship and gunnery skills, Basse's captains acquitted themselves poorly, and three of his ships were captured. Nevertheless, van Quaelbergen's fleet also suffered heavy damage, and he could not press the advantage. The battle had ended with heavy losses on each side and no definitive victor. La Haye, of course, was overjoyed to hear of this encounter several days later, as Basse's remaining ships limped into the Madras roadsteads. He immediately wrote to Langhorn again proposing an offensive alliance aimed at the VOC. Yet, even in these bleak circumstances the English Governor refused to consider the matter. Langhorn was so adamant to avoid close dealings with the French in the weeks after Petapoli—a period in which hostilities involving the English might logically have escalated into a full-blown naval and land campaign, at least in India—that he even prevented Basse from purchasing badly needed naval stores to repair his ships in San Thomé.[12]

Langhorn's attitude toward the French admirably reflected the overwhelmingly mercantile priorities of the Court of Committees during the Dutch War. The idea of forging an Asian alliance with France was never seriously considered in London. Similarly, La Haye's calls for substantial assistance in the face of the Qutb Shahi siege and Dutch aggression were a priori doomed to failure in Bombay and Madras. As Langhorn so succinctly phrased it, "The French desire no better than to have us to joyne with them. . . . We will never be drawne to doe a thing so much against our Interest and our Inclinations."[13] While Charles's ill-conceived alliance with Louis and the joint campaign in Europe had certainly complicated the issue of lending support to Colbert's *compagnie*, Langhorn proved more than able to meet this delicate challenge. The English Governor adroitly played these competing powers against one another from mid-1672, with La Haye's unwelcome arrival on the Coromandel Coast, until late 1674, when the danger of large-scale war with the Dutch was over. As Langhorn's correspondence for this tumultuous period demonstrates, his strategy was relatively simple: he subtly pressured Abul Hasan to expel the French from San Thomé; he consistently rebuffed La Haye's calls for an alliance by citing the retribution this would invite from Abul Hasan; he avoided Qutb Shahi demands for assistance against the French by citing Charles's European alliance with Louis; and he forestalled a Dutch attack on Madras by invoking the protection of Abul Hasan and entering into secret talks with Van Goens that yielded a neutrality pact of sorts and the promise of joint pressure on San Thomé. As he was able to report to London in the fall of 1673, his strategy was eminently successful: "Wee are yett safe and quiett in the midst of 3 Nations in Armes; the one our Open Enemy."[14] The English directors were no doubt encouraged by reports from Aungier and Langhorn; they were also reassured by events in London that increasingly convinced them that their belief in a short-lived alliance with His Most Christian Majesty and thus a short-lived war with the VOC would indeed prove prophetic.

As early as mid-1673, English public opinion had swung sharply against the war thanks in part to the religious imbroglio between the Crown and Parliament. This struggle revolved around Charles's Declaration of Indulgence of 1672, the retaliatory Test Act, and perhaps most importantly, James's public profession of the Catholic faith and subsequent marriage to Mary of Modena, the daughter of one of Louis's Italian clients, replete with a Bourbon dowry. Of course, the deteriorating military and diplomatic situation in the Anglo-French alliance hardly helped solidify the dubious popularity of the alliance and campaign. In the fall of that year, or at about the time that James married his Catholic princess, news reached London that Bonn had fallen to the combined forces of William of Orange and Montecuccoli and that a Dutch force had recaptured New York. Charles, rebuffed in his efforts to raise a war supply from an increasingly unruly Commons, was forced to prorogue the Parliament until January 1674. By that time, widespread opposition to the war in England, a rising in Scotland against Lauderdale's policies, and the Essex-Ranelagh dispute in Ireland had reduced Charles to a desperate man, obsessed with "finding any possible means of continuing a conflict upon which his honor had become staked" or, failing that, a means of extricating himself gracefully from the entire mess. The States General afforded him the latter with its advantageous terms for peace of 22 January 1674 (O.S.), skillfully leaked to leading MP's that same day. By 9 February (O.S.) the royal seal had been set on the so-called Treaty of Westminster, taking England out of the war without loss of territory—New York being restored—and depriving Louis of his principal ally.[15]

The directors were overjoyed with this news and promptly dispatched packets to Surat, Bombay, and Madras with the glad tidings.[16] At a crucial juncture of the company's history, when the alliance with Louis had exposed all of its valued holdings to the ravages of the VOC, prudent policies at home and in Asia, emanating from the impersonal bureaucratic structure of the company, had allowed the EIC to emerge from the Dutch War largely unscathed. None of the company's main factories had been lost, and while trade had been interrupted somewhat, it could easily be reestablished now that the conflict was over. The ability of the English Company to remain essentially a noncombatant during the Third Dutch War and the company's continued emphasis on trade over territorial expansion and military adventures would stand it in good stead as the seventeenth century progressed. This entrepreneurialism was well reflected in Langhorn's comment on the events surrounding the siege of San Thomé: while La Haye was "as desirous to embroyle us with the Moors, as the Dutch themselves . . . [o]ur business here was traffique and not warr."[17] The English Company had already abandoned the traditional mania for pepper in favor of cotton piece goods. Although these "calicoes" had long been utilized in the inter-Asiatic or country trade as a substitute for bullion or European goods, demand in Europe for them had exploded after 1650. The company had increasingly focused it activities on the loci of this trade: Gujarat, the Coromandel Coast, and Bengal. As the original correspondence reflects, Aungier was especially sensitive to price rises in calicoes engendered by the arrival of the French and feared for his key factories in light of the 1672–74 conflict. In the wake of Charles's withdrawal from the war, and given Caron's old-fashioned notions on the trade and La Haye's problems, the trade in calicoes could resume. And resume it did. Between 1668 and 1681, the company's exports in Bengal piece goods alone increased 450 percent.[18] While the English Company would also abandon its rather pristine mercantile entrepreneurialism—especially in the next century as the Mughal empire collapsed—the prudence of the London directors and men like Aungier and Langhorn during the pivotal years of the Dutch War would enable the EIC to seize every opportunity offered by future events.

In Goa, the years 1672–1674 were also crucial ones in the long history of the *Estado da India*. Following the grievous losses of 1622–1663, the Portuguese Crown was in the midst of a concerted reform program for its Asian empire at the exact time that Colbert's project began to escalate. Breaking with the policy set by his illustrious father, João IV, toward favoring the interests of the "milch-cow" of Brazil over those of the rest of the tridimensional empire, the prince regent had instead decided that the *Estado*, "the most important and glorious of all the conquests," demanded special attention for economic, religious, and historical reasons. Pedro and his Overseas Council had thereupon resolved to salvage what remained of the *Estado* by initiating reforms that would allow it to become a profitable, as well as glorious, Crown holding. The most perplexing question of course had been how to achieve these much-desired results at a time when events in Europe were clearly pointing to a renewed Dutch War that might again place the tenuous holdings of the Asian state at risk. It was at this decisive moment that Colbert and Saint-Romain had launched their diplomatic initiative to induce the Portuguese into an anti-Dutch Asian alliance.

The dismal example of the English alliance during the 1660s had been more than sufficient to convince Pedro and his closest advisors like Nuno Alvares Pereira de Melo, the duke of Cadaval, that internal regeneration, not external dependence on one of Portugal's trading rivals in Asia, was the surest means of rehabilitating the *Estado*. Despite the sustained lobbying of the French party at court, championed by his alluring bride and the marquis de Fronteira, Pedro had politely but firmly rebuffed Saint-Romain's overtures. The Lisbon hierarchy elected to remain neutral at the outset of Louis XIV's Dutch campaign and, while their European rivals in the Asian trade were busy warring with one another, to begin the timely implementation of internal reforms in the *Estado*, orchestrated by Luis de Mendonça Furtado. By early 1672, Mendonça Furtado had barely begun addressing the plethora of administrative, religious, economic, and military problems that had greeted him upon his arrival, when he was confronted with demands from La Haye and Caron for an anti-VOC alliance. For a man of Mendonça Furtado's lineage and experience, it must have been exceedingly difficult to decline this tempting offer of revenge against his old rivals. Nevertheless, he had rejected the plans of Louis XIV's viceroy, as he informed Lisbon, strictly for military and strategic reasons.[19] According to the Abbé Carré, who passed through Goa on his overland trip from Paris to the Coromandel Coast, petty jealousy may have also played a role. In his account, Carré wrote that Mendonça Furtado could "not bear any other European in India taking the name and status of Viceroy." He therefore harbored a hidden "fury" against the French campaign and did everything he could to weaken the fleet by injuring "its finances and personnel." The Portuguese viceroy had overcharged for provisions and actively encouraged desertion among the French crews and regiments. While Carré's account is clearly overwrought, significant numbers had indeed voted with their feet to embrace the charms of Golden Goa instead of renewed rigors aboard the cramped men-of-war. When the Persian squadron departed, there had been "enough Frenchmen left behind in Goa to form two companies of soldiers of whom the viceroy was very proud calling them his 'Valenters.'"[20]

After January 1672, Mendonça Furtado had monitored the movements of the fleet and the course of the French campaign as best he could. He had reacted cautiously to the unsettling news of La Haye's unexpected advances at the expense of the Dutch Company during that year. While reports on the easy occupation of Trincomalee in the face of Van Goens's fleet were no doubt puzzling, his decades of fighting experience against the VOC convinced the Portuguese viceroy that La Haye would have an exceedingly difficult time solidifying his gains on that island unless additional reinforcements arrived from Europe.[21] João Pereira de Faria's letter of July 1672, informing him of the French storming of San Thomé and the impending exodus of the exiled Portuguese merchant community in Madras to that town in search of their erstwhile property, required a more forceful response. To forestall any actions that would implicitly recognize French sovereignty over San Thomé, Mendonça Furtado had promptly issued orders specifying that the Portuguese residents in Madras should remain in the English enclave until such time as the matter could be formally addressed in Europe: "The city of San Thomé belongs to His Majesty. . . . [T]he vassals of His Majesty [should] not change the state they are in." In the meantime, Pedro's subjects were to refrain from taking up arms or engaging in any other activity that might advance the French cause in that region: "[T]hese subjects will not proceed properly in taking up arms so quickly, because in such a matter one should not do anything without precise orders from this government." In his letters to Lisbon, the viceroy advised the prince regent that he should do everything possible in Europe to obtain the rightful restitution of San Thomé to the *Estado*.[22] Evidently, Mendonça Furtado never regretted his original decision to forego a combined military campaign against the VOC. He had already concluded that "there is no doubt Majesty that the French do not have the power in India to oppose the Dutch, who are extremely powerful." Moreover, he recognized the limitation of the forces at his own command.[23]

The Portuguese viceroy had therefore devoted most of his energies during the course of war to implementing internal reforms. To bolster the military forces at his disposal, he strove to enforce Pedro's decree of April 1669, which specified that all infantrymen upon their arrival would immediately be formed into companies and dispatched to outlying forts without leave to visit Old Goa, where it was believed they were corrupted into deserting. Acting on a December 1669 *consulta* of the Overseas Council, the viceroy also formed a permanent *terco* of 500 to 600 men, with well-qualified officers, financed with the money that the *Estado* had been forced to contribute for the peace with the United Provinces. Mendonça Furtado also sought to reestablish effective control over outlying areas of the *Estado,* like Macão and Mozambique, that had largely fended for themselves during the tumultuous early years of the Restoration. Pedro and his viceroy were also determined to end some of the more glaring abuses of the Goa Inquisition and the various religious orders established in Asia. As Mendonça Furtado recognized, it was vital for the economic rehabilitation of the Eastern empire to encourage rich indigenous merchants to remain within the territorial confines of the *Estado.* The maritime interchange between Lisbon and Goa, the so-called *Carreira da India,* which was virtually moribund by 1663, also underwent a renaissance during the early 1670s, with regular sailings becoming the rule.[24] As Francis Parry, the English ambassador in Lisbon, noted, three "richly laden" ships arrived in the Tagus in the summer of 1672 alone "which is soe good a fortune as hath not been knowne here since Portugall hath been a kingdome of itselfe."[25]

In this campaign, Pedro and Mendonça Furtado were even willing to consider reforming the monarchical monopolism that had generally dominated Portuguese exploitation of the Asian trade since the days of da Gama and Albuquerque, at least in part in response to the entrepreneurial structures of the English, Dutch, and French Companies. In a 1672 move, the prince regent declared free trade *(commercio livre)* for Portuguese subjects on the east coast of Africa. There were also plans to form a joint-stock trading company for the trade to be financed largely through the contributions of the New Christians in return for protection against the Goa inquisition.[26] By 1674, as Aungier was reluctantly forced to admit with respect to the traditional problems of administrative corruption ("their evill government") and the abuses of the religious orders and nobles, which together "eat up the revenue," Mendonça Furtado "hath raised them much, both in the one and the other."[27] Between 1669 and 1672, the decision to avoid involvement in the Dutch War had allowed the Portuguese Crown to initiate reforms that were well underway by the end of Mendonça Furtado's first three-year term as viceroy. These advances would eventually alter the nature of the Portuguese presence in Asia and establish geopolitical and financial stability in the wake of decades of costly setbacks. While the *orçamento,* or state budget, for 1630 revealed a net deficit of over 150,000 xerafins, by the end of the 1670s a surplus of over 271,000 xerafins would be achieved.[28] This newfound stability would allow the *Estado da India* to continue as an economic and religious force in the Indian Ocean basin long after the fate of Colbert's project had been decided.

In Batavia, of course, the years between 1672 and 1674 constituted one of the most crucial periods in the history of the VOC, during which Maetsuycker and his council were forced to meet perhaps the most concerted commercial and military challenge to their holdings of the entire seventeenth century. At the outset of the war, two factors had combined to place the Dutch Asian empire in jeopardy. First, the symbiotic nature of Louis XIV's dynastic campaign in Europe and Colbert's predatory mercantilism in the *outre-mer* aimed at the United Provinces that allowed France to exploit the sinews of the Bourbon state for the attainment of a shared goal. The most visible manifestation of this conjuncture had been the dispatching of La Haye's grand fleet at a time judged appropriate to complement the beginning of the Continental campaign. The second factor was the overextended, and thereby vulnerable, nature of the Dutch empire by the early 1670s. In large measure, this state of affairs had resulted from the inexorable corruption of the pristine entrepreneurialism of the United Dutch Company over the course of the seventeenth century. Linschoten's *Itinerario* had warned that the company should avoid the most glaring mistakes of the Portuguese *Estado*, including inland territorial expansion and onerous military expenditures. Nevertheless, by the 1650s, the Dutch Company had fallen prey to the same vices that afflicted the monarchical monopolism of the Iberians. As Aungier noted in his perceptive letter, the VOC had risen by "their sword and violence" and were therefore doomed to "maintayne them [their places] by the same means, which will force them to continuall vast expence of men and treasure."[29] Along these lines, the Dutch experience on Ceylon had prompted Maetsuycker to lament: "I think the Company will never accomplish their proposed profit . . . for there is always one thing or another in the way which causes the profitable proposal to vanish, while the charge remaines certaine, by which the Company is burdened for what lamentable complaints are made for want of People, ready money, provisions, [and] ammunition of war."[30]

By the early 1670s, the Dutch Asian empire had therefore come to resemble the Portuguese *Estado* of a quarter-century earlier. Dangerous warfare and powerful enemies threatening the mother country in Europe, far-flung possessions to protect in Asia, a host of indigenous rulers anxious for revenge for decades of abuse at the hands of European exploiters, and a well-financed and seemingly committed rival in Asia were poised to pounce on the entire tottering edifice. The expense associated with such policies and the various wars with indigenous powers from Malabar to the Moluccas had rendered the Dutch empire extremely vulnerable to a well-coordinated attack by a vigorous rival. As the correspondence between Amsterdam and Batavia from 1670 to 1672 reflects, Maetsuycker and his council knew this, as did the Seventeen.[31] It was this inviting situation and the conjuncture of dynastic and mercantile priorities in Paris that gave the French Asian project every chance of success. Confronted by such daunting circumstances, Maetsuycker had responded with a cautious and defensive strategy at the outset of the conflict. The company's most prized possessions in Indonesia were reinforced, and fleets were organized and sent to guard Java, Bangka, and the sea routes to the north, the South China Sea, and Japan. Adriaen Roothaes's fleet guarded shipping along the Malabar Coast north to Surat and Persia, while Van Goens of course had been given the responsibility for guarding the approaches to Ceylon and monitoring the movements of La Haye's fleet.[32] In Amsterdam, meanwhile, the Seventeen recognized from the outset that their ability to reinforce Batavia would in large part be determined by the course of the war on the Continent: "[W]e must keep ourselves on the defensive, ready for any emergency, which will greatly depend on the failure or success of our armies in Europe."[33]

From 1672 to 1674, the *Heeren XVII*, Maetsuycker, and by extension, the States General all reacted with vigor and skill to the French challenge at home and in Asia. This spirited response was ultimately grounded in the unique relationship between ruling oligarchy and private enterprise that existed in the United Provinces. According to Jonathan Israel, this "high degree of interaction" between the ruling oligarchy and private enterprise allowed these groups to regulate "internal competition within the Dutch entrepôt, in the interests of the entrepôt as a whole," and to withstand a succession of economic rivals in the quest for hegemony in the world trade.[34] The example of the early years of the Dutch War also suggests that this arrangement proved equally capable in responding to overt military threats to the position of the VOC, as were embodied most menacingly in Colbert's grand design. Even during the disastrous early stages of the war, when Louis's armies advanced virtually unopposed, and it appeared that all might indeed be lost, the Dutch directors did their utmost to dispatch ships, troops, and cash to Batavia. In May 1672, a fleet departed for the East Indies carrying over 3000 men and a good deal of specie to assist Maetsuycker in the campaign. As the Seventeen noted, "by the present fleet we are sending so large a number of soldiers that Ceylon can also have its necessary share." The following fall, Batavia was informed of the election of William of Orange as stadholder and the formation of a new army, events which were hoped to "turn the tide." While lamenting that "this war has stopped trade over the greater part of Europe" and fearing that "we shall be able to dispose of but a small amount of the goods brought home by the [1672] fleet," the Seventeen had "resolved to send further reinforcements to India consisting of 5000 men. They will leave in the Spring." In 1673, stormy weather and English naval actions involving Saint Helena had taken a heavy toll on the returning fleet of that year: "These have [all] been heavy blows to the Company, which seem harder in these Sad Times. In consequence of these several calumities we find that we shall not be able to send you any ready money at present." Yet additional ships and men would sail from Amsterdam in early 1674, the Seventeen grounded in the belief that "[a]s long as by the Grace of God we keep the Supremacy in the Indian Seas . . . we need not fear any unforeseen attack from our enemies in those quarters."[35]

This overwhelming commitment toward reinforcing Batavia in the midst of the life-and-death campaign against Louis admirably demonstrates (1) the high priority placed on the Asian trade by the hybrid economic and political elite in the United Provinces and (2) the recognition in Amsterdam and The Hague that European and Asian interests were fundamentally linked. This attitude stood in marked contrast to the situation in France, where Colbert was never able to entrench such priorities among a bourgeoisie firmly wedded to sinecures and safe investments in land and venality of office that were part and parcel of the Bourbon state. Just as importantly, as the war progressed, it became obvious that the overwhelming majority of the aristocratic ruling elite in Paris discerned no vital link between interests in Europe and those in Asia. Dynastic and geopolitical goals in Europe remained dominant; *outre-mer* mercantile or even military goals in Asia remained decidedly and definitively ancillary. The Seventeen, in late 1673, may have admitted that many of their forts "would not be able to offer much resistance" should "a considerable force be brought against them." This vulnerability, however, need not have troubled Maetsuycker, since in their view—a view that ultimately proved to be correct—"there [was] very little prospect of France sending any such forces out to India [next year]."[36] In such circumstances, the governor-general was able to conclude the Third Dutch War in Asia with relative ease and peace of mind.

After receiving definitive word on the outbreak of European hostilities in October 1672, Maetsuycker had originally deviated very little from his cautious policy. A fleet of seven ships under Lucas Van der Dussen had been ordered to cruise off Pulau Tioman to convoy the much-prized annual Japan fleet. Cornelissen Van der Meer had been sent to cruise off Bangka with another seven ships, while six ships had been sent to blockade Bantam. Van Goens had been instructed to continue his patrols between Cochin and Ceylon and to avoid involvement in the initial siege of San Thomé.[37] In the early spring of 1673, the governor-general and his council had resolved to abandon this moderate strategy in favor of a much more aggressive policy, designed to clear the Asian seas of the remnants of Colbert's grand fleet and to destroy French pretensions in the trade. The welcome news of regular reinforcements from Amsterdam, combined with reports on the lack of fresh ships, men, and money that had reached La Haye from Paris and Lorient, convinced Maetsuycker that the balance of power in the Asian war had irrefutably shifted in his favor. The French viceroy's squadron had been reduced to only two serviceable men-of-war, a few supply ships, depleted stores of foodstuff and munitions, and less than 700 men. By early 1673, the governor-general and his council had also concluded that the much-feared anti-VOC triple alliance would, in all probability, not materialize. Accordingly, Dutch agents in Hyderabad were instructed to begin negotiations with Abul Hasan toward a renewed joint siege of San Thomé. A deal was swiftly concluded: the Qutb Shahi king would receive the town after its capitulation, while the Dutch would receive "all the French artillery . . . and exemption from all taxes for ten years throughout the kingdom of Golconda."[38] By mid-June, Van Goens and a fleet of sixteen ships had appeared off San Thomé, anxious to fulfill the terms of this agreement. Much to the Dutch admiral's surprise, he would discover that La Haye and his remaining men-of-war had earlier sailed north in the hope of concluding a final agreement with Abul Hasan and arranging a formal grant of San Thomé.

After lifting the initial Qutb Shahi siege in March 1673, La Haye had ordered his men to bring in supplies from the surrounding countryside, thus solving the garrison's most pressing problem. Nevertheless, he was still confronted by the disturbing lack of military and monetary reinforcements from home, a matter entirely out of his hands, as well as the necessity of reaching a formal agreement with Hyderabad that would preclude a renewed siege and a likely Qutb Shahi-VOC alliance. By the end of the month, the French viceroy had developed a plan to resolve all of these difficulties, centered around an attack on the richest port city in Abul Hasan's domains, Masulipatnam, some two hundred miles to the north. As he explained in a letter to Louis XIV, "After having defeated and razed the trenches of the Muslims . . . and obliging them to withdraw with more than 2000 horse and 10,000 infantry . . . I left for Masulipatnam . . . to oblige the king of Golconda to make a peace and [to find] in this a way to defend myself from the Dutch who threaten us, as apparently they were preparing to ally themselves with the Muslims and attack."[39] The viceroy intended to sail north with as many of his remaining ships as possible to capture all the shipping in the roadstead of Masulipatnam in order to raise needed cash and to begin a blockade of the harbor that would deprive Hyderabad of badly needed custom revenues, thereby forcing Abul Hasan and Sayyid Muzzafer to make peace. While this bold plan may have been conceptually sound, the French badly bungled the execution of its main points, thus exposing the remnants of Colbert's once grand fleet to the military and diplomatic dangers that La Haye was so intent on avoiding.

Departing from San Thomé on 10 April with the *Breton* and *Flamand,* with François Martin, his personal guards, 300 French troops, and three companies of Hindu lascars on board, the viceroy foolishly insisted on deciding matters relating to navigation, a science with which he was not altogether familiar. As a result, the French squadron overshot Masulipatnam by nearly thirty miles, thereafter encountered contrary prevailing winds, and lost any hope of surprising the shipping in Masulipatnam. A listless attack on the roadstead yielded only four paltry prizes. La Haye then dispatched Martin, an old hand at the *compagnie* factory there, ashore to negotiate affairs with Abul Hasan's local governor. An ill-advised truce resulting from these talks afforded more that adequate time for the Qutb Shahi commander and local VOC agents to reinforce the place with Persian cavalry and Dutch infantry over the ensuing weeks, effectively undermining any French plan to storm the town. Abul Hasan and Sayyid Muzzafer, irked by the expense of the first siege and ever mindful of renewed hostilities with the Marathas and Aurangzeb, made it clear in a *farman* of early May that they were willing to negotiate the matter and indeed cede San Thomé, provided suitable "gifts" and an annual rent could be arranged. La Haye, however, was either unwilling or unable to pay Hyderabad's asking price for a formal grant of the town. His unyielding stance on this crucial point not only caused a serious falling-out with Martin, by far his most able *compagnie* ally, but also ensured the failure of the negotiations and the resumption of open hostilities. The viceroy's halfhearted "embassy" to Hyderabad under M. Châteaupers, a gentleman trader from Orleans, in late May was foredoomed to failure. Châteaupers had no retinue to speak of, he had been given a mere 500 écus for expenses, neither he nor his interpreter were familiar with court protocol at Hyderabad, and the presents he carried were far from appropriate for the occasion. La Haye sent along a musket and a pair of pistols for Abul Hasan, with instructions to inform the king that "as a soldier, he had no more suitable and valuable offering to make." Most importantly, Châteaupers was ordered to reject any offer that included sizable financial gifts as a precondition.[40]

After nearly six weeks of anchoring fruitlessly off Masulipatnam, the small French squadron with two prizes sailed south on 30 May, unaware that Van Goens's fleet awaited. A fierce gale on 2 June scattered La Haye's ships.[41] Late on the afternoon of 21 June, the *Breton,* with La Haye aboard, approached San Thomé and the imposing Dutch fleet anchored offshore. The viceroy, ever anxious for military *gloire* and determined to rehabilitate his reputation after the debacle of Masulipatnam, resolved to fight his way through Van Goens's ships in order to enter the roadstead. Soon surrounded by the six Dutch ships sent out to intercept her, the *Breton* "opened fire with such effect that both [of the closest] were dismasted and shattered by these broadsides"; the other four were then received "with the same vigor and with such good result that the two nearest were dismasted and drew off." Unfortunately, a heavy squall came up that forced the *Breton* to tack and head out into the Bay of Bengal.[42] As Langhorn was grudgingly forced to admit when he subsequently described this encounter, "the Vice Roys Single Ship once baffled the whole [Dutch] fleet in our Sights, disabled one of them and [would have] forced through all 16 Sayle of them, if the wind had not turned against him."[43] After a short voyage south that included a disconcerting brush with William Basse's fleet and discussions with Bellanger de Lespinay at the fledgling post of Pondicherry, the *Breton* and her crew were able to evade the Dutch fleet searching for them and anchor before San Thomé on 5 July 1673.[44]

Upon his return, La Haye was forced to reexamine the strategic and military situation in San Thomé and on the Coromandel Coast. In his absence, the Abbé Carré had at last joined the fleet, bearing despatches from Louis XIV and Colbert on the outbreak of hostilities in Europe. The cleric had thereupon moved to Madras, where he spent the next five months valiantly struggling to arrange provisions for the French garrison, in spite of Baba Sahib's mounting threats to halt traffic between the neighboring towns and Langhorn's subtle antagonism toward La Haye's force.[45] After departing from Bombay, Baron's small naval contingent had managed to avoid Van Goens's fleet and anchored before San Thomé in early May. The reinforcements and provisions the director brought, however, were far from inspiring. As Carré described a visit to the *Bayonnais,* "I stayed some hours in private conversation with M. Baron, who astonished me by the little help in men and money he had brought." In La Haye's words, while Baron provided "some munitions," he had brought "little money and neither rice nor bread."[46] By all accounts, de Rebrey had justified his selection as governor: he had purchased provisions in surrounding villages despite increasing harassment from Baba Sahib's patrols, he had continued the work of repairing the town's defenses, he had successfully attacked a Qutb Shahi force near the town, and, most impressively, he had orchestrated the effective French resistance to Van Goens's heavy bombardment of the town on 16 June heralding the arrival of the VOC in earnest.[47] A general review of the garrison in early July also revealed that La Haye commanded over 3000 men, mostly Hindu lascars, as well as four ships, including the men-of-war *Breton* and *Bayonnais,* in the roadstead. Nevertheless, La Haye had undertaken the Masulipatnam enterprise with three objectives in mind: to arrange easy money, to force Abul Hasan into concluding a peace, and in doing so to undermine a VOC-Qutb Shahi alliance. He had failed to achieve any of these goals, and as a result a combined land and sea blockade and siege was in the offing.

For a time, events conspired to retard the prosecution of a renewed siege. Châteaupers's mission caused Abul Hasan and Sayyid Muzzafer to hesitate for a time; petty disputes also developed in the vicinity of San Thomé between Baba Sahib and Van Goens. La Haye also launched a devastating pre-emptive attack on Trimbak Bussora Raju's camp on 20 August that forced the general to withdraw with most of his remaining troops to Poonamalle.[48] By early October, however, these obstacles had been overcome, and an effective siege had been mounted. During the course of the summer, Abul Hasan and his ministers were definitively persuaded to embrace hostilities once again by the feebleness of Châteaupers's mission and the largesse of an envoy from Van Goens and other Dutch agents in Hyderabad. The overly cautious Baba Sahib was replaced by the more aggressive Chennupalli Mirza, and large-scale reinforcements were sent to Ponnamallee. Van Goens, placing van Quaelbergen in charge of the Dutch fleet with orders to intercept all vessels approaching the French-held town, organized a ground force of nearly 300 Europeans in Pulicat. This detachment reached the environs of San Thomé in mid-September, pitched camp near the pagoda of Triplicane, and in conjunction with the Qutb Shahi cavalry began to interdict all manner of provisions destined for the French garrison. By the end of October, Van Goens was convinced that it was only a matter of time before La Haye capitulated, and the siege was no longer worthy of his considerable skills. He left Antoni Paviljoen in charge of the Dutch troops and headed back to Ceylon and the continuing war with Rajah Sinha II.[49]

La Haye did his utmost to overcome the formidable challenge embodied in this siege. He had five main alternatives: substantial aid from Madras, meaningful reinforcements from France, substantial assistance from friendly indigenous rulers along the Coromandel Coast, military action on land that would break the alliance and lift the siege, and naval action that might accomplish the same result. During the next ten months, the viceroy tried to exploit all of these possibilities. La Haye's final attempt to overcome Langhorn's antipathy came in the fall of 1673 and related to Basse's squadron. Both before and after the notable engagement off Petapoli, he sought to arrange an anti-Dutch alliance and a joint attack on Van Goens's fleet, with no success whatsoever. Soon thereafter, news reached him of a meeting held in Madras between Langhorn and Van Goens, in which joint pressure on the French garrison was discussed. La Haye wrote a strongly worded letter to the English governor, complaining of duplicity, and compiled a letter to Charles II outlining Langhorn's contemptible behavior. Faced with a definitive rebuff from Madras, the viceroy could only hope that support from France would at last materialize.[50] As Aungier noted about this time, "The French at St. Thoma hitherto have held out stoutly, notwithstanding the Dutch & Mores . . . but if the French King sends them no recrutes suddenly tis thought they cannot keep the place much longer."[51] While he could not directly affect the machinations in Paris and Flanders regarding this pivotal question, La Haye did dispatch the capable Carré back to France in September 1673 to press the case for regular reinforcements with Louis XIV and Colbert. The following month, Carré reached Surat. There he found that M. de Chevreuil, sent aboard the *compagnie* ship *Soleil d'Orient* with 200,000 livres for the fleet, had wasted four months in Gujarat, where some of this money had been appropriated by the directors and the rest had been "buried in the sand" under de Chevreuil's lodgings at Swally. As the royal agent of the *marine* lamented, "How do you think I can hunt for the Viceroy in this forsaken country[?] . . . I was simply told to take this sum to Surat."[52]

News of this money reached San Thomé in late 1673, and it prompted La Haye to send out an envoy to indigenous rulers along the west coast of India in search of provisions and troops that would be paid for with promissory notes or bills of exchange to be honored in Surat. Much to his credit, the viceroy did not allow the acrimony of Masulipatnam to interfere with his judgment regarding this crucial mission, and François Martin was selected. The envoy carried a letter for the hapless de Chevreuil specifying that 70,000 livres were to be turned over to him, a sum that would be augmented by a draft for 60,000 livres that Baron stated would be honored by the directors in Surat.[53] In the months that followed, Martin held talks with Sher Khan Lodi in Valikandapuran and with Nasir Mohammed in Porto Novo. He managed to use bills of exchange to obtain an immediate loan of 1000 pagodas as well as several detachments of local cavalry. Given the severe shortage of available specie, Martin and Bellanger de Lespinay also began the policy of intercepting indigenous craft loaded with rice and other foodstuff that plied a regular trade on that coast from Pondicherry, sending these ill-gotten cargoes north toward San Thomé. The Dutch, however, were soon able to end this "pirating" and pressure local rulers like Sher Khan Lodi in order to undermine Martin's mission. A fatal blow came on 20 May 1674, when Martin learned that his bills of exchange had not been honored in Surat. Evidently, the ravages of the directors on the original 200,000 livres had not left enough money to cover the envoy's notes. In a panic, de Chevreuil had salvaged what he could in the form of cash and still more bills of exchange and, in an attempt to save what remained of his distinctly unpromising career, had begun the overland journey to Pondicherry. In early September, Martin and the *marine* agent had traveled together to Valikanpuran, but the capable Sher Khan Lodi had balked at further negotiations when the Frenchmen produced worthless bills of exchange to hire his troops.[54]

Although La Haye's attempts to use military stratagems to lift the siege were pursued with much vigor and innovation, in the end they too were ineffective against the VOC-Qutb Shahi siege. The viceroy twice tried to break the naval blockade of San Thomé and undermine what he viewed as the shaky alliance of his enemies. In late October 1673, the remaining French ships, the *Breton, Bayonnais, Guillot,* and *St-Robert,* mounted an ineffective attack on Paviljoen's anchorage off Triplicane. La Haye blamed this setback on the uninspired leadership of his captains, berating them at length upon their return to San Thomé. These officers took their revenge during a storm the following month, when they abandoned the anchorage before the town with their ships and headed south, never to return.[55] Colbert's grand squadron, perhaps the most powerful European fleet to sail in Asian waters up until that time, had been reduced to a single ship, the *Breton,* anchored before San Thomé. In March 1674, this man-of-war under the able command of de Maisonneuve tried, for the last time, to break through the blockade and make for Pondicherry to seek aid. Although de Maisonneuve acquitted himself well in an ensuing engagement with several of Paviljoen's frigates, the *Breton* was ultimately compelled to return to San Thomé. Soon after anchoring, at least fifteen men deserted, fearing that the ship would again be used in combat. Recognizing that discipline was deteriorating, La Haye henceforth made service on the *Breton* voluntary. In late March, he also had a large cache of munitions landed in order to prepare for the final option of blowing up the town and escaping with as many men as possible aboard the man-of-war. Nevertheless, even this rather desperate strategy was denied to him when the *Breton* was caught at anchor in a violent storm in early May and wrecked a short distance south of the town.[56]

On land, the results were much the same. Although La Haye led frequent sorties in an effort to retard the advance of Chennupalli's positions, the deprivations engendered inside the town by the siege intensified as time went on. These increasingly difficult conditions prompted the viceroy to propose a general attack on Chennupalli's camp and Paviljoen's positions as early as January 1674. There was, however, a good deal of opposition to this plan by the remaining French officers. After a good deal of discussion, it was decided to attempt to hold out for three more months, in the hope that reinforcements would arrive from France, or that the money believed to be in Surat could be put to efficient use. The town's defenses were still very strong, and if the "useless" people inside San Thomé's massive walls were expelled, provisions on hand would easily last that long. La Haye temporarily abandoned his plans for a general attack, and instead arranged a grant of safe conduct for the women and children inside the town from Paviljoen, with over 1200 persons departing soon after the new year.[57] During the long months that followed, La Haye frequently exhorted his men with calls for sacrifice on behalf of Louis XIV and his *gloire* in an effort to bolster their resolve. But these lofty ideals were a very poor substitute for adequate rations; desertion continued to rise, while discipline and morale deteriorated. On 19 February, La Haye led some 300 men on a raid to a nearby village and returned with over 150 bags of rice. A night raid of 3 March also yielded large quantities of rice. These actions, nonetheless, were mere stopgap measures. As it became evident that no meaningful reinforcements were going to appear from France, Surat, or Martin's mission, La Haye embraced the idea of a gradually escalating pitched battle as the only means to break the siege. Several times during the spring and summer of 1674 the viceroy attempted to lure Chennupalli Mirza and Paviljoen into such an engagement close to the bastions of the town, frequently exposing himself to capture as bait. His opponents, however, were far too experienced to fall into such an obvious trap. Instead, they were content to remain behind their fortified positions and allow the French to fall to the inexorable privations of the siege.[58]

On 13 June 1674, Paviljoen first called on the French garrison to surrender. La Haye rejected this demand with considerable élan, but his bravado was at odds with the reality of the situation: provisions were running dangerously low, disease was spreading, and desertion was climbing. Nevertheless, the viceroy remained convinced throughout that summer that a successful pitched battle with his enemies would destroy the Qutb Shahi-Dutch alliance and save what remained of the garrison. In late August, his doubts on the tenacity of the besieging army was confirmed when he attacked

Chennupalli Mirza's advanced trenches with 200 of his infantry troops and easily drove Abul Hasan's retainers off toward Triplicane. Emboldened by this victory, La Haye called the entire garrison together on 29 August. In impassioned tones, he proposed an all-out attack to decide the matter once and for all and gave his men until nightfall to render their judgment on this plan. The viceroy, however, had badly misjudged the resolve of his own command; most had had their fill of the harsh Indian climate, rationed food, tropical disease, and the elusive quest for oriental riches. By early evening many had already voted on the issue of the proposed attack by deserting the garrison. Faced with the specter of a general mutiny, La Haye abandoned his plan and instead opened negotiations with Paviljoen the following morning, with only eight days of provisions remaining inside the town.[59] By 6 September the formal articles of capitulation had been worked out and signed. As Aungier summarized the main points for his directors, "St. Thoma was surrendered to the Dutch, Mouns. La Hay the French Gen . . . being forced . . . to deliver up the Towne on Condition that the Dutch were to furnish him with 2 shipps and 8 moneths provisions to transport him and his men for Europe." Prisoners were also exchanged. As for the spoils of the siege, the Dutch had to settle merely "for the Artillery and Ammunition taken from the French," while San Thomé "was surrendered to the king of Golconda on condition that the walls and fortifications be dismantled, that it might not prove a harbor to the French, Portuguese or any other nation." "By which means," Aungier noted with much satisfaction, "wee hope the Hon. Comp. affaires at Fort-St. George will receive a great benefitt & conveniency."[60]

On the afternoon of 19 September, as the French were completing preparations for formally turning over the city, a magnificent group of Persian cavalry approached the main gate with a personal envoy from Abul Hasan. This Qutb Shahi noble presented La Haye with presents and a *farman* from the young king, who had been greatly impressed by the Frenchman's martial skill and bravery during the siege, qualities that were highly prized in a kingdom long accustomed to the looming threat of the Great Mughal's imperial army and Shivaji's periodic invasions. Abul Hasan's *farman* declared, "Wee have been glad with the information received of your great vallour and Couradge. . . . [W]e would have you come to our presence, and wee shall bestow upon you the Captainship of a quantity of horse, and the Place where you shall like the best, & you shall not want for anything your heart shall desire." Now, this was undoubtedly an intriguing offer and evidently an entirely serious one, as Chennupalli Mirza had already received orders to accompany La Haye to Hyderabad if he desired a safe escort and to provide him with 3000 to 4000 pagodas for expenses.[61] Although the viceroy must have assumed, given the exceedingly meager results of the expedition, that his reception at the Qutb Shahi court would be more gracious than the one he would receive in Paris, he nonetheless rejected Abul Hasan's offer and continued preparations to embark with what remained of his command. True to the provisions of the articles of capitulation, Paviljoen had provided the ships *Rammekin* and *Welze* to transport the Frenchmen home. On the morning of 23 September 1674, La Haye with the 530 survivors of the Persian squadron marched out of San Thomé, flags flying, trumpets blaring, and drums beating, a poignant and tragic end to Colbert's grand Asian enterprise, an enterprise that had begun so gloriously a decade before.[62]

Epilogue, 1675–1683

"France needs peace in the west, war at a distance.
War with Holland will probably ruin the new Indian companies as well as the colonies and commerce lately revived by France, and will increase
the burdens of the people while diminishing their
resources. The Dutch will retire into their maritime towns, stand there on the defensive in perfect safety, and assume the offensive on the sea
with great chance of success. If France does not
obtain a complete victory over them, she loses all
her influence in Europe, and by victory she endan-
gers that influence. In Egypt [and the East?], on
the contrary . . . victory will give the dominion of
the seas, the commerce of the East and India, the
preponderance of Christendom, and even . . . empire."

—Leibnitz, *Mémoire*, to Louis XIV

As a loyal servant of the elector of Mainz and an acquaintance of the able
German diplomat Johann Christian von Boyneburg, Leibnitz wrote both
his *Thoughts on Public Safety* (1671) and his 1672 memorial to Louis XIV as
polemics designed to divert France's growing military might away from potential conquests at the expense of the German states in the Holy Roman
Empire and to convince the French king and his ministers of the fabulous
victories that might be won at the expense of the Ottoman Turks in the
Levant, Egypt, and by extension, the Indian Ocean trade. In these tracts, he
promised Louis that "the conquest of Egypt, that Holland of the East,"
would be "infinitely easier than that of the United Provinces." Moreover, it
was "in Egypt that Holland [would] be conquered; it is there she will be
despoiled of what alone renders her prosperous, the treasures of the East."[1]
The approaching campaign against the United Provinces, strained relations

with the Porte, and earlier letters on the issue from Boyneburg and the great philosopher had resulted in a formal invitation from Arnauld de Pomponne to come to Paris in February of 1672. While Colbert may not have agreed with the emphasis Leibnitz placed on Egypt as the linchpin for dominance in the Indian Ocean trade in his *Consilium Aegyptiacum,* he no doubt shared the German's fundamental assertion that the most effective means to undermine the mercantile wealth and power of the United Provinces was to strike at the very heart of its overseas empire, its dominant position in the Asian trade. In any event, Leibnitz never received the personal audience with Louis he desired. The Egyptian project languished for another century. His *Consilium* and the reasons for his 1672 journey to Paris would remain hidden in the Hanoverian archives until they were taken by Napoleon in 1803. Nevertheless, Leibnitz's admonishments on the inherent dangers of a Continental war against the Dutch proved prophetic. The Dutch had retired "into their maritime towns" and under William of Orange had successfully resisted Louis's onslaught. Colbert's vaunted economic reforms of the previous decade had been destroyed. "Burdens" in the form of increased taxation had ensued, while the "resources" of the country were depleted.[2]

For Colbert, Leibnitz's most prophetic, albeit tragic, statement related to his plans for the Indian Ocean trade, which were indeed ruined by the war, a fact too little appreciated in the traditional historiography of the reign. Any lingering hopes that Colbert may have retained for his project following the Continental reverses of 1673–1674 and the irregular, early reports from Asia were dashed by the news in the spring of 1675 that the shattered remnants of his once grand fleet had returned to France. On the difficult voyage home, La Haye had touched at Bourbon in late 1674, only to discover that continuing reverses to indigenous chieftains had forced the *compagnie* to abandon all of its posts on Madagascar. The *Rammekin* and *Welze* had rounded the Cape early in the New Year and, after provisioning stops at Saint Helena and Ascension, were separated in a fierce storm; the *Rammekin* had anchored at Port-Louis in March, while La Haye and the *Welze* had reached Lorient only in early May. The news, which swiftly reached Paris, was decidedly unwelcome to Colbert and his directors; the costly expedition had proven to be an utter failure in its prime objective of challenging Dutch predominance in the trade and furnishing the fledgling *compagnie* with exclusive fortified settlements from Madagascar to Indonesia. As Colbert subsequently learned in a personal interview with La Haye, Fort-Dauphin was deserted, Madagascar abandoned, the *compagnie*'s trade in Persia tenuous at best, the fort at Trincomalee and French pretensions on Ceylon were ruined, Caron's grandiose plans for the Indian trade were in shambles, and Indonesia remained a virtual Dutch fiefdom, indeed, only the small factory at Surat and the new settlement at Pondicherry under Baron and Martin remained.[3]

At that moment, Colbert probably realized that his grand ambitions in the Eastern trade were irretrievably destroyed and that the favorable conjuncture of 1669–1672 had been squandered. Given the devastating news from de Maisonneuve and La Haye, the traditional apathy of the merchant classes toward the entire project, the resulting dependence on royal largesse, and Louis's escalating problems with the Continental war, it was all he could do to mount an attempt to salvage what remained of the gutted edifice of the *compagnie*. Colbert wasted no time in his feverish quest to keep a truncated *compagnie* operating. On the afternoon of 5 May 1675, the third general meeting of the *compagnie* was held at the Tuileries. It is significant that no annual meeting had been held from 1669 to 1675. During those crucial years, Colbert had entrusted the future of the Asian project and his *compagnie* to the care of La Haye's royal expedition and the victories of Louis's armies at the expense of the Hollanders in Europe. By the spring of 1675, it was obvious that this bold and timely gamble to embrace a more aggressive stance in his global mercantile war with the Dutch had failed miserably. As in 1664, all that now remained was the *compagnie* itself. But for how long? Unlike the first two general meetings, neither the king nor his secretary of state attended this third gathering, another notable point. Louis, intent on recapturing some of the lost fortresses along the Meuse, had begun the spring campaign as early as possible and thus had a legitimate excuse. Moreover, he no longer had the time or taste for such matters. Colbert may have shunned the meeting simply to avoid probing and embarrassing questions relating to the expedition and to forego the travail of personally presenting the cooked figures on the *compagnie*'s operations necessitated by the continuing financial woes, La Haye's defeat, and the unfavorable economic climate created by the Dutch War. In short, the financial statement read aloud to the shareholders constituted a primer in the type of creative accounting that the financial demands of the war had thrust upon Colbert.

In this unjustifiably optimistic document, Colbert reported that just under 9,000,000 livres had been received from the Crown and private shareholders over the years, a far cry from the 15,000,000 livres specified in the September 1664 articles, but nonetheless a respectable amount. He badly overvalued the *compagnie*'s assets at 6,325,798 livres, a figure that, for example, valued its twenty-six ships at cost price plus the costs of equipment, repairs, and even refitting! All of the *compagnie*'s factories in Asia, including Surat, Masulipatnam, Bantam, and Bandar Abbas, were valued at the total amount of capital invested in them over the years. In fact, the value of the *compagnie*'s assets in 1675 was probably less than the amount invested by the private shareholders, perhaps 3,500,000 livres. A good deal of the money from the sales of returning cargoes had already been reinvested in *compagnie* operations to very little effect; less than 1,000,000 livres remained in cash. The millions invested by the king had also been lost, as had the royal funds spent on La Haye's expedition, about 2,000,000 livres or more. Nevertheless, to revive interest in the *compagnie* in the wake of the

La Haye debacle and to obscure the harsh reality behind these figures, Colbert recommended that a dividend of 10 percent be paid. This sum would go to all shareholders who had completed payment on their stock and to those investing 8,000 livres or more. An extra 5 percent dividend was promised to the Directors for their valued services. During 1676, over 448,000 livres were distributed according to this schema to some 481 stockholders, who had invested the sum of 3,353,966 livres.[4]

However, not even these desperate financial maneuverings could salvage the *compagnie*. Crown and merchant interest in the venture continued to decline during the remainder of the 1670s and into the 1680s, while mercantile interchange with the surviving factories in Asia remained at best sporadic. No *compagnie* ships returned from the Indies in 1675. Between 1677 and 1678 not a single ship departed from Lorient, nor did any return there from Surat or Pondicherry. The year 1680 "represented a low ebb in the financial state of the company." Of the twenty-six ships listed by Colbert in his 1675 balance sheet, one had already been captured by the VOC, five had been sold at Surat, another three had been auctioned off in Le Havre for cash, and most of the rest were hardly fit to attempt the arduous Cape voyage. Louis still owed the *compagnie* over 330,000 livres for advances made to La Haye's squadron on its voyage and "unpaid import and export bounties." The directors had to plead with Colbert to secure them 150,000 livres so that they could attempt to dispatch two ships the following year. The year 1681 also proved to be bittersweet, as a valuable cargo and an impressive embassy from the king of Siam bound for Paris aboard the lumbering *Soleil d'Orient* were lost when this ship sank on the passage, at a loss of over 600,000 livres to the *compagnie*. By 1682, Colbert was finally forced to suspend its monopoly privileges "on condition always that as soon as it is in a position to sustain itself, by itself, no other person will be admitted to it." This reorganized *compagnie* would never achieve sufficient financial strength to regain its erstwhile exclusionism. In the twilight of his great career, Colbert died the following year. Despite the best efforts of his son, the marquis de Seignelay, who succeeded his father as minister of the marine, and the efforts of Baron, Martin, and others in Asia, the *compagnie* could simply not compete with the entrenched corporate edifices of the Dutch and English, as well as with a reforming *Estado*.[5]

In the end, therefore, Colbert's notable Asian project failed at a high cost to future French ambitions in that trade, just as Louis's dynastic dreams in Europe were ultimately frustrated at a tremendous cost to his subjects and kingdom. On the level of *l'histoire événementielle* there can be little doubt that the mistakes of Colbert, Caron, La Haye, and other members of the French *compagnie* hierarchy contributed to this defeat. The vast expenditures made by Colbert and the directors on the initial *compagnie* fleets were certainly ill advised. La Haye's disastrous campaign on Madagascar, Blot's staunch opposition and obstructionism in Surat, Caron's enigmatic policy of nonaggression off Cape Comorin and at Trincomalee, and the ill-conceived decision to storm San Thomé, all played a role in the debacle. Conversely, the skilled response of Maetsuycker and Van Goens to the challenge certainly exacerbated the strategic errors of the French leadership and hastened the project's downfall.

On a structural level, the valiant response of the *Heeren XVII,* which emanated from the merchant capitalism that flourished in the United Provinces and the unique merging of political elite and private enterprise in that country, also proved decisive, with huge levels of reinforcements dispatched even during the bleakest stages of the war. In contrast, Colbert was simply unable to exploit such priorities in France, since they had not been sufficiently entrenched in the Bourbon state machinery under Louis XIII and Louis XIV. According to William Beik, seventeenth-century France possessed a political system "in which royal institutions developed the conditions necessary to continue to prosper in the Europe of expanding merchant capitalism while extending the membership of the dominant class to new groups and slowly pulling old and new together."[6] Nevertheless, the *mechanism* employed in this vital process sought to wed the merchant classes to the expanding centralized state and royal authority by offering safe investments in venality of office, aristocratic privilege, and rural property.

As the example of Colbert's grand Eastern strategy suggests, those merchant capitalists who may have been integrated into the dominant class during the seventeenth century not only came to embrace the landed wealth, titles, and privileges of the nobility; they also came to embrace many of the societal and foreign policy priorities of the aristocracy and Crown. The lack of substantial private investment in the *compagnie* that in part resulted from this development, when combined with the traditional priorities of Louis XIV and most of his principal ministers, put France at a decided disadvantage in any competition with rival powers whose dominant class had already embraced the economic imperatives of merchant capitalism in a global context and rejected the outmoded quest for geopolitical and dynastic goals in Europe alone. The political system of seventeenth-century France thus may have embodied a transitional arrangement in the shift from feudalism to capitalism, as Beik and others have suggested, but in doing so this system still ensured a society that was much more willing to embrace traditional European struggles championed by a strong king than to support the mercantile struggles in *outre-mer* that Colbert was seeking and that his rivals had already embraced. For all his genius, all his hours of tedious bureaucratic work in Paris and Sceaux, his supreme organizational efforts, not to mention his extreme good fortune in the timing of the mercantile offensive against the Dutch, Colbert was never able to overcome the societal constraints imposed upon him and his economic reforms by this fundamental reality of Bourbon absolutism and the structures of the early modern French state. The great inroads into the global trading position of the

United Provinces, and particularly the VOC, that the French *compagnie*, La Haye's squadron, and Louis's 1672 spring offensive portended were never obtained by the king's great minister.[7]

Increasingly forced to embrace the more traditional aspects of such a state, Colbert found himself at the most crucial moment of the entire campaign unable to match the spirited response of the Hollanders. Louis XIV's dynastic priorities and the escalating demands of the Continental campaign predictably won out: the Asian campaign atrophied after 1672 and ultimately succumbed to the forceful response of the exceedingly anxious merchants of Amsterdam. In the face of continued dynastic warfare on the Continent, the *Compagnie royale des Indes Orientales* withered on the vine in the 1680s. In the midst of the War of the Spanish Succession, its operations would finally grind to a whimpering halt. Louis's continuing thirst for Continental *gloire* in the years after 1674 precluded any renascent quest for Asian trade and wealth for what remained of the long reign. The force of Colbert's challenge, based on the shifting blend of capitalist and aristocratic wealth found in Louis XIV's France, was simply not sufficient to overcome the entrenched merchant capitalism of the United Provinces and the resolute commitment of its bourgeois burghers to defend the very lifeblood of their increasingly vulnerable empire. Only in the years after the king's death would a revitalized *compagnie* again compete for the type of economic power in *les Indes Orientales* that Colbert had hoped to achieve, as a cornerstone of his mercantilist economic system, half a century earlier.

Notes

ABBREVIATIONS

AAE   Archives des affaires étrangères

AC   Archives coloniales

AHU   Arquivo Historico Ultramarino

AM   Archives nationales: Dépôt du service historique de la marine

ANTT   Arquivo Nacional da Torre do Tombo

BN   Bibliothèque Nationale

BNL   Biblioteca Nacional, Lisbon

CC   Correspondance consulaire, AAE

CCC   Manuscrits Cinq Cents Colbert, BN

DAI   Documentos avulsos relativos à Índia, AHU

FF   Fonds français, BN

FR   Factory Records, IOL

HAG   Historical Archive of Goa

HT   The Hague Transcripts, IOL

IOL   India Office Library

MC   Mélanges Colbert, BN

MR   Livros das Monções do Reino, HAG

NAF   Nouvelles acquisitions françaises, BN

OC   Original Correspondence, IOL

PRO   Public Record Office

SPF   State Papers, Foreign, PRO

PREFACE

1. For Pearson's views, see *The Age of Partnership* (Honolulu, 1979), 3–4; *Merchants and Rulers in Gujurat* (Berkeley, 1975), 4–6; and *Coastal Western India* (New Delhi, 1981), xii–xvii, 19–20. For examples of this tendency in the literature, see W. W. Hunter, *England's Work in India* (London, 1881); *A History of British India*, 2 vols. (London, 1899–1900); F. C. Danvers, *The Portuguese in India*, 2 vols. (London, 1894); G. B. Malleson, *History of the French in India* (London, 1869); and Vincent E. Smith, *The Oxford History of India* (Oxford, 1919).

2. Boxer's vast contribution to the field is summarized in S. George West's *A*

Complete Bibliography of the Works of C. R. Boxer, 1926–83 (London, 1984).

3. See Pearson, *Merchants and Rulers in Gujurat* (Berkeley, 1975); *Coastal Western India* (New Delhi, 1981); and *The Portuguese in India* (Cambridge, 1987); T. R. de Souza, *Medieval Goa: A Socio-Economic History* (New Delhi, 1979); "Goa-based Seaborne Trade in the Early Seventeenth Century," *The Indian Economic and Social History Review* 12 (1975): 433–42; "Glimpses of Hindu Dominance of Goan Economy in the 17th Century," *Indica* 12 (1975): 27–35; A. R. Disney, *Twilight of the Pepper Empire: Portuguese Trade in Southeast India in the early Seventeenth Century* (Cambridge, MA, 1978); Subrahmanyam, *The Political Economy of Commerce: Southern India, 1500–1800* (Cambridge, 1990); *The Portuguese Empire in Asia, 1500–1700* (London, 1993); K. N. Chaudhuri, *Asia before Europe: Economy and Civilization of the Indian Ocean from the Rise of Islam to 1750* (Cambridge, 1990); and *The Trading World of Asia and the English East India Company, 1660–1760* (Cambridge, 1978).

4. See John E. Wills, Jr., "Maritime Asia, 1500–1800: The Interactive Emergence of European Domination," *American Historical Review* 98, no. 1 (1993): 83–105. Recent scholarly conferences on these issues have yielded very useful collections of essays on the general topic, including James D. Tracy, ed., *The Rise of Merchant Empires: Long-Distance Trade in the Early Modern Period* (Cambridge, 1990) and *The Political Economy of Merchant Empires: State Power and World Trade, 1350–1750* (Cambridge, 1991); and Roderick Ptak and Dietmar Rothermund, eds., *Emporia, Commodities and Entrepreneurs in Asian Maritime Trade, c. 1400–1700* (Stuttgart, 1991).

5. See, for example, Jonathan I. Israel, *Dutch Primacy in World Trade, 1585–1740* (Oxford, 1989); and Om Prakash, *The Dutch East India Company and the Economy of Bengal, 1630–1720* (Princeton, 1985).

6. See Jules Sottas, *Histoire de la Compagnie royale des Indes orientales: Un escadre français aux Indes en 1690* (Paris, 1905); Paul Kaeppelin, *La Compagnie des Indes orientales et François Martin* (Paris, 1908); H. Weber, *La Compagnie française des Indes, 1604–1875* (Paris, 1904); and H. Castonnet des Fosses, *L'Inde française avant Dupleix* (Paris, 1887).

7. The few exceptions are S. P. Sen, *The French in India: First Establishment and Struggle* (Calcutta, 1947); Lotika Varadarajan's translation with notes of Martin's *Mémoires* with the title *India in the Seventeenth Century: Social, Economic, and Political*, 2 vols. (New Delhi, 1981); and Philippe Haudrère "La Compagnie française des Indes, 1719–1795," (*Thèse d'État*, University of Paris VI, 1986).

8. At times, even the French archives were not exhaustively examined. While Kaeppelin's work is perhaps the most careful to date on the 1664 *compagnie*, his chapter on Colbert's Persian squadron, *Compagnie des Indes*, pp. 79–116, is based almost exclusively on one series: AC C2–62. He therefore overlooked some important documents found in the AC B1–B6 series and the AM B2–7 through B2–30 series.

9. In particular the correspondence between Fort-St. George and the Golcondan court in Hyderabad found in G/9/26 of the IOL. The *Reis Vizinhos* series of the HAG contains the correspondence between the Portuguese viceroy in Goa and the "neighboring kings" of India and the rest of the *Estado da India*. Codices 970 and 971 of the HAG cover the years between 1662 and 1668 and 1677 and 1681.

Summaries of these documents can be found in the *Boletim da Filmoteca Ultramarina Portuguesa* 11 (1959): 165–296, and 13 (1959): 527–605.

INTRODUCTION: EUROPEAN POWERS AND THE ASIAN TRADE

1. *The Travels of Marco Polo [The Venetian]*, ed. Manuel Komroff (New York, 1926, 1982), 3.

2. See J. H. Parry, *The Age of Reconnaissance: Discovery, Exploration, and Settlement, 1450–1650* (London and Berkeley, 1963, 1981), 6–8.

3. See John Mandeville, *Mandeville's Travels*, ed. M. Letts (London, 1953); and Parry, *Age of Reconnaissance*, 8.

4. For a recent discussion of the motivations for this process in Lisbon, see Pearson, *The Portuguese in India*, 5–11.

5. For details on Portuguese exploration along the African coast and the discovery of the sea route to India, see V. M. Godinho, *A Economia dos descobrimentos Henriquinos* (Lisbon, 1962); B. W. Diffie and G. D. Winius, *Foundations of the Portuguese Empire, 1415–1580* (Minneapolis, 1977); C. R. Boxer, *The Portuguese Seaborne Empire, 1415–1825* (New York, 1969); R. S. Whiteway, *The Rise of Portuguese Power in India, 1497–1550* (London, 1899, 1967); F. C. Danvers, *The Portuguese in India*, 2 vols. (London, 1894, 1966); E. Prestage, *The Portuguese Pioneers* (London, 1923); and M. N. Pearson, *The Portuguese in India* (Cambridge, 1987).

6. For a recent discussion of the motivations for this process in Lisbon, see Pearson, *The Portuguese in India*, 5–11.

7. On the establishment of the Portuguese empire in Asia, see Alfonso Albuqurque, *The Commentaries of the Great Afonso Dalboquerque* (London, 1875–83); Boxer, *Portuguese Seaborne Empire*, 39–64; and Pearson, *The Portuguese in India*, 30–39. On Columbus, the New World, and Habsburg Spain, among others, see J. H. Elliot, *Imperial Spain, 1469–1716* (London, 1963); Henry Kamen, *Spain, 1469–1714: A Society of Conflict* (London, 1983); S. E. Morison, *Admiral of the Ocean Sea*, 2 vols. (Boston, 1942); and *The Journal of Christopher Columbus*, trans. Cecil Jane, ed. L. A. Vigneras (London, 1960).

8. Boxer, *Portuguese Seaborne Empire*, 37.

9. Parry, *Age of Reconnaissance*, 168–69.

10. For the various estimates on the level of spice imports for this period, see F. C. Lane, "The Mediterranean Spice Trade: Its Revival in the Sixteenth Century," in *Venice and History* (Baltimore, 1966); V. M. Godinho, *L'èconomie de l'empire portugais aux XVe et XVIe siècles* (Paris, 1969), 674–704; C. H. H. Wake, "The Changing Pattern of Europe's Pepper and Spice Imports, ca. 1400–1700," *The Journal of European Economic History* 8 (1979); Bal Krishna, *Commercial Relations between England and India, 1601–1757* (London, 1924); and Niels Steensgaard, "The Return Cargoes of the *Carreira* in the 16th and Early 17th Century," in *Indo-Portuguese History: Old Issues, New Questions* (New Delhi, 1985), 13–31.

11. On the flow of precious metals from the New World to Europe and the debate over the causes of the price revolution, see E. J. Hamilton, *American Treasure and the Price Revolution in Spain, 1501–1650* (Cambridge, MA, 1934); Pierre Vilar, "Problems of the Formation of Capitalism," *Past and Present* 10 (1956): 15–38, and *Or et monnaie dans l'histoire* (Paris, 1974); F. Braudel and F. C.

Spooner, "Les métaux monétaires et l'économie du XVIe siècle," *X Congresso Internazionale di Scienze Storiche, Roma, Relazioni* (Florence, 1955), 233–64; and Dennis Flynn, "Sixteenth Century Inflation from a Production Point of View," in *Inflation through the Ages* (Brooklyn, 1982).

12. Quoted in Boxer, *Portuguese Seaborne Empire*, 1.

13. *An Inquiry into the Nature and Causes of the Wealth of Nations*, 2 vols. (Chicago, 1976), 2:141.

14. On the victory of the Protestant capitalist companies over the monarchical monopolism of the Portuguese in Asia, see Niels Steensgaard, *The Asian Trade Revolution of the Seventeenth Century: The East India Companies and the Decline of the Caravan Trade* (Chicago, 1974), originally published as *Carracks, Caravans, and Companies: The Structural Crisis in the European-Asian Trade in the Early 17th Century* (Copenhagen, 1973).

15. For the "decline of Spain" debate, see J. H. Elliot, "The Decline of Spain," *Past and Present* 20 (1961): 52–75; Henry Kamen, "The Decline of Spain: A Historical Myth?" *Past and Present* 81 (1978): 24–50; and J. I. Israel, "The Decline of Spain: A Historical Myth?" *Past and Present* 91 (1981): 170–80, with a rejoinder by Kamen in ibid.: 181–85.

16. See Perry Anderson, *Lineages of the Absolutist State* (London, 1987), 35–37, 196–99.

17. For details on the theoretical underpinnings of mercantilism and Colbertism, see C. W. Cole, *Colbert and a Century of French Mercantilism*, 2 vols. (New York, 1939), especially 1:278–355; and Anderson, *Lineages*, 35–37. On Colbert's network among the French financial community, see D. Dessert and J. L. Journet, "Le lobby Colbert: Un royaume, ou une affaire de famille?" *Annales ESC* 30 (1975): 1303–1336.

18. See Malleson, *History of the French in India*, 9; and Michel Mollat, "Passages français dans l'Ocean Indien au temps de François Ier," *Studia* 11 (1963): 239–50.

19. See *The Voyage of François Pyrard of Laval to the East Indies, the Maldives, the Moluccas, and Brazil*, 2 vols. (London, 1887–1889); and J. Barassin, "Compagnies de navigation d'expéditions françaises dans l'Ocean Indien au XVIIe siècle," *Studia* 11 (1963): 373–76.

20. See Weber, *Compagnie française*, 55–63; and J. Barbier, "La Compagnie française des Indes," *Revue historique de l'Inde française* 3 (1919): 6–7.

21. See Barbier, "La Compagnie française des Indes," *Revue historique de l'Inde française* 3 (1919): 7–9; and Barassin, "Compagnies de navigation," *Studia* 11 (1963): 383–85.

22. Classic treatments in the vast and divided historiography include Christopher Hill, *The Century of Revolution, 1603–1714* (Edinburgh, 1961); and Charles Wilson, *England's Apprenticeship, 1603–1763* (London, 1965).

23. On the institutional model of the EIC, see Chaudhuri, *The Trading World of Asia*, 19–39.

24. This term and model are advanced in Israel, *Dutch Primacy*, 5–17. See also volume 3 of Fernand Braudel's, *Civilization and Capitalism* (London, 1984), 175–276.

25. Braudel, *Civilization and Capitalism* 3: 190. These figures were based on a *mémoire* of May 1669 written by the French ambassador to the United

Provinces, Arnauld de Pomponne, found in AEE B1–619.

26. Femme Gaastra, "The Shifting Balance of Trade of the Dutch East India Company," in *Companies and Trade* (Leiden, 1981), 55–56.

27. See Israel, *Dutch Primacy,* 16–17.

28. Based on figures from table 3, "The Financial Results of the VOC in Asia, 1613–1696," from Gaastra's "The Shifting Balance of Trade," 62.

29. For the impressive results these reforms had yielded by 1680, see Glenn J. Ames "The *Estado da India,* 1663–1677: Priorities and Strategies in Europe and the East," *Revista Portuguesa de História* 22 (1987): 31–46; and "The *Carreira da India,* 1668–1682: Maritime Enterprise and the Quest for Stability in Portugal's Asian Empire," *The Journal of European Economic History* 20 (1991): 7–27. See also T. Bentley Duncan, "Navigation between Portugal and Asia in the Sixteenth and Seventeenth Centuries," in *Asia and the West* (Notre Dame, 1986), 3–25.

30. For the crucial importance of the Dutch War in Louis XIV's reign, see Pierre Goubert, *Louis XIV and Twenty Million Frenchmen,* trans. Anne Carter (London, 1970), 121ff.

31. According to Dessert and Journet, Parisian and provincial merchants combined contributed less than 20 percent of the money invested in the *compagnie.* See Dessert and Journet, "Le lobby Colbert," 1331–32.

CHAPTER 1: PARIS, 1665

1. For details on the 1665 expedition and the first meeting of the *compagnie* stockholders, see Kaeppelin, *Compagnie des Indes,* 7–12; Weber, *La Compagnie française,* 133–38; Sottas, *Compagnie royale,* 15–19; Pauliat, *Louis XIV et la Compagnie,* 143–56; and Cole, *Colbert* 1:503–4.

2. Cole, *Colbert* 1:278.

3. For background on Colbert's early life and career to 1661, see the traditional view found in Cole, *Colbert* 1:278–88; Pierre Clément, *Histoire de la vie et administration de Colbert* (Paris, 1846); and P. Boissonnade, *Colbert, le triomphe de l'étatisme, 1661–1683* (Paris, 1932), as well as the revisionist view given concisely, for example, in Dessert and Journet, "Le lobby Colbert," 1304–11.

4. Cole, *Colbert* 1:355. The best treatment of early French mercantilist theories remains Cole, *French Mercantilist Doctrine before Colbert* (New York, 1931). See also his sections in *Colbert* 1:27–109, 135–64, and 208–34; Henri Hauser's article "Le Colbertisme avant Colbert et la liberté du travail sous Henri IV, Lyons et Tours, 1596–1601," *Revue bourguignonne de l'ens. sup.* 8, 3–69; and Roger Mettam, *Power and Faction in Louis XIV's France* (Oxford, 1988), 189. The standard treatment of mercantilism remains E. F. Heckscher, *Mercantilism,* 2 vols. (London, 1955).

5. Quoted in Cole, *Colbert* 1:476. For Colbert's estimates on the importance of the Indian Ocean trade for the Dutch, see Colbert, *Lettres* II/1:cclxvi; BN CCC 204, fol. 7; BN MC 119 *bis,* fols. 842–43, 872–73.

6. Colbert, *Lettres* VI:260–70.

7. In their critique of Colbert and his economic policies, Dessert and Journet argue that "his pessimistic and aggressive economic conceptions" resulted in international tension that was highly unfavorable to the success of his commercial companies (see "Le lobby Colbert," p. 1328). In the Asian context, this somewhat Whiggish

view seemingly overlooks the fact that commercial and military bellicism had been part of the Indian Ocean trade at least since the arrival of da Gama. Moreover, the tensions engendered by six decades of nearly continual open and sub rosa warfare in Asia could hardly have been exacerbated or assuaged by anything Colbert did at this time. It is important to remember that Colbert's form of mercantilism emanated precisely from such contemporary realities of political economy and not those governing some post-Smithian, idealized free market that appears to underlie some of the recent revisionism.

8. Cole, *Colbert* 1:301–2.

9. For details on the activities of the *Chambre de justice,* see Cole, *Colbert* 1:302–3; D. Dessert, "Finances et société au XVIIe siècle: à propos de la Chambre de justice de 1661," *Annales ESC* 29 (1974): 849–69; and Julian Dent, *Crisis in Finance: Crown, Financiers, and Society in Seventeenth Century France* (New York, 1973), 106ff.

10. Cole, *Colbert* 1:303. For additional details on the *rentes* question, see Dent, *Crisis in Finance,* 52–54; G. Martin and M. Bezançon, *L'histoire du crédit en France sous le règne de Louis XIV* (Paris, 1913), 85–110; and R. M. Jennings and A. P. Trout, "Internal Control: Public Finance in 17th Century France," *The Journal of European Economic History* 1 (1972): 647–60.

11. See Cole, *Colbert* 1:303–4.

12. For details on Colbert's tariffs of the 1660s, see among others Cole, *Colbert* 1:415–33; and S. Elzinga, "Le tariff de Colbert de 1664 et celui de 1667 et leur signification," *Economisch-historisch Jaarboek* 15 (1929): 221–73.

13. Colbert, *Lettres* II/1:cclxiii ff., and VII:240ff., quoted in Cole, *Colbert* 1:437–38.

14. Cole, *Colbert* 1:438.

15. Quoted in Cole, *Colbert* 1:439.

16. Colbert, *Lettres* VII:250–51.

17. For details, see Cole, *Colbert* 1:477–78.

18. The travails of the early French East India Companies are outlined in Weber, *Compagnie;* Castonnet des Fosses, *L'Inde;* J. Barassin, "Compagnies de navigation," 373–88; and J. Barbier, "La Compagnie française des Indes," 5–96.

19. Colbert, *Lettres* II/1:50.

20. See Charles de La Roncière, *Histoire de la marine française,* 6 vols. (Paris, 1899–1932), 5:331 and 5:332, n.1.

21. Quoted in Cole, *Colbert* 1:477. For Colbert's views on the wealth of the Dutch Company, see *Lettres* II/1:cclxvi; VII:240, 244; BN CCC 204, fol. 7; BN MC 119 *bis,* fols. 842–43, 872–73.

22. *The French in India,* 17.

23. Cole, *Colbert* 1:477.

24. See Holden Furber, *Rival Empires of Trade in the Orient, 1600–1800* (Minneapolis, 1976), 186–91, 201–5.

25. For a copy of the articles, see BN FF 16,738, fol. 173. For details on the formation of the *compagnie,* see Cole, *Colbert* 1:475–501; L. Pauliat, *Louis XIV,* 79–100; and Kaeppelin, *La Compagnie,* 1–7.

26. François Charpentier, *Discours d'un fidèle sujet* (Paris, 1664), 7. The swift appearance of a London edition of 1664 titled *A Treatise Touching the East India Trade: or Discourse concerning the establishment of a French Company for the Com-*

merce of the East Indies attests to the great interest and anxiety among the English mercantile community toward Colbert's project from the outset.

27. Charpentier, *Discours d'un fidèle sujet,* 57.

28. Cole, *Colbert* 1:483; Dessert and Journet, "Le lobby Colbert," 1313.

29. Ibid.

30. In the view of Barbier, "La Compagnie française," 10.

31. For details on the 1664–1665 subscription campaign, see Cole, *Colbert* 1:483–96; P. Boissonnade, *Colbert et la souscription aux actions de la compagnie des Indes* (Poitiers, 1909); Colbert, *Lettres* II/2:428, 439; BN MC 34, fols. 94–100; MC 100, fols. 200–202; MC 122, fols. 116, 483–86, 856; MC 123 *bis,* fols. 667–68, 886–87; and Pauliat, *Louis XIV,* 101–12.

32. See Boissonade, *Colbert et la souscription,* 5ff., summarized in Cole, *Colbert* 1:488–89.

33. BN MC 126, fol. 629, cited in Cole, *Colbert* 1:491.

34. BN MC 127, fols. 126–27, cited in Cole, *Colbert* 1:493.

35. See Cole, *Colbert* 1:493–96 and the manuscript sources cited therein.

36. For details on the subscription amounts, see AC C2–2, fol. 257, and C2–4, fol. 251. Dernis, *Recueil et collection des titres, etc. concernant la Compagnie des Indes orientales,* 2 vols. (Paris, 1755–56) 1:84–87, also contains a *liste des intéressés en la Compagnie* through March 1665, and 1:170–72 contains a similar list through July 1667. For an analysis of the social and economic background of the subscribers, see Dessert and Journet, "Le lobby Colbert," 1313–17.

37. See Dessert and Journet, "Le lobby Colbert," 1317.

38. Cole, *Colbert* 1:498–501, provides a useful summary of the problems associated with collecting on the original subscriptions, including a contemporary list of dilatory investors. See also BN *Collection Clairambault* 532, fols. 79–111.

39. On d'Estrades's actions in the United Provinces at this time relating to the *compagnie,* see BN MC 199 *bis,* fols. 994–95; 123 *bis,* fols. 693–700; and BN CCC 207, fols. 105–6.

40. On these negotiations, see BN MC 122, fols. 553–56, 779, cited in Cole, *Colbert* 1:498.

41. The best source for details on Caron's career with the Dutch Company is found in C. R. Boxer's introductory notes to François Caron, *A True Description of the Mighty Kingdoms of Japan and Siam* (London, 1935), xv–cxxi, 147–52.

42. *A True Description of the mighty Kingdoms of Japan and Siam* (London, 1663).

43. According to François Martin's *Mémoires.* See François Martin, *Mémoires de François Martin, fondateur de Pondichéry,* 3 vols. (Paris, 1931–34), 1:97–99.

44. See AC B1, fols. 26v–27, Colbert to Caron, 31/III/1669; Colbert *Lettres,* III/2:471 and 504–6; François Caron, *A True Description,* civ, 150–51; Cole, *Colbert* 1:506; Martin, *Mémoires* 1:99; and Dernis, *Recueil* 1:87.

45. On this initial advice, see *Letter from Mr. Carron to Mr. d'Thou, Count of Meslay and Director of the East India Company of France, with Instructions concerning the Commerce* dated Paris, 29 May 1665, and an addendum found in Jean Chardin's *Travels in Persia, 1673–1677* (New York, 1988), 17–26.

46. For details, see AC C2–62, Caron to Colbert: fols. 27–36, 21/IV/1668; fols. 42–43, 9/I/1669; fols. 45–46, 12/IV/1669; and fols. 53–53v, 22/VIII/1669.

47. For example, governor-general and council in Batavia to *Heeren XVII*, IOL HT I/3/56, 734, 25/I/1667; HT I/3/58, 740, 18/X/1668; and 752, 31/I/1670.

48. AC C2–62, Caron to Colbert: fols. 45–46, 12/IV/1669; and fols. 64–65, 1/I/1670.

CHAPTER 2: SURAT, 1668

1. For biographical information on Bernier, see François Bernier, *Travels in the Mogul Empire* (London, 1891), xix–xxii.

2. Bernier, *Travels,* 110–312 passim. For background on the internal situation in India during the late seventeenth century, and especially Aurangzeb and Shivaji, among others, see William Irvine, *The Army of the Indian Moghuls* (New Delhi, 1962); W. H. Moreland, *From Akbar to Aurangzeb: A Study in Indian Economic History* (London, 1923); I. R. Qureshi, *The Administration of the Mughal Empire* (Karachi, 1966); M. Athar Ali, *The Mughal Nobility under Aurangzeb* (Bombay, 1968); Iran Habib, *The Agrarian System of Mughal India* (Bombay, 1963); Satish Chandra, *Parties and Politics at the Mughal Cour* (New Delhi, 1972); J. F. Richards, *Mughal Administration in Golconda* (Oxford, 1975); Jadunath Sarkar, *Shivaji and His Times* (Calcutta, 1961); S. N. Sen *Foreign Biographies of Shivaji* (Calcutta, 1947); Bal Krishna, *Shivaji the Great* 2 vols. (Kolhapur, 1939); and M. N. Pearson, "Shivaji and the Decline of the Mughal Empire," *Journal of Asian Studies* 35 (1976): 221–35.

3. For details on the 1665 fleet, see Cole, *Colbert* 1:504; Sottas, *Histoire,* 15–19; Pauliat, *Louis XIV,* 143–56; Weber, *Compagnie,* 133–38; and Kaeppelin, *La Compagnie,* 7–12. The *Aigle Blanc,* after stopping at the nearby island of Bourbon, or Réunion, had only reached Fort-Dauphin in November.

4. According to Kaeppelin, *La Compagnie,* 653, these ships, the *St-Louis* and *St-Jacques,* had departed from Le Havre.

5. Expenditure figures for the Compagnie's early years can be found in Dernis, *Recueil* 1:170–72.

6. Cole *Colbert* 1:504. For additional details on the first stockholders meeting, see BN FF 21,778, fols. 226–28; Sottas, *Histoire,* 20–21; and Pauliat, *Louis XIV* pp. 187–94.

7. These decrees are found in BN FF 21,778, fols. 226ff.

8. Cole, *Colbert* 1:507–8.

9. From his letter of 29 May 1665 cited in Chardin, *Travels,* 17ff.

10. For details on Mondevergue's fleet, see Pauliat, *Louis XIV,* 211–27; Sottas, *Histoire,* 24–25; Weber, *Compagnie,* 141, 269; Castonnet des Fosses, *L'Inde,* 59; Cole, *Colbert* 1:506–7; and Dernis, *Recueil* 1:170–72.

11. Colbert, *Lettres* II/2:437.

12. Malleson, *History of the French in India,* 15.

13. For information on Madagascar during this period, see Hubert Deschamps, *Histoire de Madagasca* (Paris, 1961); P. M. Mutibwa, *The Malagasy and the European* (London, 1974); and R. K. Kent, *Early Kingdoms in Madagascar, 1500–1700* (New York, 1970). During the mid-seventeenth century, these kingdoms included the Antemoro and Antesaka on the eastern coast, the Betsileo and Sakalava in the southwest, the Merina, or Imerina, on the large central plateau, and

the Anosi and Antandroy in the southeast region bordering Fort-Dauphin.

14. On the policy of pillaging local cattle and poor relations with the Madagascans, see BN NAF 9342, fol. 63; Sottas, *Histoire,* 16–18; and Pauliat, *Louis XIV,* 226–40.

15. It should be noted that the Crown originally supported Caron in this dispute with the Capuchins. As late as December 1670, Louis XIV advised, "[A]s [the Capuchins] . . . have strongly supported the French who are disposed against the Sieur Caron, in which his religion has swayed them . . . I will be grateful if they are able to convert him; but I wish that, without considering his unpleasant religion, they follow his sentiments completely on economic matters." See AC B2, fols. 160v–61, Louis XIV to La Haye, 27/XII/1670.

16. For biographical information on Marcara, his recruitment by the *compagnie,* and his arrival in Fort-Dauphin, see Cole, *Colbert* 1:513–15; Castonnet des Fosses, *L'Inde,* 78–82; and the manuscript sources cited therein.

17. Castonnet des Fosses, *L'Inde,* 78–79; Martin, *Mémoires* 1:106; Kaeppelin, *La Compagnie,* 55–56; and Sottas, *Histoire,* 27–28.

18. On Surat's trade during the late seventeenth century, see John Ovington, *A Voyage to Surat in the Year 1689 by John Ovington* (London, 1929), 131–34; Castonnet des Fosses, *L'Inde,* 79; Kaeppelin, *La Compagnie,* 52; Sottas, *Histoire,* 45; W. H. Moreland, *India at the Death of Akbar* (London, 1920), 46–50; Bal Krishna, *Commercial Relations between India and England,* 15–18; and Ashin Das Gupta, *Indian Merchants and the Decline of Surat* (Wiesbaden, 1979).

19. Pearson, "Shivaji and the Decline of the Mughal Empire," 227.

20. Cited in Castonnet des Fosses, *L'Inde,* 79.

21. For details on the European presence in Gujarat at this time, see C. J. Hamilton, *Trade Relations between England and India* (New Delhi, 1975), 16ff.; Philip Anderson, *The English in Western India* (Bombay, 1854); Moreland, *From Akbar to Aurangzeb,* 39–41; M. N. Pearson, *Coastal Western India,* 104–6; and Martin, *Mémoires,* 1:237–39.

22. See François Bernier, *Travels; Indian Travels of Thevenot and Careri,* ed. S. Sen (New Delhi, 1949); Jean-Baptiste Tavernier, *Travels in India* (London, 1889); and LaBoullaye, *Les voyages et observations du sieur de La Boullaye Le Gouz* (Paris, 1653). For an overview, see George A. Rothrock, "Seventeenth Century India through French Eyes," *The Historian* 22 (1959): 163–84.

23. From a model letter proffered by Caron to Louis on the style the king should utilize in his intitial embassies to the emperors of Persia, China, and Japan. See Chardin, *Travels,* 26–39. For details on the formation of the embassy by Colbert, see Castonnet des Fosses, *L'Inde,* 74–77; Martin, *Mémoires,* 1:204–5; Kaeppelin, *La Compagnie,* 54; and Adrian Duarte, *Les premières relations entre les français et les princes indigènes dans l'Inde au XVIIe siècle* (Paris, 1932), 18–22.

24. On the events in Isfahan, see Chardin, *Travels,* 40–45; and Castonnet des Fosses, *L'Inde,* 75.

25. There are differing versions on the reception that La Boullaye Le Gouz and Beber received in Agra. Castonnet des Fosses suggests that the pair cut a poor figure at the Mughal court, that their embassy was indeed modest, and that they bragged excessively about the power of the ships their king possessed and would eventually send to India. See *L'Inde,* 76–78. On the other hand, Niccolāo Manucci, a Venetian physician in Agra at the time, noted that the French envoys were well

received. See Niccolão Manucci, *Storia do Mogor or Mogul India by Niccolão Manucci*, 4 vols. (London, 1907–1908), 2:150–52. For a French translation of Aurangzeb's *farman* of 11 August 1666, see A. Martineau, ed., *Lettres et conventions des governeurs de Pondichéry* (Pondicherry, 1914), 1–3.

26. Castonnet des Fosses, *L'Inde*, 77; Kaeppelin, *La Compagnie*, 54; Martin, *Mémoires* 1:204; and Duarte, *Relations*, 22.

27. IOL OC 3144, Surat presidency to directors, 11/I/1666, fol. 4.

28. IOL FR G/36/105, fols. 125–26, Bantam to Surat, 10/IX/1668.

29. IOL OC 3144, Surat presidency to directors, 11/I/1666, fol. 1.

30. On the fundamental shift in the trade from pepper and other spices to cotton piece goods and tea during the period 1660–1730, see Furber, *Rival Empires of Trade*, 234–45.

31. De Flacourt and two *compagnie* clerks reached the Malabar Coast in late 1668 and soon after the New Year arranged for the establishment of a factory at the village of Alicot. As Henry Oxenden noted on these talks with the Zamorin from aboard the ship *Bantam* in January 1669, "[T]he Evening before our departure from Callicut arrd . . . 3 French merchants onshoare desiring licence to trade and settle a factory. . . . [T]hey are gone to the Samorine with the Presents . . . & pretend to ask leave to build a fort upp the River of Cranganore above the Dutch fort of Cranganore to prevent the Dutches invasions into the Samorins Country." See IOL FR G/36/105, fol. 81.

32. For Caron's strategy in the Ceylon trade as outlined in 1668, see AC C2-62, Caron to Colbert, fols. 27–36, 21/IV/1668; and C. R. Boxer, "The Third Dutch War in the East, 1672–74," *The Mariner's Mirror* 16 (1930): 345.

33. Detailed in IOL OC 3491, Surat to Alex Grigbie on Malabar Coast, 14/X/1670, fol. 1. Aungier reported to the Directors: "There are now 2 French ships . . . in this road. . . . [T]heire goods for Europe consist of Cloth, Druggs, Indico, Cloth yarne all which were bought in the dearest time." See IOL OC 3385, Surat presidency to directors, 2/I/1670, fol. 2.

34. The potential horrors of the Cape passage, especially for the Portuguese *Carreira da India*, were originally delineated in graphic detail in works like Bernado Gomes de Brito's *Historia tragico-maritima*, 2 vols. (Lisbon, 1735–1736); and Fernão de Queyroz, *Relación de las grandes perdidas* (Madrid, 1651). Modern works on the subject include James Duffy's, *Shipwreck and Empire* (Cambridge, MA, 1955); and the various works of C. R. Boxer, including *The Portuguese Seaborne Empire*, 205–27; *From Lisbon to Goa, 1500–1750: Studies in Portuguese Maritime Enterprise* (London, 1984); and "The *Carreira da India*, 1650–1750," *The Mariner's Mirror* 46 (1960): 35–54.

35. See "Journal du pilotage du vaisseau la Force, envoyé avec l'Aigle d'or, sa conserve, à l'isle Bourbon, à Madagascar, et dans l'Hindoustan, par la Compagnie des Indies Orientales," found in BN MC 62, fols. 1–135.

36. Of the fifty-six French ships (both *compagnie* and royal) that made the passage from Europe to the *Indes Orientales* between 1665 and 1682, only twenty-six, or 37.4 percent, made it back to France. See Kaeppelin, *La Compagnie*, 654–55. In comparison, in a reforming *Carreira da India*, from 1668 to 1682, 96.8 percent of the thirty-one ships sailing from Lisbon reached India, while 82.8 percent of the twenty-eight ships departing from Goa made the return voyage to Europe successfully. See Glenn J. Ames, "The *Carreira da India*, 1668–1682,"

The Journal of European Economic History 20 (1991): 7–27.

37. Given in Chardin, *Travels,* 22–23.

38. IOL OC 3515, Surat presidency to directors, 30/XI/1670, fol. 2.

39. For details on how Aungier and the English Company exploited the abuses of the Goa Inquisition in an attempt to lure rich indigenous merchants to Bombay during the late 1660s and early 1670s, see Glenn J. Ames, "*Estado da India,* 1663–1677," *Revista Portuguesa de História* 22: 35, 41–42.

40. From his letter of 29/V/1665 given in Chardin, *Travels,* 18.

41. As described by Cole, *Colbert* 1:513.

42. On this dispute, see Cole, *Colbert* 1:513–15; Malleson, *French in India,* 16–17; Martin, *Mémoires* 1:231–90; and Kaeppelin, *La Compagnie,* 67–68. For Marcara's side of the story, see AC C2–62, fols. 67–68, Marcara to Colbert, 12/I/1670; and BN, Collection Morel de Thoisy 377, fols. 66ff.

43. IOL OC 3515, Surat presidency to directors, 30/I/1670, fol. 21.

44. IOL HT I/3/58; 752, Batavia to *Heeren XVII,* 31/I/1670, fol. 3.

45. On the cargo and return voyage of the *St-Jean-Baptiste,* see AC C2–62, fols. 27–36, Caron to Colbert, 21/IV/1668; and Cole, *Colbert* 1:509.

46. Bernier's *mémoire* is found in AC C2–62, fols. 14–25. See also his more detailed letter (n.d.) to Colbert found in *Travels,* 200–238.

47. AC C2–62, fol. 14.

48. AC C2–62, fols. 14–15.

49. AC C2–62, fols. 14–20v.

50. AC C2–62, fols. 21–25.

51. See the addendum to his letter of 29/V/1665 found in Chardin's *Travels,* 21.

52. See AC C2–62, fols. 27–36, Caron to Colbert, 21/IV/1668.

53. AC C2–62, fols. 30–31.

CHAPTER 3: PARIS, 1669

1. See Cole, *Colbert* 1:289 and the manuscript sources cited therein.

2. For details on Colbert's financial reforms of the 1660s, among others, see Goubert, *Louis XIV,* 114–27; and Cole, *Colbert* 1:356–474. A critique of these policies and their impact on the French financial system can be found in Dessert and Journet, "Le lobby Colbert," 1328–29.

3. For background on Colbert's activities as superintendent of buildings, see Orest Ranum, *Paris in the Age of Absolutism* (New York, 1968), 256–82; Cole, *Colbert* 1:314–15; Goubert, *Louis XIV,* 80–81; and Andrew Trout, *Jean-Baptiste Colbert* (Boston, 1978), 53–77.

4. Colbert, *Lettres* VI:xxxvi, 269–70. On Versailles, among others, see Ranum, *Paris in the Age of Absolutism,* 267–69; Robert W. Berger, *Versailles: The Chateau of Louis XIV* (College Park, MD, 1985); and Guy Walton, *Louis XIV's Versailles* (Chicago, 1986).

5. Quoted in Trout, *Colbert,* 180.

6. On royal expenditures on Versailles during this period, see Trout, *Colbert,* 181; and François Bluché, *Louis XIV* (New York, 1990), 171–72, 195.

7. Cole, *Colbert* 1:314–15.

8. Ranum, *Paris in the Age of Absolutism,* 262.

9. See Cole, *Colbert* 1:319–20.

10. On the academies, see Goubert, *Louis XIV*, 81–85; Cole, *Colbert* 1:314–20; and Bluché, *Louis XIV*, 157–59.

11. See Mettam, *Power and Faction in Louis XIV's France*, 189.

12. For details on Colbert's tariff policies of the 1660s, see Cole, *Colbert* 1:415–36; and S. Elizinga, "Le tarif de Colbert de 1664 et celui de 1667 et leur signification," 221–73. On the struggle against internal tariffs and tolls, see J. F. Bosher, *The Single Duty Project* (London, 1964).

13. Based on the financial data relating to subsequent negotiations for an Anglo-French commercial treaty found in BN MC 34, fols. 3–4, 68–83. For the reaction of the English merchants to Colbert's 1667 tariff, see Maurice Lee, *The Cabal* (Urbana, IL, 1965), 98–99, 105–6; and Cole, *Colbert* 1:431–32. See also Dessert and Journet, "Le lobby Colbert," 1328.

14. According to Cole, *Colbert* 1:450.

15. Colbert, *Lettres* II/1:50.

16. See Colbert, *Lettres* II/1:50; III/2:699; La Roncière, *Histoire de la Marine française* 5:325–31; and Cole, *Colbert* 1:201–2, 451–52.

17. La Roncière, *Histoire de la Marine française* 5:331.

18. Cole, *Colbert* 1:454.

19. Cited in Cole, *Colbert* 1:453.

20. On the "Ordinance of Waters and Forests" of 1669 and Colbert's attempt to ensure adequate timber supplies for the navy, see BN CCC 207, fols. 6–8; Colbert *Lettres* II/2, fols. 534–35, 578, 622–23; III/1, fols. 42–43, 76–79, 136, 148–50, 196, 212–22, 233, 239–40, 256, and 270–71; and Paul W. Bamford, *Forests and French Seapower, 1660–1789* (Toronto, 1956).

21. According to Auguste Jal, *Glossaire nautique* (Paris, 1848), 1517. See also Cole, *Colbert* 1:456–57.

22. Paul Sonnino, *Louis XIV and the Origins of the Dutch War* (Cambridge, 1988), 53, 58.

23. John B. Wolf, *Louis XIV* (New York, 1968), 219. On this tendency, see also André Corvisier, *Louvois* (Paris, 1983), 288–89.

24. See Paul W. Bamford, *Privilege and Profit* (Philadelphia, 1988), xiii–xiv.

25. For the Third Republic view of these tendencies, see Charles de La Roncière, *Colbert* (Paris, 1919); discussed more recently in Fernand Braudel, *The Identity of France* (New York, 1988), 1:327–28.

26. See Eugene L. Asher, *The Resistence to the Maritime Classes* (Berkeley, 1960), 37–41.

27. Cole, *Colbert* 1:499, based on figures in BN Collection Clairambault 532, fols. 79–111.

28. BN Collection Clairambault 532, fols. 79–111.

29. According to figures given in Dessert and Journet, "Le lobby Colbert," 1331–32, the merchant community in France ultimately contributed some 1,465,910 livres of 8,919,284 livres to the *compagnie*, or less than 20 percent.

30. See, for example, *Dutch Primacy in World Trade*, 16–17.

31. Cole, *Colbert* 1:502.

32. For details on the second stockholders meeting, see BN FF 16,738, fols. 24–26; Sottas, *Histoire*, 30–38; and Cole, *Colbert* 1:508–9.

33. Cole, *Colbert* 1:507–8.

34. Cole, *Colbert* 1:509.

35. AC C2–62, fols. 4–6, La·Boullaye Le Gouz to Colbert, 1/IV/1666.

36. For details on Vieira's arrival in Paris, see ANTT ME/LPP 1, fols. 36–36v, Duarte Ribeiro de Macedo to Prince Regent Pedro, 23/XII/1668. For the Jesuit projects, see BN MC 31, fols. 297–99 *Devis d'une expédition navale contre les Hollandais au Cap et aux Indes, avec une carte des possessions hollandaises et portugaises dans l'Inde;* and fols. 300–310v, *Mémoire de l'Éstat présent des affaires des Indes, pour ce qui concerne le commerce des diverses nations des l'Europe, et les facilitez, et moyens d'éstablir, et affermir celuy de la France en ce pays là, tiré des relations du R. P. Damianus Vieyra, d'Aureou, Portugais.* Vieira's eventual return to Lisbon and his actions toward facilitating a Franco-Portuguese Asian alliance are detailed in AE CC B1–644, fols. 159–59v, Saint-Romain to Louis XIV, 16/V/1670; fols. 161–62, Saint-Romain to Colbert, 30/V/1670; and fol. 165, Vieira to Colbert, 28/V/1670.

37. AC B1, fols. 43–59v.

38. AC B1, fol. 43v.

39. AC B1, fols. 49v–59v.

40. Wolf, *Louis XIV,* 214.

41. On Louis XIV's impatience for war and on Louvois's position in the ruling elite in early 1669, see Sonnino, *Origins,* 6–7, 52, 58, 82. For details on the king's largesse to Colbert during the 1660s and early 1670s, see Cole, *Colbert* 1:288–89, 296–99. On Louis's relationship with Colbert, see Bluché, *Louis XIV,* 133–56.

42. See the plethora of Louis's letters relating to the royal Asian fleet found in AM B2–9, B2–10, and B2–11.

43. AM B2–9, fols. 130v–32.

44. AM B2–9, fol. 131.

45. See AM B2–9, fol. 131 for Colbert's original suggestions and AM B2–9, fol. 151, Colbert to Colbert de Terron, 27/V/1669, for his final choices.

46. AM B2–9, fols. 151–51v.

47. Cole, *Colbert* 1:459.

48. AM B2–9, fol. 392, Colbert to Dumas, 26/IX/1669; and fols. 401–1v, Colbert to Colbert de Terron, 30/IX/1669.

49. AM B2–9, fol. 458v, Colbert to Colbert de Terron, 1/XI/1669.

50. For a brief description of La Haye's background, see Weber, *Compagnie,* 161, n. 3.

51. AM B2–10, fols. 7–7v, 5/I/1670.

52. See Castonnet des Fosses, *L'Inde,* 63.

53. Colbert, *Lettres* III/2:462.

54. Colbert, *Lettres* III/2:463–67.

55. Colbert, *Lettres* III/2:467.

56. Colbert, *Lettres* II/2:467. On the embarkation of the infantry troops, see AM B2–10, fols. 5–5v. In January 1670, commissions were first issued for the two marine regiments that Colbert had formed; the *régiment royal de la marine* under the marquis de Lavardin and the *régiment de l'Admiral de France* under the chevalier de Martignon. See AM B2–8, fols. 229–45.

57. AM B4–4, fols. 166–89v.

58. AC B2, fols. 79–80.

59. These building materials included about 40,000 bricks, 500 hoes and picks, 150 axes, and a wide assortment of masonry and carpentry tools; see AC B2, fols. 79–80v. Colbert had earlier written to Colbert de Terron on La Haye, stating, "[A]s the principal aim of his voyage consists in landing and constructing establishments, it is necessary to examine what is needed to accomplish this task." See AC B1, fols. 190–92v, 3/XII/1669.

CHAPTER 4: LONDON AND LISBON, 1670

1. See Ronald Hutton, *Charles II: King of England, Scotland, and Ireland* (Oxford, 1989), 254–55.

2. Hutton *Charles II*, 256–62.

3. See Ronald Hutton, "The Making of the Secret Treaty of Dover, 1668–1670," *The Historical Journal* 29, no. 2 (1986): 298.

4. Among others, see Hutton, *Charles II*, 262–63.

5. On the financial problems of the English Crown in the years before the Dutch War, see Hutton, "The Making of the Secret Treaty of Dover," 304–5; C. D. Chandaman, *The English Public Revenue, 1660–1688* (Oxford, 1975), 218–21; and Maurice Lee, *Cabal*, 128–55.

6. For details on English complaints against the provisions of Colbert's 1667 tariff, see BN MC 34, fols. 3–4, 68–83.

7. See Charles II, *The Letters, Speeches, and Declarations of King Charles II*, ed. Arthur Bryant (New York, 1968), 203–28.

8. Charles II to Louis XIV, 3 February 1667/8, given in *Letters*, 213. Charles had already informed his sister that while she might be a "little surprised" at the treaty with the Dutch, the "effect of it is to bring Spain to consent to the peace, upon the terms the King of France hath avowed he will be content with, so I have done nothing to prejudice France in this agreement." See *Letters*, 211.

9. On the problems affecting the Triple Alliance, see Hutton, *Charles II*, 265–66; Lee, *Cabal*, 95–100; and Keith Feiling, *British Foreign Policy, 1660–1672* (London, 1930).

10. On Colbert de Croissy's mission, see F. A. M. Mignet, *Négociations relatives à la succession d'Espagne*, 4 vols. (Paris, 1835–42), 3:44–46; and for Louis's instructions of 2/VIII/1668 to his ambassador, see *Recueil des instructions données aux ambassadeurs et ministres de France depuis les traités de Westphalie jusqu'à la révolution française: Angleterre*, ed. J. J. Jusserand, 2 vols. (Paris, 1929), 2:54–92.

11. Charles II to Madame, 8 July 1668 (O.S.), given in *Letters*, 222.

12. For details on Colbert de Croissy's arrival and initial foray into court life, see John Evelyn, *The Diary of John Evelyn*, ed. E. S. de Beer, 6 vols. (Oxford, 1955), 3:513.

13. *Letters*, 224–25.

14. See *Recueil* 2:54–92.

15. Historical Manuscript Commission, *Report on the Manuscripts of the Duke of Buccleuch and Queensberry* (London, 1899–1926), 1:422; Montagu to Arlington, 3 May 1669 (O.S.).

16. From a letter of December 1668 to Colbert de Croissy, given in Mignet, *Négociations* 3:62–63.

17. See Lee, *Cabal*, 98–99, 146.

18. Furber's *Rival Empires of Trade,* 38–44, 64–76, 89–103, and 186–201, constitutes perhaps the most concise summary of the fortunes of the EIC during the seventeenth century.

19. Furber, *Rival Empires of Trade,* 92–93.

20. From a letter of 28 January 1664, given in Tavernier, *The English Factories in India 1661–1664,* ed. William Foster (Oxford, 1923), 264.

21. For details, see Furber, *Rival Empires of Trade,* 92–94.

22. Furber, *Rival Empires of Trade,* 91. For additional details on the company's trade during this period, see James Mill's *The History of British India* (New York, 1968), 1:74–77.

23. See Lee, *Cabal,* 99.

24. IOL E/3/87, fol. 59, directors to Fort-St. George, 3/II/1667.

25. IOL E/3/87, fols. 112v–13, directors to Surat, 20/III/1668.

26. IOL E/3/87, fol. 113, directors to Surat, 20/III/1668, and fol. 159v, directors to Surat, 26/II/1669.

27. PRO SPF 78/128, fols. 129–31v, 25/XII/1669, and SPF 78/129, fols. 21–22, 23–24v, Perwich to Arlington, 29/I/1670.

28. PRO SPF 78/128, fols. 21–22v, Vernon to Williamson, 13/XI/1669.

29. IOL E/3/87, fol. 162v, directors to Surat, 26/II/1669.

30. On Arundell's mission and the "meeting" of 25 January 1669, see Lee, *Cabal,* 102; and Hutton, *Charles II,* 263–64.

31. On the negotiations culminating in the Treaty of Dover, see Lee, *Cabal,* 102–12; Hutton, *Charles II,* 263–74; and Feiling, *British Foreign Policy,* 269–319, for the English perspective. Mignet, *Négociation* 3:40ff., and more recently Sonnino, *Dutch War,* 60–113 passim, provide the French prespective on the process.

32. According to Lee, *Cabal,* 102–3.

33. From a letter of 20 November 1673, given in Mignet, *Négociations,* 4:236.

34. HMC, *Buccleuch and Queensberry Mss.* 1:423, Montagu to Arlington, 3 May 1669 (O.S.).

35. C. H. Hartmann, *Charles II and Madame* (London, 1934), 277–81.

36. For details, see Lee, *Cabal,* 106–12.

37. This view has most recently been restated by Sonnino, *Dutch War,* 60–64.

38. Charles II to Madame, 2 September 1668 (O.S.), given in *Letters,* 224–25.

39. Sonnino, *Dutch War,* 70.

40. BN CCC 204, fols. 9v–11v.

41. BN CCC 204, fols. 70–71, Colbert to Colbert de Croissy, 27/IV/1669.

42. IOL FR G/19/17, fol. 9, Langhorn to English agent at Hyderabad, 21/III/1673.

43. See Glenn J. Ames, "A Portuguese Perspective on the Emerging French Presence in the East, c. 1670," *Studia* 46 (1987): 255–86, and "The *Estado da India,* 1663–1677," 31–46.

44. For details on events in Lisbon from 1640 to 1668, see H. V. Livermore, *A New History of Portugal* (Cambridge, 1987), 173–94; A. H. Oliveira Marques, *History of Portugal* 2 vols. (New York, 1972), 1:322–33; C. R. Boxer, *Salvador de Sá and the Struggle for Brazil and Angola, 1602–1686* (London, 1952), 333–56; and Carl A. Hanson, *Economy and Society in Baroque Portugal, 1668–1703* (Minneapolis, 1981), 5–17.

208

45. The most concise treatment of Portuguese foreign policy during these decades remains Edgar Prestage, *The Diplomatic Relations of Portugal with France, England, and Holland from 1640–1668* (Watford, 1925).

46. Among others, see Boxer, *Salvador de Sá*, 339–56; Livermore, *New History*, 185–94; and Oliveira Marques, *Portugal* 1:332–33.

47. For a published version of the treaty, see George Forrest, *Selections from the Letters, Despatches, and other State Papers Preserved in the Bombay Secretariat, Home Series*, 2 vols. (Bombay, 1887), 2:362–81.

48. The letter from Afonso and the Overseas Council to Mello de Castro was dated 8/II/1664 and can be found in HAG MR/29, fol. 13. Although a large quantity of documents on this dispute can be found in the HAG, AHU, IOL, and PRO, no detailed analysis of the transfer of Bombay has yet been completed. The issues have, however, been touched upon in *The English Factories in India, 1661–1664*, ed. Foster, 123–44, 214–18, 332–41, and *The English Factories in India, 1665–1667*, ed. William Foster (Oxford, 1925), 37–75, 180–200, 287–313; S. A. Khan, "Anglo-Portuguese Negotiations Relating to Bombay, 1660–1677," *Journal of Indian History*, 3d series (1922): 419–570; and J. G. da Cunha, *The Origin of Bombay* (Bombay, 1900), 239–79.

49. On the marriage of Marie-Françoise to Afonso VI and the new queen's initial actions at court, see Prestage, *Diplomatic Relations*, 84–88, 166–69; Boxer, *Salvador da Sá*, 352–59; and Livermore, *New History*, 192–94.

50. For the disposition of Afonso VI and the assumption of power by Pedro, see Oliveira Marques, *Portugal* 1:332–33; Livermore, *New History*, 194–97; and Boxer, *Salvador da Sá*, 358–74. The 1668 treaty ending the Restoration struggle can be found in J. F. Borges de Castro, *Colleção dos tratados, convenções, contratos, e actos publicos celebrados entre a Coroa de Portugal e as mais potencias desde 1640 até o presente*, 8 vols. (Lisbon, 1856–58), 1:357–409.

51. See Ames, "The *Estado da India*, 1663–1677;" and Hanson, *Baroque Portugal*, 141–259.

52. Given in Colbert, *Lettres* II/2:456–59.

53. See James C. Boyajian, *Portuguese Bankers at the Court of Spain, 1626–1650* (New Brunswick, NJ, 1983), 7.

54. For details, see Alfredo Botelho de Sousa, *Subsídios para a história militar marítima da India, 1585–1650*, 4 vols. (Lisbon, 1930–56); and N. Macleod, *De Oost-Indische Compagnie als zeemongeheid in Azie, 1602–1652*, 2 vols. (Rijswijk, 1927), both based on the relevant archival collections; and Boxer, *Portuguese Seaborne Empire*, 106–27.

55. On Mendonça Furtado's background, see Boxer, *A Índia Portuguesa em meados do século XVII* (Lisbon, 1982), 59–61, and *Salvador da Sá*, 374–76; Fernão de Queyroz, *The Temporal and Spiritual Conquest of Ceylon*, trans. S. G. Perera (Colombo, 1930), 987–92, 1000–1002.

56. AAE CC B1–644, fols. 119–20, Saint-Romain to Colbert, 4/II/1670. See also AAE CC B1–644, Saint-Romain to Louis XIV, fol. 98v, 15/IV/1670, and fol. 111, 22/I/1670.

57. AAE CC B1–644, fols. 103–5v, Saint-Romain to Colbert, 30/XII/1669.

58. AAE CC B1, fols. 105–5v.

59. The *Instrucção* is found in BNL Codex 748, fols. 130–165. For Fronteira's views, see fols. 154–54v.

60. BNL Codex 748, fols. 137–38.

61. The *consulta* of the Overseas Council is found in AHU DAI, box 28, document 71.

62. For Colbert's letters to Saint-Romain on these negotiations, see BN CCC 204, fols. 131–33, 10/VI/1669; fols. 133v–34v, 11/VI/1669; fols. 278v–82, 27/X/1669; fols. 312–13v, 21/XI/1669; and fols. 330–31, 7/XII/1669. See also G. B. Depping, *Correspondance administrative sous le règne de Louis XIV,* 4 vols. (Paris, 1850–55), 3:494–95; and Colbert, *Lettres* III/2:494–95, letter of 27/VIII/1670.

63. AAE B1–644, fols. 103–5v, Saint-Romain to Colbert, 30/XII/1669.

64. AAE B1–644, fol. 142v, Saint-Romain to Louis XIV, 18/IV/1670.

65. BN CCC 204, fols. 312–13v, Colbert to Saint-Romain, 21/XI/1669.

66. PRO SPF 89/10, fols. 117–18, Parry to Arlington, 13/VIII/1669.

67. PRO SPF 89/11, Parry to Arlington, fols. 5–5v, 21/XI/1670, and fol. 14, 29/XI/1670.

CHAPTER 5: SURAT, 1671

1. On these early complaints against Caron's behavior, see Castonnet des Fosses, *L'Inde,* 78–90; Cole, *Colbert* 1:512–15; and for Colbert's reasons for appointing the new directors, see AC B2, fols. 151v–58, *Mémoire pour la Compagnie des Indes Orientales* of December 1670, also given in *Lettres* III/2:506–8.

2. IOL FR G/36/105 (2), fols. 157–58, Child to Surat Council, 2/V/1671. The new director evidently reached Bandar Abbas on 17 April. For details on Baron's background, see Kaeppelin, *La Compagnie,* 65–66.

3. See La Haye, *Journal* 1:97–98.

4. AM B2–9, Colbert to Dumas: fol. 220, 25/VI/1669; fol. 392, 26/IX/1669; fol. 412v, 5/X/1669; fos. 444–44v, 25/X/1669; fol. 461, 1/XI/1669; fol. 495, 15/XI/1669; and fol. 548, 27/XII/1669.

5. PRO SPF 78/129, fols. 21–22, Perwich to Arlington, 29/I/1670.

6. AM B2–9, fols. 18–18v, *Lettre du Roy à M. duc de St. Aignan pour arrêster le Captaine Magnou,* 21/I/1670; and AM B2–10, fols. 41–41v, Louis XIV to Colbert de Terron, 27/II/1670.

7. See AM B2–10, fols. 4v–6v, Colbert to Colbert de Terron, 5/I/1670; Louis XIV to Colbert de Terron: fols. 20–22, 21/I/1670; fols. 26v–28v, 3/II/1670; fols. 10–10v, *Ordres du Roy,* 8/I/1670; B2–11, Colbert to Colbert de Terron, fols. 71–74, 9/II/1670; fols. 74–78v, 13/II/1670; fols. 112–15v, 7/III/1670; fols. 146v–49, 24/III/1670; and fols. 149–51, 28/III/1670. The *Europe* was expected to carry the same number of men as the ill-fated *Breton.* The *Flamand* sailed from Le Havre on 9 February 1670.

8. See AAE B1–644, fol. 145, Saint-Romain to Louis XIV, 9/V/1670; fols. 148–49, des Granger to Colbert, 9/V/1670; fols. 158v–59, Saint-Romain to Louis XIV, 16/V/1670; and La Haye *Journal* 1:2–6.

9. For details on this part of the voyage, see portions of La Haye's log, found in AM B4–4, fols. 54–61; and in the *Journal* 1:17–43. The fleet passed the equator on 5 July and sighted the "montaigne du lion" near the Cape of Good Hope on 24 August 1670. The *Flamand* reached Saldanha on 22 August, while the *Bayonnais, Navarre,* and *Jules* anchored there three days later.

10. La Haye, *Journal* 1:47–54.

11. For La Haye's early actions on the island and his relations with the

Malagasy tribes, see *Journal* 1:47–54. The relevant section of Colbert's instructions on this matter can be found in *Lettres* III/2:466.

12. La Haye, *Journal* 1:54.

13. Carré, *Travels* 2:386–87.

14. The *Journal* entry for 5/I/1671 noted that "M. l'Admiral has ordered that powder, shot, fuses, wine & brandy be sent to him, and that a surgeon go to Andravoulle as quickly as possible to see him, he has been attacked by a *colique*, which is very common and dangerous in this land"; see *Journal* 1:54–55. Carré, *Travels* 2:386–87, puts the French losses at one thousand in this campaign. Kaeppelin rightly criticized this number as exaggerated and offered the more reasonable one of a few hundred; see *La Compagnie*, 51, n. 1.

15. On the voyage to Bourbon and the dispatching of the *Jules* and *Diligente*, see La Haye, *Journal* 1:65–76, and AM B4–4 fols. 314–15. During his stay on the island, La Haye helped plan the defensive works for Saint Denis. It appears he only began using the title of viceroy after his arrival in India; see *Journal* 1:97.

16. For details, see La Haye, *Journal* 1:62, 66–76. The three *compagnie* ships had separated soon after leaving Port-Louis in April 1670. The *Dauphin* stopped in Brazil and then spent several months in Mozambique before reaching Fort-Dauphin in the spring of 1671. The *Phoenix*, carrying the bishop of Heliopolis, M. Pallu, to missionary work in Siam, nearly lost her entire crew to sickness at Saldanha before the arrival of the *Indienne*. The *Vautour* bypassed Fort-Dauphin and anchored at Swally in February 1671.

17. Colbert replied by ordering the ships to make the second rendezvous at Saldanha. Du Trembley was also instructed to send regular reports to Paris on the state of all the ships in the squadron, their crews, and the number of men fit for service. Forrand was charged with reconnoitering all the coasts he visited with great care. See AC B2, fols. 162–62v, Colbert to Du Trembley, 27/XII/1670, and fols. 162v–63, Colbert to Forrand, 27/XII/1670.

18. AAE CC B1–644, fol. 159v, Saint-Romain to Louis XIV, 19/V/1670. The *consulta* of August 1669 is found in AHU DAI, box 28, document 71.

19. The letters of Antonio Alvares Pereira and Antonio de Mello de Castro on this subject are found in HAG MR/28, fols. 150–50v, and HAG MR/28A, fol. 149. On increased Portuguese interest in the region in response to Colbert's initiative, see AHU DAI, box 28, document 94, *Consulta of the Overseas Council on the Rios de Cuama*, 17/X/1669; and HAG MR/36, fols. 318–19, Pedro to Mendonça Furtado, 20/III/1671; discussed in Ames, "A Portuguese Perspective on the Emerging French Presence in the East," 42–45.

20. AAE CC B1–644, fols. 123v–24, 19/II/1670.

21. AM B2–11, fol. 148, Colbert to Colbert de Terron, 24/III/1670.

22. For details on the voyages of the *Triomphe, Sultane,* and *Indienne* from Lisbon to Fort-Dauphin, see AAE CC B1–644, fols. 166–66v, des Granger to Colbert, 10/VII/1670; La Haye, *Journal* 1:62–63; and portions of Du Trembley's journal found in AM B4–4, fols. 64–93.

23. HAG MR/36, fol. 319, Mendonça Furtado to Pedro, 3/X/1671.

24. HAG MR/36, fol. 319.

25. *Colbert* 1:515–16.

26. See AC B4, fols. 82v–83v, Louis XIV to de Turelle (signed by Marie-Thérèse), 23/VI/1672; fols. 83v, Colbert to de Turelle, 26/VI/1672; and fols. 81v–82v, Colbert to Du Trembley, 23/VI/1672.

27. *Journal* 1:80. La Haye, however, was also instructed to mend his ways in a letter from Colbert of 30 June 1672, found in AC B4, fols. 74v–81v.

28. See Henri Froidevaux, "Un mémoire inédit de M. de La Haye sur Madagascar," *Bulletin du comité de Madagascar* 3 (1897): 110–29; and La Haye, *Journal* 1:80. The *Sultane* and *Indienne* did not sail until several weeks later.

29. Carré, *Travels* 2:389.

30. "The noise which the French fleet made in the Court of Agra causes the Mogull to send another Governor with two thousand horse." See IOL OC 3611, Surat presidency to directors, 20/I/1672, fol. 13.

31. IOL OC 3594, Surat presidency to directors, 17/XI/1671, fols. 6–7. As Maetsuycker informed the *Heeren XVII*, "The Portuguese in October last received a great relief from Lisbon. . . . [F]rom their great sea preparations and other signs we have long been of the opinion that they intend to join with the French ships . . . jointly to fall upon us at Malabar or Ceylon." See IOL OC 3661, governor-general and council in Batavia to *Heeren XVII*, 31/VII/1672.

32. AC C2–62, fols. 79–81v, Baron to Colbert, 8/VI/1671.

33. The best description of de Faye's voyage from Fort-Dauphin to Surat can be found in Martin, *Mémoires* 1:145–46, 175–98.

34. For details on Marcara's mission to Golconda, see Malleson, *History of the French in India*, 16; Martin, *Mémoires* 1:231–90; Kaeppelin, *La Compagnie*, 67–78; and AC C2–62, fols. 67–68, Marcara to Colbert, 12/I/1670. The Dutch and English were extremely wary of Marcara's discussions with the Qutb Shahi court and French designs on the Coromandel trade. Anthonie Pavillion, or Paviljoen, advised Batavia in early 1670 that "the French do not much business as yet in these parts, but they make much show and spend much money. They have an agent at St. Thomé, an Armenian by birth, who buys for them, mostly fine muslins for France." See IOL HT I/3/58, 757, 13/II/1670, fol. 3. Marcara failed in his attempt to extend the terms of the *farman* he received to San Thomé. As Pavillion noted, "[T]he French have sent a copy of their firman to the Nawalder of St. Thomé expecting to be admitted free of tolls in that port. But as the firman only mentioned this privilege for Masulipatam, he [Marcara] could not extend it." See IOL HT I/3/58, 755, Pavillion to Batavia, 29/X/1669, fol. 1. As William Jearsey, the English factory chief in Masulipatam wrote, the Dutch agents in Hyderabad did everything they could to undermine French negotiations there. "Mons. Marcara, who was designed chiefe here is yet at Gulcondah, negotiating his business at Court . . . which he hath not done yet, nor will hardly be. . . . [T]he Dutch would given him [Abdullah] 15,000 Pag. rather than he should do it." See IOL FR G/36/105, fol. 185, Jearsey to Surat presidency, 3/XI/1669.

35. Cole, *Colbert* 1:512–13. De Faye evidently died from dysentery; see Martin, *Mémoires* 1:221–23.

36. "They are doing no business whatever. Mr. Caron and his first advisor are still quarreling, they even go so far as to indulge in free fights among themselves and partisans." See IOL HT I/3/58, 752, Batavia to *Heeren XVII*, 31/I/1670, fol. 3.

37. Cole, *Colbert* 1:514; Colbert, *Lettres* III/2:427–31, 461–62; AC B1, fols. 20–22, Louis XIV to Caron, 31/III/1669; and fols. 27–32v, Colbert to de Faye, 31/III/1669.

38. AC B1, fols. 174–75v.

39. AC B2, fols. 158–61, Louis XIV to La Haye, 27/XII/1670.

40. Castonnet des Fosses *L'Inde*, 90; and Kaeppelin, *La Compagnie*, 80–81.

41. See Martin, *Mémoires* 1:248–90; and Kaeppelin, *La Compagnie,* 67–70. Marcara launched an ill-fated lawsuit upon his return to France. Goujon died in Masulipatnam in September 1671.

42. For details on the Bantam-Bangka enterprise, see AC C2–62, fols. 72–75, Caron to Colbert, 15/I/1670.

43. IOL OC 3546, Surat presidency to directors, 5/II/1671, fol. 1v.

44. IOL OC 3566, Surat presidency to directors, 17/IV/1671, fol. 2.

45. IOL OC 3566, fols. 2–3.

46. On Caron's voyage to Indonesia, see IOL OC 3610, Bantam factors to Surat presidency, 8/I/1672; IOL FR G/36/106, fols. 23–24, Bantam to Surat, 26/VIII/1672; and IOL FR G/21/4, fol. 89, Bantam to directors, 8/VIII/1672. The treaty between the rajah of Bangka and the Dutch is described in IOL HT I/3/58, 744.

47. On the *Vautour*'s cargo, see IOL OC 3594, Surat presidency to directors, 17/XI/1672, fol. 21v.

48. IOL OC 3610, Bantam factors to Surat presidency, 8/I/1672, fol. 5.

49. See IOL OC 3594, Surat presidency to directors, 17/XI/1671, fols. 6–7; IOL FR G/36/105, fols. 5–6, Grigby at Swally to Surat, 14/X/1671; and Boxer, "The Third Dutch War in the East," 344.

50. La Haye, *Journal* 1:100–110; and IOL OC 3594, Surat presidency to directors, 17/XI/1671, fol. 21.

51. On these conferences, see La Haye, *Journal* 1:100–110. Caron's experiences on Ceylon during the 1640s are described in Furber, *Rival Empires of Trade,* 54–56; and Boxer, "The Third Dutch War in the East," 345. For details on the director's plans for Ceylon, see AC C2–62, Caron to Colbert, fols. 27–36, 21/IV/1668; fols. 53–53v, 22/VIII/1669; and fols. 64–65, 1/I/1670.

52. S. P. Sen, *The French in India,* 85.

53. Carré, *Travels* 2:142–43.

54. AM B4–4, fols. 332–35, La Haye to Louis XIV, 29/XII/1671.

55. AM B4–4, fols. 332–35.

56. AM B4–4, La Haye to Colbert, fols. 336–39, 13(?)/XII/1671; and fols. 525–26, 6/I/1672.

57. "The French Directors for their East India Company here have Sent one shipp called the *Dauphin* for France being little more than half laden. Her Cargo consissting of Saltpeter, Indico, some Agra, Ahmadabad & Hundrabad cloath, great quantities of Cuttanees . . . and allso druggs of Severall Sorts with Some Pepper. . . . They have a shipp now intended in a few dayes for Bantam, called the *Vulture,* whose Cargo consiste of the Same goodes which you have [ordered] & wee feare will do you much prejudice in the sale of your goods there." See IOL OC 3624, Surat presidency to directors, 13/II/1672. The *Dauphin* reached France in May 1673. See Kaeppelin, *La Compagnie,* 654. On the departure of the main fleet from Surat, see La Haye, *Journal* 1:109.

58. IOL OC 3611, Surat presidency to directors, 20/I/1672, fol. 13.

CHAPTER 6: BATAVIA AND THE MALABAR COAST, 1672

1. IOL HT I/3/94, 177, fol. 2.

2. IOL HT I/3/94, 179, *Heeren XVII* to Batavia, 5/IX/1670, fols. 1–2.

3. For background on Maetsuycker, see Furber, *Rival Empires of Trade,* 63–64, 79–87. On the expulsion of the Portuguese from Ceylon, see Sinnappah Arasaratnam, *Dutch Power in Ceylon, 1658–1687* (Amsterdam, 1958); P. E. Pieris, *Portugal in Ceylon, 1505–1658* (Cambridge, 1937), and *Some Documents Relating to the Rise of Dutch Power in Ceylon, 1602–1670* (Colombo, 1929); R. G. Anthonisz, *The Dutch in Ceylon* (Colombo, 1929); K. W. Goonwardena, *The Foundation of Dutch Power in Ceylon, 1638–58* (Amsterdam, 1958); and G. D. Winius, *The Fatal History of Portuguese Ceylon* (Cambridge, MA, 1971).

4. See Steensgaard, *The Asian Trade Revolution of the Seventeenth Century* (Chicago, 1974), and "The Dutch East India Company as an Institutional Innovation," in *Dutch Capitalism and World Capitalism,* ed. Maurice Aymard (Cambridge, 1982).

5. Discussed in Ames, "The *Carreira da India,* 1668–1682," 25–27.

6. A concise overview of the activities of the VOC during the seventeenth century can be found in Furber, *Rival Empires of Trade,* 31–38, 44–64, 76–89, and 186–91.

7. For background on Van Goens, see Arasaratnam, *Dutch Power,* 22, n. 9; Boxer, "The Third Dutch War in the East," 344; and Furber, *Rival Empires of Trade,* 80–87.

8. IOL HT I/3/56, 732, Batavia to *Heeren XVII,* 30/I/1666. On Dutch fears resulting from the appearance of the *Anne,* see Arasaratnam, *Dutch Power,* 19–21. For details on a 1667 Portuguese fleet gathering at Goa that was believed to be destined for an attack on Ceylon, see IOL HT I/3/56, 737, Vingurla to Batavia, 20/III/1667.

9. IOL HT 732.

10. For details on this campaign, see Arasaratnam, *Dutch Power,* 31–47.

11. IOL HT I/3/58, 740, Batavia to *Heeren XVII,* 18/X/1668.

12. On Rajah Sinha II's counterattack and the financial drain of this warfare, see Arasaratnam, *Dutch Power,* 48–61; IOL OC 3749, Batavia to *Heeren XVII,* 31/I/1673, fols. 1–1v; and Furber, *Rival Empires of Trade,* 80–82. For Caron's negotiations, see his letters to Colbert, found in AC C2–62, fols. 53–53v, 22/VIII/1669, and fols. 64–65, 1/I/1670.

13. IOL FR G/36/105 (2), fol. 29, Petit to Surat presidency, 14/III/1670.

14. IOL FR G/36/105 (2), fol. 26, Petit to Surat presidency, 15/V/1670.

15. For details on de Flacourt's original negotiations with the Zamorin, see IOL FR G/36/105 (1), fol. 81, Oxinden to Surat presidency, 10/I/1669. On the stopover the *St-Paul* and *François* on the Malabar Coast on the return voyage from Bantam, see IOL OC 3594, Surat presidency to directors, 17/XI/1671, fols. 21–22; and La Haye, *Journal* 1:141–43.

16. IOL OC 3749, Batavia to *Heeren XVII,* 31/I/1672, fols. 1–1v.

17. For the amount of pepper carried by the 1670 fleet, see Furber, *Rival Empires of Trade,* 236. IOL OC 3770 provides the following geographic breakdown of the 68 fighting ships at Maetsuycker's disposal in 1672–1673: Batavia (11), Malacca (5), Sumatra (6), Bengal (4), Turatta (1), Japan (1), Timor (2), Macassar (7), Spice Islands (13), and Ceylon (18). On the period in Dutch trade see also Israel, *Dutch Primacy in World Trade,* 197–291.

18. IOL HT I/3/94, 174, *Heeren XVII* to Batavia, 9/V/1669.

19. "The prospect becomes more certain daily that our State will again

become involved in war. . . . You will take every necessary precaution and be quite prepared for the event, and in the meantime secure the possession of all those islands which produce cloves and spices." IOL HT I/3/94, 179, *Heeren XVII* to Batavia, 5/IX/1670, fols. 1–2.

20. IOL HT I/3/94, 182, *Heeren XVII* to Batavia, 24/XI/1671.

21. IOL HT I/3/94, 183, *Heeren XVII* to Batavia, 14/V/1672, fols. 1–2.

22. IOL OC 3646, Bantam factors to directors, 14/VI/1672, fol. 4.

23. IOL OC 3661, Batavia to *Heeren XVII,* 31/VII/1672, fols. 5–15v, summarizes Maetsuycker's military preparations. See also Bantam factors to directors: IOL OC 3646, 14/VI/1672, and 3660, 4/VIII/1672.

24. IOL OC 3661, fols. 9–11. On the offer of brass cannon, see IOL OC 3641, Petit to Surat presidency, 30/V/1672, fol. 2.

25. IOL FR G/36/106, fols. 103–4, Fort-St. George to Surat, 22/III/1672.

26. IOL FR G/36/106, Calicut to Surat presidency, fols. 63–64, 10/I/1672, fols. 81–82, 11/II/1672; and fols. 83–85, 13/II/1672 and 7/III/1672.

27. See Furber, *Rival Empires of Trade,* 92–93.

28. HAG MR/36, fols. 259–59v.

29. HAG Codex 782, fols. 103–14 contains a list of properties valued at nearly 159,000 xerafins that were "usurped without cause by the English" in Bombay between 1666 and 1668.

30. IOL OC 3624, Surat presidency to directors, 13/II/1672, fol. 3.

31. For a description of this town and the short stay of the fleet, see La Haye, *Journal* 1:109–24. Manuel de Mendonça Furtado, a kinsman of the viceroy, had been appointed governor of this town in November 1671; see HAG Codex 1258, *Livro de Homenagens* (3).

32. IOL OC 3624, Surat presidency to directors, 13/II/1672, fols. 2–2v.

33. Mendonça Furtado's voyage included a long stopover in Mozambique and the loss of the *Nossa Senhora dos Remedios* en route. For details on his voyage and arrival in Goa, see HAG MR/36, fol. 405, Mendonça Furtado to Pedro, 14/X/1671.

34. HAG MR/28A, fol. 157, Mello de Castro to queen regent, 29/XII/1662.

35. Mendonça Furtado's initial analysis of the plethora of problems that confronted him are contained in his October 1671 letters to the Crown found in HAG MR/36. The reform campaign of the viceroy and prince regent have been detailed in Ames, "The *Estado da India,* 1663–1677," 31–46 and "The *Carreira da Indi,* 1668–1682," 7–27.

36. HAG MR/37, fol. 130, Baron to Mendonça Furtado, 7/XII/1671.

37. AAE B1–644, fols. 119–20, Saint-Romain to Colbert, 4/II/1670; and B1–644, fols. 110–13v, Saint-Romain to Louis XIV, 22/I/1670.

38. HAG MR/37, fols. 139–39v, Mendonça Furtado to Pedro, 24/VIII/1672.

39. HAG MR/36, fol. 319, Mendonça Furtado to Pedro, 3/X/1671.

40. HAG MR/37, fols. 129–29v, Mendonça Furtado to Pedro, 24/VIII/1672.

41. Martin, *Mémoires* 1:322. The exact date that the fleet reached "Goa" is not entirely clear. La Haye, *Journal* 1:126–27, gives 25 January 1672. The log of

the *Breton* indicates, however, that this man-of-war anchored at "Goa" on that same day, and that the main body of the squadron did not arrive until 28 January. See AM B4–5, fols. 375–76. The confusion can perhaps be resolved by utilizing a letter from Mendonça Furtado to Lisbon of 25 January (HAG MR/36, fol. 459) that states that both La Haye's ships and the *Breton* were in "Goa" on that date. It is likely that the *Breton*, arriving from the south, anchored at Mormugão and for several days was unaware of La Haye's presence several miles to the north, near Panjim.

42. HAG MR/37, fols. 129–29v, Mendonça Furtado to Pedro, 24/VIII/1672.

43. IOL OC 3624, Surat presidency to directors, 13/II/1672, fol. 3.

44. IOL OC 3661, Batavia to *Heeren XVII*, 31/VII/1672, fol. 12v.

45. See Mendonça Furtado to Pedro, HAG MR/36, fol. 459, 25/I/1672; and MR/37, fols. 129–29v, 24/VIII/1672. La Haye's statement that Mendonça Furtado was extremely jealous of his claim to an equal title and increasing French pretensions in the trade is supported by a report from the English Malabar factors to Aungier: "[B]ut their Generall & the Vice Roy both standing upon their punctillioes (sic); neither of them would [at first] condicend to give the other a Visitt. . . . The Portugalls were very Jealous dureing their aboade there, keepeing a very strict watch along the shoar; and at severall Castles to seaward." See IOL FR G/36/106, fols. 72–73.

46. AHU DAI, box 29, document 171.

47. IOL FR G/36/106, fols. 72–73, Carwar to Surat presidency, 19/II/1672.

48. See La Haye, *Journal* 1:127–30.

49. For construction data on the *Breton*, see The Society for Nautical Research Occasional Publications, *Lists of Men-of-War, 1650–1700, part 2, French Ships, 1648–1700*, comp. Pierre Le Conte, no. 5 (London, 1935), 9. Outfitting expenditures on this small fleet can be gleaned from the "List of Expenses on the Two Squadrons Sent to the East Indies under the Command of M. de La Haye," in AM B4–4, fols. 166–89v. For du Clos's instructions, see AC B2, fols. 106–6v. The log of the *Breton* is found in AM B4–5, fols. 332–565v; see especially fols. 374–80 for the arrival and stay in Goa. The stopover in Goa was not without drawbacks, including a fair amount of desertion. See Martin, *Mémoires* 1:323; and Carré, *Travels* 2:399–400. Although Carré did not join the fleet until April 1673, he ascribed rather nefarious motives to Mendonça Furtado during La Haye's stay: "All this apparent friendship and courtesy hid his fury against our nation and his underhanded game. He could not bear any other European in India taking the name and status of Viceroy. He thought of every possible way of weakening our fleet, and the rising glory of our Viceroy, and believed there was no better means of gaining his ends than to injure the squadron in its finances and personnel."

50. IOL FR G/36/106, fols. 81–82, Petit to Surat presidency, 11/II/1672.

51. For details on the departure from Goa, the voyage south, and negotiations with the Zamorin, see La Haye, *Journal* 1:140–50; Martin, *Mémoires* 1:323–24; Carré, *Travels* 2:400–401; and AM B4–5, fols. 381–85.

52. IOL OC 3661, Batavia to *Heeren XVII*, 31/VII/1672, fol. 12.

53. For the French version of the "capture" of Alicot, see La Haye, *Journal* 1:148–49; AM B4–5, fols. 380–84v.; Martin, *Mémoire* 1:324–25; and Duarte, *Relations*, 50–51.

54. On the encounter off Cape Comorim, see La Haye, *Journal* 1:149; AM B4–5, fols. 385–86; Martin, *Mémoires* 1:325–27; Carré, *Travels* 2:400–402; and L'Estra, *Relation*, 93–94. The relevant passage from Colbert's instructions can be found in *Lettres* III/2:462.

55. Carré, *Travels* 2:401.

56. By the fall of 1672, La Haye would inform Paris of his suspicion that Caron was receiving bribes from the VOC. See AM B4–4, fols. 523–23v, La Haye to Louis XIV, 14/IX/1672. The viceroy's sentiments on this matter largely set the tone for Caron's treatment in the historiography of the Third Republic. See Kaeppelin, *La Compagnie*, 95–97; Sottas, *Histoire*, 49–50; Castonnet des Fosses, *L'Inde*, 96–99; and Delort, "La première escadre de la France dans les Indes orientales," *Revue maritime et coloniale* 47 (1875): 458.

CHAPTER 7: PARIS, THE LOW COUNTRIES, AND TRINCOMALEE, 1672

1. On the military and diplomatic preparations for the Dutch War of 1672 and its outbreak, see among others Mignet, *Négociations* 4:3ff.; Goubert, *Louis XIV*, 98–114, 128–29; Ekberg, *The Failure of Louis XIV's Dutch War* (Chapel Hill, NC, 1979), 13–14; Sonnino, *Dutch War*, pass.; Bluché, *Louis XIV*, 246–50; and Hutton, *Charles II*, 271–92.

2. Herbert H. Rowen, *John de Witt, Grand Pensionary of Holland, 1625–1672* (Princeton, 1978), 809–11.

3. Goubert, *Louis XIV*, 128.

4. See Rowen, *John de Witt*, 811–18.

5. On Holmes's surprise attack on the Smyrna fleet, see Rowen, *John de Witt*, 815–16; and Hutton, *Charles II*, 288.

6. For details on the battle of Sole Bay and the early stages of the naval war, see among others A. T. Mahan, *The Influence of Sea Power upon History, 1660–1783* (Boston, 1928), 140–50; and Rowen, *John de Witt*, 816–24.

7. On the early stages of the land campaign, see Goubert, *Louis XIV*, 128–29; Bluché, *Louis XIV*, 248–50; and Rowen, *John de Witt*, 824–39.

8. Goubert, *Louis XIV*, 129.

9. Goubert, *Louis XIV*, 129–30; Bluché, *Louis XIV*, 249–50; and Rowen, *John de Witt*, 837–39.

10. On these negotiations, see Mignet, *Négociations* 4:30–40; and Rowen, *John de Witt*, 837–50. The additional French demands included the provinces of Utrecht, Overijssel, Gelderland, the Generality Lands east of the Maas, 16,000,000 guilders, an annual Dutch embassy to Paris to present Louis with a gold medal expressing contrition for their unwarranted hosility, the free practice of Catholicism, and the supression of all edicts harming French trade since 1662.

11. For details on the deteriorating military and diplomatic situation confronting Louis and Charles II by the fall of 1672 and on the rise of William of Orange, see Rowen, *John de Witt*, 851–94; Hutton, *Charles II*, 288–97; Ekberg, *Failure of Louis XIV's Dutch War*, 14–15, 48–51, 77–81 and 112–14; and Bluché, *Louis XIV*, 250–51.

12. Colbert's writings leave little doubt that he indeed supported the war against the United Provinces for reasons of political economy; see his *Mémoire au roi sur les finances* (1670), given in *Lettres* VII:251; Clément's analysis of the controller-general's actions in *Lettres* II:cxxxv, as well as sentiments expressed in *Mé-*

moires, found in II/2:448–49, 481, 571–74, 604, and 658ff. See also Cole, *Colbert* 1:345; Goubert, *Louis XIV,* 127; Wolf, *Louis XIV,* 214; and Bluché, *Louis XIV,* 247. Paul Sonnino has attempted to challenge this formidable orthodoxy in his article "Jean-Baptiste Colbert and the Origins of the Dutch War," *European Studies Review* 13 (1983): 1–11, and *Louis XIV and the Origins of the Dutch War.* Although Sonnino provides a useful political narrative for the years 1668–1672, his efforts to portray Colbert as a narrow-minded bureaucrat cowered by Louis into supporting the war is less than convincing. Nevertheless, see also Andrew Lossky, *Louis XIV and the French Monarchy* (New Brunswick, NJ, 1994), 100–1.

13. In his *The Ambassador Prepares for War: The Dutch Embassy of Arnauld de Pomponne, 1669–1671* (The Hague, 1957), 195, Rowen argued that Colbert had made no long-term plans between 1668 and 1670 to exploit the economic "potentialities" of a military victory over the United Provinces.

14. See Colbert's *Mémoire* of 8/VII/1672 in *Lettres* II/2:658–60.

15. Ames, "*Carreira da India,* 1668–1682," 20–23.

16. On the *compagnie*'s continuing problems, see Cole, *Colbert* 1:498–510; and Furber, *Rival Empires of Trade,* 202–3. According to the *procès verbal* of the *Assemblée générale* of 8/V/1675, the total had reached 8,919,284 livres. See Dessert and Journet, "Le lobby Colbert," 1314–15.

17. AC B2, fols. 106–9v, "Instructions to Régnier Du Clos," 19/IX/1670; fols. 109v–10, Louis XIV to La Haye, 19/IX/1670; and fols. 110–10v, Colbert to La Haye, 19/IX/1670.

18. AC B2, fols. 158–58v.

19. AC B4, fols. 14v–18v.

20. AC B4, fols. 27v–28v.

21. AC B4, fols. 91–93v.

22. La Haye, *Journal* 1:152–53.

23. For details on the squadron's arrival and early activities on Ceylon, see La Haye, *Journal* 1:151–69; and Carré, *Travels* 2:405–6. In a letter of April 1668, Caron favored Batticaloa over Trincomalee as the site for a French entrepôt and fortress. See AC C2–62, fols. 27v–28, Caron to Colbert.

24. IOL FR G/36/106, Bombay to Surat, 18/VII/1672, fol. 114.

25. IOL OC 3649, Bombay to directors, 22/IV/1672, fol. 5.

26. HAG MR/37, Mendonça Furtado to Pedro, fols. 129–29v, 24/VIII/1672; and fols. 203–3v, 15/IX/1672.

27. On these initial negotiations, see La Haye, *Journal* 1:169–71; Martin, *Mémoires* 1:339–40; and AC C2–62, fols. 116–17, La Haye to Boisfontaine, n.d.

28. AC C2–62, fols. 118–18v, La Haye to Boisfontaine, 7/V/1672; La Haye, *Journal* 1:171–203; Martin, *Mémoires* 1:341–49; Carré, *Travels* 2:421; "Mémoires de L. A. Bellanger de Lespinay," ed. Henri Froidevaux, *Bulletin de la Société archéologique du Vendômois* 33 (1894) and 34 (1895): 61–74; Arasaratnam, *Dutch Power,* 62–63; and Robert Knox, *An Historical Relation of Ceylon* (Glasgow, 1911), 294–96. Bellanger de Lespinay was one of La Haye's private guards on the voyage. Knox was an Englishman from the ship *Anne,* who had been captured in 1660 and remained a prisoner at the court of Kandy for the next twenty years.

29. AC C2–62, fols. 116–18.

30. According to Martin, *Mémoires* 1:330–31.

31. Martin, *Mémoires* 1:338.

32. AC C2 62, fols. 90–91, summary of La Haye's letters from Malabar and

Ceylon (compiled in Surat?), n.d. The *Phoenix* and *St-Louis* were *compagnie* ships, whereas the *Europe* was a royal vessel. Added military precautions were taken in outfitting these ships, including embarking an infantry company aboard the *Phoenix*. See Carré, *Travels* 2:333; and Martin, *Mémoires* 1:330.

33. IOL OC 3661, Batavia to *Heeren XVII*, 31/VII/1672, fols. 9–10.

34. IOL OC 3639, "Extract of General Resolution of Batavia Council," 12/VII/1672.

35. IOL OC 3639.

36. IOL OC 3661, fols. 8v–10.

37. IOL OC 3639, Van Goens to La Haye, 15/V/1672.

38. IOL OC 3639, La Haye to Van Goens, 16/V/1672.

39. IOL OC 3639, Van Goens to La Haye, 20/V/1672.

40. IOL OC 3639, La Haye to Van Goens, 27/V/1672.

41. For details on these land skirmishes, see La Haye, *Journal* 1:180–200; Martin, *Mémoires* 1:341–48; Carré, *Travels* 2:417–18; and Bellanger de Lespinay, *Mémoires*, 70–72. In a letter to Colbert of July 1672, Caron maintained that there were 360 men who were sick and another 340 too weak to fight. See *Journal* 2, app. 28.

42. On the debate surrounding the capture of the *Phoenix* and *Europe* by Van Goens's ships, see Carré, *Travels* 2:334–35, 408–10; La Haye, *Journal* 1:189–98; Martin, *Mémoires* 1:330, 346–47; L'Estra, *Relation*, 105, 131–34; and Bellanger de Lespinay, *Mémoires*, 69–70.

43. La Haye, *Journal* 1:221–22; Carré, *Travels* 2:411–12; Martin, *Mémoires* 1:348; and L'Estra, *Relation*, 135–37. L'Estra's account, however, mistakenly states that the *St-Louis* was able to rejoin the fleet inside the inner bay.

44. On this decision, see La Haye, *Journal* 1:192, 219–29; Martin, *Mémoires* 1:349–50.

45. La Haye, *Journal* 1:201–2; Martin, *Mémoires* 1:349–50; and Carré, *Travels* 2:422–24.

46. Carré, *Travels* 2:427.

47. Carré, *Travels* 2:425; Martin, *Mémoires* 1:350; Bellanger de Lespinay, *Mémoires*, 76–77; and La Haye, *Journal* 1:226–27. This envoy, M. de La Norelle, was instructed to make it clear that the main reason for La Haye's departure was the inadequate level of supplies forthcoming from Kandy. On de La Norelle's reception by Rajah Sinha II, see Knox, *Historical Relation*, 295–99.

48. La Haye, *Journal* 1:231; Carré, *Travels* 2:427; Martin, *Mémoires* 1:351; and Bellanger de Lespinay, *Mémoires*, 77–78.

49. Carré, *Travels* 2:427–31; Martin, *Mémoires* 1:366–71; L'Estra, *Relation*, 164–69; and Kaeppelin, *La Compagnie*, 94–95.

50. AM B4–4, fols. 523–24v, 529–31, La Haye to Louis XIV, 14/IX/1672.

51. AC C2–62, fols. 145–62, given in La Haye, *Journal* 2, app. 1–30.

CHAPTER 8: THE COROMANDEL COAST, PARIS, AND FLANDERS, 1673

1. La Haye, *Journal* 1:232–37; Martin, *Mémoires* 1:352; and Bellanger de Lespinay, *Mémoires*, 81–82. The Danes had received Tranquebar from the naik of Tanjore in 1620 for an annual rent of 2000 pagodas. For details on Colbert's 1669 attempt to procure the town from Denmark, see Henri Froidevaux, "Un projet

d'acquisition de Tranquebar par la France en 1669," *Revue de géographie* 41 (1897), 88–96.

2. AC C2–62, fols. 166–67, Blot to Colbert, 29/III/1672; and Chardin, *Travels*, 4–5.

3. AC B2, fols. 166v–67, Louis XIV to La Haye, 20/VI/1671.

4. See AC B4, fols. 14v–18v, Louis XIV to La Haye, 11/II/1672. La Haye originally argued that the delayed packets had adversely affected the squadron's fortunes in a letter to the king of 14/IX/1672; see AM B4–4, fols. 523–24v. His sentiments set the tone for the traditional Third Republic literature on this episode, found in Sottas, *Histoire*, 49–50; Kaeppelin, *La Compagnie*, 95–96; Castonnet des Fosses, *L'Inde*, 96–98; and Henri Froidevaux, "The French Factories in India," in *The Cambridge History of India*, ed. H. H. Dodwell (Cambridge, 1929), 67–70.

5. La Haye, *Journal* 1:242.

6. John Fryer, *A New Account of East India and Persia*, ed. William Crooke, 3 vols. (London, 1909–15), 1:115.

7. For details on San Thomé during the seventeenth century, see Lotika Varadarajan, "San Thomé—Early European Activities and Aspirations," in Luis Albuquerque and Inacio Guerreiro, *Actas de II Seminário Internacional de Historia Indo-Portuguesa* (Lisbon, 1985), 432–41; H. D. Love, *Vestiges of Old Madras, 1640–1800*, 3 vols. (London, 1913), 1:286–310; H. K. Sherwani, *History of the Qutb Shahi Dynasty* (Delhi, 1974), 480–515; and "Reign of Abdu'l-lah Qutb Shah (1626–1672)" *Journal of Indian History* 45 (1967): 115–60; and Foster, ed., *The English Factories in India, 1661–1664*, 146.

8. IOL HT I/3/58, 757, Paviljoen to Batavia, 13/II/1670, fol. 3. See also HT I/3/58, 755, Paviljoen to Batavia, 29/X/1670, fols. 1–2.

9. On the Ceylon discussions, see AM B4–4 fol. 524, La Haye to Louis XIV, 14/IX/1672. Martin, *Mémoires* 1:300–302 suggests that Caron's plans to capture San Thomé were well known on the Coromandel Coast, while Carré, *Travels* 2:433, argues that the squadron arrived before the town with no intention of attacking it.

10. IOL FR G/36/87, fols. 71–72, Langhorn to Aungier, 5/VIII/1672.

11. Richards, *Golconda*, 14–15; and Shah Manzur Alam, "Masulipatam—A Metropolitan Port in the Seventeenth Century," *Islamic Culture* 33 (1959): 169–87.

12. For details on events from 21 to 24 July, see La Haye, *Journal* 1:242–48; Martin, *Mémoires* 1:353–56; Carré, *Travels* 2:437–39; and Bellanger de Lespinay, *Mémoires*, 111.

13. On the capture of San Thomé, see La Haye, *Journal* 1:248–52; Martin, *Mémoires* 1:357–59; L'Estra, *Relation*, 170–80; Carré, *Travels* 2:441–44; Bellanger de Lespinay, *Mémoires*, 113–15; Love, *Vestiges* 1:314; and *The English Factories in India, 1670–1677*, ed. Charles Fawcett, 2 vols. (Oxford, 1936–52), 2:45–47.

14. IOL FR G/19/1, fols. 18–20. Fort-St. George was judged to have sufficient artillery, including forty-nine cannon and fourteen hundred iron shot, to meet this threat. But Langhorn and his councilors decided that the gates of the fort needed strengthening, the town's outworks needed repair, and the wall facing San Thomé should be raised by five feet. See IOL OC 3721, Langhorn to directors, 26/XII/1672, fol. 2v.

15. HAG MR/37, fol. 203v, Mendonça Furtado to Pedro, 13/IX/1672; and AHU DAI, box 29, document 131, "*Consulta* of the Overseas Council on the

French Capture of San Thomé," 2/IX/1673; and MR/37, fol. 212, João Pereira de Faria to Mendonça Furtado, 30/VII/1672. No copy of the first evidently survives, although there are indirect references to its contents in a letter from Mendonça Furtado to Pedro of 11/X/1673, found in HAG MR/38A, fols. 243. The only extant copy of the 19 October letter appears to be in AC C2–62, fol. 186.

16. Richards, *Golconda*, 1, 14–15, 34–35.

17. Richards, *Golconda*, 14–15; H. K. Sherwani, "The Reign of Abu'l Hasan Qutb Shah," *Journal of Indian History* 46 (1968): 315–16; Carré, *Travels* 2:447–48; Martin, *Mémoires* 1:393–94. For Langhorn's estimate, see IOL OC 3721, Langhorn to directors, 26/XII/1672, fol. 1v.

18. Martin, *Mémoires* 1:387–88; La Haye, *Journal* 2:4–5; Carré, *Travels* 2:452–54; and Bellanger de Lespinay, *Mémoires,* 115–16. For the superiority of Qutb Shahi heavy cavalry, see Richards, *Golconda*, 14.

19. La Haye, *Journal* 2:10–18; Love, *Vestiges* 1:321–22; and Carré, *Travels* 2:454–55. According to Martin, *Mémoires* 1:391–92, some three thousand cavalry appeared in the western suburbs on 3 September 1672.

20. La Haye, *Journal* 1:252; Love, *Vestiges* 1:44–45, 304, 311–15; and L'Estra, *Relation*, 175–77. The town's bastions were rather predictably given names like *Colbert, Bourbon, La Haye, de Rebrey,* and *Dauphin.*

21. See La Haye, *Journal* 2:4–18; Martin, *Mémoires* 1:388–97; and Carré, *Travels* 2:453–56.

22. On the dispatch of these ships and the granting of Pondicherry, see La Haye, *Journal* 2:13–15, 40,48; Martin, *Mémoires* 1:394–99, 416; and Bellanger de Lespinay, *Mémoires,* 211–21, 278–97.

23. La Haye, *Journal* 2:44; Carré, *Travels* 2:484–85; and Martin, *Mémoires*˙ 1:388–90, 398–99, 406, 419–20, and 425.

24. *The Dictionary of National Biography*, ed. Sidney Lee (London, 1892), 32:103–4.

25. IOL OC 3729, Langhorn to directors, 6/II/1673, fol. 2v.

26. IOL FR G/19/17, fol. 7, Langhorn to Abul Hasan, 16/II/1673. The question of how far the English went in attempting to undermine the French presence at San Thomé is one of the more controversial issues surrounding the Third Dutch War in Asia. Carré wrote that Langhorn tried to subvert the French by supplying arms, advice, and provisions to Abul Hasan's armies; see *Travels* 2:448–49. English historians have traditionally downplayed such activities, arguing that, faced with three potential enemies, Langhorn did everything he could to remain neutral. See Fawcett, ed., *The English Factories, 1670–1677*, 2:vi–x, and his notes in Carré, *Travels* 2:448–49. Fawcett's argument that the determining factor in Langhorn's behavior was his desire to maintain English trading interests rings true. However, his statement that Carré's charges "are not supported by the Madras records in the India Office" rests on the dubious assumption that the astute governor would have left written records of his most controversial decisions. The most logical approach is to compromise and suggest that, while the English did everything they could to avoid war, Abul Hasan's power and the dread of a French settlement so close to their own ensured that Langhorn made far more concessions to the Qutb Shahi army than to La Haye. He did, however, allow "private" merchants to sell goods surreptitiously to San Thomé during the initial siege. See IOL OC 3729, Langhorn to directors, 6/II/1673.

27. AM B4–5, fol. 311, La Haye to Louis XIV, 9/II/1673. For details on this attack, see La Haye, *Journal* 2:19–20; Martin, *Mémoires* 1:397–98 and Carré, *Travels* 2:461–64.

28. La Haye, *Journal* 2:20–30; Martin, *Mémoires* 1:404–5, 420; Carré, *Travels* 2:465–66, 469–71, 473–77.

29. For details, see Carré, "Suite de l'histoire de Sevagy," in S. N. Sen, *Foreign Biographies of Shivaji* (London, 1930), 255–67; *Travels* 2:485–91; Martin, *Mémoires* 1:496–97; Richards, *Golconda*, 35–38; and Love, *Vestiges* 1:339–40, 343–47.

30. AM B4–5, fol. 313v, La Haye to Louis XIV, 9/II/1673.

31. On these negotiations, see AM B4–5, fol. 313v, La Haye to Louis XIV, 9/II/1673; La Haye, *Journal* 2:37–39; Martin, *Mémoires* 1:408–15; and Carré, *Travels* 2:478–79.

32. AM B4–5, fol. 313v.

33. On La Haye's growing suspicions of Caron, see AM B4–4, fols. 523–23v, La Haye to Louis XIV, 14/IX/1672. For details on the director-general's departure, see *Journal* 2:10–11.

34. On Caron's voyage and death in the Tagus, see Carré, *Travels* 2:458; AAE B1–645, fols. 174–76, "Report on the Loss of the *Jules,* Lisbon," 10/IV/1673; fols. 165–68v, d'Aubeville to Seignelay, 4/IV/1673; and fol. 179, "*Mémoire* to Seignelay," 10/IV/1673.

35. According to Carré, *Travels* 2:459–60, the *St-Louis* was captured in December 1672, and Van Goens confiscated Caron's gold and silver plate. Citing IOL HT I/3/60, 785, fol. 13, Batavia to *Heeren XVII,* 11/XII/1672, Fawcett attempts to refute these charges against Van Goens; see *Travels* 2:459, n. 3. Martin, *Mémoires* 1:413, suggests that the officers of the *St-Louis* and the Dutch divided the booty.

36. Carré, *Travels* 2:494–95.

37. IOL FR G/19/17, fol. 6v, Langhorn to English agent at Hyderabad, 16/III/1673.

38. For details on this engagement, see La Haye, *Journal* 2:55–62; Carré, *Travels* 2:497–508; Martin, *Mémoires* 1:425–28; and L'Estra, *Relation,* 180. On 14 March, Langhorn wrote: "I look forward to the time when I can send one of our messengers to congratulate the happy success of your arms without giving a pretext to the Moslems to do prejudice to our trade. I entreat you to accept the good will with the grand desire that I possess to render assistance to you in everything which depends on me." See IOL FR G/19/17, fol. 4v, Langhorn to La Haye, 14/III/1673.

39. AM B4–5, fol. 531, La Haye to Louis XIV, 14/IX/1672.

40. AM B4–5, fols. 311–13v, La Haye to Louis XIV, 9/II/1673; and fols. 315–16, La Haye to Colbert, 9/II/1673.

41. AM B4–5, fols. 317–18, La Haye to Louis XIV, 14/III/1673.

42. Colbert, *Lettres* II/2:658–60.

43. Ekberg, *Failure of Louis XIV's Dutch War,* 15.

44. Louis XIV, *Oeuvres,* ed. P. H. Grimoard and P. A. Grouvelle, 6 vols. (Paris, 1806), 3:303–6.

45. On the early stages of the 1673 campaign, see Ekberg, *Failure of Louis XIV's Dutch War,* 14–21.

46. See Louis XIV, *Oeuvres* 3:412–13; quoted in Ekberg, *Failure of Louis XIV's Dutch War,* 21.

47. The best treatment of the deterioration of the Dutch War in 1673 remains Ekberg's *Failure of Louis XIV's Dutch War*, especially pp. 48–75 and 110–50.

48. For Croissy's letters, see Mignet, *Négociations* 4:247ff. On the events culminating in the Westminster Treaty, see Ekberg, *Failure of Louis XIV's Dutch War*, 152–71; and Hutton, *Charles II*, 297–319.

49. R. B. Bingham has even gone so far as to call this debate "a dead end in historical research." See his commentary in the *Proceedings of the 3rd Annual Meeting of the Western Society for French History* (1975), 81.

50. Ekberg, *Failure of Louis XIV's Dutch War*, 11.

51. Based mainly on court memoirs, Sonnino, *Origins of the Dutch War*, 172–73, has sought to elevate this episode, the supposed "octave de M. Colbert," into a seminal event in the relationship between the king and his chief minister. Perhaps the only thing that descriptions like Montagu's convincingly demonstrate is that Louvois and his supporters sought to make as much of the episode as possible in an attempt to undermine Colbert's position ("being in the hands and power of one man, for his finances") with the king. See Montagu to Arlington, 1/XII/1671, *Buccleuch and Queensberry Mss.* 1:505–6. The extant evidence tells us little about Louis's thought on the matter.

52. Cole, *Colbert* 1:297–98. See also p. 293 on Colbert's ministerial dominance.

53. Among others, see Cole *Colbert* 2:551; and Goubert, *Louis XIV*, 131–141.

54. Discussed in Sonnino, *Origins of the Dutch War*, 116–18.

55. Colbert, *Lettres* II/2:676–78.

56. See *Lettres* II/1:ccxxxiv, Colbert to Louis XIV, 1/VIII/1673.

57. Goubert, *Louis XIV*, 131–41.

58. AC B4, fols. 14v–18v, Louis XIV to La Haye, 11/II/1672.

59. AC B4, fols. 27v–28v, Louis XIV to La Haye, 15/III/1672.

60. AC B5, fols. 4v–7v, Louis XIV to La Haye, 27/II/1673. On the gradual diminuation in the king's estimation of the Asian project, see also AC B4, fols. 91–93v, Louis XIV to La Haye, 19/X/1672.

61. See AC B2, fols. 166v–67v, Louis XIV to La Haye, 20/VI/1671; and AC B4, fols. 14v–15v, Louis XIV to La Haye, 11/II/1672.

62. For example, see AM B2–23, Colbert to Colbert de Croissy, fols. 108v–9v, 26/VII/1673; fols. 132v–35v, 13/IX/1673; and AM B2–24, fols. 255–57v, Colbert to Colbert de Croissy, 17/VI/1673.

63. AAE CC B1–645, fols. 174–76, "Report on the Loss of the *Jules,* Lisbon," 10/IV/1673; fols. 165–68v, d'Aubeville to Seignelay, 4/IV/1673; and fol. 179, *"Mémoire* to Seignelay on Loss of *Jules,"* 10/IV/1673.

64. AC B5, fols. 21–21v,*"Mémoire* to King on the Subject of the Shipwreck of the Man-of-War *Jules."*

65. AC B4, fols. 79–80v, Colbert to La Haye, 30/VI/1672. See also fols. 73–74v, Louis XIV to La Haye (Signed by Marie-Thérèse and Colbert), 30/VI/1672.

66. AC B5, fol. 21v.

67. Ekberg, *Failure of Louis XIV's Dutch War*, 22.

68. AC B5, fols. 32–34, Louis XIV to La Haye, 23/VIII/1673.

69. See AC B5, fols. 8–9, Colbert to Lesboris, 27/II/1673; fols. 9–10, "Pro-

visions on the Government of the Island of Soleil," 27/II/1673; fols. 10–11, "Orders to M. de la Hure and the Inhabitants of Bourbon," 27/II/1673; and fols. 11–12v, "Instructions to le Sr. Beauregard," 27/II/1673.

70. See B5, fols. 39–41v, "Cargo of the flute *Eléphant,* charged with refitting the vessels of the Persian Squadron," October 1673. In April 1674, the *Rubis* sailed from Rochefort with 100,000 livres and some troops to assist La Haye. See AC B6, fols. 8v–10, "Cargo of the *Rubis* bound for the East Indies," 12/II/1674.

71. AM B2–23, fols. 132–35v.

72. See Sonnino, *Origins of the Dutch War,* 6–7.

73. Colbert de Croissy had forwarded copies of the letters from the Court of Committees to Langhorn on this matter to Paris. See AM B2–23, fols. 135–35v. In a letter of October 1673, the London directors revealed their priorities, instructing Langhorn, "Wee therefore require that you exercise such Caution and prudence, as not to give, any European just occasion of affronte, But in a more especial manner that you provoke not the Natives."

CHAPTER 9: *LES INDES ORIENTALES* AND PARIS, 1674

1. "Wee still have reasonable hopes that the god of peace will dispose his Majestie, and the States of Holland to a lasting peace, and friendship." See IOL OC 3682, Bombay to Surat, 14/X/1672, fol. 1v; and OC 3683, president and council in Bombay to directors, 7/X/1672, fol. 2.

2. HAG Codex 782, fols. 103–14.

3. HAG MR/36, fols. 259–59v, "Petition of the Hindus of Baçaim to Luis de Mendonça Furtado," 19/VI/1671. As this petition pointed out, the influx of such merchants into the English enclave had incresed tax-farming receipts on the tobacco *renda* sixfold in less than six years.

4. For details, see Furber, *Rival Empires of Trade,* 31–94.

5. See, for example, Chaudhuri, *The Trading World of Asia,* 19–21.

6. IOL OC E/3/87, fol. 159v, directors to Surat presidency, 26/II/1669. See also fol. 112v, directors to Surat presidency, 20/III/1668.

7. The convoy policy was originally engendered by rumors regarding the formation of the Persian squadron, see IOL OC E/3/87, fol. 173, directors to Bantam, 6/III/1669.

8. IOL FR G/3/6 (2), fol. 185, Aungier to Langhorn, 13/IX/1673. See also IOL OC 3779, fol. 3, Bombay to directors (?), 11/XI/1673; and OC 3872, fol. 3v, Bombay to directors, 3/XII/1673.

9. IOL OC E/3/88, fol. 35, directors to Fort-St. George, 9/X/1673.

10. IOL OC 3966, fol. 1v, Langhorn to Aungier, 30/V/1674.

11. On Baron's expedition, see AC C2–62, fols. 177–78, Gueston to Colbert, 15/X/1672; fols. 179–80, Baron to Colbert, 18/X/1672; fols. 181–81v, directors in Surat to Colbert, 16/XI/1672; IOL FR G/3/6 (2), Aungier to Langhorn, fols. 80–84, 11/III/1673; fols. 97–105, Bombay to directors, 7/IV/1673; Carré, *Travels* 2:512–15; Martin, *Mémoires* 1:449–50; and La Haye, *Journal* 2:72. The threat to French trading activities in Persia was evidently quite real. As John Child, an English factor in Bandar Abbas wrote in May 1671, "[I]ts Credible reported that if they [the French] have not Shipps & an Embassador come here next yeare, that the Persian will take from them Customes for all goods, they have export & imported since they

have bin in Persia." See IOL FR G/36/105 (2), fols. 157–58. On Shah Abbas II's death and activities at the Safavid court from 1672 to 1674, see Chardin, *Travels.*

12. On the battle of Petapoli and its significance, see Boxer, "The Third Dutch War in the East," which includes descriptions of the encounter by van Quael-bergen and Basse; La Haye, *Journal* 2:87–92; Martin, *Mémoires* 1:501–3; Carré, *Travels* 2:602; Fawcett, *The English Factories in India, 1670–1677* 2:240–41; IOL FR G/26/9, fols. 17–21v, Langhorn to Mohun, 14–17/VII/1673; and OC 3992, Langhorn to directors, VIII–IX/1674.

13. IOL FR G/19/17, fol. 9, Langhorn to English agent in Hyderabad, 21/III/1673.

14. IOL OC 3849, fol. 1, Langhorn to directors, 22/IX/1673.

15. Hutton, *Charles II*, 295–318.

16. IOL OC E/3/88, fols. 46v, directors to Fort-St. George, 23/III/1674; and fols. 51–51v, directors to Surat presidency, 23/III/1674.

17. IOL OC 3992, fols. 4–5, Langhorn to directors, 30/VIII/1674.

18. Furber, *Rival Empire of Trade*, 242.

19. On this reform campaign and the proposed alliance with France, see Ames, "The *Estado da India,* 1663–1677," 35–46, and "A Portuguese Perspective on the Emerging French Presence in the East, c. 1670."

20. Carré, *Travels* 2:399–400.

21. HAG MR/37, Mendonça Furtado to Pedro, fol. 203, 13/IX/1672; and fols. 129–29v, 24/VIII/1672.

22. See HAG MR/37, fol. 212, João Pereira de Faria to Mendonça Furtado, 30/VII/1672; Mendonça Furtado to Pedro, fol. 211, 29/IX/1672; fols. 203–3v, 15/IX/1672; MR/38A, fol. 243, 11/X/1673; MR/38A, fols. 244–44v, João Coelho to Mendonça Furtado, 14/VII/1673; AHU DAI, box 29, document 131, "*Consulta* of the Overseas Council on the French Capture of San Thomé," 2/IX/1673; and AC C2–62, fol. 186, Mendonça Furtado to Coelho, 19/X/1672.

23. See AHU DAI, box 29, document 171, Mendonça Furtado to Pedro, 18/II/1673.

24. See Ames, "The *Estado da India,* 1663–1677," 39–46, and "The *Carreira da India,* 1668–1682," 20–27.

25. See PRO SPF 89/12, fols. 134–34v, Parry to Williamson, 30/VIII/1672.

26. For details on this project, see PRO SPF 89/12, fols. 186–87, Parry to Arlington, 26/XI/1672; and Parry to Williamson, fols. 248–49, 18/VII/1673; fols. 252–53, 15/VIII/1673; fols. 279–79v, 5/XII/1673; and Hanson, *Baroque Portugal*, 89–99.

27. IOL OC 3929, Aungier to directors, 25/I/1674.

28. HAG Codex 2316, fol. 27, discussed in Ames, "The *Estado da India,* 1663–1677," 45–46.

29. IOL OC 3929.

30. IOL OC 3749, fols. 1–2, Batavia to *Heeren XVII,* 31/I/1673.

31. See IOL HT I/3/58–60, "Letters from India to the *Heeren XVII,* 1667–1673"; HT I/3/93–94, "Letters from *Heeren XVII* to India, 1666–1700"; and I/3/104, "Letters from Batavia to dependent factories, 1668–1680."

32. See IOL OC 3661, Batavia to *Heeren XVII,* 31/VII/1672.

33. IOL HT I/3/94, 183, *Heeren XVII* to Batavia, 14/V/1672.

34. See Israel, *Dutch Primacy in World Trade,* 16–17.

35. See IOL I/3/94, 183, 185, 187, 188, *Heeren XVII* to Batavia, 14/V/1672, 20/IX/1672, 30/IX/1673, and 4/XI/1673.

36. IOL HT I/3/94, 188, *Heeren XVII* to Batavia, 4/XI/1673.

37. See IOL OC, Batavia to *Heeren XVII,* 3661, 31/VII/1672; and 3749, 31/I/1673.

38. See IOL HT, Batavia to *Heeren XVII,* I/3/59, 785, 11/XII/1672; I/3/60, 794, 31/I/1673; I/3/60, 795, 13/XI/1673. On the terms of the alliance, see Carré, *Travels* 2:531.

39. AM B4–5, fols. 321–21v, La Haye to Louis XIV, 20/IX/1673.

40. On the Masulipatnam enterprise, see La Haye, *Journal* 2:66–76; Martin, *Mémoires* 1:443–83; and Carré, *Travels* 2:532–55.

41. AM B4–5, fol. 323, La Haye to Louis XIV, 20/IX/1673; La Haye, *Journal* 2:80; Carré, *Travels* 2:559–60; Martin, *Mémoires* 1:535, 538–41; L'Estra, *Relation,* 185–86; and Boxer, "Third Dutch War in the East," 360. The two prizes sought shelter on the Gingalee Coast and were reclaimed by their Muslim owners; the *Flamand* lost sight of the *Breton* and was captured a month later cruising the Balasore Coast of Orissa by three Dutch ships.

42. For differing descriptions of the encounter, see AM B4–5, fols. 323–24, La Haye to Louis XIV, 20/IX/1673; Carré, *Travels* 2:560–63, who watched the fight from the bastions of Fort-St. George; and Martin, *Mémoires* 1:486–88, who was aboard the *Breton* at the time.

43. IOL FR G/26/9 (3), fol. 15, Langhorn to Mohun, 7/VII/1673.

44. La Haye, *Journal* 2:78–79; Martin, *Mémoires* 1:487–92; Carré, *Travels* 2:574–75; and Bellanger de Lespinay, *Mémoires,* 120–22.

45. La Haye's initial meetings with the cleric are described in the *Journal* 2:79–80 and Carré, *Travels* 2:575–80. Copies of the letters that Carré carried to India can be found in AM B4, fols. 14v–18v. For details on the cleric's activities in Madras during the summer and early fall of 1673, see *Travels* 2:577–675.

46. Carré, *Travels* 2:523; and AM B4–5, fol. 322, La Haye to Louis XIV, 20/IX/1673.

47. See Carré, *Travels* 2:510–21, 546; Martin, *Mémoires* 1:489–93; and La Haye, *Journal* 2:69–76.

48. For details, see La Haye, *Journal* 2:92–100; Martin, *Mémoires* 1:507–10; and Carré, *Travels* 2:618–22.

49. On the erection of the second siege, see La Haye, *Journal* 2:105–10; Martin, *Mémoires* 1:517–21; Carré, *Travels* 2:672–73; and IOL OC 3853, Langhorn and council to directors, 30/IX/1673.

50. See AM B4–5, fols. 329–30, La Haye to Louis XIV, 20/IX/1673; IOL OC 3992, fols. 3–5, Langhorn to directors, 30/VIII/1674; Carré, *Travels* 2:667–68; and Fawcett, *The English Factories in India, 1670–1677* 2:76–77.

51. IOL OC 3918, fol. 2, "Bombay Occurences, 1674."

52. Carré, *Travels* 3:771–72.

53. Martin, *Mémoires* 1:550–60; and La Haye, *Journal* 2:150–53.

54. For details on Martin's mission, see his *Mémoires* 1:556–617.

55. La Haye, *Journal* 2:124–27; Martin, *Mémoires* 1:527–48. The officers from the *Bayonnais* were evidently killed while crossing the kingdom of Bijapur.

56. On de Maisonneuve's attack and the eventual loss of the *Breton,* see La

Haye, *Journal* 2:170–80; Martin, *Mémoires* 1:591–95, 609–20.

  57. See La Haye, *Journal* 2:149–53.

  58. La Haye, *Journal* 2:164–70; and Martin, *Mémoires* 1:572, 586–90.

  59. La Haye, *Journal* 2:185–86; Martin, *Mémoires* 1:658–59.

  60. IOL OC 3918, fol. 3, "Bombay Occurences, 1674." The articles of capitulation can be found in La Haye, *Journal* 2:189–99.

  61. IOL OC 3994, *farmans* of Abul Hasan to Chennupalli Mirza, 2/IX/1674 and 11/IX/1674; and *farman* of Abul Hasan to La Haye, 2/IX/1674.

  62. On the French departure from San Thomé, see IOL OC 3992, fols. 10–11, Langhorn to directors, 23–26/IX/1674; and La Haye, *Journal* 2:206–10.

EPILOGUE, 1675–1683

  1. The historical context of Leibnitz's *mémoire* to Louis XIV is discussed in Mahan, *The Influence of Sea Power upon History, 1660–1783*, 106–7, 141–43.

  2. See Goubert, *Louis XIV*, 137–44; and Cole, *Colbert* 2:551.

  3. The best source for the return voyage to France is Bellanger de Lespinay, *Mémoires*, 189–200. La Haye ultimately fell victim to his king's love for dynastic war. After his discussions with Colbert, he headed north to Flanders, where he was well received by Louis XIV and given command of a cavalry regiment. La Haye was killed the following year during an attack on a Dutch convoy. See Martin, *Mémoires* 1:673–74.

  4. On the 1675 stockholders meeting, see Colbert, *Lettres* II/2:635; III/2:554, 581–83; Sottas, *Histoire*, 54–64; Cole, *Colbert* 1:517–18; and Dessert and Journet, "Le lobby Colbert," 1314–15.

  5. For details on the *compagnie*'s continued decline in the late 1670s and early 1680s, see Cole, *Colbert* 1:518–24; Furber, *Rival Empires of Trade*, 112–13, 203–4. For information on the sailings of this period, see Kaeppelin, *La Compagnie*, 654–55.

  6. William Beik, *Absolutism and Society in Seventeenth-Century France*, 336.

  7. Perry Anderson notes on French Absolutism: "The late feudal French state was stopped in its path by two capitalist states of unequal power—England, Holland—assisted by its Austrian counterpart. . . . The strenuous inner preparations of Louis XIV's reign for outer dominion proved vain. The hour of supremacy for Versailles, which seemed so near in the Europe of the 1660s [and the Asian trade of the 1670s ?], never struck." See *Lineages of the Absolutist State*, 106. For the shift from feudalism to capitalism argument, see Beik, *Absolutism and Society in Seventeenth-Century France*, 336–39.

Bibliography

PRIMARY WORKS

Manuscript Sources

Archives Nationales, Dépot du Service Historique de la Marine, Paris
Series B2 (Letter Books and Registers): B2–7, B2–9, B2–10, B2–11, B2–13, B2–14, B2–16, B2–23, B2–26, B2–29, B2–30. Orders, despatches, and mémoires of Louis XIV and Colbert concerning the navy, 1669–1675.
Series B4 (Campaigns): B4–4 and B4–5. Indes Orientales, 1670–1674.

Archives Coloniales, Paris
Series B (Registers, Letter Books, Despatches): B1–B6. Ordres du Roy concernant la Compagnie des Indes Orientales, 1663–1674.
Series C (Correspondence): C2–62. Indes Orientales, 1666–1676.

Archives des Affaires Étrangères, Correspondance consulaire located at the Archives Nationales, Paris
B1 series, Aff. Etr.: B1–644 and B1–645 (Correspondence from Lisbon, 1667–1675); B1–754 and B1–755 (Correspondence from London, 1668–1678); B1–619 and B1–620 (Correspondence from The Hague, 1663–1673).

Bibliothèque Nationale, Paris
Manuscrits Cinq Cents Colbert, 201, 204, 206.
Mélanges Colbert, 31, 34, 62, 84, 122, 176, 177.
Collection Dupuy, 939.
Collection Clairambault, 532, 1016.
Collection Morel de Thoisy, 377.
Fonds français, 16,738; 21,778.
Nouvelles Acquisitions françaises, 9342, 9387.

India Office Library, London
Series E/3 (Original Correspondence): E/3/29–E/3/35 (documents 3057–4086, correspondence from Asia, 1665–1675); E/3/87–E/3/88 (despatch books from the company directors, 1666–1678).
Series G (Factory Records): Bombay—G/3/1 (consultations, 1670, 1672–1674), G/3/6 (letters despatched, 1670, 1672–1674), G/3/19 (letters received 1670); Fort-St. George (Madras)—G/19/1 (consultations, 1672–1673, 1675–1676), G/19/17 (letters despatched, 1673–1675), G/19/26 (correspondence with the king of Golconda, 1669–1674); Java—G/21/4 (extracts of letters to company, 1664–1674), G/21/6 (consultations, 1670–1680); Masulipatnam—G/26/6 (letters despatched 1672–1673), G/26/9 (letters received, 1670–1673); Surat—G/36/2 (consultations, 1666–1668), G/36/3 (consultations, 1669–1670, 1672–1675), G/36/87 (letters despatched, 1671–1674), G/36/104 (letters received, 1664–1666), G/36/105 (letters received, 1668–1671), G/36/106 (letters received, 1671–1673).
Series I (The French, Dutch, and Portuguese in India): I/1/1 (French in India, 1664–1810, misc. correspondence); I/3 (The Hague Transcripts—

this series contains transcriptions and partial translations of the major series from the Colonial Archive Section (KA) at the *Algemeen Rijksarchief* carried out under the supervision of F. C. Danvers. The equivalent AR reference is provided); I/3/56–I/3/62 (K. A. 1110–K. A. 1322) (*Overgekomen Brieven em Papieren*—letters from subordinate settlements forwarded to Batavia and then Amsterdam with reports from the Governor-General, 1665–1675); I/3/94 (K. A. 456–K. A. 460) (*Brieven van Heeren Zeventhienen naer Indien*—orders of the *Heeren* XVII for Batavia and dependent settlements, 1666–1700); I/3/104 (K. A. 785–K. A. 816) (*Bataviaesch Utgaende Briefboek*—letters from the governor-general to subordinate settlements, 1668–1680).

Public Record Office, London
    State Papers, Foreign: SP 89 (Portugal), vols. 8–12 (consular correspondence from Lisbon, 1667–1674); SP 78 (France), vols. 127–135, (consular correspondence from Paris, 1669–1674).

Arquivo Historico Ultramarino, Lisbon
    Codices 16–17 (consultations of the Overseas Council, 1661–1684).
    Codex 208 (register of royal letters, 1660–1677).
    Codices 211–212 (register of consultations on India, 1644–1711).
    Documentos avulsos relativos à Índia [DAI]: Boxes 25–30 (unbound documents relating to India, 1661–1678).

Biblioteca Nacional, Lisbon
    Fundo Geral Mss. 218, no. 127.
    Codex 748.

Arquivo Nacional da Torre do Tombo, Lisbon
    Foreign Ministry Documents
    ME III, documents 1 and 2 (despatches from the legation in France, 1668–1677).

Historical Archive of Goa, Panjim, India
    Livros das monçoes do Reino (Monsoon Books), vols. 28A–40 (official correspondence between Lisbon and Goa, 1660–1676).
    Codices 970–71, *Livros das Reis Vizinhos* (correspondence between the viceroy in Goa and the "neighboring kings" of India, 1662–1668 and 1677–1681).
    Codices 782, 1258, 2316.

Maharastra State Archive, Bombay
    Surat Presidency Records
    Secretariat Outward or Order Books, 1 and 2 (correspondence for the years 1663–1677).

Printed Sources

Albuquerque, Afonso. *The Commentaries of the Great Afonso Dalboquerque, by his son Afonso Braz de Alboquerque.* Ed. W. de G. Birch. 4 vols. London, 1875–1883.
——. *A Calendar of The Court Minutes etc. of the East India Company, 1660–1679.* Ed. E. B. Sainsbury. 6 vols. London, 1922–1938.

Barbosa, Duarte. *The Book of Duarte Barbosa: An Account of the Countries Bordering on the Indian Ocean and their Inhabitants, Written by Duarte Barbosa and Completed about the Year 1518 A. D.* Trans. and ed. M. L. Dames. 2 vols. London, 1918–1921.

Bellanger de Lespinay, Auguste. *Mémoires.* Ed. Henri Froidevaux. Vols. 33 and 34 of *Bulletin de la société archélogique scientifique et literaire du Vendômois.* 1894–1895.

Bernier, François. *Travels in the Mogul Empire, A.D. 1656–1668, by François Bernier.* Trans. Irving Brock. Ed. Archibald Constable. London, 1891.

Bowery, Thomas. *A Geographical Account of the Countries Round the Bay of Bengal, 1669 to 1679.* Ed. Richard Temple. Cambridge, 1905.

Caron, François. *A True Description of the Mighty Kingdoms of Japan and Siam, by François Caron and Joost Schouten.* Ed. C. R. Boxer. 1663. Reprint. London, 1935.

Carré, Bartelemy. *The Travels of the Abbé Carré in India and the Near East, 1672 to 1674.* Trans. Lady Fawcett. Ed. Charles Fawcett. 3 vols. London, 1947–1948.

Chardin, John. *Travels in Persia, 1673–1677.* 1720. Reprint of 1927 ed. New York, 1988.

Charles II. *The Letters, Speeches and Declarations of King Charles II.* Ed. Arthur Bryant. 1935. Reprint. New York, 1968.

Charpentier, François. *Discours d'un fidèle sujet du roi touchant l' établissement d'une Compagnie françoise pour le commerce des Indes Orientales.* Paris, 1664.

———. *Relation de l'établissement de la Compagnie françoise pour le commerce des Indes Orientales.* Paris, 1665.

Colbert, Jean-Baptiste. *Lettres, instructions, et mémoires.* Ed. Pierre Clément. 7 vols. Paris, 1861–1882.

Depping, G. B. *Correspondance administrative sous le règne de Louis XIV.* 4 vols. Paris, 1850–1855.

Dernis. *Receuil et collection des titres, édits, déclarations, arrêts, règlements, & autres pièces concernant la Compagnie des Indes Orientales.* 4 vols. Paris, 1755–1756.

The English Factories in India, 1661–1669. Ed. William Foster. 3 vols. Oxford, 1923–27.

The English Factories in India, 1670–1677. Ed. Charles Fawcett. 2 vols., Oxford, 1936–52.

Evelyn, John. *The Diary of John Evelyn.* Ed. E. S. de Beer. 6 vols. Oxford, 1955.

Fryer, John. *A New Account of East India and Persia.* Ed. William Crooke. 3 vols. London, 1909–1915

Gomes de Brito, Bernando. *História tragico-maritima, em que se escrevem chronologicamente os naufragios que tiverão as naos de Portugal, depois que se poz em exercicio a navegação da India.* 2 vols. Lisbon, 1735–1736.

Knox, Robert. *An Historical Relation of Ceylon, together with Somewhat Concerning Severall Remarkable Passages of my Life.* Glasgow, 1911.

La Haye, Jacob Blanquet de. *Journal du voyage des grandes Indes.* 2 vols. Orléans, 1697.

———. Historical Manuscripts Commission of Great Britain. *Report on the Manuscripts of the Duke of Buccleuch and Queensberry.* 4 vols. in 3. London, 1899–1920.

L'Estra, François. *Relation; ou journal d'un voyage fait aux Indes Orientales.* Paris, 1677.

Linschoten, Jan Huyghen van. *The Voyage of John Huyghen van Linschoten to the East Indies.* Ed. A. C. Burnell and P. A. Tiele. London, 1885.

Louis XIV. *Mémoires.* Ed. Jean Longnon. Paris, 1927.

———. *Oeuvres.* Ed. P. H. Grimoard and P. A. Grouvelle. 6 vols. Paris, 1806.

Mandeville, John. *Mandeville's Travels.* Trans. M. Letts, London, 1953.

Manucci, Niccolão. *Storia do Mogor or Mogul India by Niccolão Manucci.* Trans. and ed. William Irvine. 4 vols. London, 1907–1908.

Martin, François. *Mémoires de François Martin, fondateur de Pondichéry.* Ed. A. Martineau. 3 vols. Paris, 1931–1934.

Ovington, John. *A Voyage to Surat in the Year 1689 by John Ovington.* Ed. H. G. Rawlinson. London, 1929.

Pires, Tome. *The Suma Oriental of Tome Pires.* Trans. and ed. João Cortesão. London, 1944.

Polo, Marco. *The Travels of Marco Polo [The Venetian].* Rev. ed., ed. Manuel Komroff. New York, [1926] 1983.

Pyrard, François. *Selections from the Letters, Despatches, and other State Papers Preserved in the Bombay Secretariat.* Ed. G. W. Forrest. 2 vols. Bombay, 1887.

———. *The Voyage of François Pyrard of Laval to the East Indies, the Maldives, the Moluccas, and Brazil.* Trans. and ed. Albert Gray and H. C. P. Bell. 2 vols. in 3. London, 1887–1890.

Queyroz, Fernão de. *The Temporal and Spiritual Conquest of Ceylon.* Trans. S. G. Perera. Colombo, 1930.

Recueil des instructions données aux ambassadeurs et ministres de France depuis les traités de Westphalie jusqu'à la révolution française: Angleterre. Ed. J. J. Jusserand. 2 vols. Paris, 1929.

Relación de las grandes perdidas de naos y galeones, que han tenido los Portugueses en la India Oriental. Madrid, 1651.

Tavernier, Jean-Baptiste. *Travels in India by Jean-Baptiste Tavernier.* Trans. and ed. V. Ball. 2 vols. London, 1889.

SECONDARY WORKS

Alam, S. M. "Masulipatnam—A Metropolitan Port in the Seventeenth Century." *Islamic Culture* 33 (1959): 169–87.

Albuquerque, Luis de, and Inacio Guerreiro. *Actas de II Seminário Internacional de História Indo-Portuguesa.* Lisbon, 1985.

Ali Athar, M. *The Mughal Nobility under Aurangzeb.* Bombay, 1968.

Ames, Glenn J. "The *Carreira da India,* 1668–1682: Maritime Enterprise and the Quest for Stability in Portugal's Asian Empire." *The Journal of European Economic History* 20, no. 1 (1991): 7–27.

———. "Colbert's Grand Asian Fleet of 1670." *The Mariner's Mirror* 76, no. 3. (1990): 227–40.

———. "Colbert's Indian Ocean Strategy of 1664–1674: A Reappraisal." *French Historical Studies* 16, no. 3. (1990): 536–59.

———. "The *Estado da India,* 1663–1677: Priorities and Strategies in Europe and the East." *Revista Portuguesa de História* 22 (1987): 31–46.

———. "A Portuguese Perspective on the Emerging French Presence in the East, c. 1670." *Studia* 46 (1987): 255–87.

Anderson, Perry. *Lineages of the Absolutist State*. 4th ed. London, 1987.

Anderson, Philip. *The English in Western India: being the Early History of the Factory of Surat, of Bombay, and the subordinate factories on the West Coast*. Bombay, 1854.

Anthonisz, R. G. *The Dutch in Ceylon*. Colombo, 1929.

Arasaratnam, Sinnappah. *Dutch Power in Ceylon, 1658–1687*. Amsterdam, 1958.

——. *Merchants, Companies and Commerce on the Coromandel Coast, 1650–1740*. Delhi, 1986.

Asher, Eugene. *The Resistance to the Maritime Classes: The Survival of Feudalism in the France of Colbert*. Berkeley and Los Angeles, 1960.

Axelson, Eric. *The Portuguese in South-East Africa, 1600–1700*. Johannesburg, 1960.

Baker, J. N. L. *A History of Geographical Discovery and Exploration*. London, 1937.

Bamford, Paul W. *Fighting Ships and Prisons: The Mediterranean Galleys of Louis XIV*. Minneapolis, 1973.

——. *Forests and French Seapower, 1660–1789*. Toronto, 1956.

——. *Privilege and Profit: A Business Family in Eighteenth-Century France*. Philadelphia, 1988.

Barassin, J. "Compagnies de navigation et expéditions françaises dans l'Ocean Indien au XVIIe siècle." *Studia* 11 (1963): 373–88.

Barber, William. *British Economic Thought and India, 1600–1858*. Oxford, 1975.

Barbier, J. "La Compagnie française des Indes." *Revue historique de l'Inde française* 3 (1919): 50–96.

Beazley, R. *The Dawn of Modern Geography*. 3 vols. Oxford, 1896–1906.

Beik, William. *Absolutism and Society in Seventeenth-Century France: State and Provincal Aristocracy in Languedoc*. Cambridge, 1985.

Bentley, Duncan, T. "Navigation between Portugal and Asia in the Sixteenth and Seventeeth Centuries." In *Asia and the West*, ed. C. K. Pulliapilly and E. J. Van Kley, 3–25. Notre Dame, IN, 1986.

Berger, R. W. *Versailles: The Chateau of Louis XIV*. College Park, MD, 1985.

Bluché, François. *Louis XIV*. Trans. Mark Greengrass. New York, 1990.

Blussé, L., and F. Gaastra, eds. *Companies and Trade: Essays on Overseas Trading Companies during the Ancien Régime*. Leiden, 1981.

Boissonnade, P. *Colbert et la souscription aux actions de la Compagnie des Indes*. Poitiers, 1909.

——. *Colbert: le triomphe de l'étatisme*. Paris, 1932.

Boiteux, L. A. *Richelieu: grand maître de la navigation et du commerce de France*. Paris, 1955.

Borges de Castro, J. F. *Colleção de tratados, convençoes, contratos, e actos publicos celebrados entre a Coroa de Portugal desde 1640 até o presente*. 8 vols. Lisbon, 1856–1858.

Bosher, J. F. *The Single Duty Project: A Study of the Movement for a French Customs Union in the Eighteenth Century*. London, 1964.

Botelho de Sousa, A. *Subsídios Para a Historia Militar Marítima da India*. 4 vols. Lisbon, 1930–1956.

Boxer, C. R. *The Dutch Seaborne Empire, 1600–1800*. New York, 1965.

——. *Four Centuries of Portuguese Expansion, 1415–1825: A Succinct Survey*. Berkeley and Los Angeles, 1969.

——. *A India Portuguesa em Meados do Seculo XVII*. Lisbon, 1982.

——. "Portuguese and Dutch Colonial Rivalry." *Studia* 2 (1958): 7–42.

——. *The Portuguese Seaborne Empire, 1415–1825.* New York, 1969.

——. *Salvador da Sá and the Struggle for Brazil and Angola, 1602–1686.* London, 1952.

——. "The Third Dutch War in the East, 1672–1674." *The Mariner's Mirror* 16 (1930): 341–86.

——. "Vicissitudes of the Anglo-Portuguese Alliance." *Revista da Faculdade de Letras* (Lisbon) 3rd ser., no. 2 (1958): 5–36.

Boyajian, J. C. *Portuguese Bankers at the Court of Spain, 1626–1650.* New Brunswick, NJ, 1983.

——. *Portuguese Trade in Asia under the Habsburgs, 1580–1640.* Baltimore, 1993.

Braudel, F. *Civilization and Capitalism, Fifteenth to Eighteenth Century.* 3 vols. London, 1984.

——. *The Identity of France.* Trans. Sian Reynolds. 2 vols. New York, 1988.

Braudel, F., and F. C. Spooner. "Les métaux monétaires et l'économie du XVIe siècle." In *X Congresso Internazionale di Science Storiche, Roma Relazoni.* Florence, 1955.

Burn, R., ed. *The Cambridge History of India IV (The Mughal Period).* Cambridge, 1937.

Castonnet des Fosses, Henri. *La Boullaye Le Gouz: sa vie et ses voyages.* Angers, 1891.

——. *François Bernier: ses voyages dans l'Inde.* Angers, 1888.

——. *L'Inde française avant Dupleix.* Paris, 1887.

——. *L'Inde française au XVIIe siècle.* Paris, 1899.

Chandaman, C. D. *The English Public Revenue, 1660–1688.* Oxford, 1975.

Chandra, Satish. *Parties and Politics at the Mughal Court.* New Delhi, 1972.

Chaudhuri, K. N. *The Trading World of Asia and the English East India Company, 1660–1760.* Cambridge, 1978.

Church, William. *Louis XIV in Historical Thought.* New York, 1976.

Cipolla, Carlo. *European Culture and Overseas Expansion.* London, 1970.

——. *Guns, Sails, and Empires: Technological Innovation and the Early Phases of European Expansion, 1400–1700.* New York, 1965.

Clément, Pierre. *Histoire de Colbert et de son administration.* 2 vols. Paris, 1874.

——. *Histoire de la vie et administration de Colbert.* Paris, 1846.

Cole, C. W. *Colbert and a Century of French Mercantilism.* 2 vols. New York, 1939.

——. *French Mercantilist Doctrine before Colbert.* New York, 1931.

Corvisier, André. *Louvois.* Paris, 1983.

da Cunha, J. G. *The Origin of Bombay.* Bombay, 1900.

Danvers, F. C. *The Portuguese in India.* 2 vols. London, 1894.

Das Gupta, Ashin. *Indian Merchants and the Decline of Surat.* Wiesbaden, 1979.

Davies, D. W. *A Primer of Dutch Seventeenth-Century Overseas Trade.* The Hague, 1961.

Delort, Theodore. "La première escadre de la France dans les Indes." *Revue maritime et coloniale* 47 (1875): 29–63, 443–71, 841–66.

Dent, Julian. *Crisis in Finance: Crown, Finances and Society in Seventeenth-Century France.* New York, 1973.

Deschamps, H. *Histoire de Madagascar.* Paris, 1961.

De Souza, T. R. "Glimpses of Hindu Dominance of Goan Economy in the 17th Century." *Indica* 12 (1975): 27–35.

——. "Goa-based Portuguese Seaborne Trade in the Early Seventeenth Century."

The Indian Economic and Social History Review 12 (1975): 433–42.

———, ed. *Indo-Portuguese History: Old Issues, New Questions.* New Delhi, 1985.

———. *Medieval Goa: A Socio-Economic History.* New Delhi, 1985.

Dessert, D. *Argent, pouvoir, et société au Grand Siècle.* Paris, 1985.

———. "Finances et société au XVIIe siècle: À propos de la Chambre de justice de 1661." *Annales, ESC* 29 (1974): 849–69.

———. "Les Groupes financiers et Colbert." *Bulletin de la Société d'histoire moderne.* 80 (1981): 19–29.

Dessert, D., and J. L. Journet. "Le lobby Colbert: Un royaume ou une affaire de famille?" *Annales, ESC* 30 (1975): 1303–36.

Disney, A. R. *Twilight of the Pepper Empire.* Cambridge, MA, 1978.

Dodwell, H. H., ed. *The Cambridge History of India.* Vol. 5, *British India, 1497–1858.* Cambridge, 1929.

Duarte, Adrian. *Les premières relations entre les français et les princes indigènes dans l'Inde au XVII siècle, 1666–1706.* Paris, 1932.

Duffy, James. *Shipwreck and Empire: Being an Account of Portuguese Maritime Disasters in a Century of Decline.* Cambridge, MA, 1955.

Ekberg, Carl, J. *The Failure of Louis XIV's Dutch War.* Chapel Hill, NC, 1979.

Elizinga, S. "Le prélude de la guerre de 1672." *Revue d'histoire moderne* 2 (1927): 349–66.

———. "Le tarif de Colbert de 1664 et celui de 1667 et leur signification." *Economisch-historisch Jaarboek* 15 (1929): 221–73.

Elliot, J. H. "The Decline of Spain." *Past and Present* 20 (1961): 52–75.

———. *Imperial Spain, 1469–1716.* London, 1963.

Feiling, Keith. *British Foreign Policy, 1660–1672.* London, 1930.

Flynn, Dennis. "Sixteenth-Century Inflation from a Production Point of View." In *Inflation Through the Ages,* ed. N. Schmukler and E. Marcus. Brooklyn, 1982.

Frémy, Elphège. "Causes économiques de la guerre de Hollande, 1664–1672." *Revue d'histoire diplomatique* 28 (1914–1915): 523–55.

Froidevaux, Henri. "Un memoire inèdit de M. de La Haye sur Madagascar." *Bulletin du comité de Madagascar* 3 (1897): 110–29.

———. "Un projet d'acquisition de Tranquebar par la France en 1669." *Revue de géographie* 41 (1897): 88–96.

Furber, Holden. *Rival Empires of Trade in the Orient, 1600–1800.* Minneapolis, 1976.

Gaastra, F. "The Shifting Balance of Trade of the Dutch East India Company." In *Companies and Trade: Essays on Overseas Trading Companies and Trade during the Ancien Régime,* ed. L. Blussé and F. Gaastra, 47–69. Leiden, 1981.

Glamann, Kristof. *Dutch Asiatic Trade, 1620–1740.* The Hague, 1958.

Godinho, V. M. *A Economia dos Descobrimentos Henriquinos.* Lisbon, 1962.

———. *L'Économie de l'empire portugais aux XVe et XVIe siècles.* Paris, 1969.

Goonatilleka, M. H. "A Portuguese Creole in Sri Lanka: A Brief Socio-Linguistic Survey." In *Indo-Portuguese History: Old Issues, New Questions,* ed. T. R. de Souza, 147–80. New Delhi, 1985.

Goonewardena, K. W. *The Foundation of Dutch Power in Ceylon, 1638–1658.* Amsterdam, 1958.

Goubert, Pierre. *Louis XIV and Twenty Million Frenchmen.* Trans. Anne Carter. London, 1970.

Habib, Irfan. *The Agrarian System of Mughal India*. Bombay, 1963.

Hamilton, C. J. *The Trade Relations between England and India, 1600–1896*. 1919. Reprint. Delhi, 1975.

Hamilton, E. J. *American Treasure and the Price Revolution in Spain, 1501–1650*. Cambridge, MA, 1934.

Hanson, C. A. *Economy and Society in Baroque Portugal, 1668–1703*. Minneapolis, 1981.

Haring, C. H. *The Spanish Empire in America*. New York, 1947.

Hartmann, C. H. *Charles II and Madame*. London, 1934.

Hasan, Ibn. *The Central Structure of the Mughal Empire*. 1936. Reprint. Karachi, 1967.

Hatton, Ragnhild, ed. *Louis XIV and Europe*. Columbus, 1976.

Haudrère, Philippe. "La Compagnie française des Indes: 1719–1795." Thèse d'État, University of Paris, 1986.

Heckscher, E. F. *Mercantilism*. 2 vols. Rev. ed. London, 1958.

Hill, Christopher. *The Century of Revolution, 1603–1714*. Edinburgh, 1961.

Hunter, W. W. *A History of British India*. 2 vols. London, 1899–1900.

Hutton, Ronald. *Charles II: King of England, Scotland, and Ireland*. Oxford, 1989.

———. "The Making of the Secret Treaty of Dover, 1668–1670." *The Historical Journal* 29 (1986): 297–318.

Irvine, William. *The Army of the Indian Moghuls: Its Organization and Administration*. 1903. Reprint. New Delhi, 1962.

Israel, Jonathan I. *Dutch Primacy in World Trade, 1585–1740*. Oxford, 1989.

Jal, Auguste. *Glossaire nautique*. Paris, 1848.

Jennings, R. M., and A. P. Trout. "Internal Control: Public Finance in 17th Century France." *The Journal of European Economic History* 1 (1972): 647–60.

Kaeppelin, Paul. *La Compagnie des Indes Orientales et François Martin*. Paris, 1908.

Kamen, Henry. "The Decline of Spain: A Historical Myth?" *Past and Present* 81 (1978): 24–50.

———. *Spain, 1469–1714: A Society of Conflict*. London, 1983.

Kent, R. K. *Early Kingdoms in Madagascar, 1500–1700*. New York, 1970.

Khan, S. A. *Anglo-Portuguese negotiations relating to Bombay*. Allahabad, 1922.

———. *The East India Trade in the XVII Century*. London, 1923.

Krishna, Bal. *Commercial Relations between India and England, 1601–1757*. London, 1924.

———. *Shivaji the Great*. 2 vols. Kolhapur, 1939.

La Roncière, Charles de. *Histoire de la marine française*. 6 vols. Paris, 1899–1932.

———. "Les précurseurs de la Compagnie des Indes orientales." *Revue de l'histoire des colonies française* (1913): 39–72.

Lach, Donald, and Edwin J. Van Kley. *Asia in the Making of Europe*. Vol. 3, *A Century of Advance*. Chicago, 1993.

Lachs, P. S. *The Diplomatic Corps of Charles II and James II*. New Brunswick, NJ, 1965.

Lane, F. C. "The Mediterranean Spice Trade: Its Revival in the Sixteenth Century." In *Venice and History: The Collected Papers of Frederic C. Lane*. Baltimore, 1966.

Lee, Maurice. *The Cabal*. Urbana, IL, 1965.

Livermore, H. V. *A New History of Portugal*. Cambridge, 1967.

———. *Shivaji the Great*. 2 vols. Kolhapur, 1939.

Lohuizen, J. V. *The Dutch East India Company and Mysore*. The Hague, 1961.

Lossky, Andrew. *Louis XIV and the French Monarchy*. New Brunswick, NJ, 1994.

Love, Henry D. *Vestiges of Old Madras, 1600–1800*. 4 vols. London, 1913.

Macleod, N. *De Oost-Indische Compagnie als Zeemongeheid in Azie, 1602–1652*. 2 vols. Rijswick, 1927.

Mahan, A. T. *The Influence of Sea Power Upon History, 1660–1783*. Boston, 1928.

Malleson, George B. *History of the French in India*. Edinburgh, 1909.

Martin, G., and M. Bezançon. *L'Histoire du crédit en France sous le règne de Louis XIV*. Paris, 1913.

Martineau, A., ed. *Lettres et conventions des gouverneurs de Pondichéry avec différents princes Hindous, 1666–1793*. Pondicherry, 1914.

Mauro, Fredric. *L'expansion européen, 1600–1870*. Paris, 1964.

Meilink-Roelofsz, M. A. P. *Asian Trade and European Influence in the Indonesian Archipelago between 1500 and about 1630*. The Hague, 1962.

Mettam, Roger. *Power and Faction in Louis XIV's France*. Oxford, 1988.

Mignet, F. A. M. *Négociations relatives à la succession d'Espagne sous Louis XIV*. 4 vols. Paris, 1835–1842.

Mill, James. *History of British India*. 6 vols. in 4. 1858. Reprint. New York, 1968.

Mollat, Michel. "Passages françaises dans l'Océan Indien au temps de François Ier." *Studia* 11 (1963): 239–50.

Moreland, W. H. *From Akbar to Aurangzeb: A Study in Indian Economic History*. London, 1923.

———. *India at the Death of Akbar*. London, 1920.

———. *Relations of Golconda in the Early Seventeenth Century*. London, 1931.

Morison, S. E. *Admiral of the Ocean Sea*. 2 vols. Boston, 1942.

Mutibwa, P. M. *The Malagasy and the Europeans*. London, 1974.

Oliveira Marques, A. H. *History of Portugal*. 2 vols. New York, 1972.

Oliver, Pasfield S. *The Voyages made by the Sieur D. B. to the Islands Dauphine or Madagascar and Bourbon or Mascarenne in the Years 1669, 70, 71, and 72*. London, 1897.

Panikkar, K. M. *Asia and Western Dominance*. London, 1959.

Parry, J. H. *The Age of Reconnaissance*. London, 1963.

Pauliat, Louis. *Louis XIV et La Compagnie des Indes Orientales de 1664*. Paris, 1886.

Pearson, M. N. *The Age of Partnership*. Honolulu, 1974.

———. *Coastal Western India*. New Delhi, 1981.

———. *Merchants and Rulers in Gujarat: The Response to the Portuguese in the 16th Century*. Berkeley, 1975.

———. *The Portuguese in India*. Cambridge, 1987.

———. "Shivaji and the Decline of the Mughal Empire." *Journal of Asian Studies* (1976): 221–35.

———. "Wealth and Power: Indian Groups in the Portuguese Indian Economy." *South Asia* 3 (1973): 36–44.

Pieris, P. E. *Ceylon and the Portuguese, 1505–1658*. Tellippalai, 1920.

———. *Some Documents Relating to the Rise of Dutch Power in Ceylon, 1602–1670*. Colombo, 1929.

———. *Portugal in Ceylon, 1505–1658*. Cambridge, 1937.

Pissurlencar, P. S. S. "Portugueses et Maratas." *Boletim do Instituto Vasco da Gama* 1 (1926): 48–98; 2 (1927): 66–92; 3 (1928): 66–92; and 6 (1931): 80–89.

——. *Shivaji and the Portuguese*. Bombay, 1927.

Poonen, T. I. *A Survey of the Rise of Dutch Power in Malabar, 1603–78*. Trichinopoly, 1948.

Poujade, Jean. *La route des Indes et ses navires*. Paris, 1946.

Prakash, Om. *The Dutch East India Company and the Economy of Bengal, 1630–1720*. Princeton, 1985.

Prescott, W. H. *History of the Reign of Ferdinand and Isabella*. Boston, 1937.

Prestage, E. *The Diplomatic Relations of Portugal with France, England, and Holland from 1640 to 1668*. Watford, 1925.

——. *The Portuguese Pioneers*. London, 1933.

Qureshi, I. H. *The Administration of the Mughal Empire*. Karachi, 1966.

Ranum, O. *Paris in the Age of Absolutism*. New York, 1968.

Raychaudhuri, Tapan. *Jan Company in Coromandel, 1605–1690*. The Hague, 1962.

Richards, J. F. *Mughal Administration in Golconda*. Oxford, 1975.

Rothrock, G. A. "Seventeenth-Century India through French Eyes." *The Historian* 22 (1959): 163–81.

Rowen, Herbert. *The Ambassador Prepares for War: The Dutch Embassy of Arnauld de Pomponne, 1669–1671*. The Hague, 1957.

——. "Arnauld de Pomponne: Louis XIV's Moderate Minister." *American Historical Review* 61 (1956): 531–49.

——. *John de Witt: Grand Pensionary of Holland, 1625–1672*. Princeton, 1978.

Santarem, M. F. de Barros. *Quadro elementar das relaçoes politicas e diplomaticas de Portugal com as diversas potencias do mundo, desde o principio da monarchia portuguesa até aos nossos dias*. 18 vols. in 13. Paris, 1842–1876.

Saran, P. *The Provincial Government of the Mughals*. Allahabad, 1941.

Sarkar, J. *House of Shivaji*. 3d ed. Calcutta, 1955.

——. *Shivaji and his Times*. 6th ed. Calcutta, 1961.

See, Henri. "Que fait-il penser de l'oeuvre de Colbert?" *Revue historique* 152 (1926): 181–93.

Sen, S. N. *Administrative System of the Marathas*. Calcutta, 1925.

——. *Foreign Biographies of Shivaji*. London, 1930.

——. *Military System of the Marathas*. Calcutta, 1928.

Sen, S. P. *The French in India: First Establishment and Struggle*. Calcutta, 1947.

Sherwani, H. K. *History of the Qutb Shahi Dynasty*. Delhi, 1974.

——. "Reign of Abdu'l-lah Qutb Shah (1626–1672): Political and Military Aspects." *Journal of Indian History* 45 (1967): 115–60.

——. "The Reign of Abu'l-Hasan Qutb Shah." *Journal of Indian History* 46 (1968): 315–56.

Sherwani, H. K., and P. M. Joshi. *History of Medieval Deccan, 1295–1724*. 2 vols. Hyderabad, 1943–58.

Siddiqui, A. M. *History of Golconda*. Hyderabad, 1956.

Smith, Adam. *An Inquiry into the Nature and Causes of the Wealth of Nations*. Ed. Edwin Cannan. 2 vols. in 1. Chicago, 1976.

Smith, Vincent E. *The Oxford History of India*. Oxford, 1919.

Sonnino, Paul. "Hugues de Lionne and the Origins of the Dutch War." *Proceedings of the Western Society for French History* 1 (1974): 49–60.

——. "Jean-Baptiste Colbert and the Origins of the Dutch War." *European Studies Review* 13 (1983): 1–11.

———. "Louis XIV and the Dutch War." In *Louis XIV and Europe,* ed. Ragnhild Hatton, 153–78. Columbus, 1976.

———. *Louis XIV and the Origins of the Dutch War.* Cambridge, 1988.

———. "The Marshal de Turenne and the Origins of the Dutch War." *Studies in Politics and History* 4 (1985): 125–36.

Sottas, Jules. *Histoire de la Compagnie royale des Indes orientales, 1664–1719.* Paris, 1905.

Steensgaard, Neils. "Asian Trade and World Economy." In *Indo-Portuguese History,* ed. T. R. de Souza, 225–35. New Delhi, 1985.

———. *The Asian Trade Revolution of the Seventeenth Century.* Chicago, 1974.

———. "The Companies as a Specific Institution in the History of European Expansion." In *Companies and Trade: Essays on Overseas Trading Companies and Trade during the Ancien Régime,* ed. L. Blussé and F. Gaastra, 245–64. Leiden, 1981.

———. "The Dutch East India Company as an Institutional Innovation." In *Dutch Capitalism and World Capitalism,* ed. M. Aymard. Cambridge, 1982.

———. "The Return Cargoes of the *Carreira* in the 16th and Early 17th Century." In *Indo-Portuguese History,* ed. T. R. de Souza, 13–31. New Delhi, 1985.

Subrahmanyam, Sanjay. *The Political Economy of Commerce: Southern India, 1500–1800.* Cambridge, 1990.

———. *The Portuguese Empire in Asia, 1500–1700.* London, 1993.

Tracy, James D., ed. *The Political Economy of Merchant Empires: State Power and World Trade, 1350–1750.* Cambridge, 1991.

———, ed. *The Rise of Merchant Empires: Long Distance Trade in the Early Modern World.* Cambridge, 1990.

Trout, Andrew. *Jean-Baptiste Colbert.* Boston, 1978.

Varadarajan, Lotika. *India in the Seventeenth Century: Social, Economic and Political.* 2 vols. New Delhi, 1981.

———. "San Thomé—Early European Activities and Aspirations." In *Actas de II Seminario Internacional de Historia Indo-Portuguesa,* ed. Luis de Albuquerque and Inacio Guerreiro, 432–41. Lisbon, 1985.

Vilar, Pierre. *Or et monnaie dans l'histoire.* Paris, 1974.

———. "Problems of the Formation of Capitalism." *Past and Present* 10 (1956): 15–38.

Wake, C. H. H. "The Changing Pattern of Europe's Pepper and Spice Imports, ca. 1400–1700." *The Journal of European Economic History* 8 (1979): 361–403.

Wallerstein, I. *The Modern World System II: Mercantilism and the Consolidation of the European World Economy, 1650–1750.* New York. 1981.

Walton, G. *Louis XIV's Versailles.* Chicago, 1986.

Weber, Henry. *La Compagnie française des Indes, 1604–1875.* Paris, 1904.

West, S. George. *A Complete Bibliography of the Works of C. R. Boxer, 1926–1983.* London, 1984.

Whiteway, R. S. *The Rise of Portuguese Power in India, 1497–1550.* London, [1899] 1967.

Wills, John E., Jr. "Maritime Asia, 1500–1800: The Interactive Emergence of European Domination." *American Historical Review* 98, no. 1 (1993): 83–105.

Wilson, C. *England's Apprenticeship, 1603–1763.* London, 1965.

——. *Profit and Power: A Study of England and the Dutch Wars.* London, 1957.

Winius, George D. *The Fatal History of Portuguese Ceylon: Transition to Dutch Rule.* Cambridge, MA, 1971.

Winius, George D., and B. W. Diffie. *Foundations of Portuguese Empire, 1415–1825.* Minneapolis, 1977.

Wolf, John B. *Louis XIV.* New York, 1968.

Zeller, Gaston. *Aspects de la politique française sous l'Ancien Régime.* Paris, 1964.

——. "Politique extérieure et diplomatie sous Louis XIV." *Revue d'histoire moderne* 6 (1931): 124–43.

Index